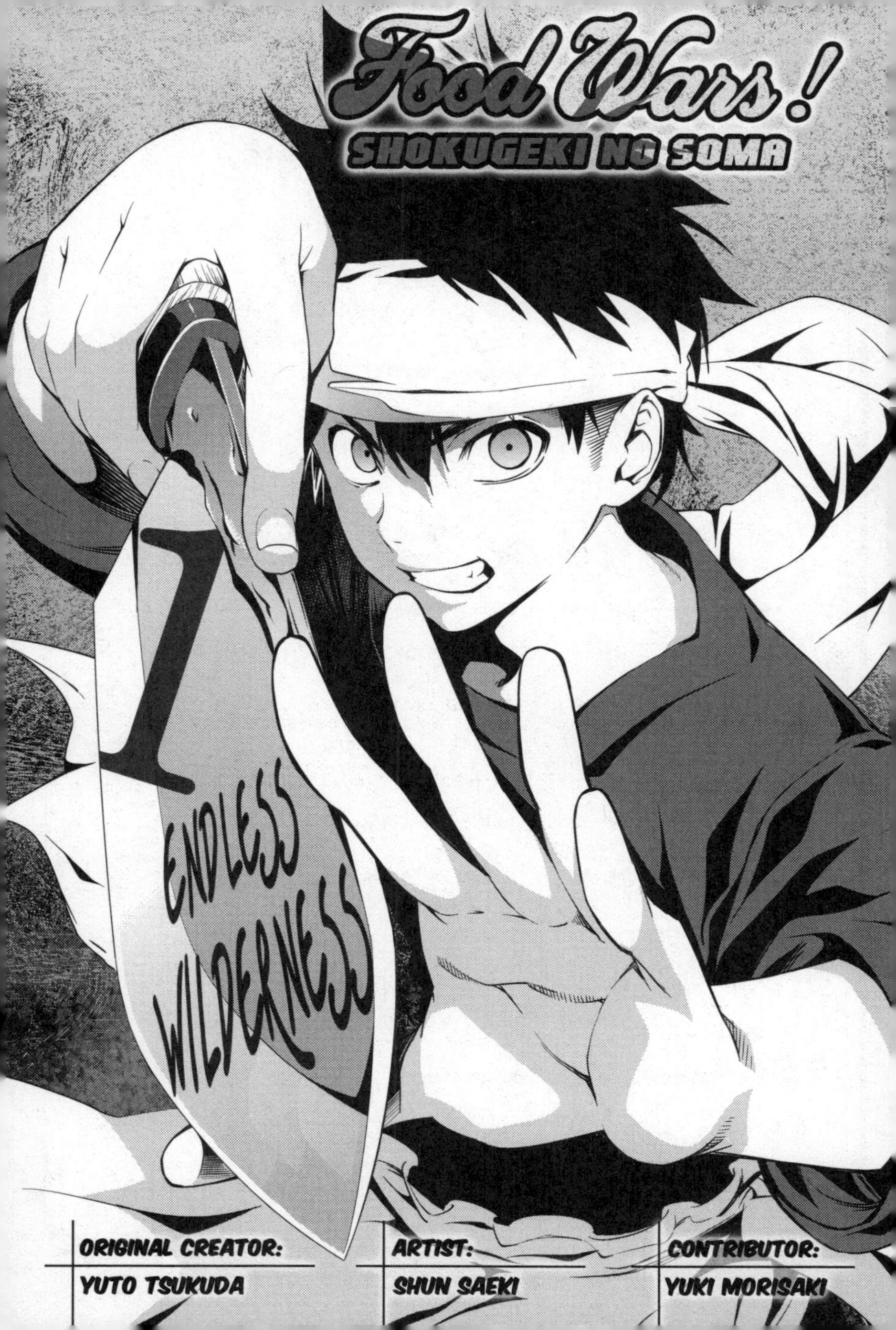
Food Wars!
SHOKUGEKI NO SOMA
1
ENDLESS WILDERNESS
ORIGINAL CREATOR:
YUTO TSUKUDA
ARTIST:
SHUN SAEKI
CONTRIBUTOR:
YUKI MORISAKI

SHOKUGEKI NO SOMA

Food Wars!

1

Table of Contents

1. Endless Wilderness 5

2. Divine Tongue 61

3. "Morphing" Furikake 87

4. The Godfather Speaks of Diamonds 111

5. The Chef Who Never Smiles 131

Special Short—
Food Wars!: Shokugeki no Soma 151

Side Story—Kurase's Diary 203

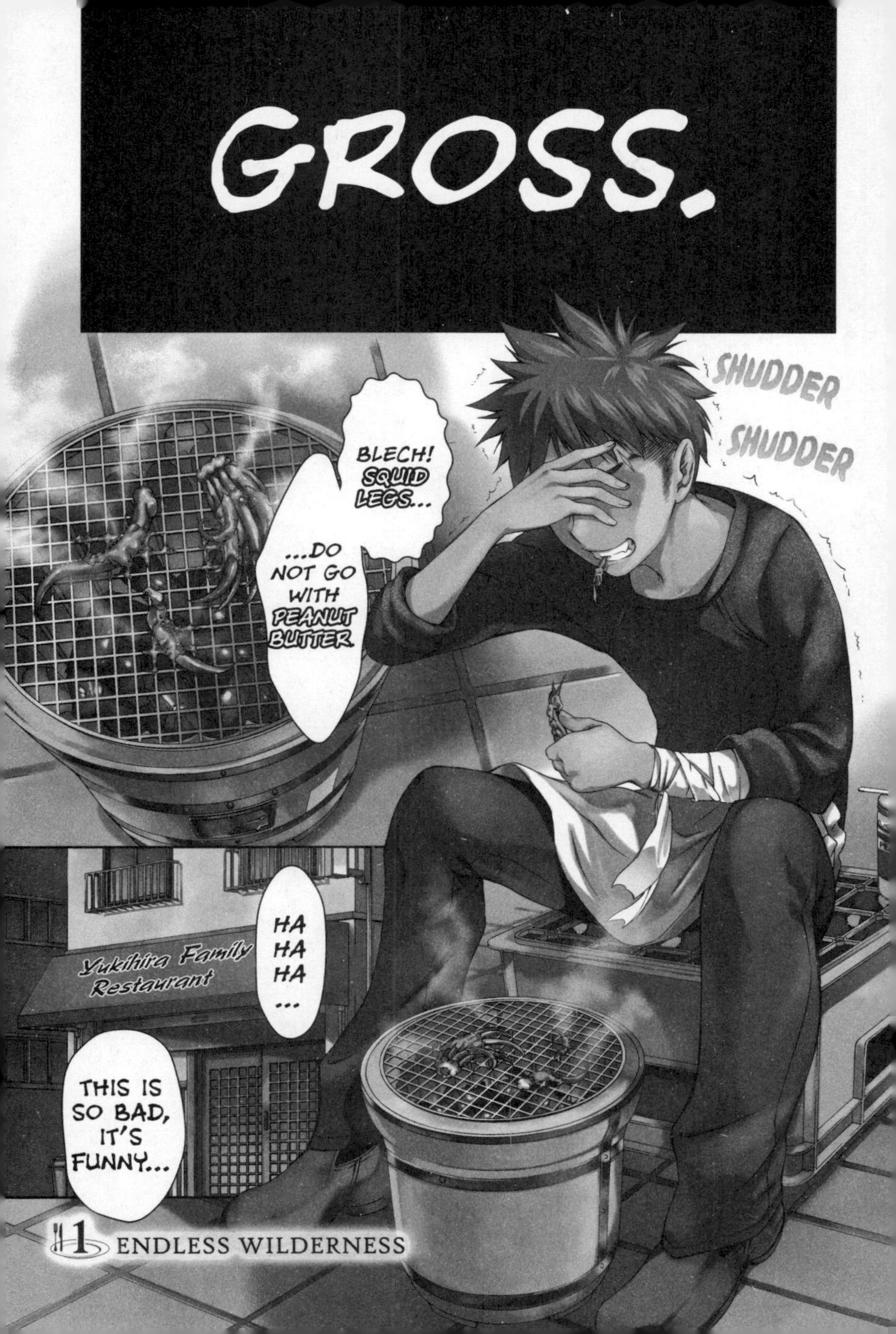
GROSS.
SHUDDER
SHUDDER
BLECH! SQUID LEGS...
...DO NOT GO WITH PEANUT BUTTER
HA HA HA ...
THIS IS SO BAD, IT'S FUNNY...
Yukihira Family Restaurant
1 ENDLESS WILDERNESS

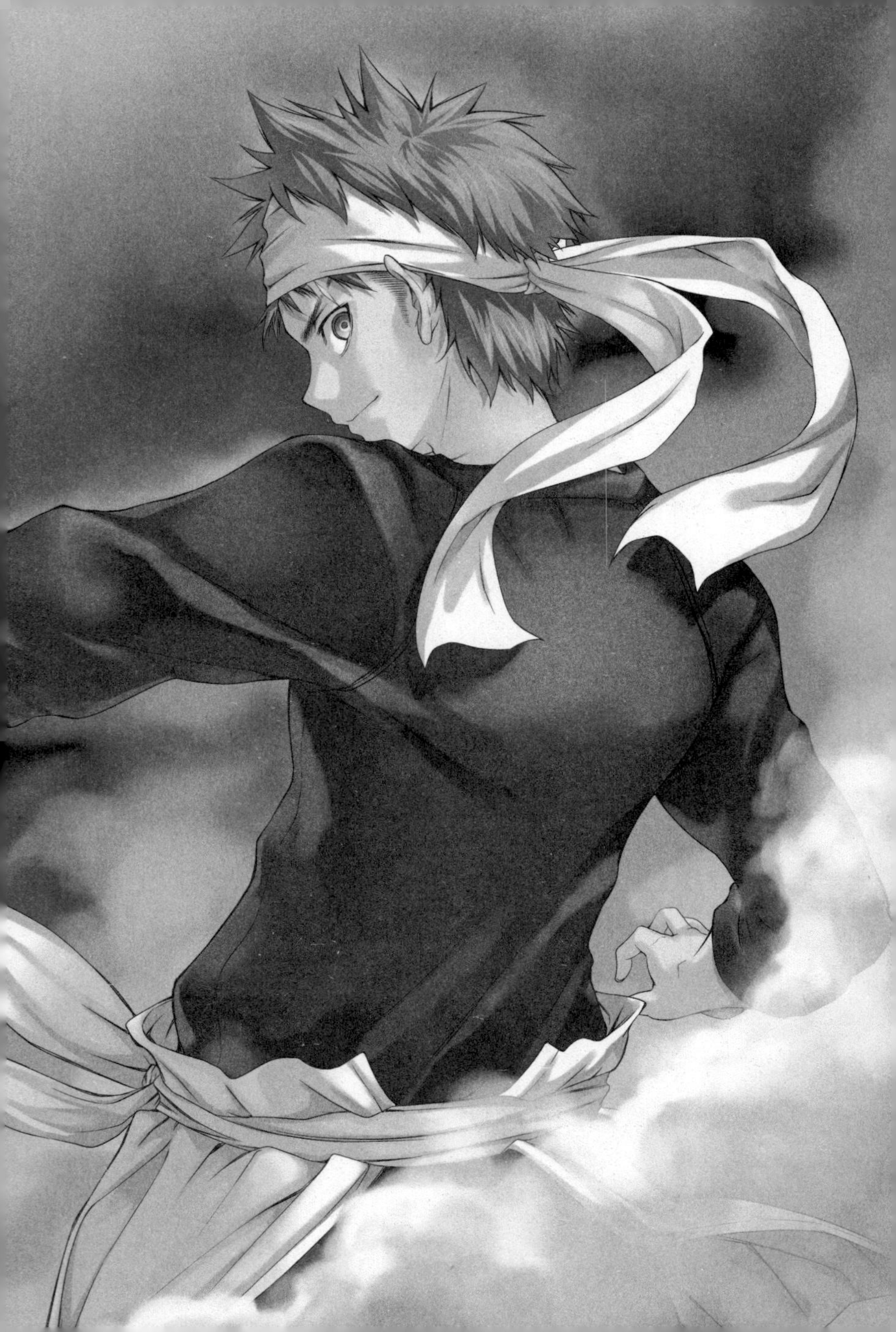

1 ENDLESS WILDERNESS

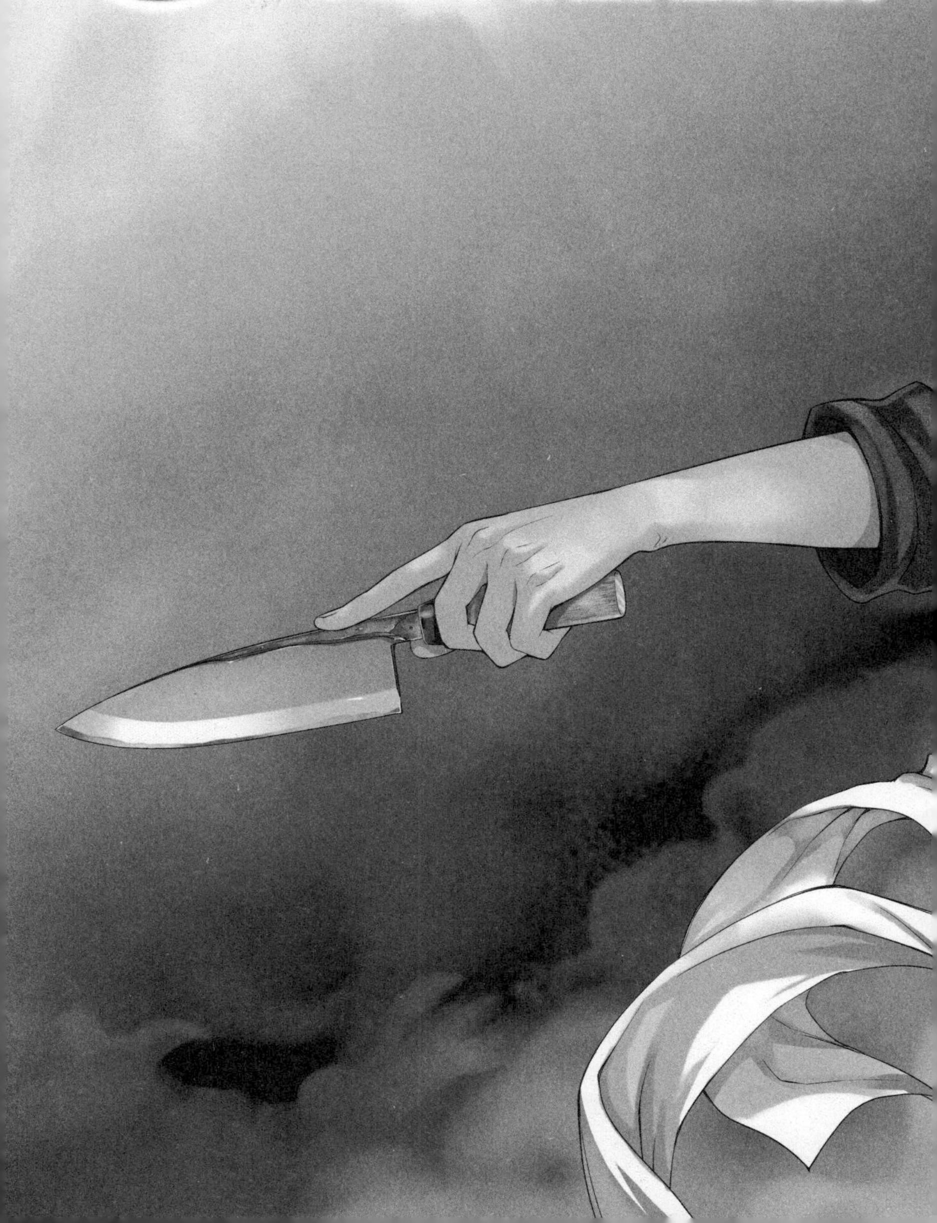

Food Wars!
SHOKUGEKI NO SOMA

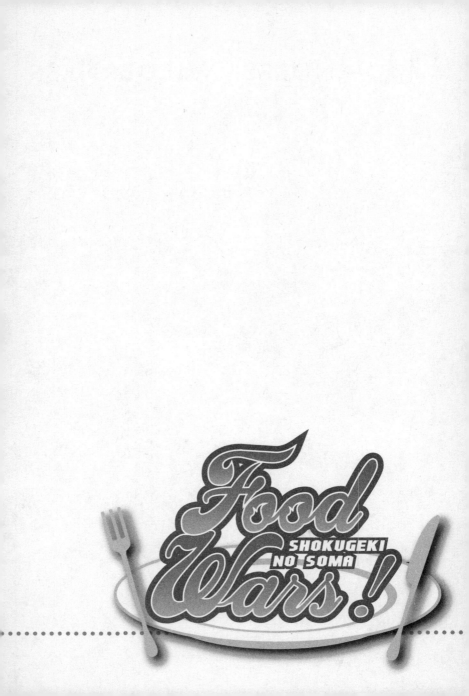

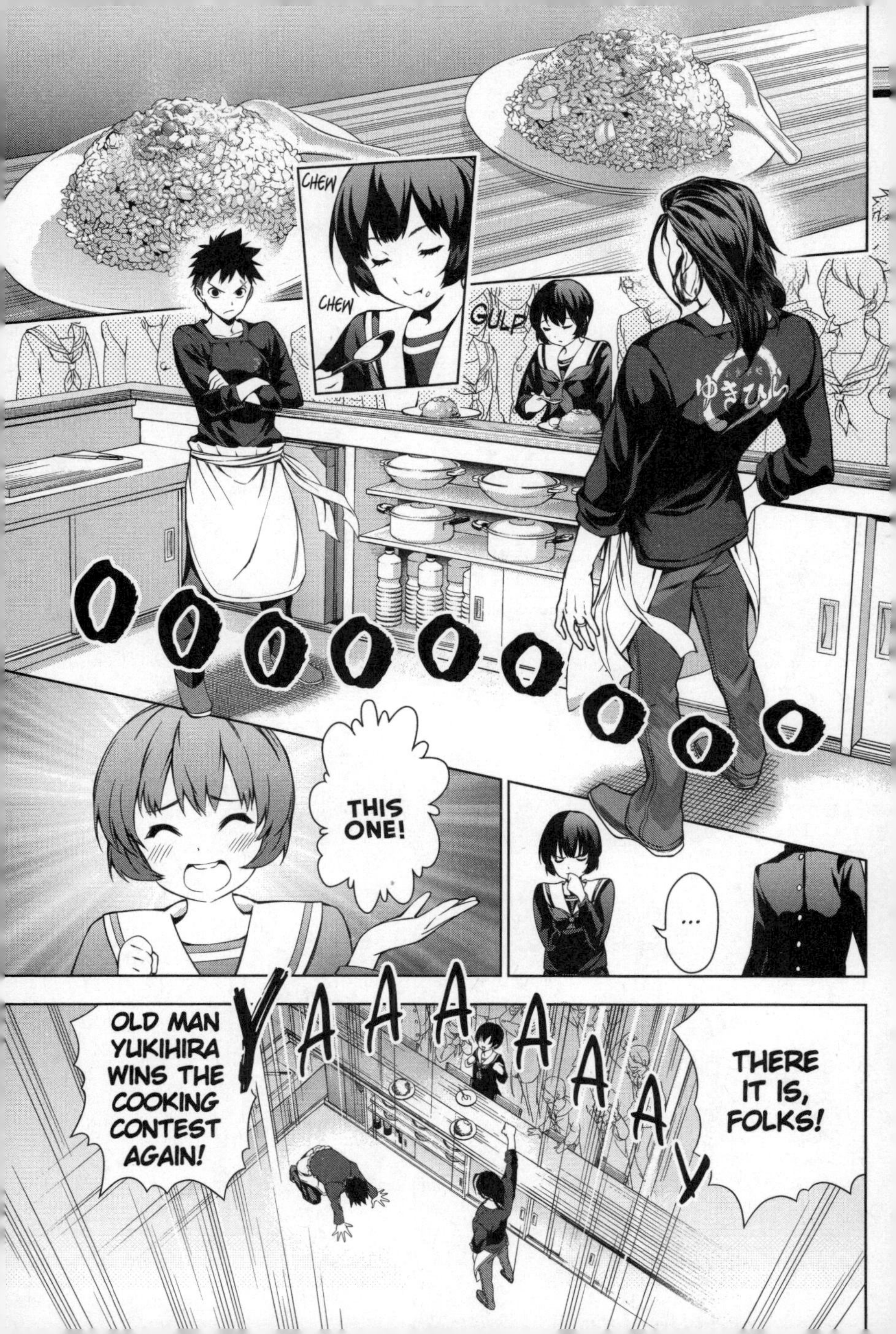
CHEW
CHEW
GULP
OOOOOOOOO
...
THIS ONE!
THERE IT IS, FOLKS!
YAAAAAAY
OLD MAN YUKIHIRA WINS THE COOKING CONTEST AGAIN!

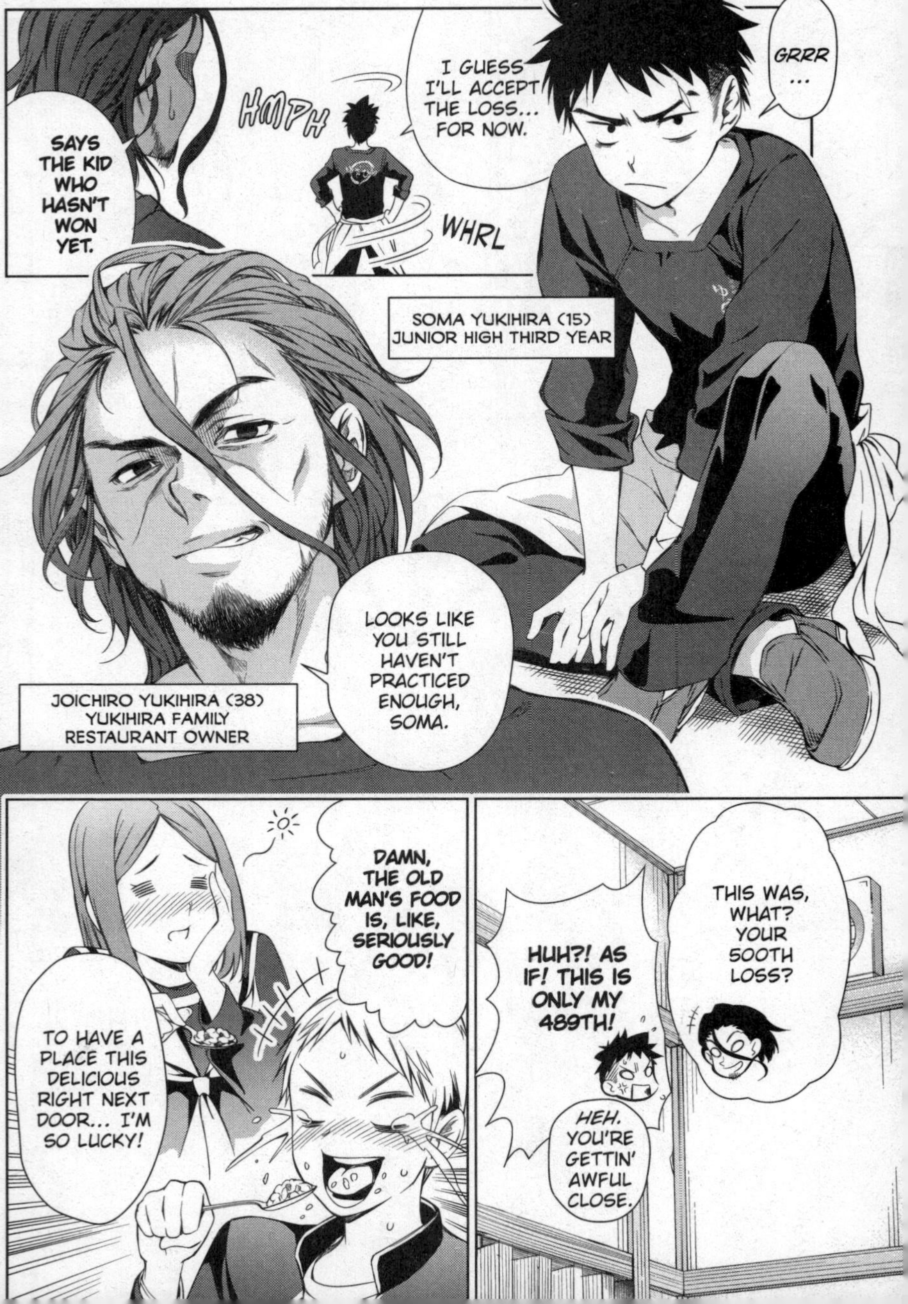
GRRR...
I GUESS I'LL ACCEPT THE LOSS... FOR NOW.
HMPH
WHRL
SAYS THE KID WHO HASN'T WON YET.
SOMA YUKIHIRA (15) JUNIOR HIGH THIRD YEAR
LOOKS LIKE YOU STILL HAVEN'T PRACTICED ENOUGH, SOMA.
JOICHIRO YUKIHIRA (38) YUKIHIRA FAMILY RESTAURANT OWNER
THIS WAS, WHAT? YOUR 500TH LOSS?
HUH?! AS IF! THIS IS ONLY MY 489TH!
HEH. YOU'RE GETTIN' AWFUL CLOSE.
DAMN, THE OLD MAN'S FOOD IS, LIKE, SERIOUSLY GOOD!
TO HAVE A PLACE THIS DELICIOUS RIGHT NEXT DOOR... I'M SO LUCKY!

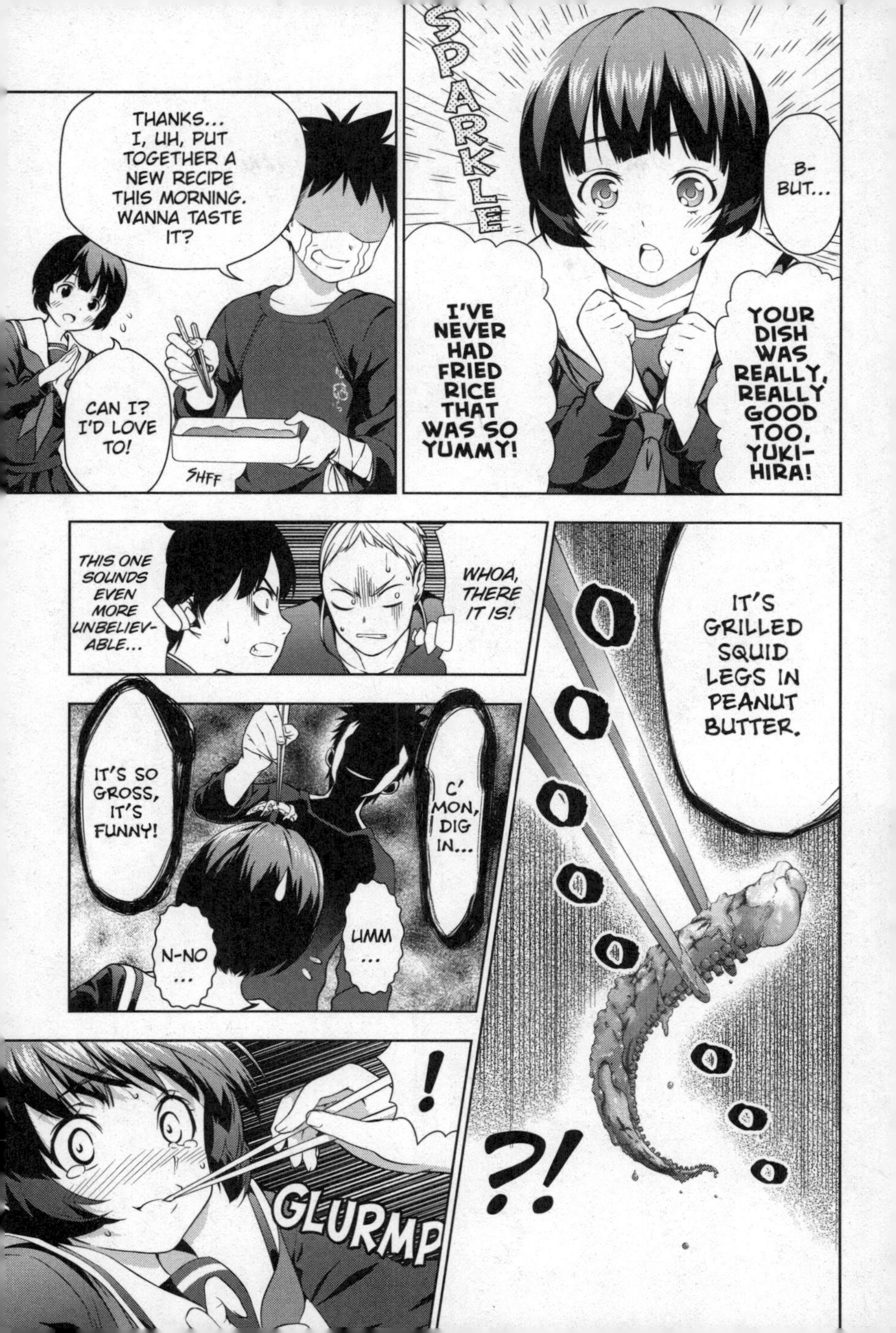
B- BUT...
SPARKLE
YOUR DISH WAS REALLY, REALLY GOOD TOO, YUKI-HIRA!
I'VE NEVER HAD FRIED RICE THAT WAS SO YUMMY!
THANKS... I, UH, PUT TOGETHER A NEW RECIPE THIS MORNING. WANNA TASTE IT?
CAN I? I'D LOVE TO!
SHFF
IT'S GRILLED SQUID LEGS IN PEANUT BUTTER.
?!
WHOA, THERE IT IS!
THIS ONE SOUNDS EVEN MORE UNBELIEV-ABLE...
C' MON, DIG IN...
IT'S SO GROSS, IT'S FUNNY!
UMM ...
N-NO ...
!
GLURMP

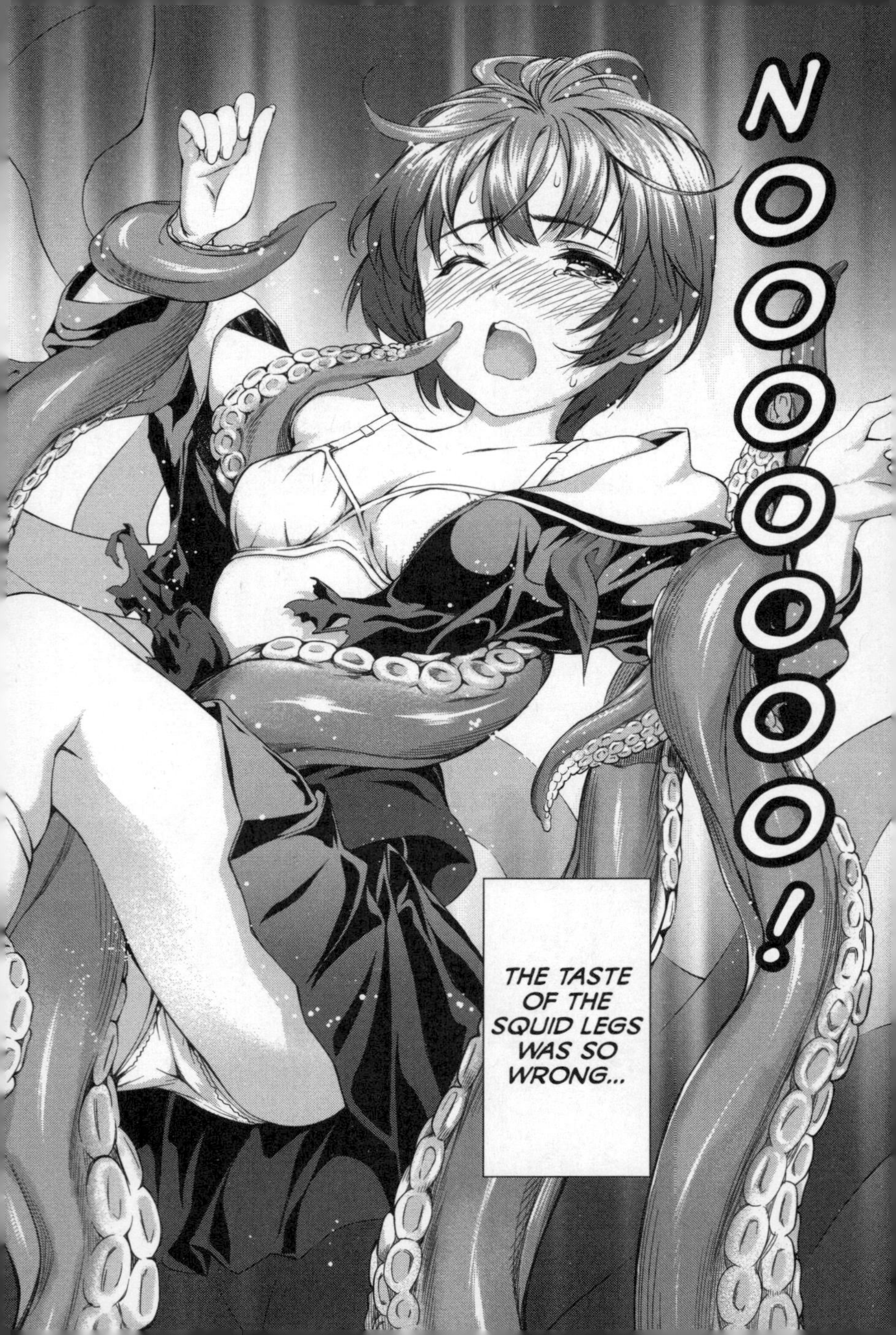
NOOOOOOOO!
THE TASTE OF THE SQUID LEGS WAS SO WRONG...

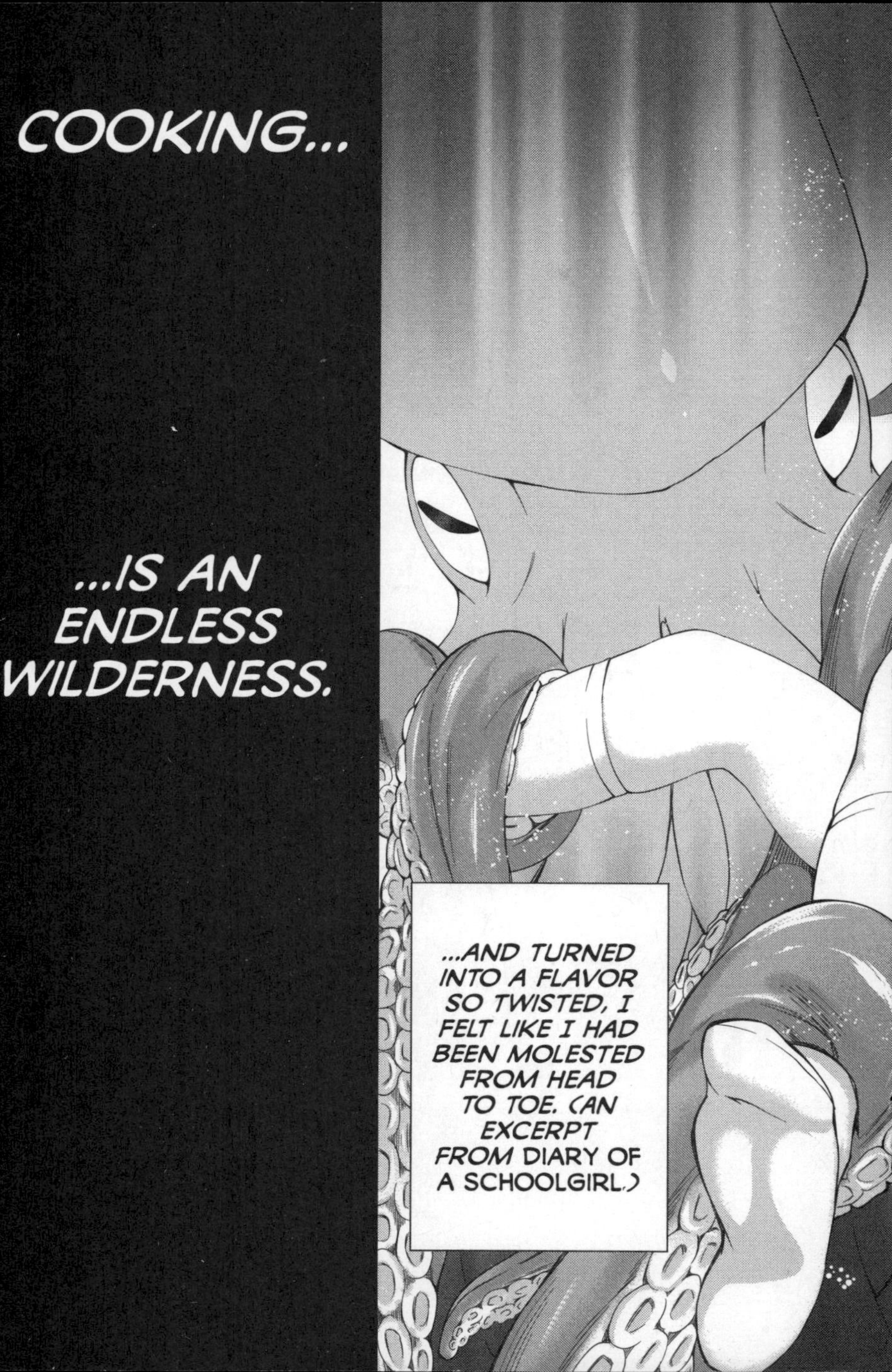
...AND TURNED INTO A FLAVOR SO TWISTED, I FELT LIKE I HAD BEEN MOLESTED FROM HEAD TO TOE. (AN EXCERPT FROM DIARY OF A SCHOOLGIRL.)
COOKING...
...IS AN ENDLESS WILDERNESS.

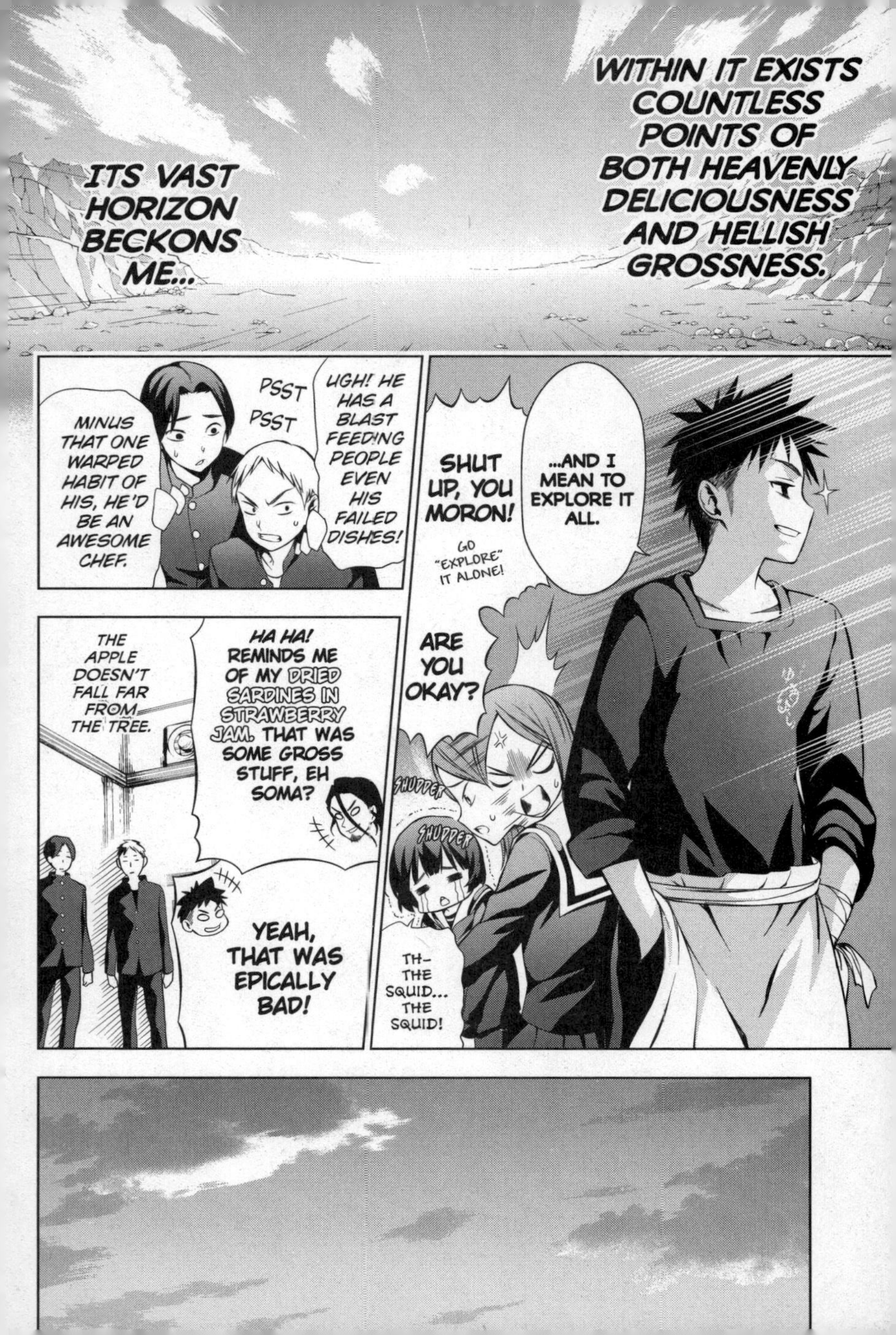
WITHIN IT EXISTS COUNTLESS POINTS OF BOTH HEAVENLY DELICIOUSNESS AND HELLISH GROSSNESS.
ITS VAST HORIZON BECKONS ME...
...AND I MEAN TO EXPLORE IT ALL.
SHUT UP, YOU MORON!
GO "EXPLORE" IT ALONE!
ARE YOU OKAY?
SHUDDER
SHUDDER
TH-THE SQUID... THE SQUID!
UGH! HE HAS A BLAST FEEDING PEOPLE EVEN HIS FAILED DISHES!
PSST
PSST
MINUS THAT ONE WARPED HABIT OF HIS, HE'D BE AN AWESOME CHEF.
HA HA! REMINDS ME OF MY DRIED SARDINES IN STRAWBERRY JAM. THAT WAS SOME GROSS STUFF, EH SOMA?
THE APPLE DOESN'T FALL FAR FROM THE TREE.
YEAH, THAT WAS EPICALLY BAD!

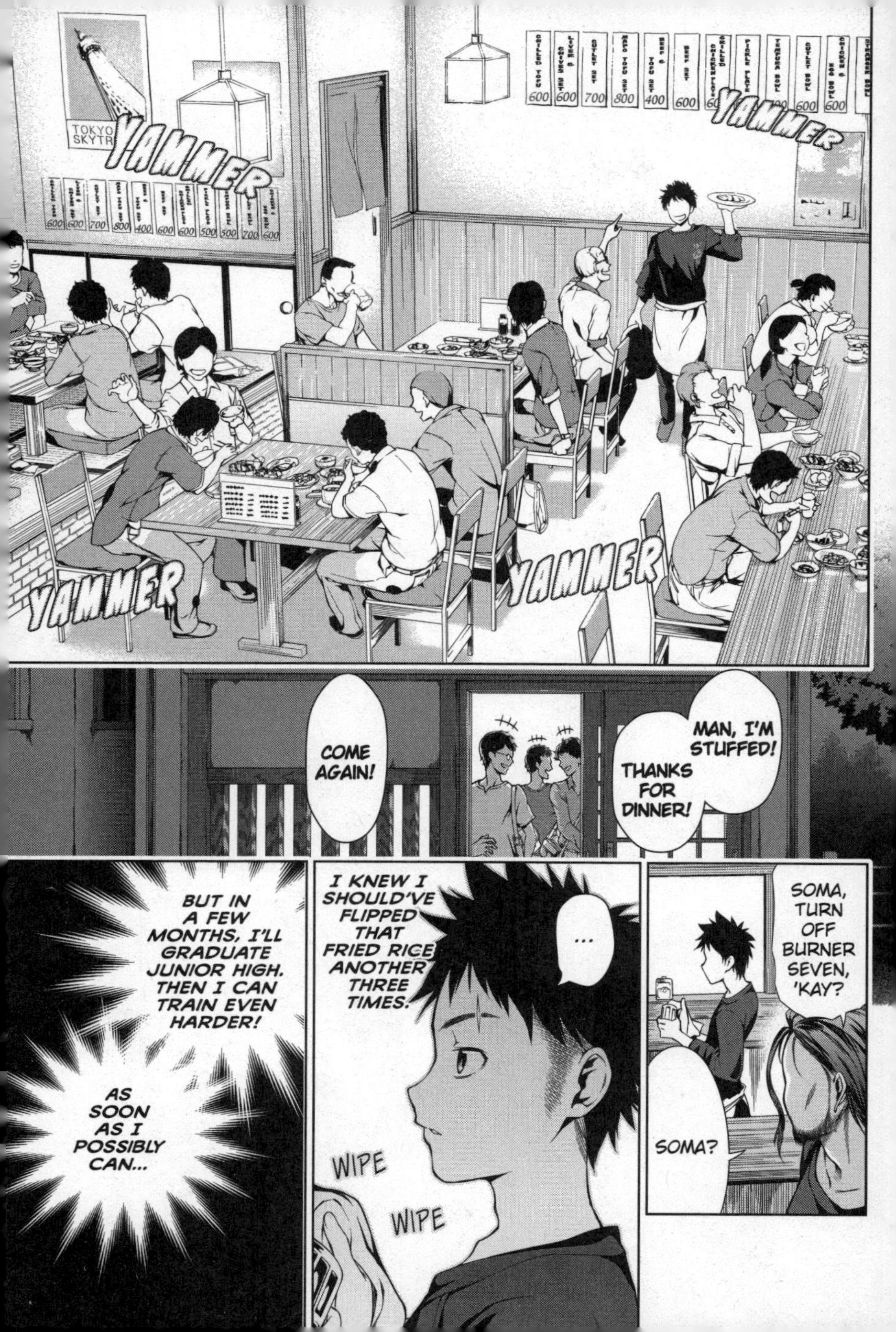
YAMMER
YAMMER
YAMMER
YAMMER
MAN, I'M STUFFED!
THANKS FOR DINNER!
COME AGAIN!
SOMA, TURN OFF BURNER SEVEN, 'KAY?
SOMA?
...
I KNEW I SHOULD'VE FLIPPED THAT FRIED RICE ANOTHER THREE TIMES.
WIPE
WIPE
BUT IN A FEW MONTHS, I'LL GRADUATE JUNIOR HIGH. THEN I CAN TRAIN EVEN HARDER!
AS SOON AS I POSSIBLY CAN...

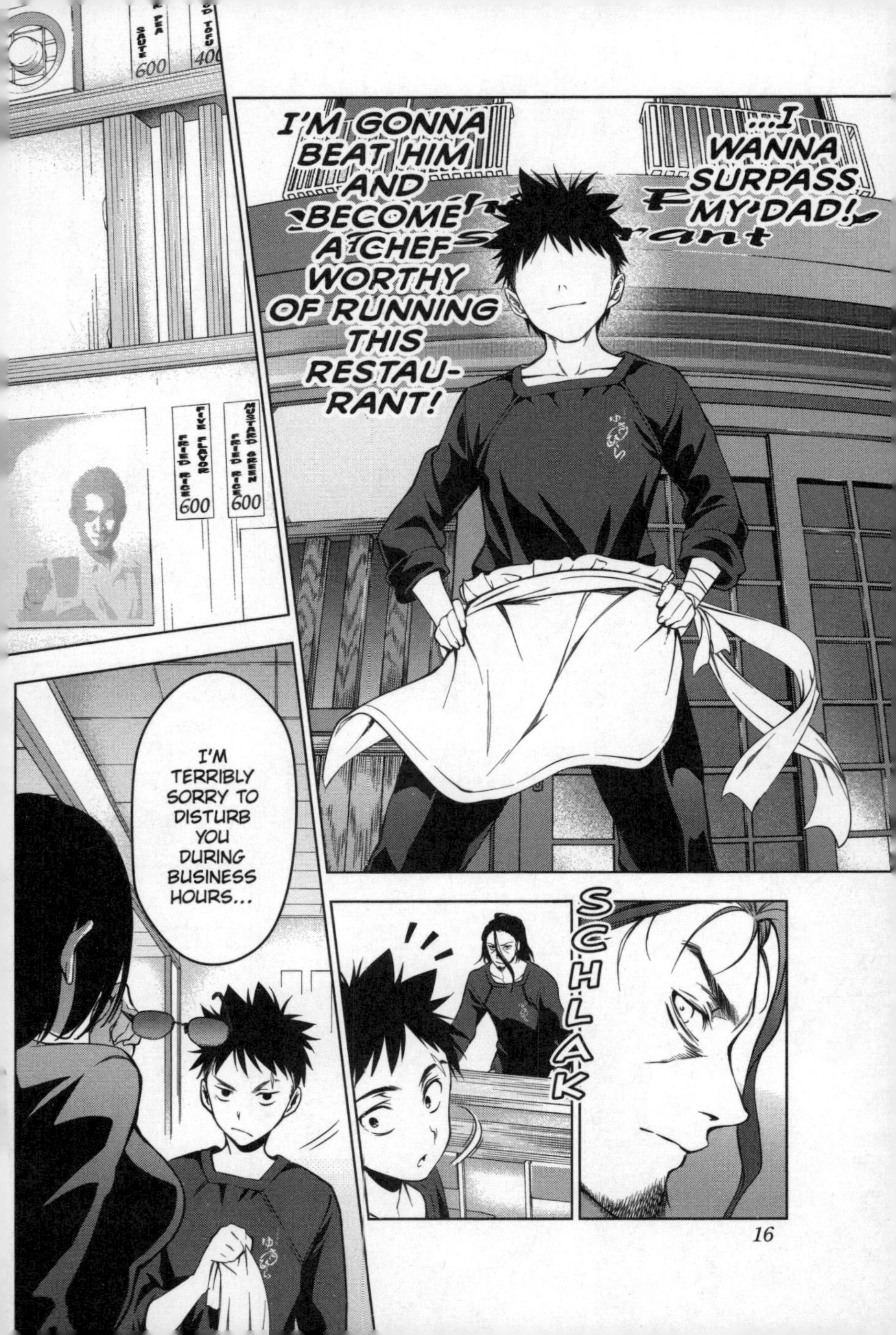
...I WANNA SURPASS MY DAD!
I'M GONNA BEAT HIM AND BECOME A CHEF WORTHY OF RUNNING THIS RESTAU-RANT!
PEA SAUTE 600
TOFU 400
FIVE FLAVOR FRIED RICE 600
MUSTARD GREEN FRIED RICE 600
SCHLAK
I'M TERRIBLY SORRY TO DISTURB YOU DURING BUSINESS HOURS...

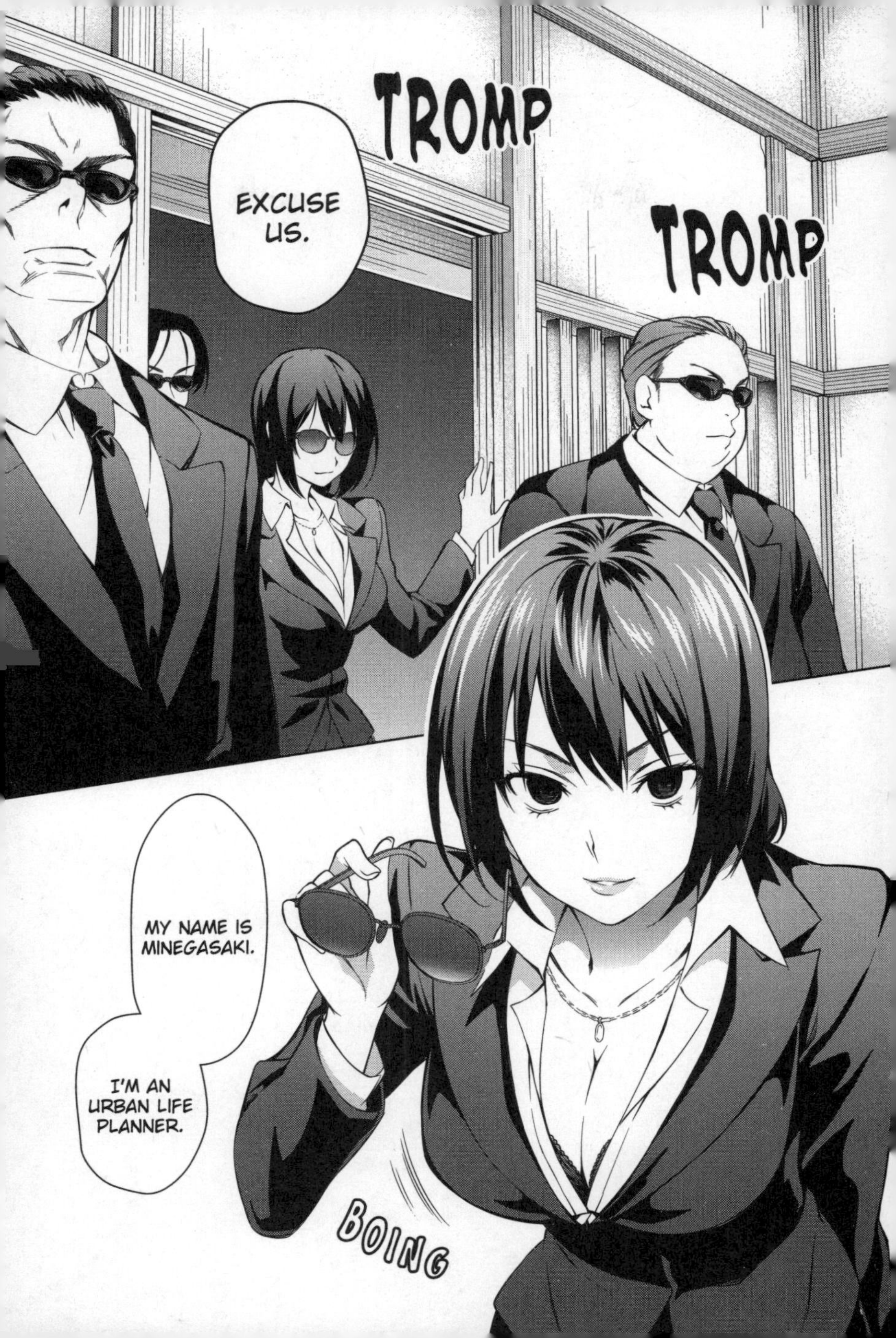
TROMP
TROMP
EXCUSE US.
MY NAME IS MINEGASAKI.
I'M AN URBAN LIFE PLANNER.
BOING

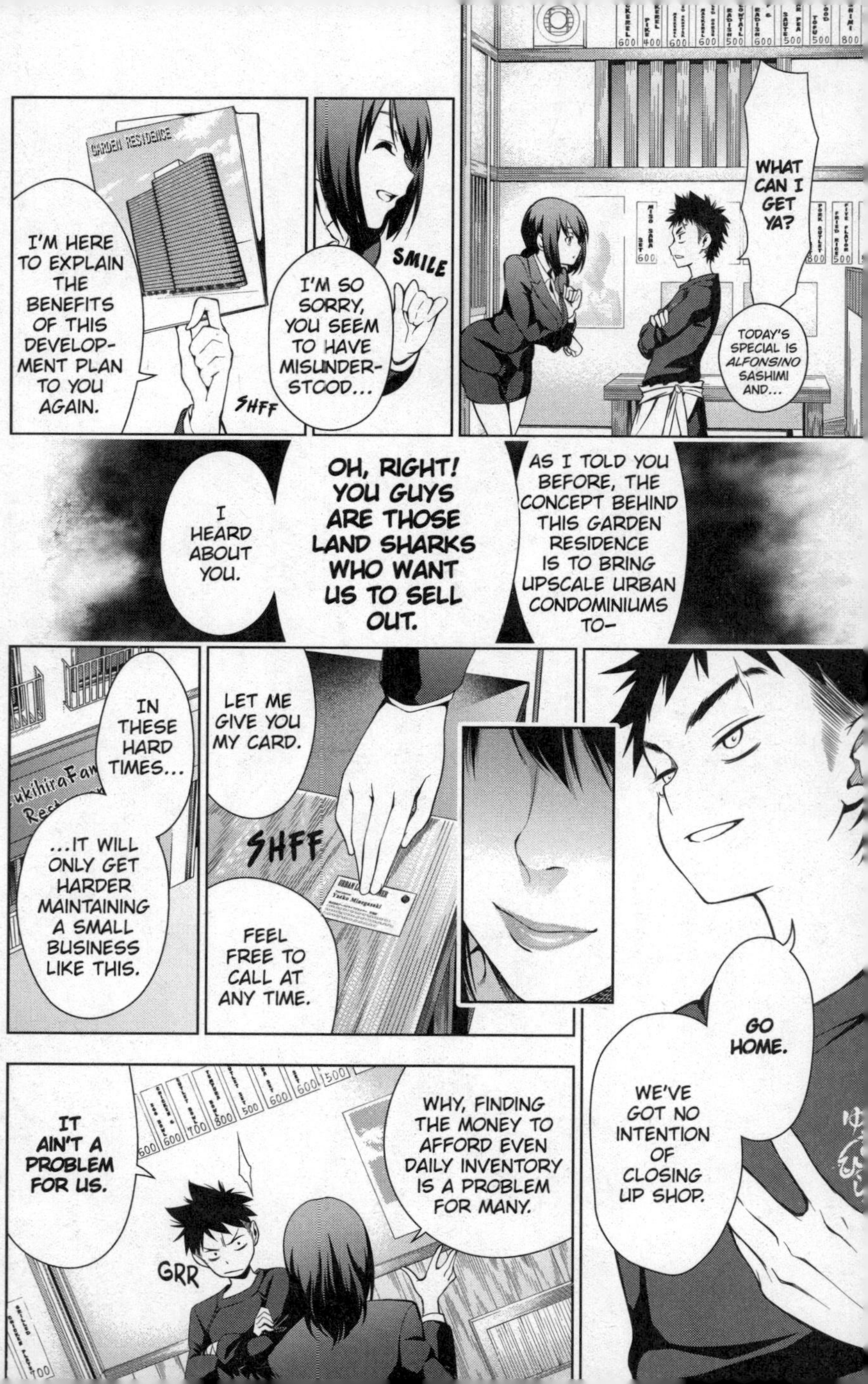
WHAT CAN I GET YA?
TODAY'S SPECIAL IS ALFONSINO SASHIMI AND...
SMILE
I'M SO SORRY, YOU SEEM TO HAVE MISUNDERSTOOD...
I'M HERE TO EXPLAIN THE BENEFITS OF THIS DEVELOPMENT PLAN TO YOU AGAIN.
SHFF
AS I TOLD YOU BEFORE, THE CONCEPT BEHIND THIS GARDEN RESIDENCE IS TO BRING UPSCALE URBAN CONDOMINIUMS TO–
OH, RIGHT! YOU GUYS ARE THOSE LAND SHARKS WHO WANT US TO SELL OUT.
I HEARD ABOUT YOU.
GO HOME.
WE'VE GOT NO INTENTION OF CLOSING UP SHOP.
LET ME GIVE YOU MY CARD.
SHFF
FEEL FREE TO CALL AT ANY TIME.
IN THESE HARD TIMES...
...IT WILL ONLY GET HARDER MAINTAINING A SMALL BUSINESS LIKE THIS.
WHY, FINDING THE MONEY TO AFFORD EVEN DAILY INVENTORY IS A PROBLEM FOR MANY.
IT AIN'T A PROBLEM FOR US.
GRR

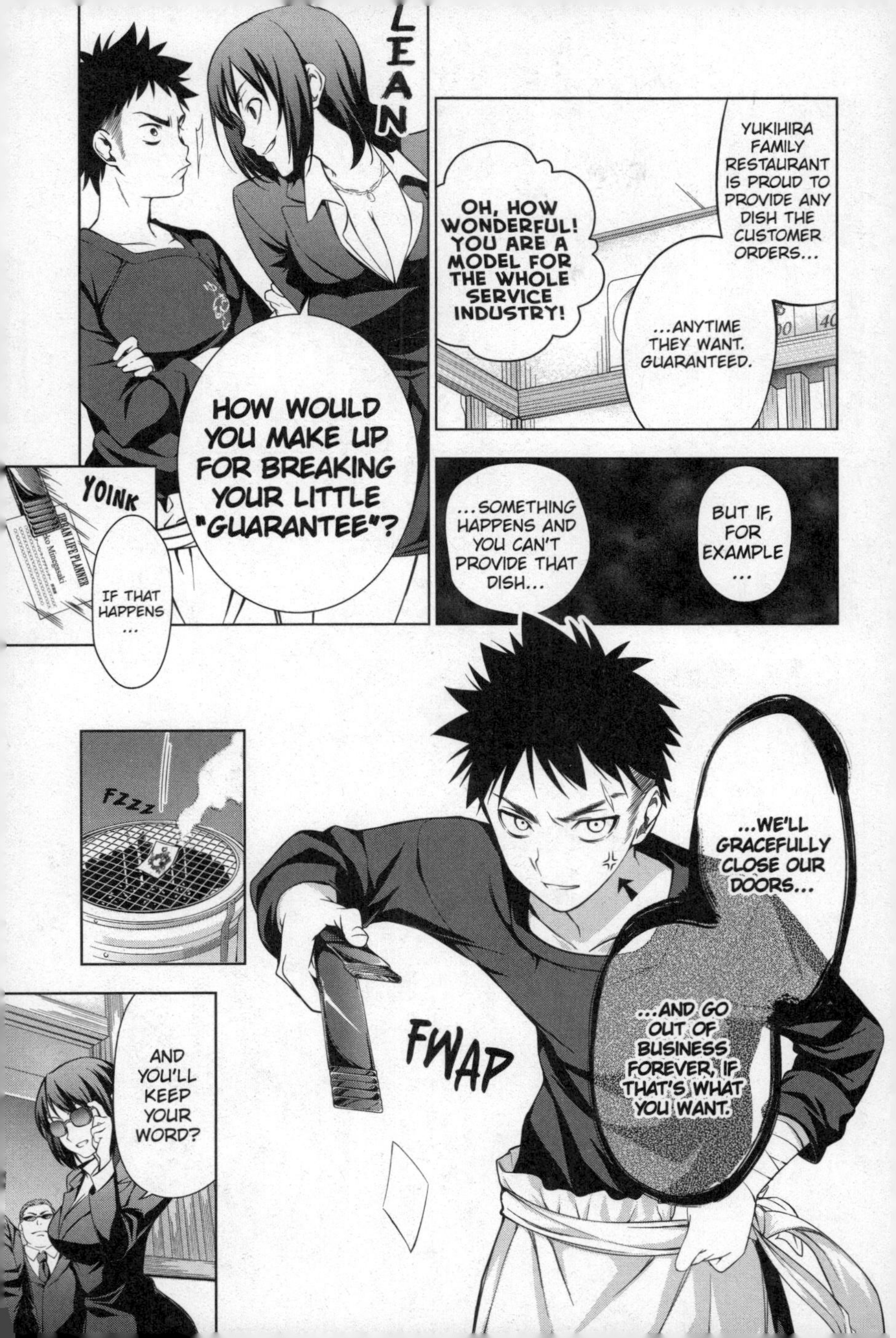
YUKIHIRA FAMILY RESTAURANT IS PROUD TO PROVIDE ANY DISH THE CUSTOMER ORDERS...
...ANYTIME THEY WANT. GUARANTEED.
OH, HOW WONDERFUL! YOU ARE A MODEL FOR THE WHOLE SERVICE INDUSTRY!
BUT IF, FOR EXAMPLE...
...SOMETHING HAPPENS AND YOU CAN'T PROVIDE THAT DISH...
LEAN
HOW WOULD YOU MAKE UP FOR BREAKING YOUR LITTLE "GUARANTEE"?
YOINK
IF THAT HAPPENS...
...WE'LL GRACEFULLY CLOSE OUR DOORS...
FWAP
...AND GO OUT OF BUSINESS FOREVER, IF THAT'S WHAT YOU WANT.
FZZZ
AND YOU'LL KEEP YOUR WORD?

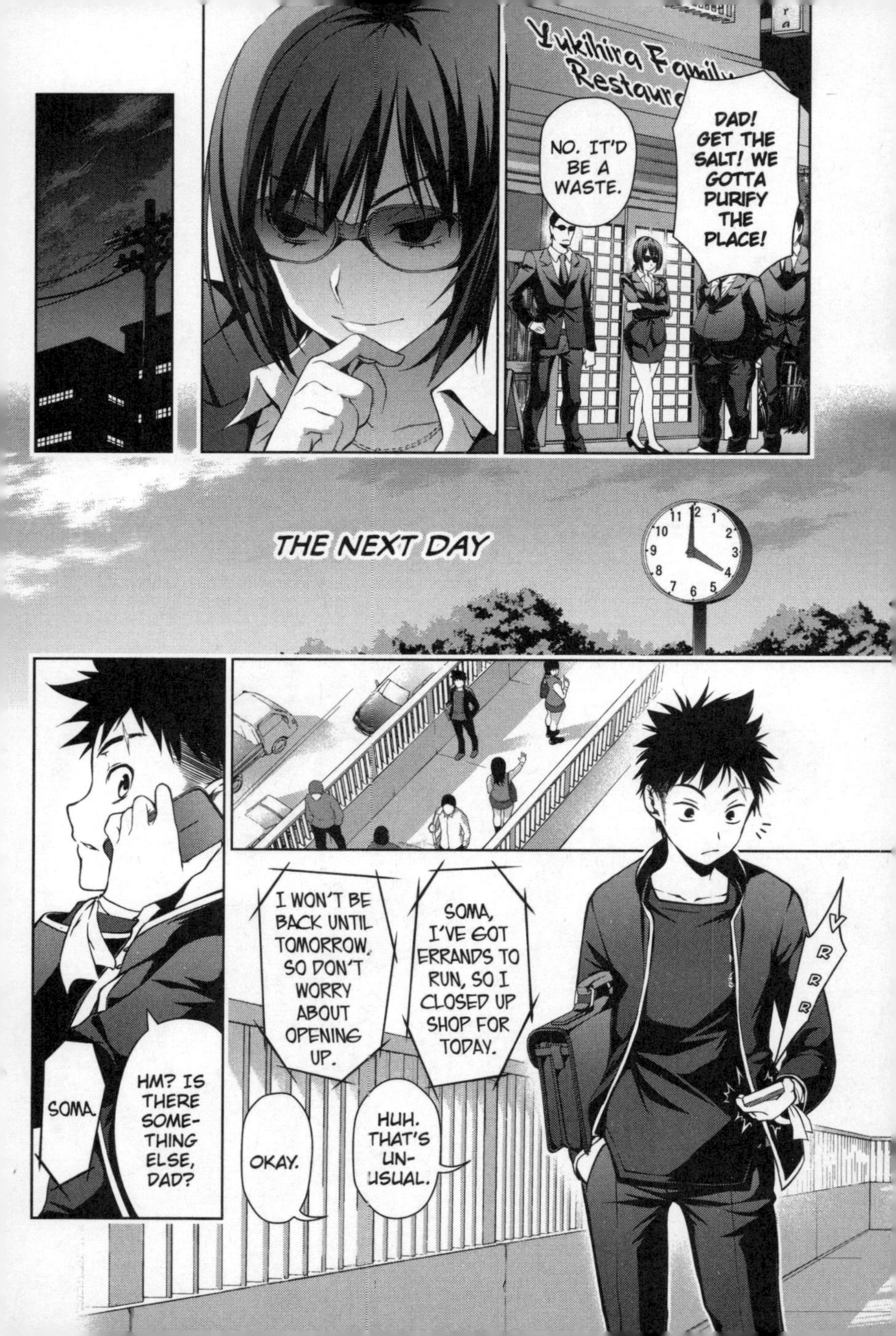
DAD! GET THE SALT! WE GOTTA PURIFY THE PLACE!
NO. IT'D BE A WASTE.
THE NEXT DAY
VRRRR
SOMA, I'VE GOT ERRANDS TO RUN, SO I CLOSED UP SHOP FOR TODAY.
I WON'T BE BACK UNTIL TOMORROW, SO DON'T WORRY ABOUT OPENING UP.
HUH. THAT'S UN-USUAL.
OKAY.
HM? IS THERE SOME-THING ELSE, DAD?
SOMA.

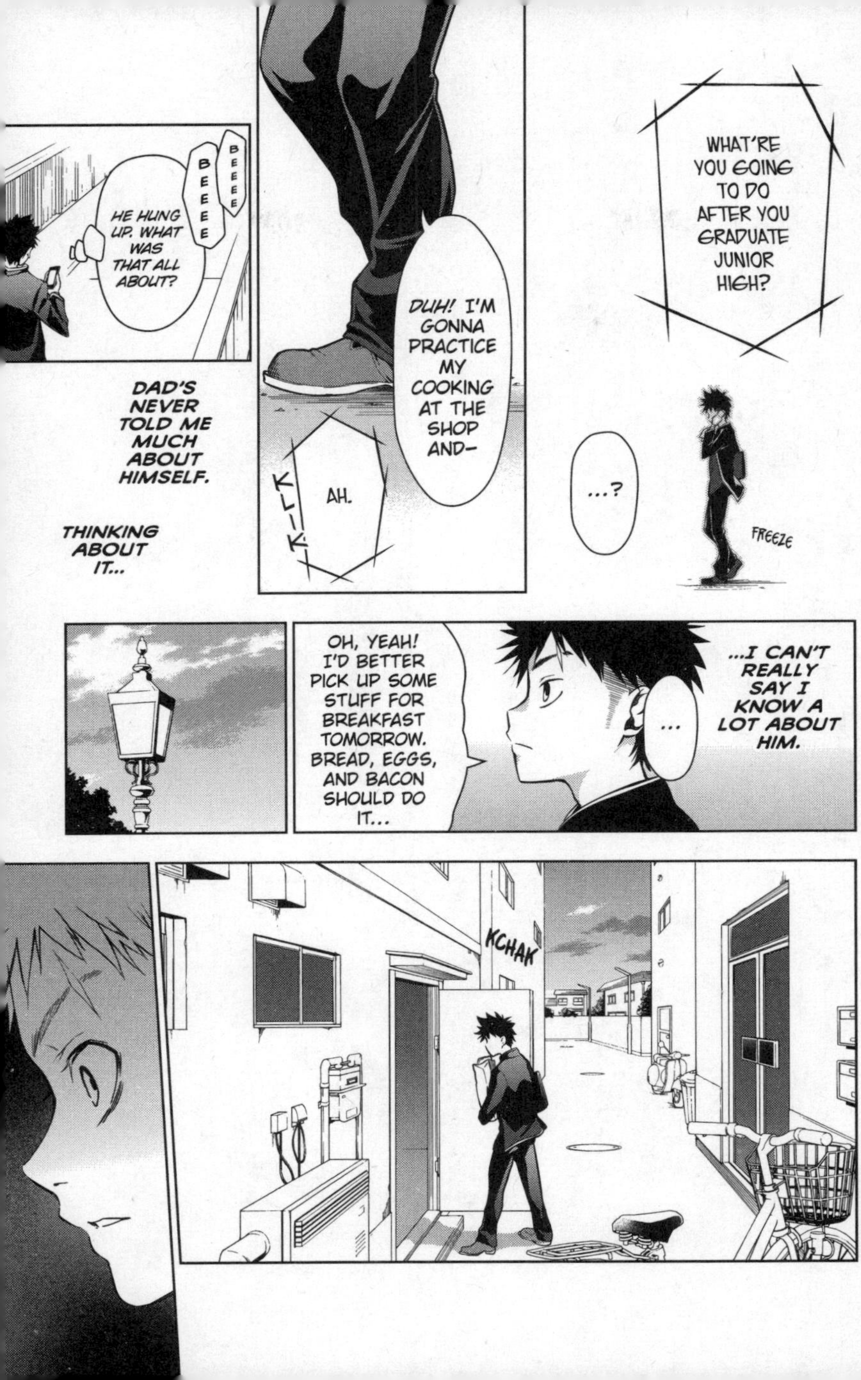
WHAT'RE YOU GOING TO DO AFTER YOU GRADUATE JUNIOR HIGH?
...?
FREEZE
DUH! I'M GONNA PRACTICE MY COOKING AT THE SHOP AND—
AH.
KLIK
BEEEE
BEEEE
HE HUNG UP. WHAT WAS THAT ALL ABOUT?
DAD'S NEVER TOLD ME MUCH ABOUT HIMSELF.
THINKING ABOUT IT...
...I CAN'T REALLY SAY I KNOW A LOT ABOUT HIM.
...
OH, YEAH! I'D BETTER PICK UP SOME STUFF FOR BREAKFAST TOMORROW. BREAD, EGGS, AND BACON SHOULD DO IT...
KCHAK

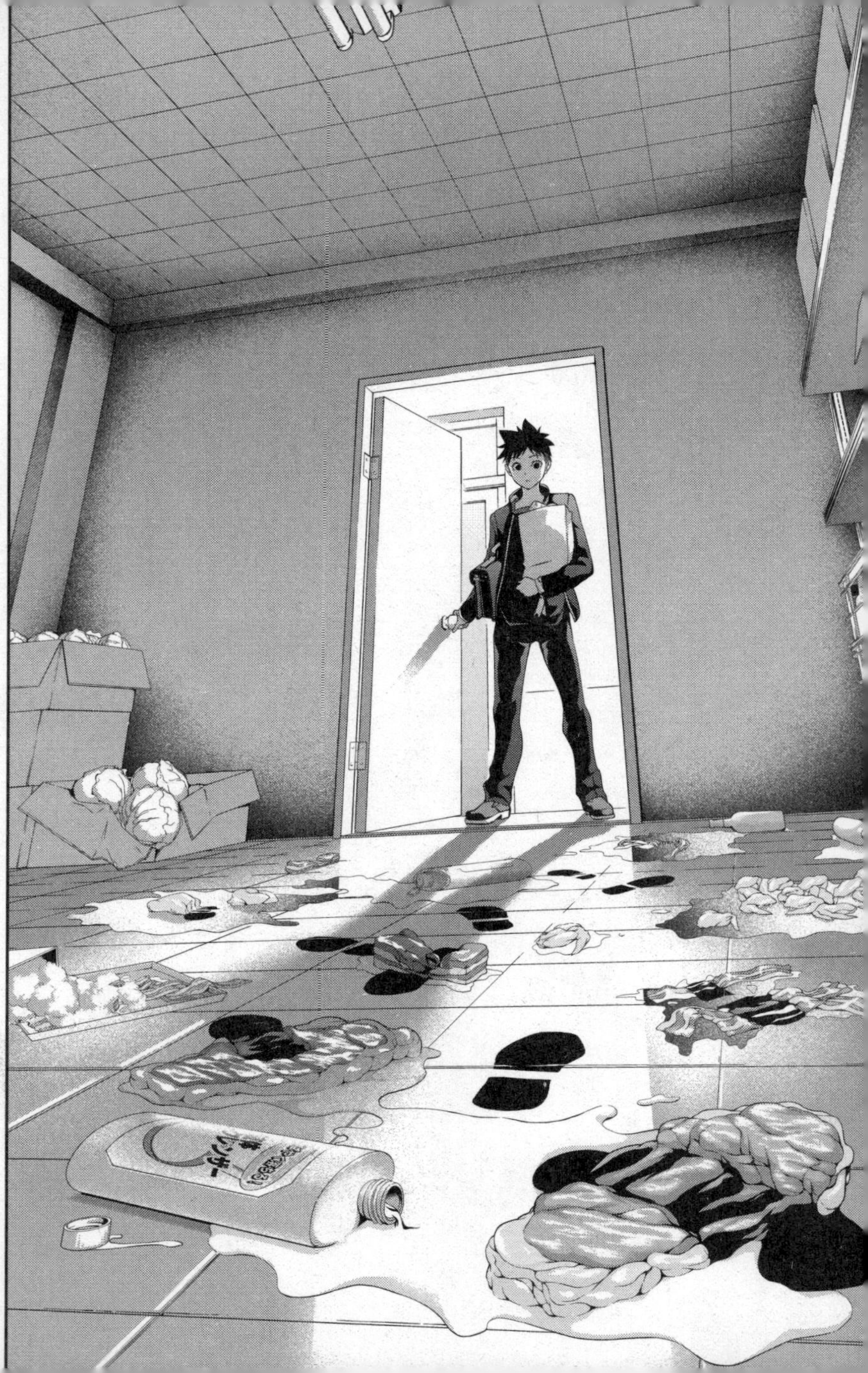

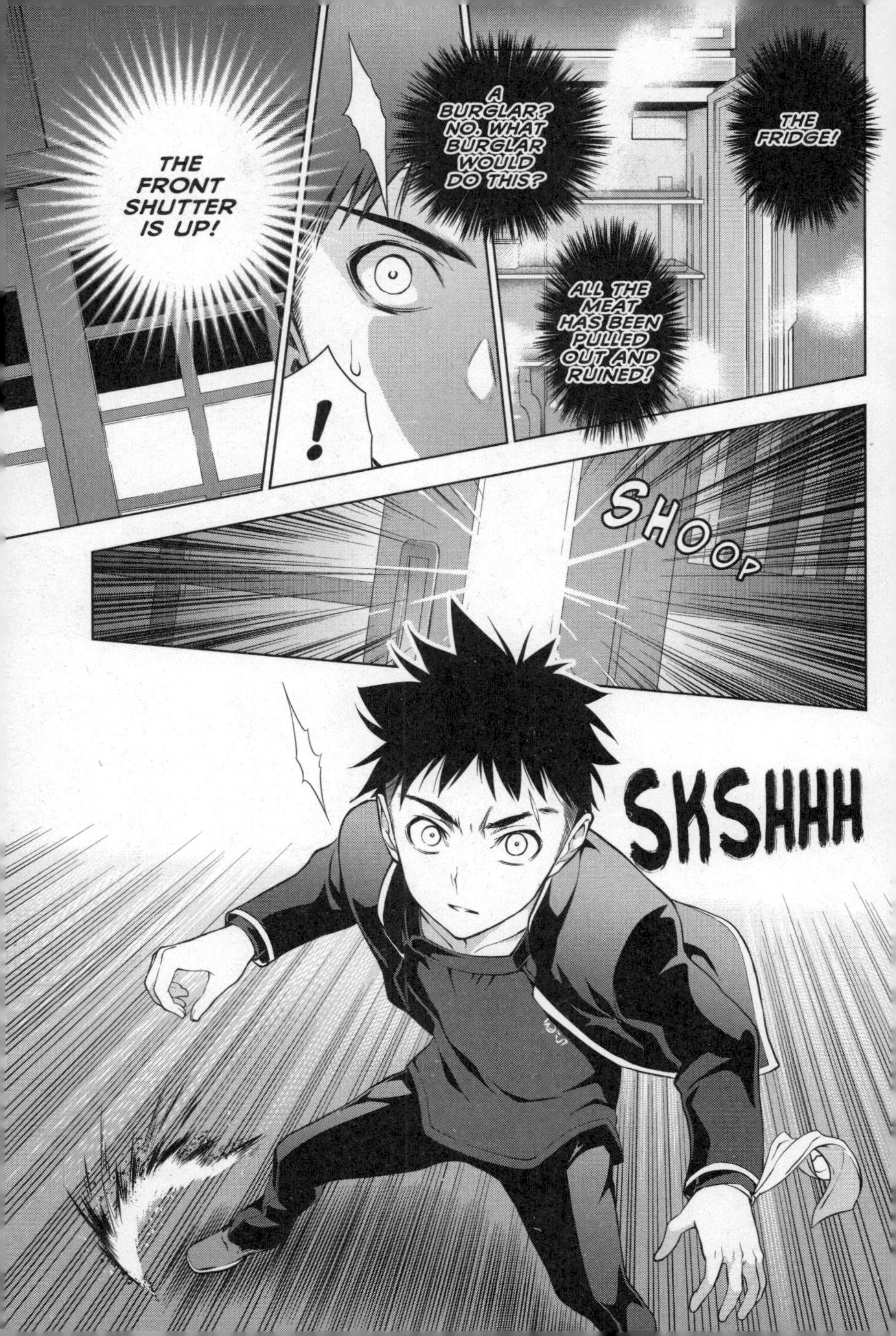
THE FRIDGE!
ALL THE MEAT HAS BEEN PULLED OUT AND RUINED!
A BURGLAR? NO. WHAT BURGLAR WOULD DO THIS?
!
THE FRONT SHUTTER IS UP!
SHOOP
SKSHHH

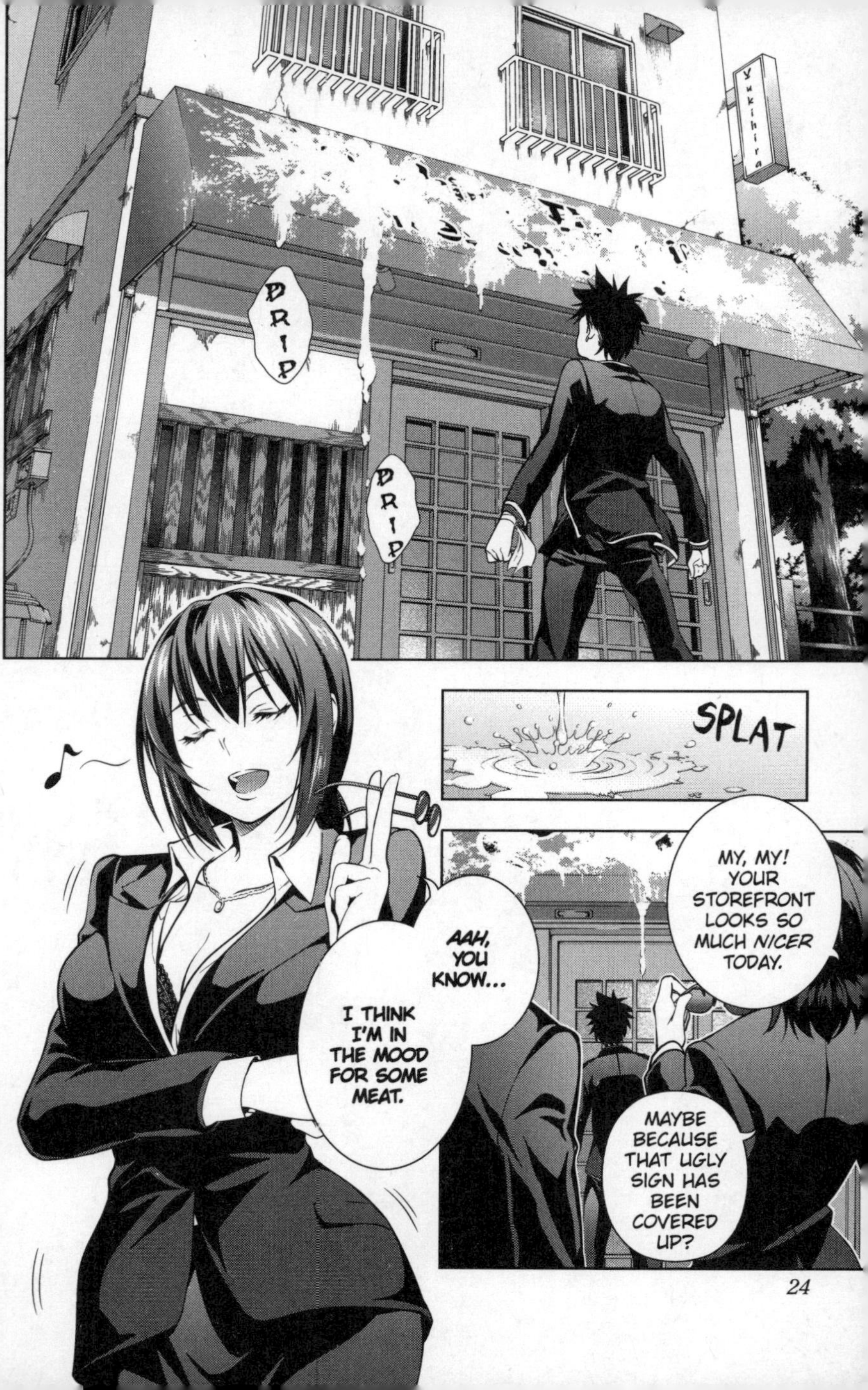
Yukihira
DRIP
DRIP
SPLAT
MY, MY! YOUR STOREFRONT LOOKS SO MUCH *NICER* TODAY.
MAYBE BECAUSE THAT UGLY SIGN HAS BEEN COVERED UP?
AAH, YOU KNOW...
I THINK I'M IN THE MOOD FOR SOME MEAT.

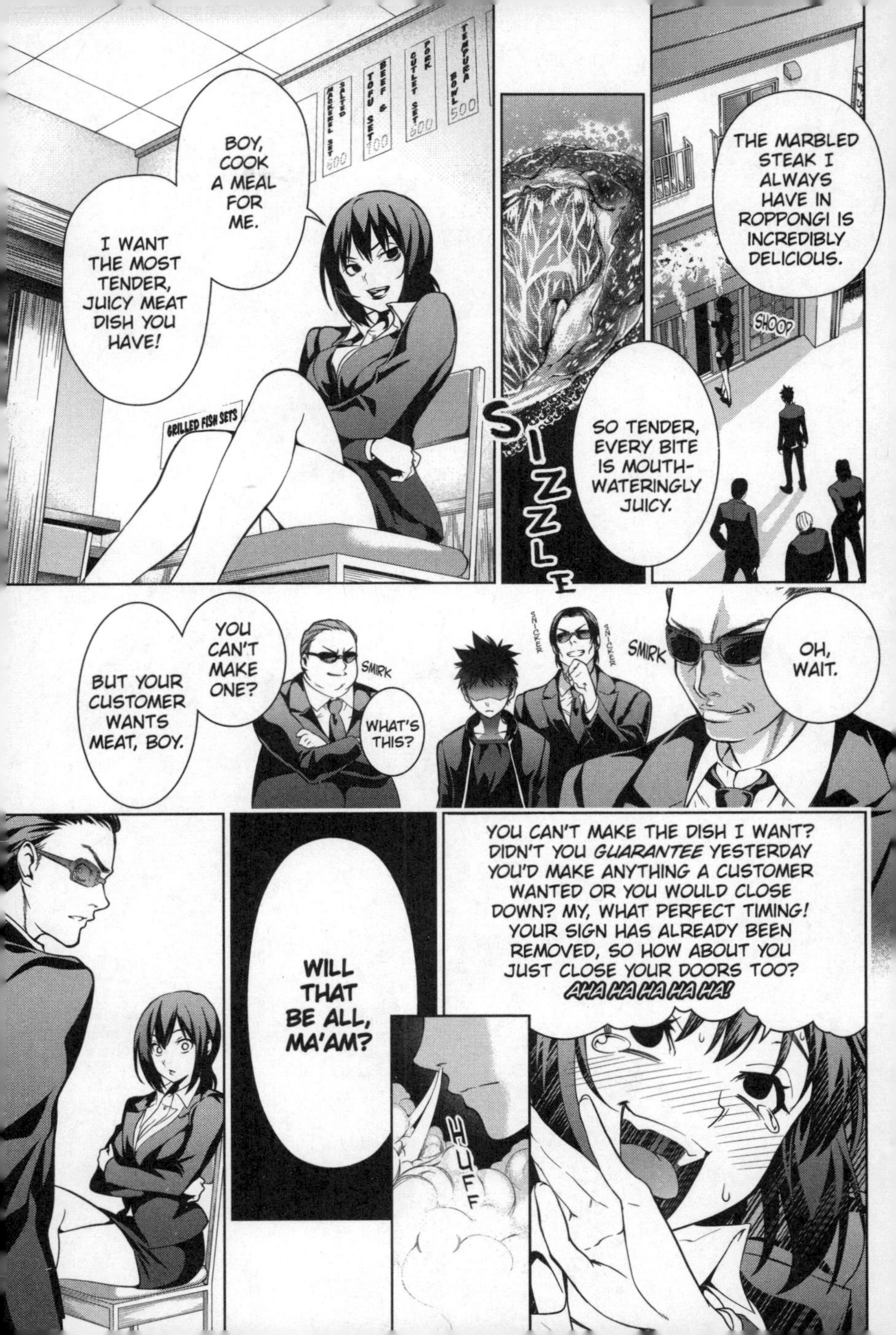
THE MARBLED STEAK I ALWAYS HAVE IN ROPPONGI IS INCREDIBLY DELICIOUS.
SHOOP
SO TENDER, EVERY BITE IS MOUTH-WATERINGLY JUICY.
SIZZLE
TEMPURA BOWL 500
PORK CUTLET SET 600
BEEF & TOFU SET 700
SALTED MACKEREL SET 600
BOY, COOK A MEAL FOR ME.
I WANT THE MOST TENDER, JUICY MEAT DISH YOU HAVE!
GRILLED FISH SETS
OH, WAIT.
SMIRK
SNICKER
SNICKER
WHAT'S THIS?
SMIRK
YOU CAN'T MAKE ONE?
BUT YOUR CUSTOMER WANTS MEAT, BOY.
YOU CAN'T MAKE THE DISH I WANT? DIDN'T YOU *GUARANTEE* YESTERDAY YOU'D MAKE ANYTHING A CUSTOMER WANTED OR YOU WOULD CLOSE DOWN? MY, WHAT PERFECT TIMING! YOUR SIGN HAS ALREADY BEEN REMOVED, SO HOW ABOUT YOU JUST CLOSE YOUR DOORS TOO?
AHA HA HA HA HA HA!
HUFF
WILL THAT BE ALL, MA'AM?

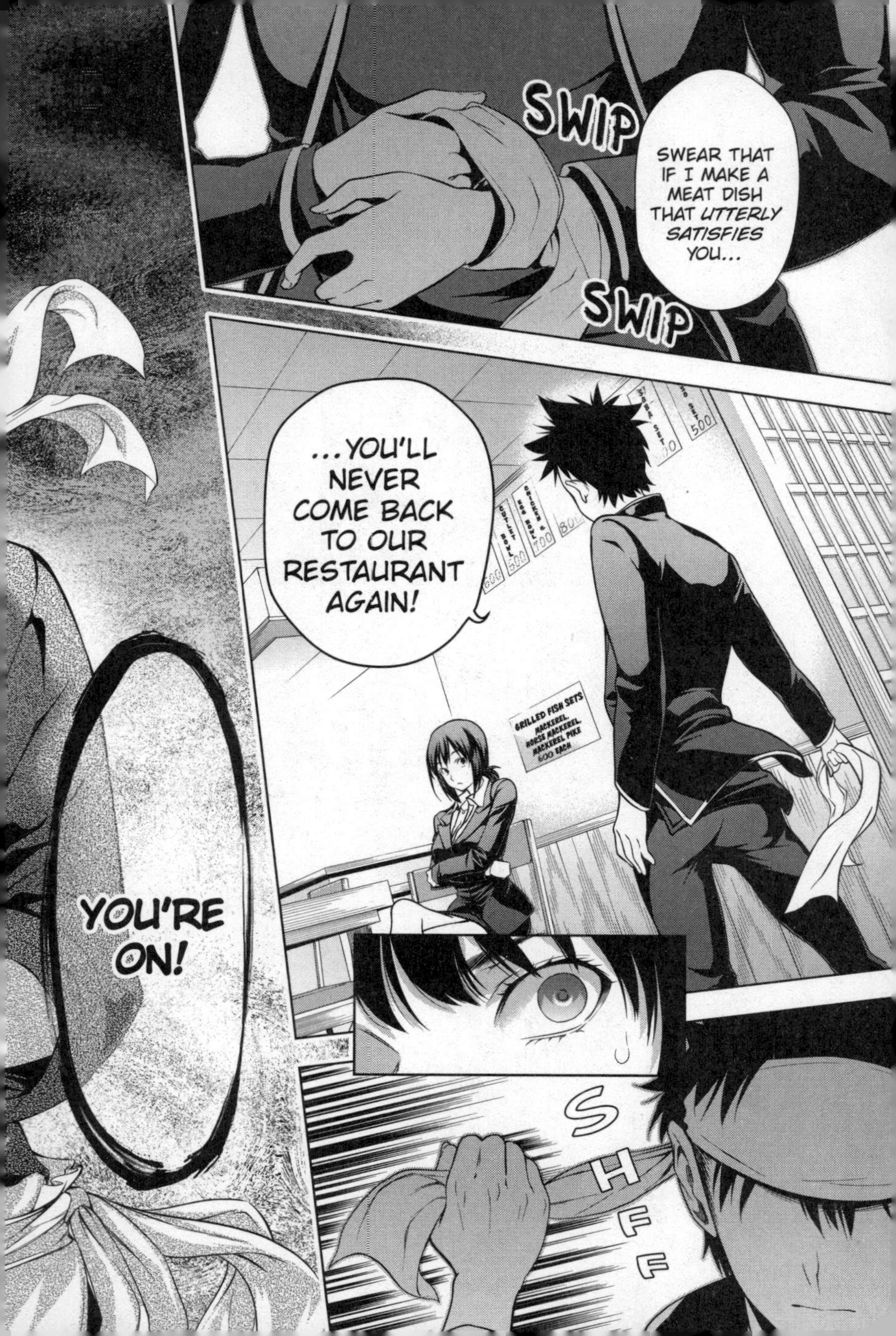
SWIP
SWEAR THAT IF I MAKE A MEAT DISH THAT *UTTERLY SATISFIES* YOU...
SWIP
...YOU'LL NEVER COME BACK TO OUR RESTAURANT AGAIN!
GRILLED FISH SETS MACKEREL, HORSE MACKEREL, MACKEREL PIKE 600 EACH
SHFF
YOU'RE ON!

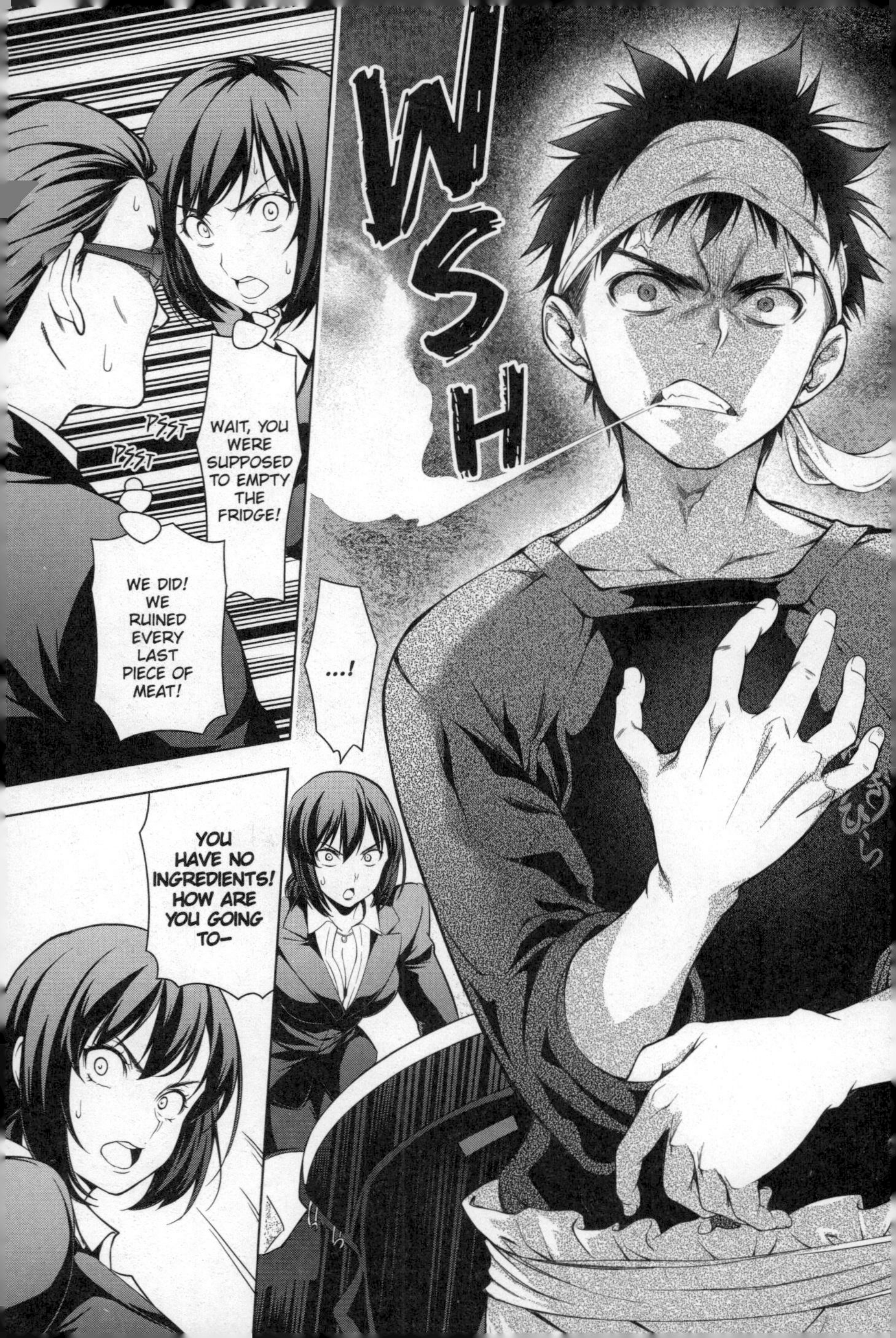
WSH
...!
PSST
PSST
WAIT, YOU WERE SUPPOSED TO EMPTY THE FRIDGE!
WE DID! WE RUINED EVERY LAST PIECE OF MEAT!
YOU HAVE NO INGREDIENTS! HOW ARE YOU GOING TO-

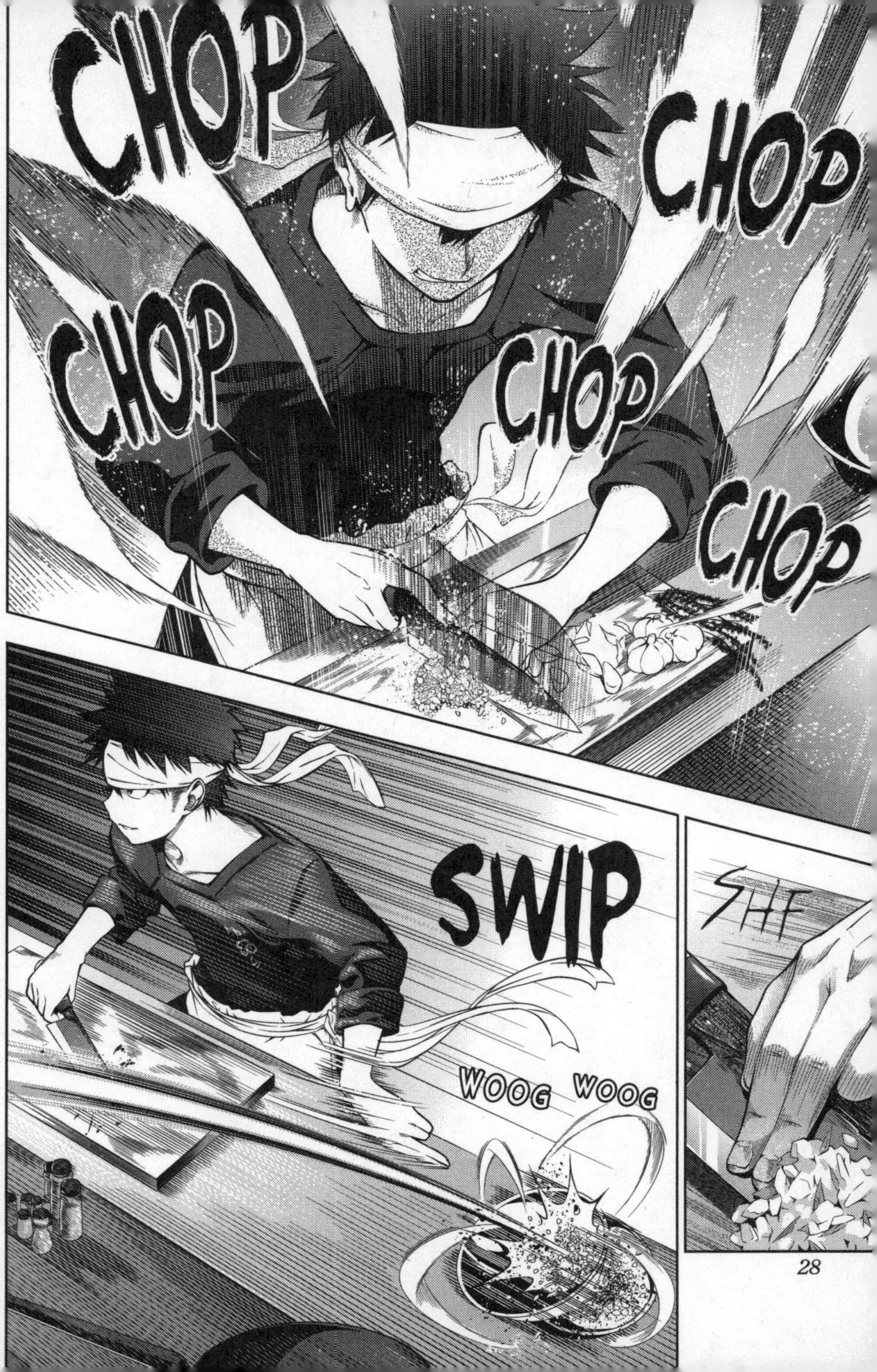
CHOP
CHOP
CHOP
CHOP
CHOP
SHF
SWIP
WOOG WOOG

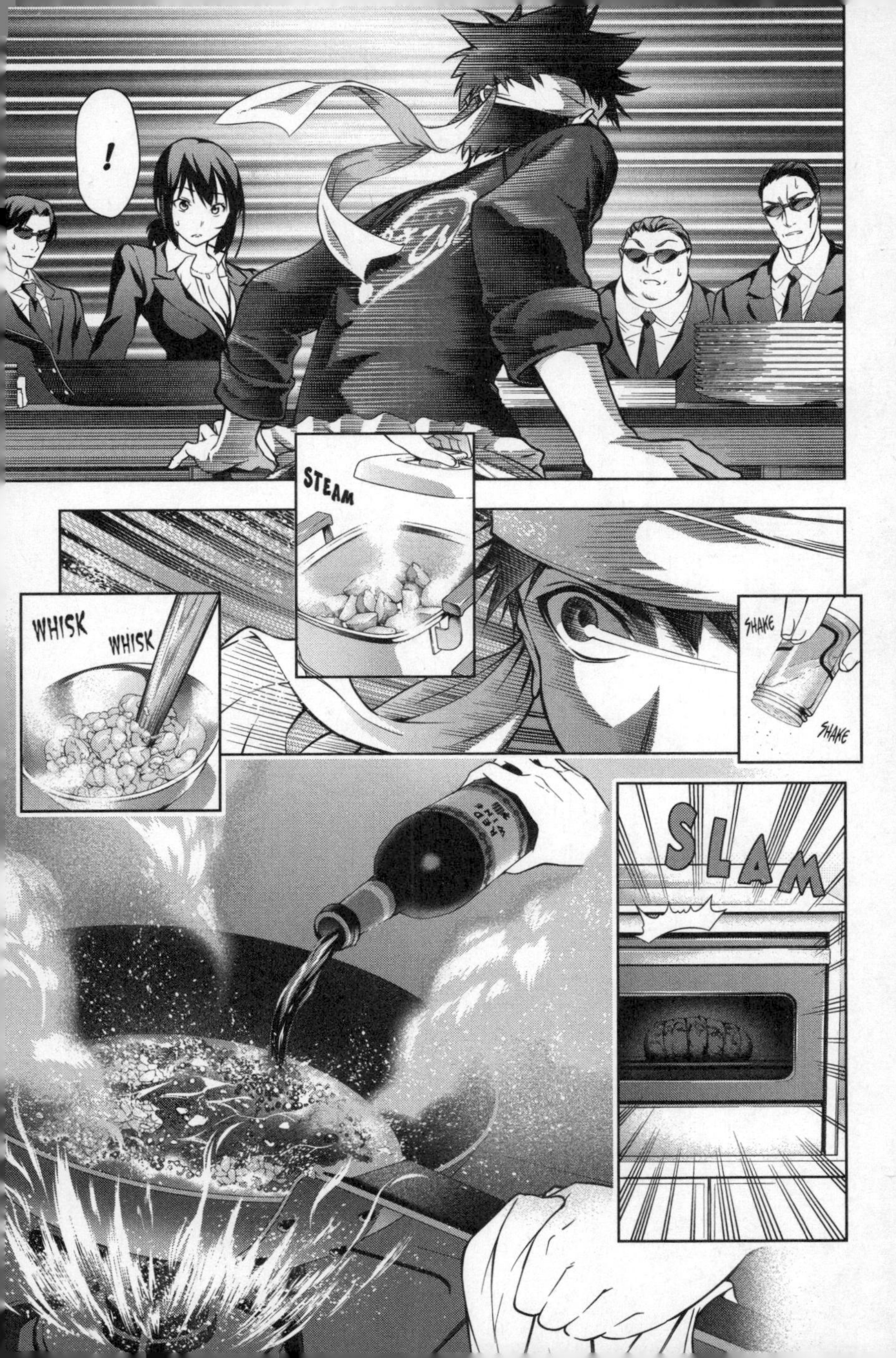
!
STEAM
SHAKE
SHAKE
WHISK
WHISK
SLAM

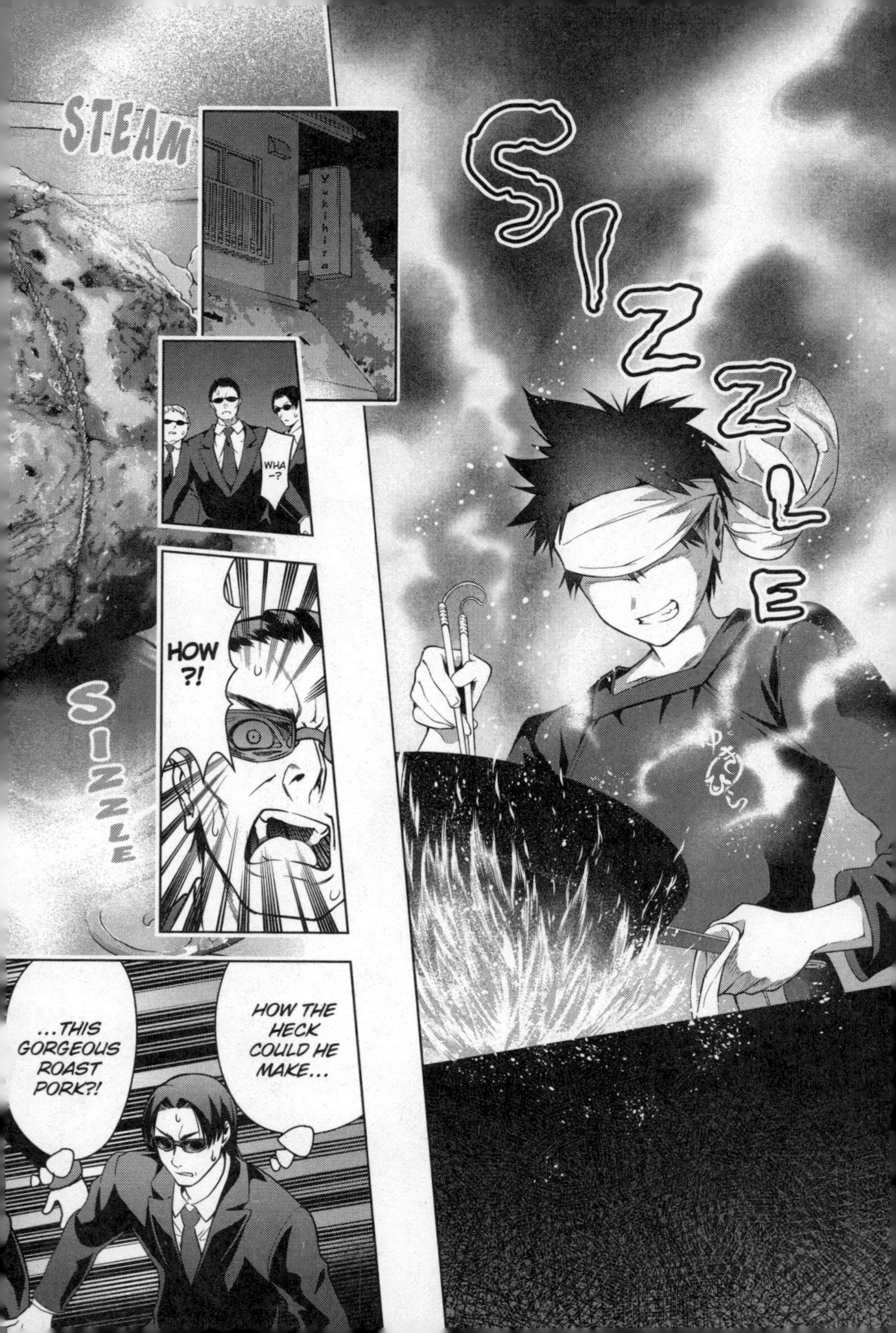
SIZZLE
STEAM
Yukihira
WHA
-?
HOW
?!
SIZZLE
HOW THE HECK COULD HE MAKE...
...THIS GORGEOUS ROAST PORK?!

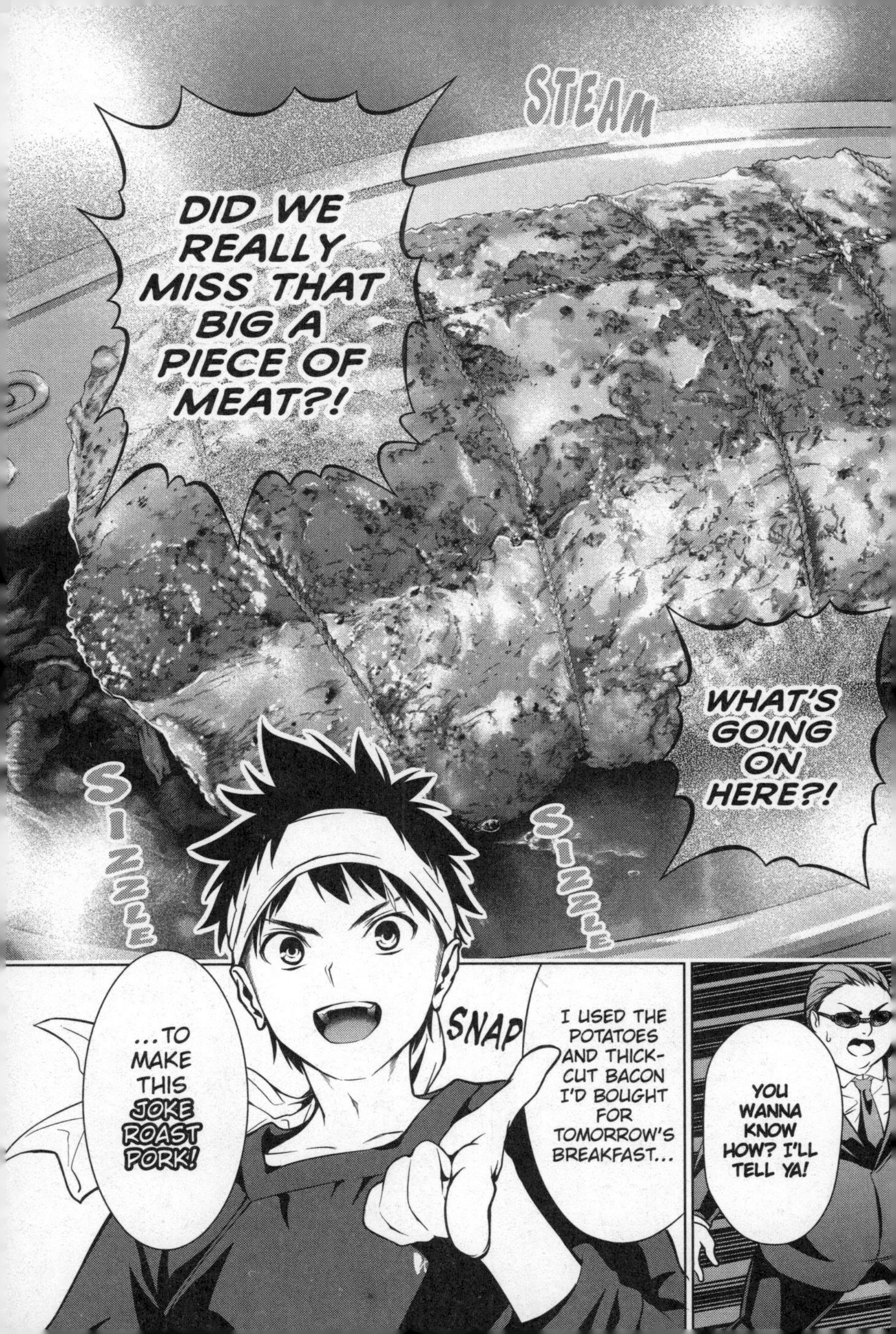
STEAM
DID WE REALLY MISS THAT BIG A PIECE OF MEAT?!
WHAT'S GOING ON HERE?!
SIZZLE
SIZZLE
YOU WANNA KNOW HOW? I'LL TELL YA!
I USED THE POTATOES AND THICK-CUT BACON I'D BOUGHT FOR TOMORROW'S BREAKFAST...
SNAP
...TO MAKE THIS JOKE ROAST PORK!

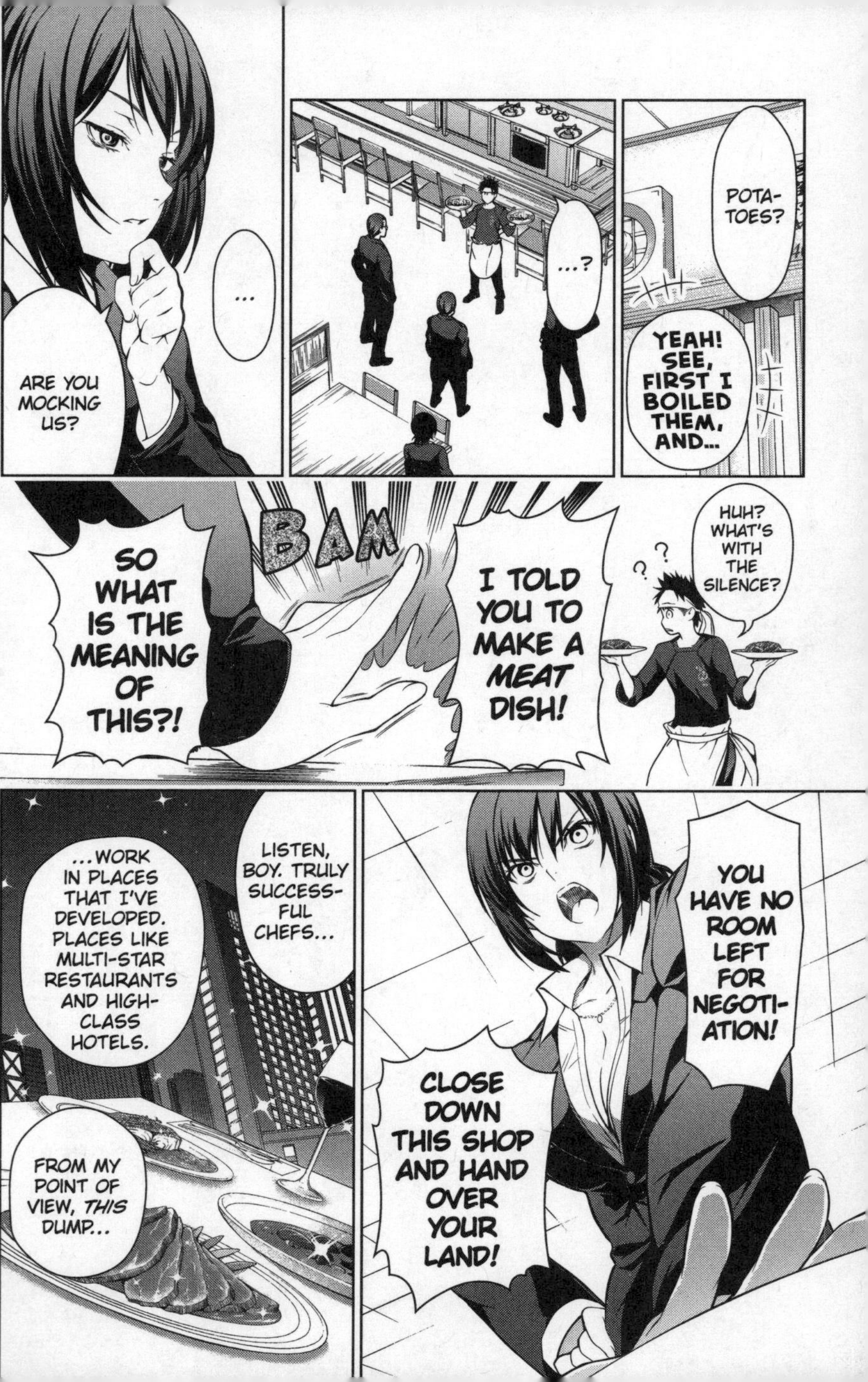
POTATOES?
YEAH! SEE, FIRST I BOILED THEM, AND...
...?
...
ARE YOU MOCKING US?
HUH? WHAT'S WITH THE SILENCE?
I TOLD YOU TO MAKE A *MEAT* DISH!
BAM
SO WHAT IS THE MEANING OF THIS?!
YOU HAVE NO ROOM LEFT FOR NEGOTIATION!
CLOSE DOWN THIS SHOP AND HAND OVER YOUR LAND!
LISTEN, BOY. TRULY SUCCESSFUL CHEFS...
...WORK IN PLACES THAT I'VE DEVELOPED. PLACES LIKE MULTI-STAR RESTAURANTS AND HIGH-CLASS HOTELS.
FROM MY POINT OF VIEW, *THIS* DUMP...

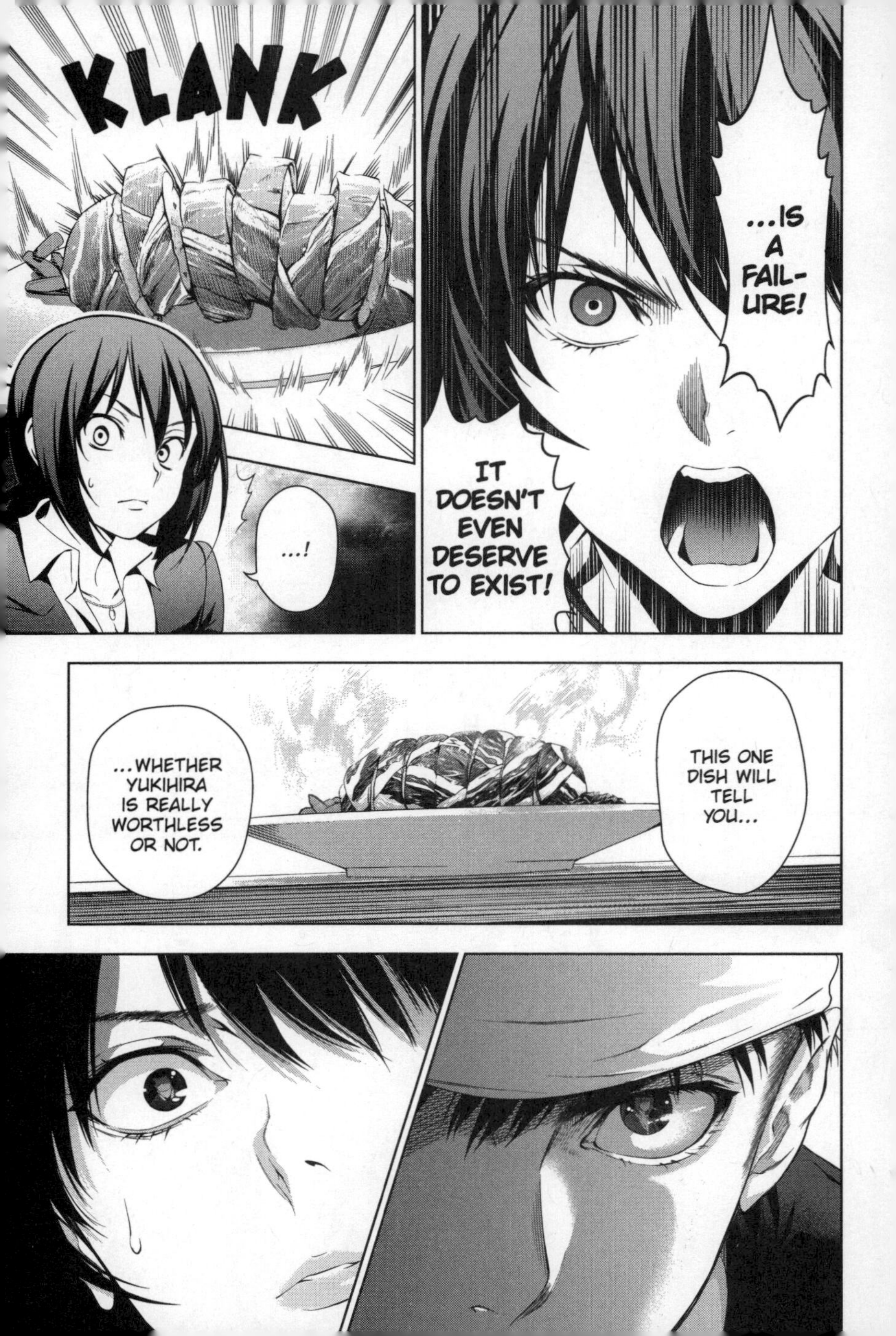

...IS A FAIL-URE!
IT DOESN'T EVEN DESERVE TO EXIST!
KLANK
...!
THIS ONE DISH WILL TELL YOU...
...WHETHER YUKIHIRA IS REALLY WORTHLESS OR NOT.

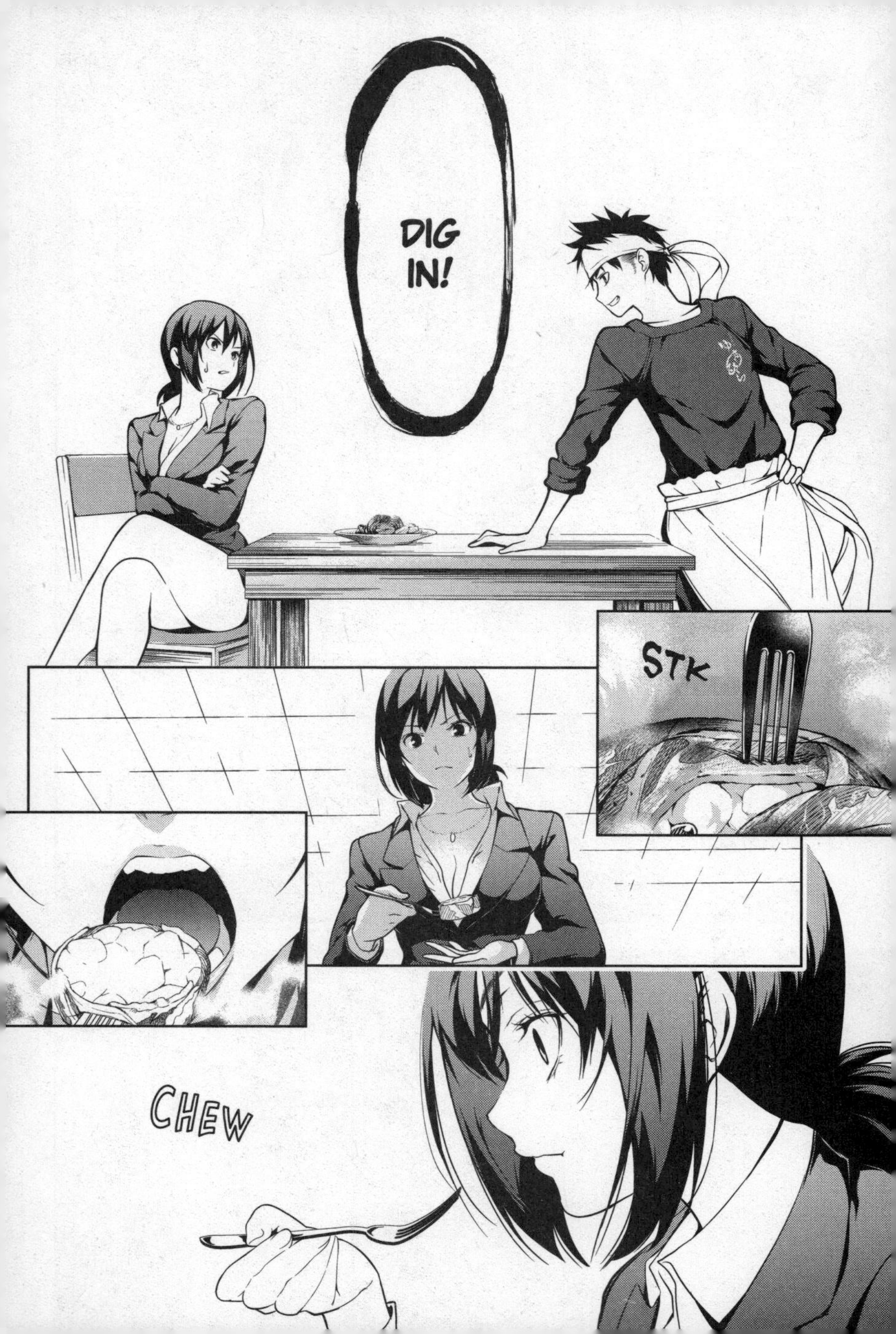
DIG IN!
STK
CHEW

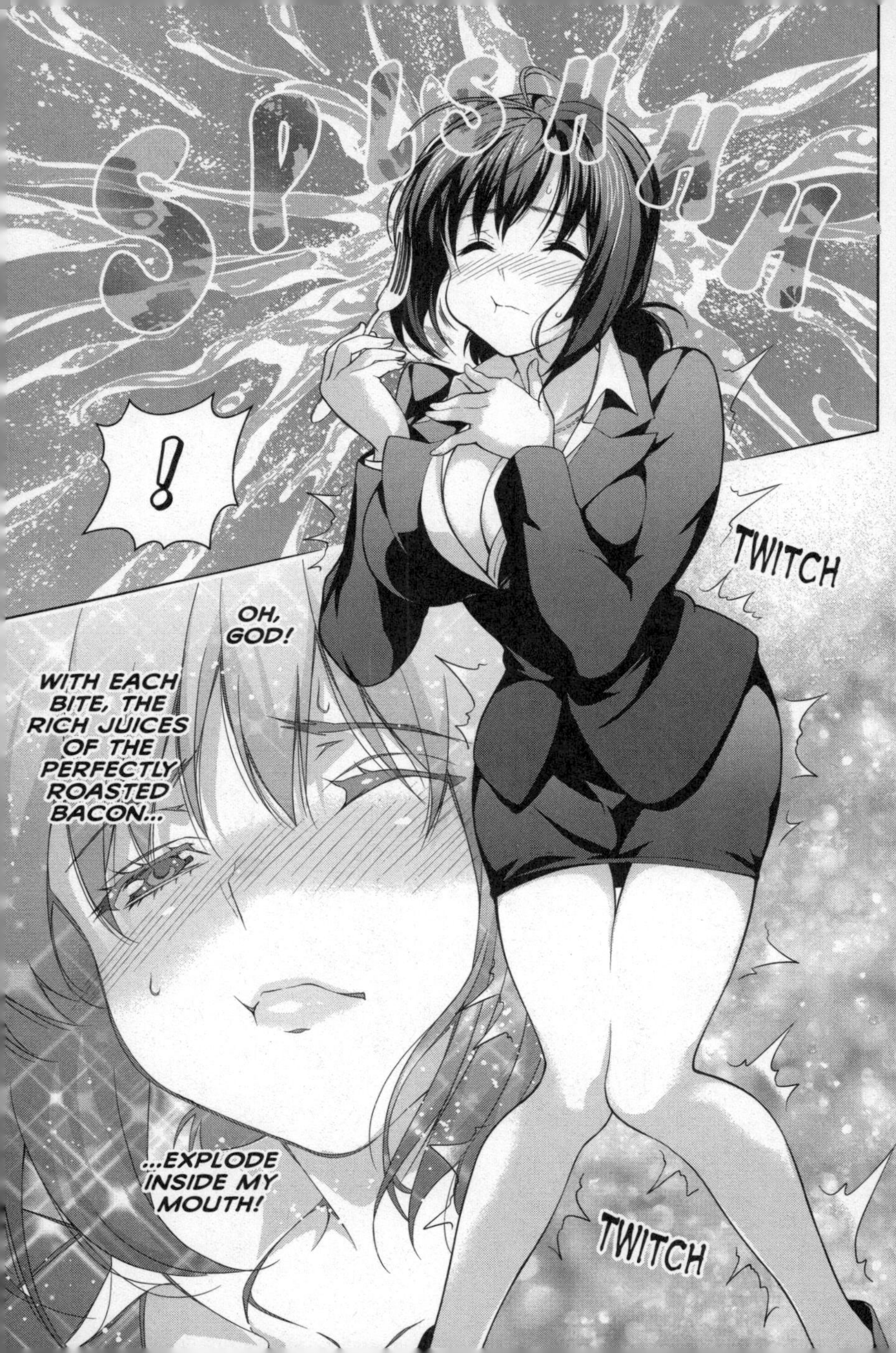

SPLSHHH
!
TWITCH
OH, GOD!
WITH EACH BITE, THE RICH JUICES OF THE PERFECTLY ROASTED BACON...
...EXPLODE INSIDE MY MOUTH!
TWITCH

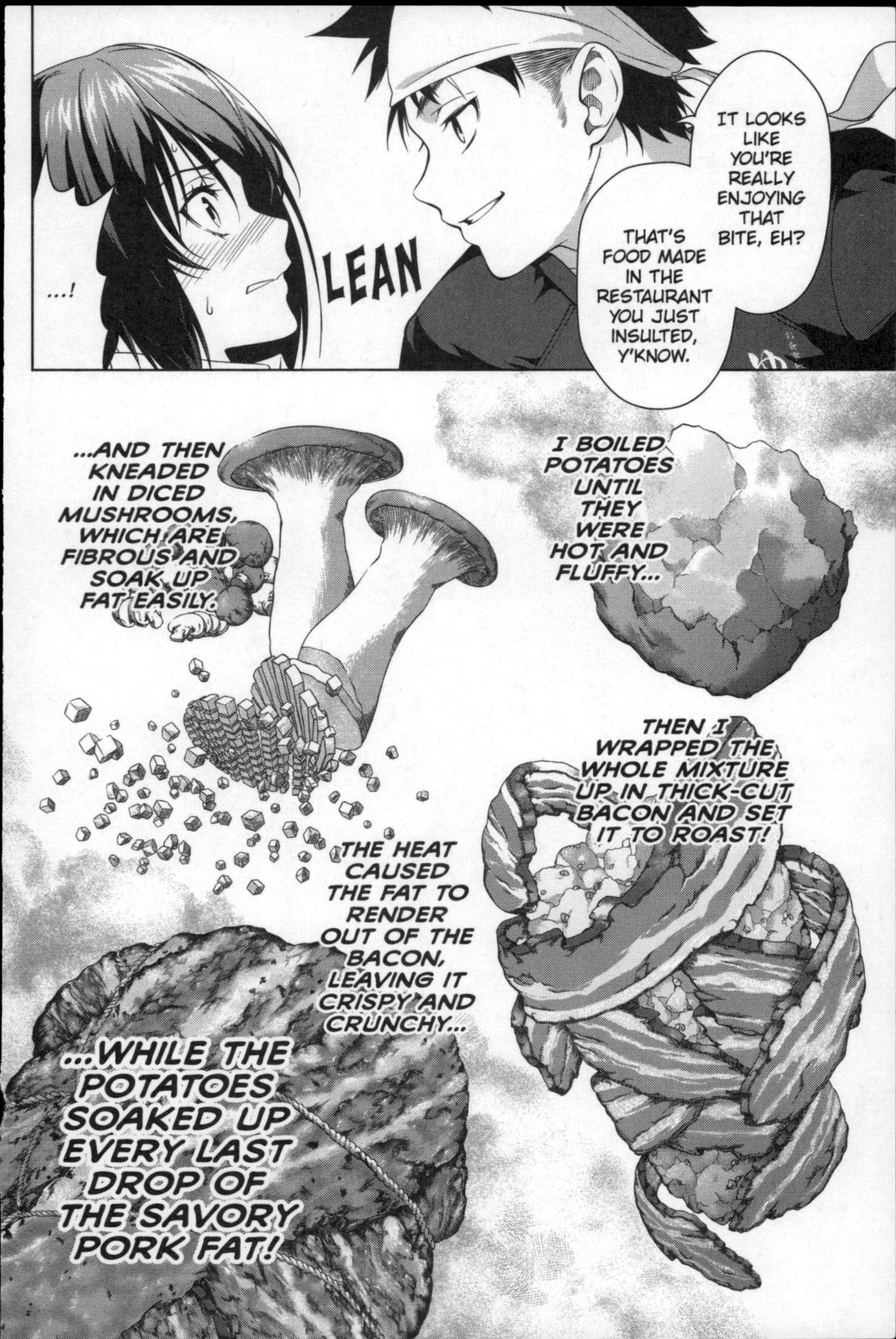
IT LOOKS LIKE YOU'RE REALLY ENJOYING THAT BITE, EH?
THAT'S FOOD MADE IN THE RESTAURANT YOU JUST INSULTED, Y'KNOW.
LEAN
...!
I BOILED POTATOES UNTIL THEY WERE HOT AND FLUFFY...
...AND THEN KNEADED IN DICED MUSHROOMS, WHICH ARE FIBROUS AND SOAK UP FAT EASILY.
THEN I WRAPPED THE WHOLE MIXTURE UP IN THICK-CUT BACON AND SET IT TO ROAST!
THE HEAT CAUSED THE FAT TO RENDER OUT OF THE BACON, LEAVING IT CRISPY AND CRUNCHY...
...WHILE THE POTATOES SOAKED UP EVERY LAST DROP OF THE SAVORY PORK FAT!

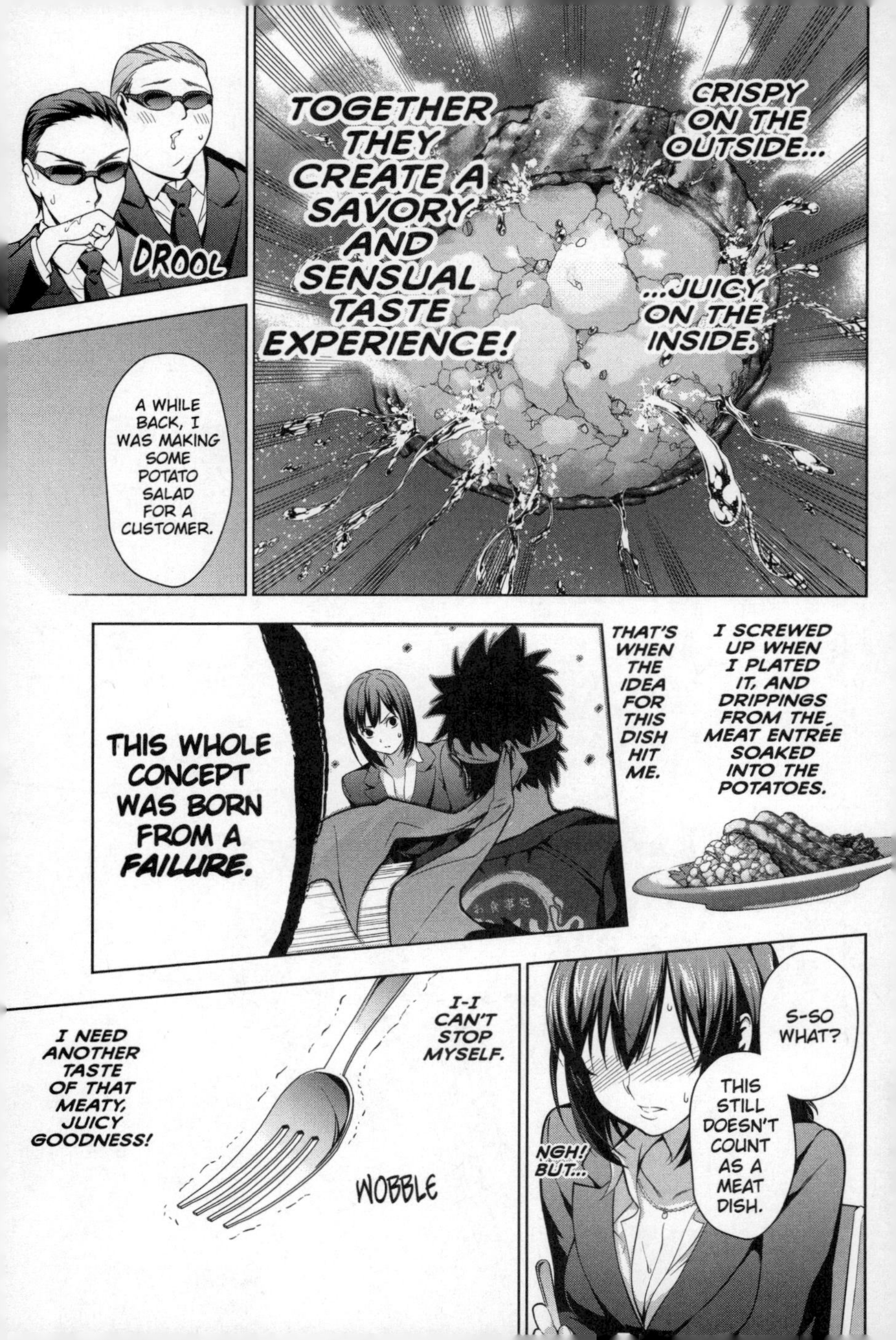
CRISPY ON THE OUTSIDE...
...JUICY ON THE INSIDE.
TOGETHER THEY CREATE A SAVORY AND SENSUAL TASTE EXPERIENCE!
DROOL
A WHILE BACK, I WAS MAKING SOME POTATO SALAD FOR A CUSTOMER.
I SCREWED UP WHEN I PLATED IT, AND DRIPPINGS FROM THE MEAT ENTRÉE SOAKED INTO THE POTATOES.
THAT'S WHEN THE IDEA FOR THIS DISH HIT ME.
THIS WHOLE CONCEPT WAS BORN FROM A FAILURE.
S-SO WHAT?
THIS STILL DOESN'T COUNT AS A MEAT DISH.
NGH! BUT...
I-I CAN'T STOP MYSELF.
I NEED ANOTHER TASTE OF THAT MEATY, JUICY GOODNESS!
WOBBLE

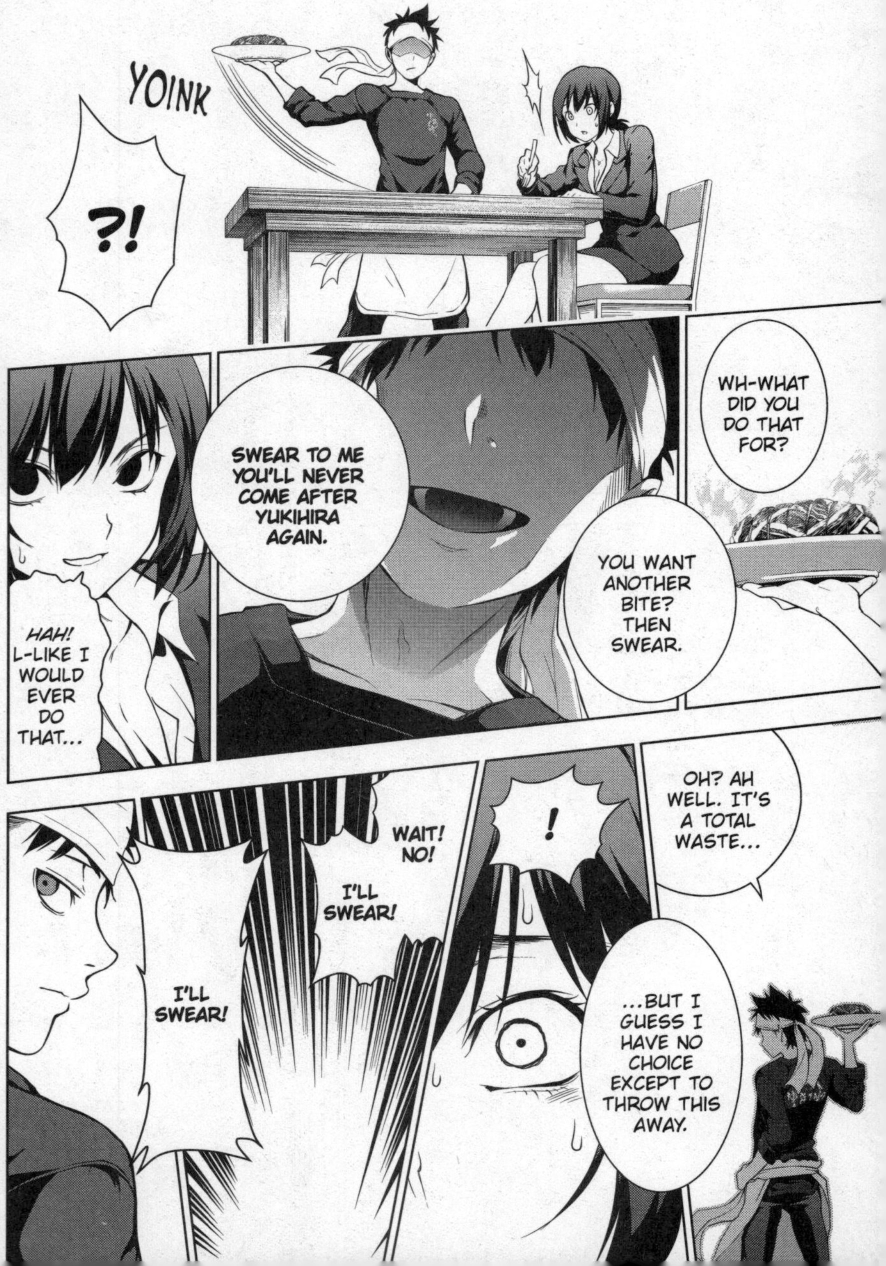
YOINK
?!
WH-WHAT DID YOU DO THAT FOR?
YOU WANT ANOTHER BITE? THEN SWEAR.
SWEAR TO ME YOU'LL NEVER COME AFTER YUKIHIRA AGAIN.
HAH! L-LIKE I WOULD EVER DO THAT...
OH? AH WELL. IT'S A TOTAL WASTE...
...BUT I GUESS I HAVE NO CHOICE EXCEPT TO THROW THIS AWAY.
!
WAIT! NO!
I'LL SWEAR!
I'LL SWEAR!

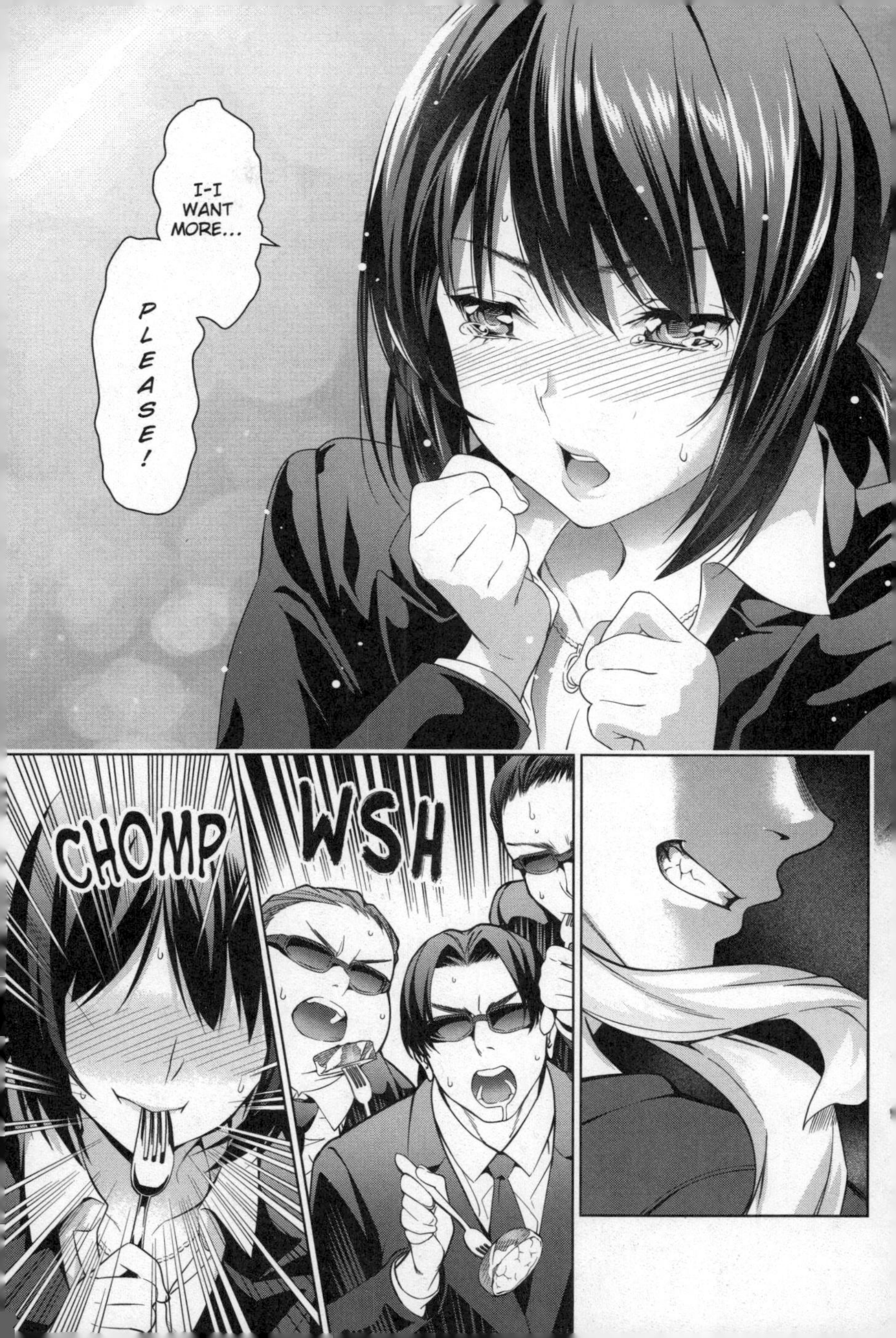
I-I WANT MORE...
PLEASE!
WSH
CHOMP

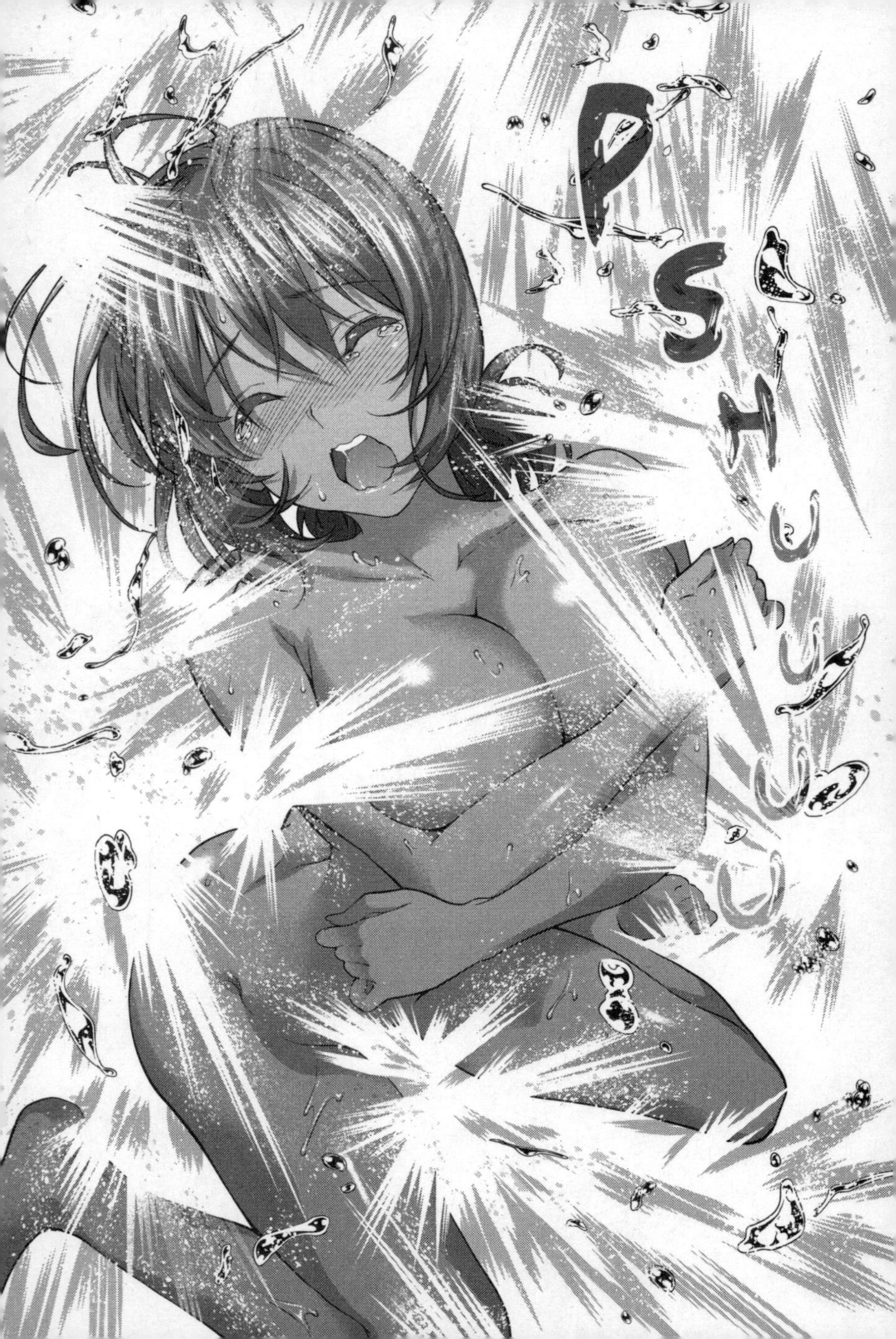
PSHUUUU

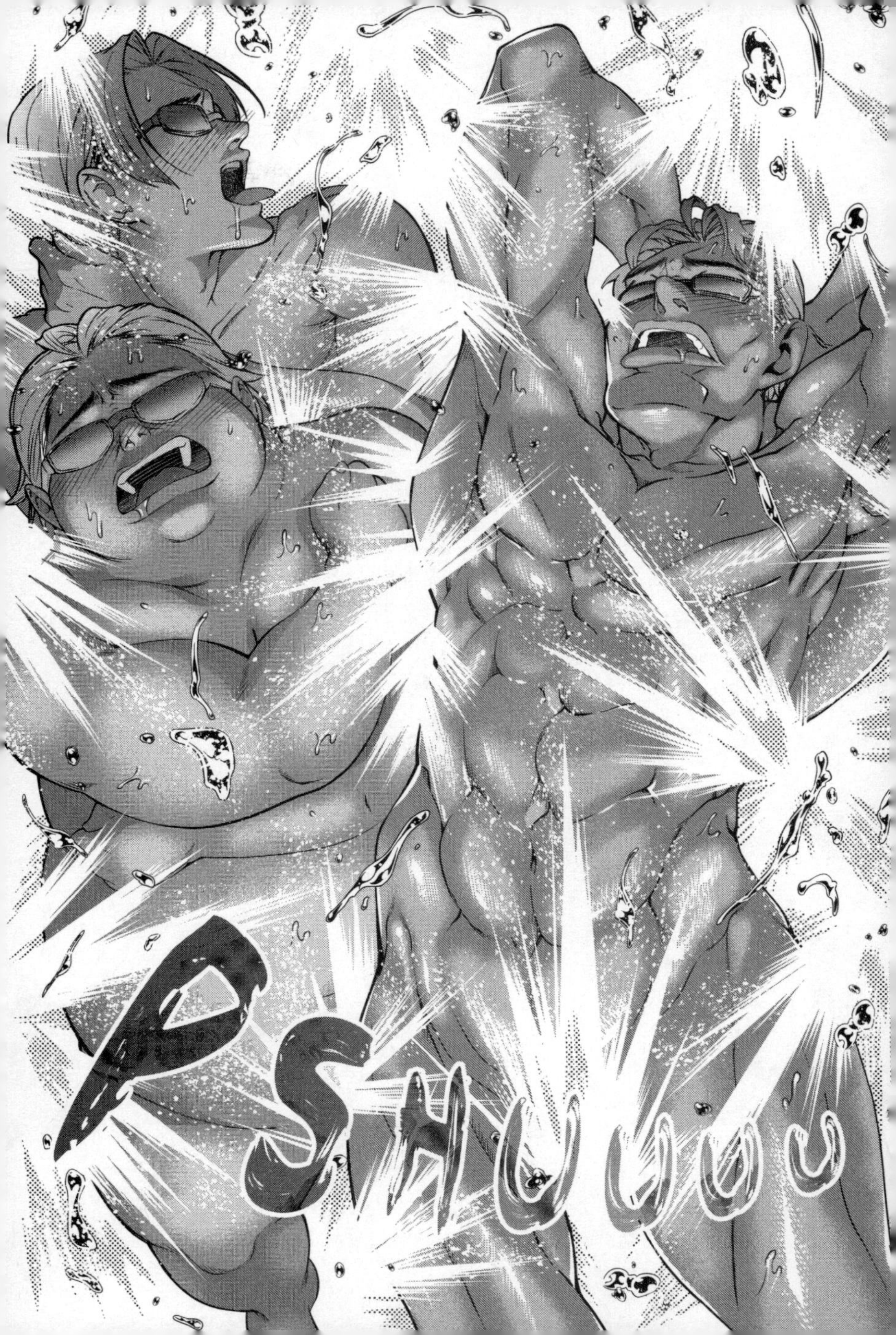
PSHUUUU

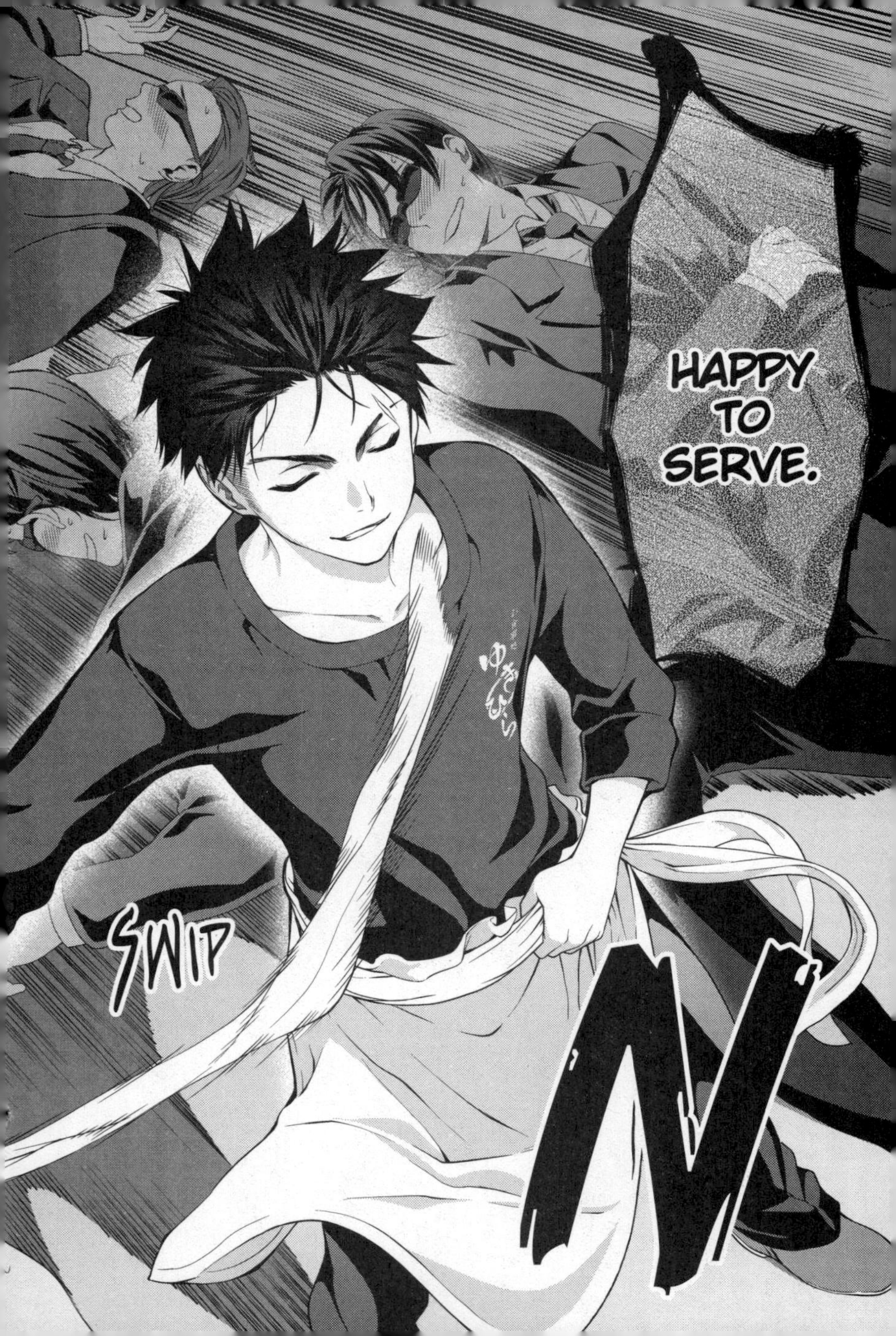
HAPPY TO SERVE.
SWIP
N

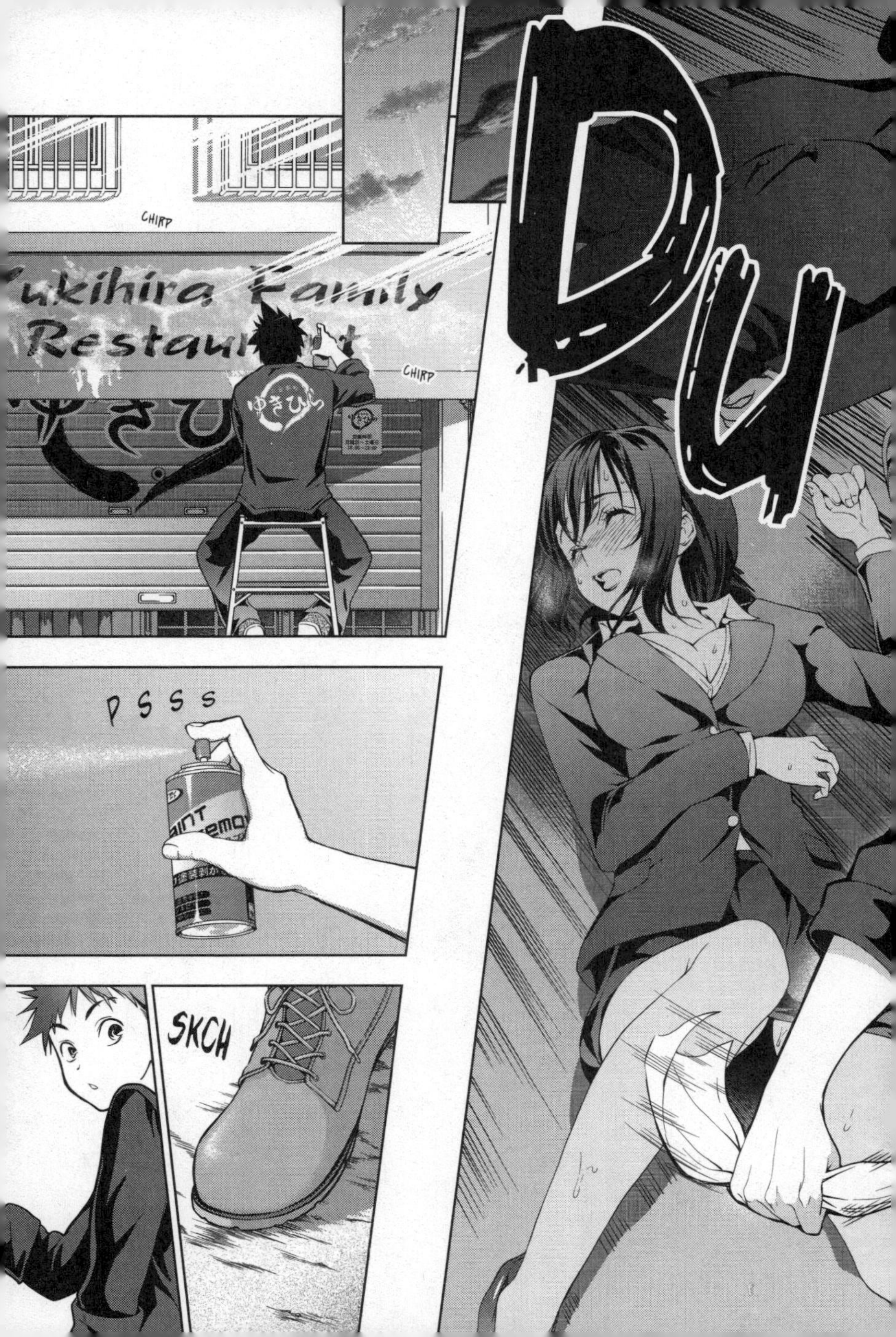
DU
CHIRP
CHIRP
PSSS
SKCH

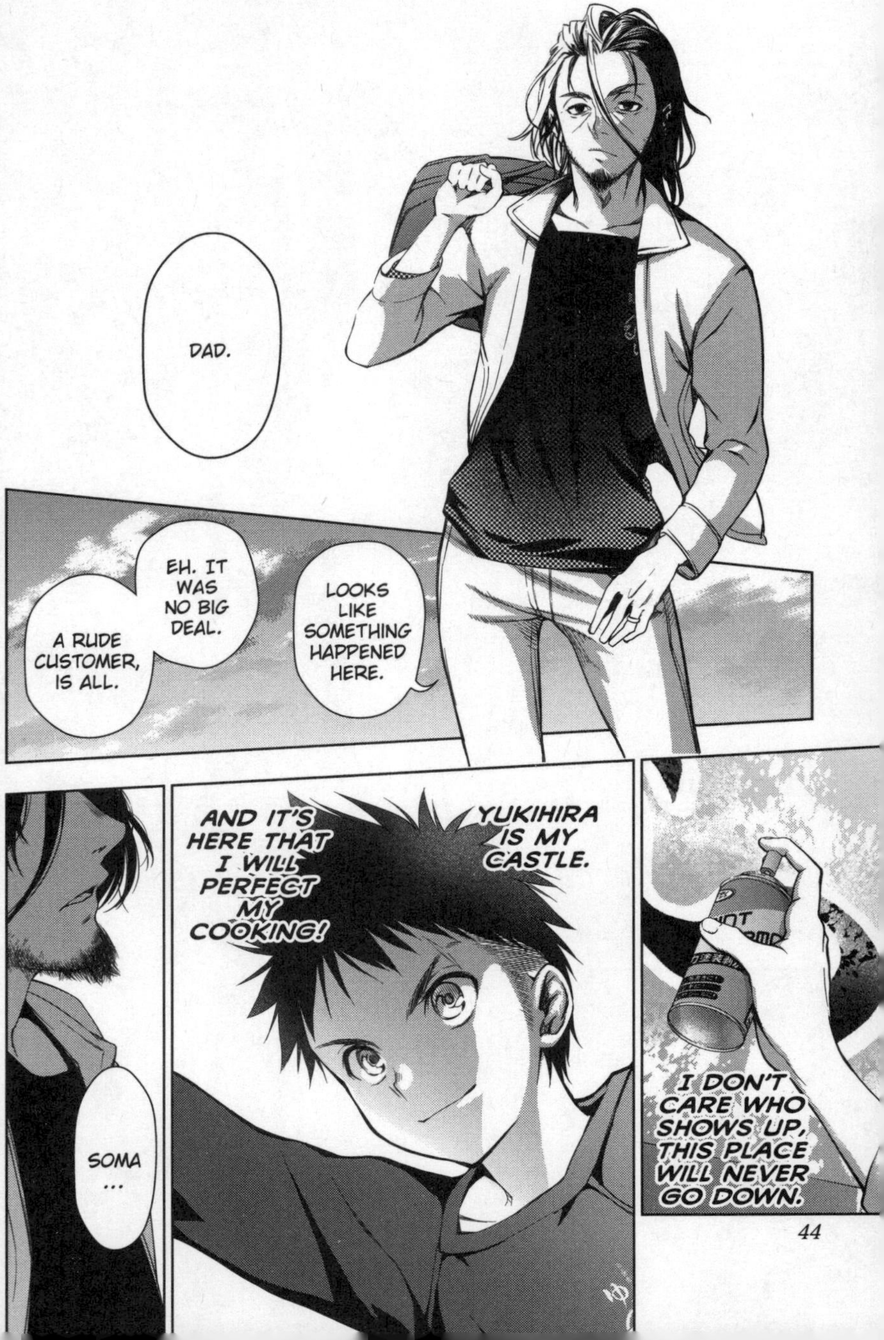
DAD.
LOOKS LIKE SOMETHING HAPPENED HERE.
EH. IT WAS NO BIG DEAL.
A RUDE CUSTOMER, IS ALL.
I DON'T CARE WHO SHOWS UP, THIS PLACE WILL NEVER GO DOWN.
YUKIHIRA IS MY CASTLE.
AND IT'S HERE THAT I WILL PERFECT MY COOKING!
SOMA ...

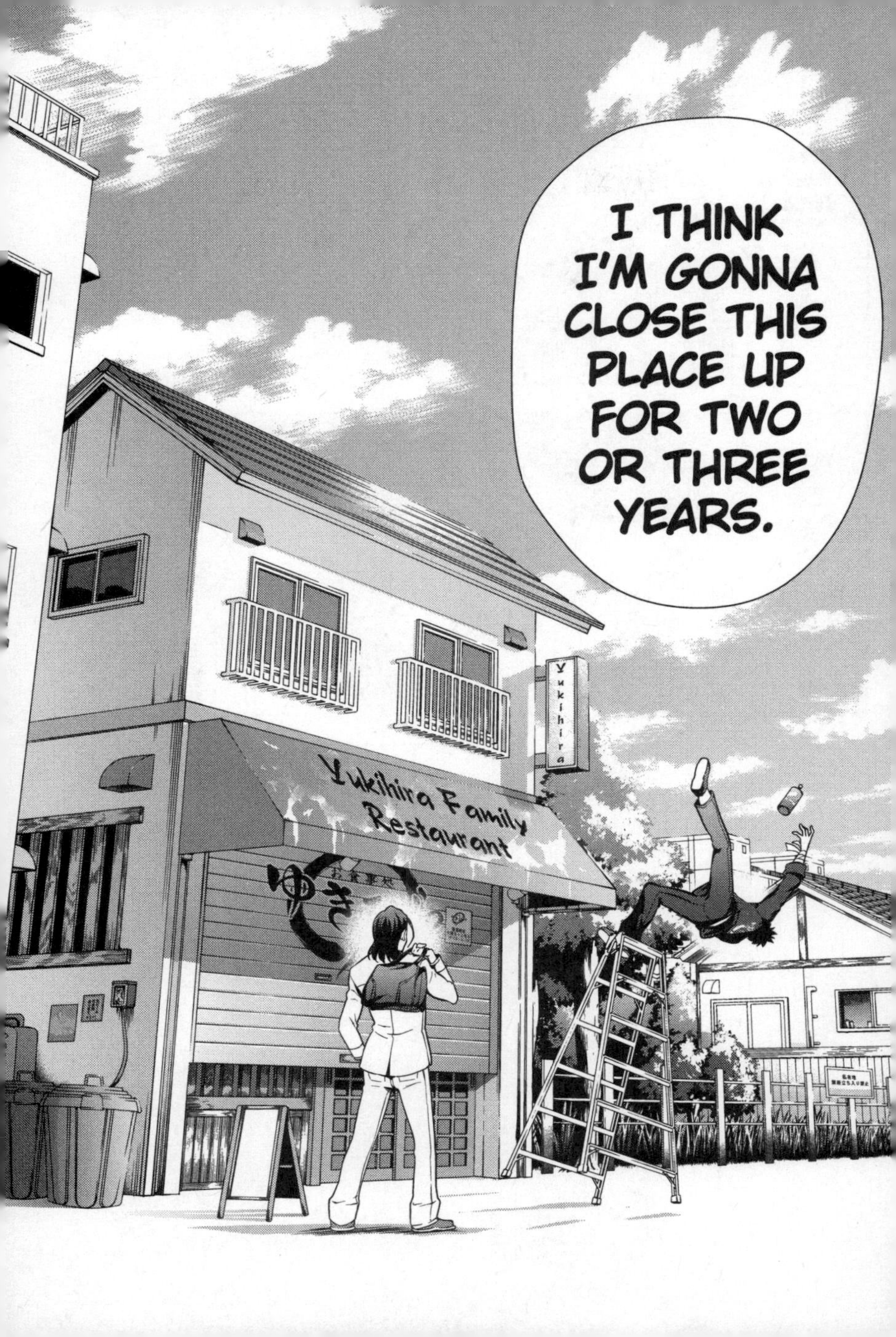
I THINK I'M GONNA CLOSE THIS PLACE UP FOR TWO OR THREE YEARS.
Yukihira
Yukihira Family Restaurant

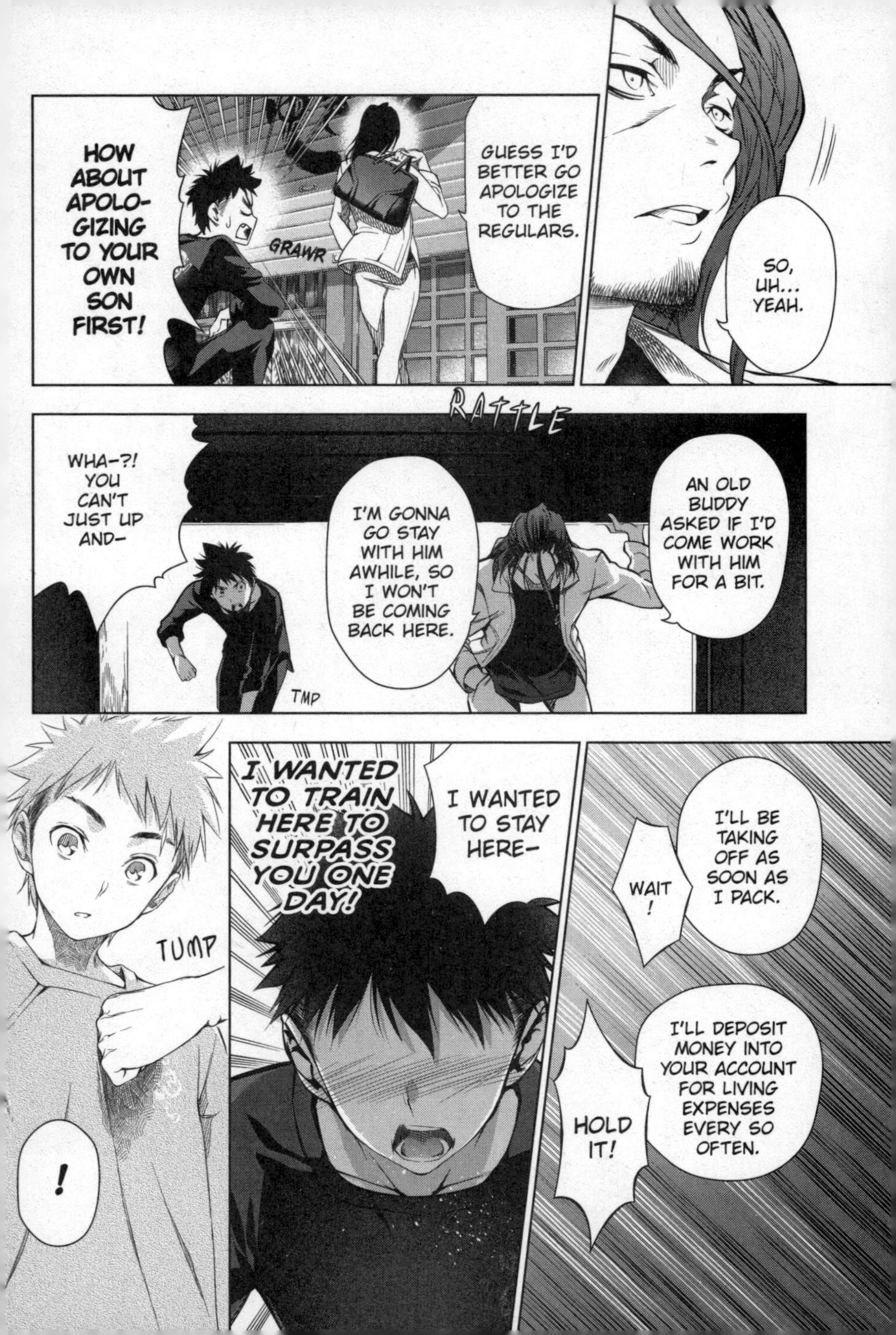
SO, UH... YEAH.
GUESS I'D BETTER GO APOLOGIZE TO THE REGULARS.
HOW ABOUT APOLO-GIZING TO YOUR OWN SON FIRST!
GRAWR
RATTLE
AN OLD BUDDY ASKED IF I'D COME WORK WITH HIM FOR A BIT.
I'M GONNA GO STAY WITH HIM AWHILE, SO I WON'T BE COMING BACK HERE.
TMP
WHA-?! YOU CAN'T JUST UP AND-
I'LL BE TAKING OFF AS SOON AS I PACK.
WAIT!
I'LL DEPOSIT MONEY INTO YOUR ACCOUNT FOR LIVING EXPENSES EVERY SO OFTEN.
HOLD IT!
I WANTED TO STAY HERE-
I WANTED TO TRAIN HERE TO SURPASS YOU ONE DAY!
TUMP
!

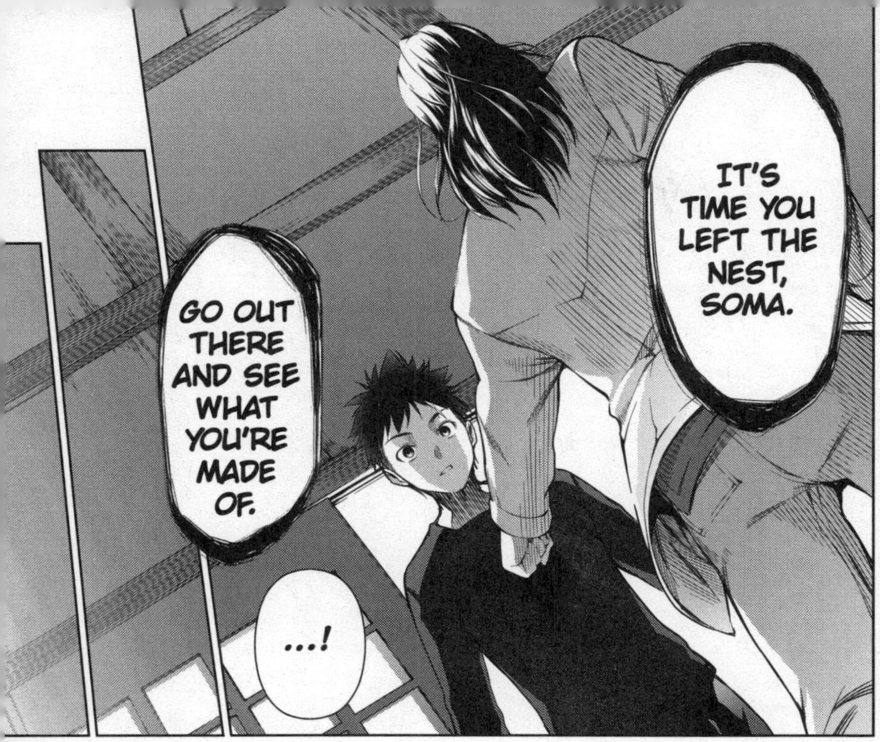
IT'S TIME YOU LEFT THE NEST, SOMA.
GO OUT THERE AND SEE WHAT YOU'RE MADE OF.
...!

SEVERAL WEEKS LATER...

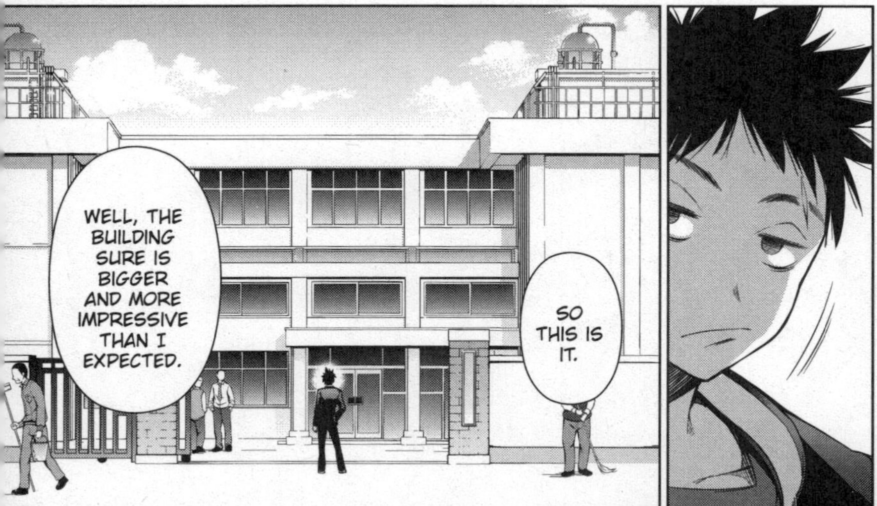
SO THIS IS IT.
WELL, THE BUILDING SURE IS BIGGER AND MORE IMPRESSIVE THAN I EXPECTED.

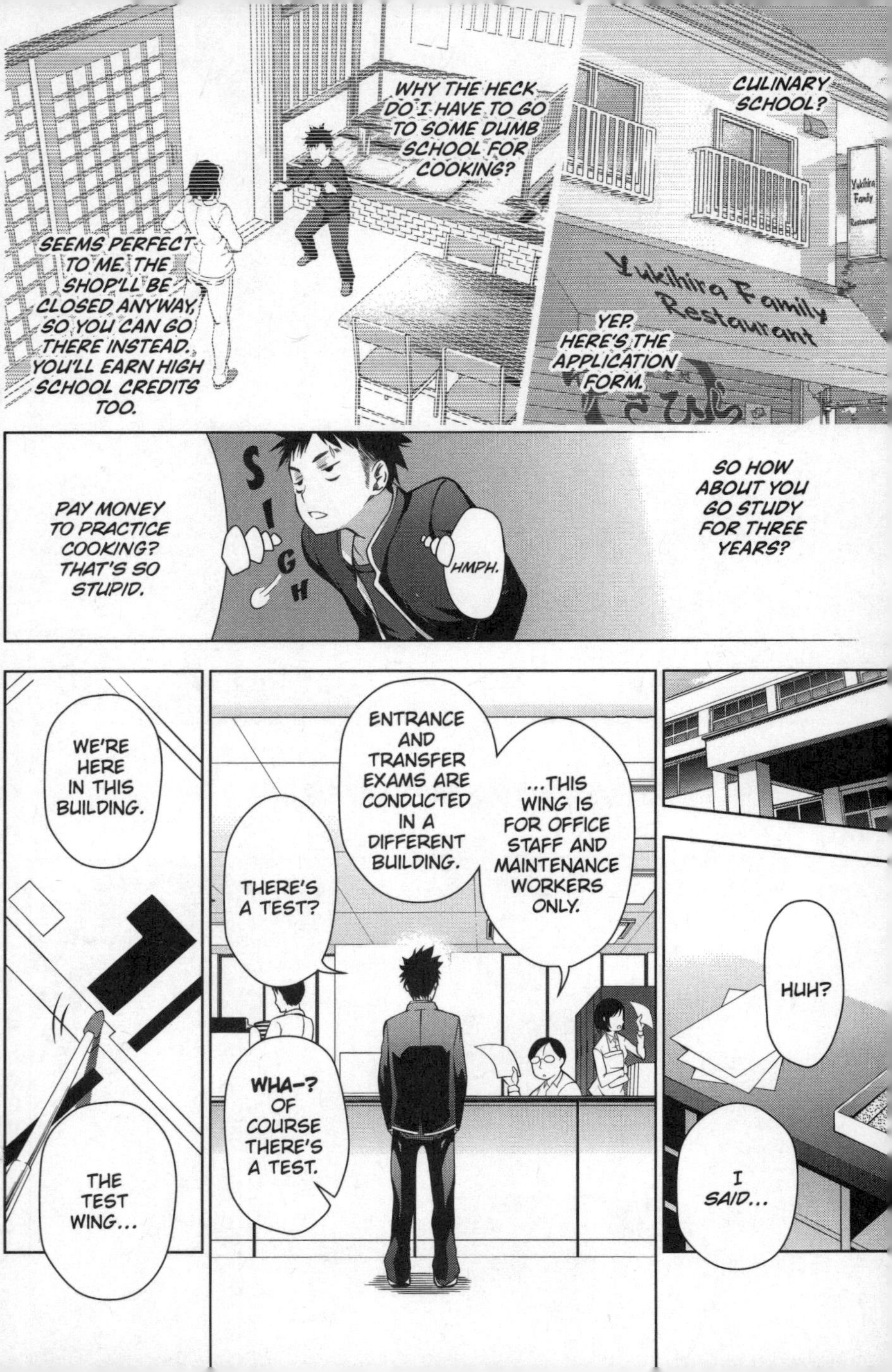
CULINARY SCHOOL?
Yukihira Family Restaurant
Yukihira Family Restaurant
YEP. HERE'S THE APPLICATION FORM.
WHY THE HECK DO I HAVE TO GO TO SOME DUMB SCHOOL FOR COOKING?
SEEMS PERFECT TO ME. THE SHOP'LL BE CLOSED ANYWAY, SO YOU CAN GO THERE INSTEAD. YOU'LL EARN HIGH SCHOOL CREDITS TOO.
SO HOW ABOUT YOU GO STUDY FOR THREE YEARS?
HMPH.
SIGH
PAY MONEY TO PRACTICE COOKING? THAT'S SO STUPID.
HUH?
I SAID...
...THIS WING IS FOR OFFICE STAFF AND MAINTENANCE WORKERS ONLY.
ENTRANCE AND TRANSFER EXAMS ARE CONDUCTED IN A DIFFERENT BUILDING.
THERE'S A TEST?
WHA-? OF COURSE THERE'S A TEST.
WE'RE HERE IN THIS BUILDING.
THE TEST WING...

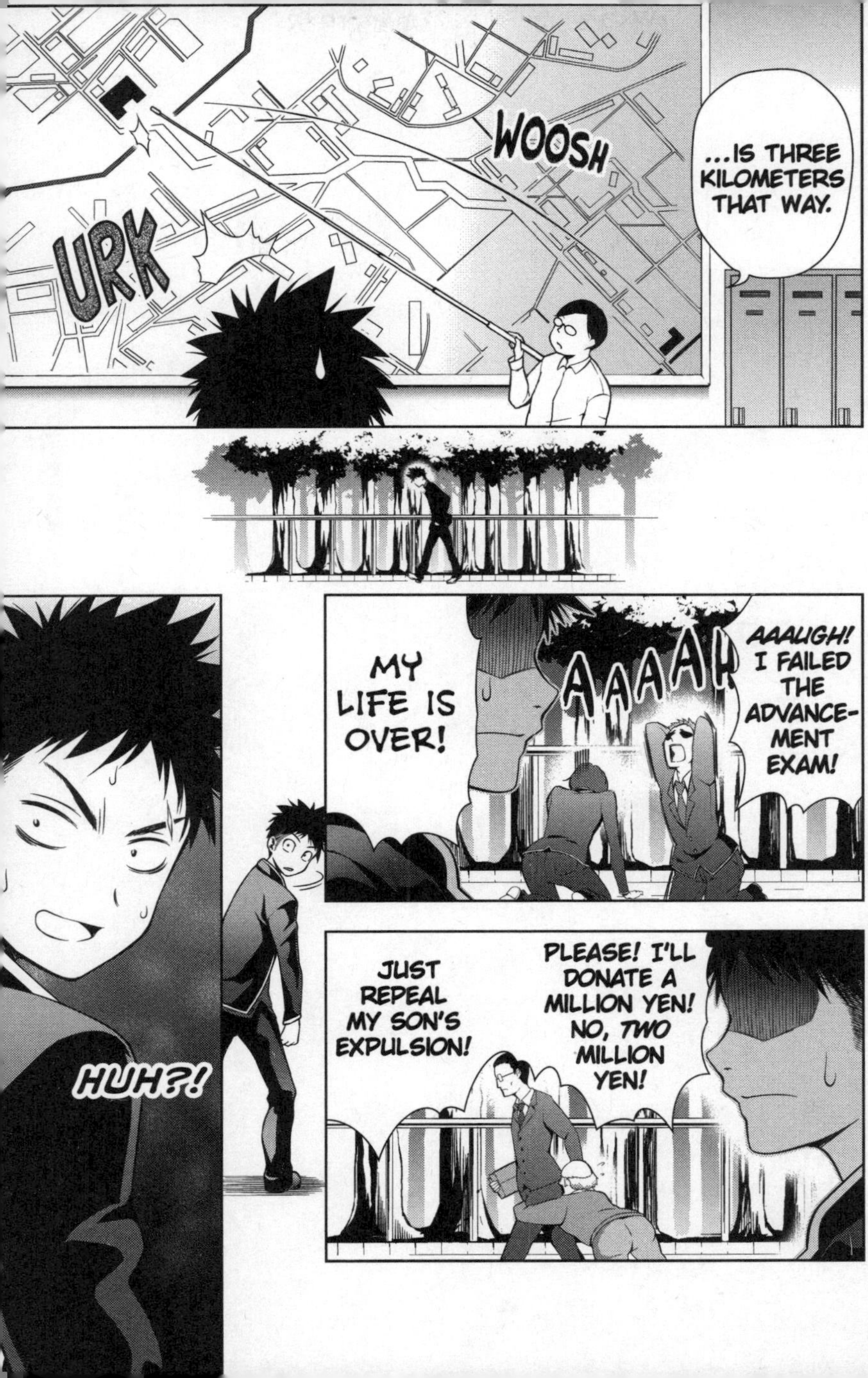
...IS THREE KILOMETERS THAT WAY.
WOOSH
URK
AAAUGH! I FAILED THE ADVANCEMENT EXAM!
AAAAH
MY LIFE IS OVER!
PLEASE! I'LL DONATE A MILLION YEN! NO, *TWO* MILLION YEN!
JUST REPEAL MY SON'S EXPULSION!
HUH?!

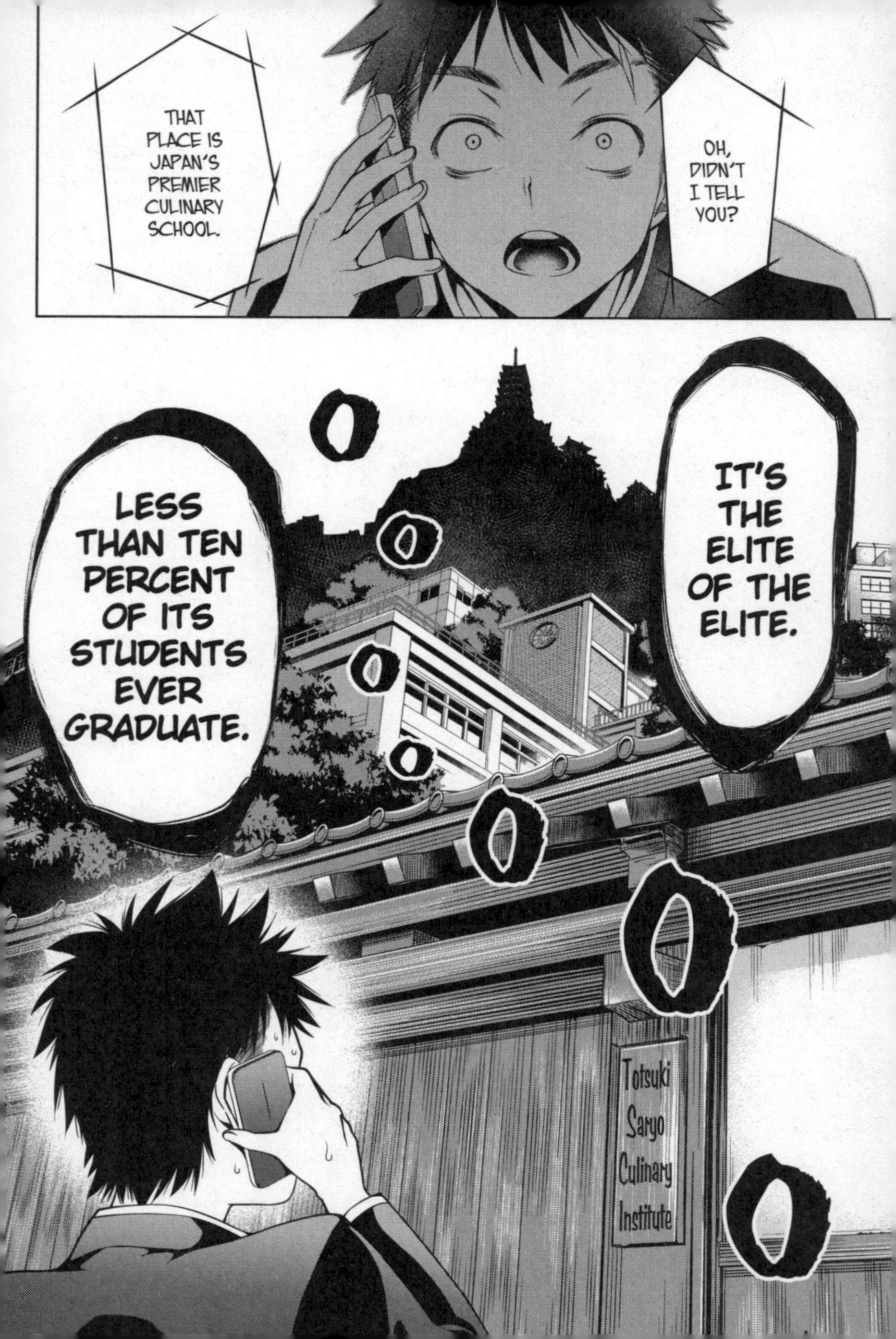
OH, DIDN'T I TELL YOU?
THAT PLACE IS JAPAN'S PREMIER CULINARY SCHOOL.
IT'S THE ELITE OF THE ELITE.
LESS THAN TEN PERCENT OF ITS STUDENTS EVER GRADUATE.
Totsuki Saryo Culinary Institute

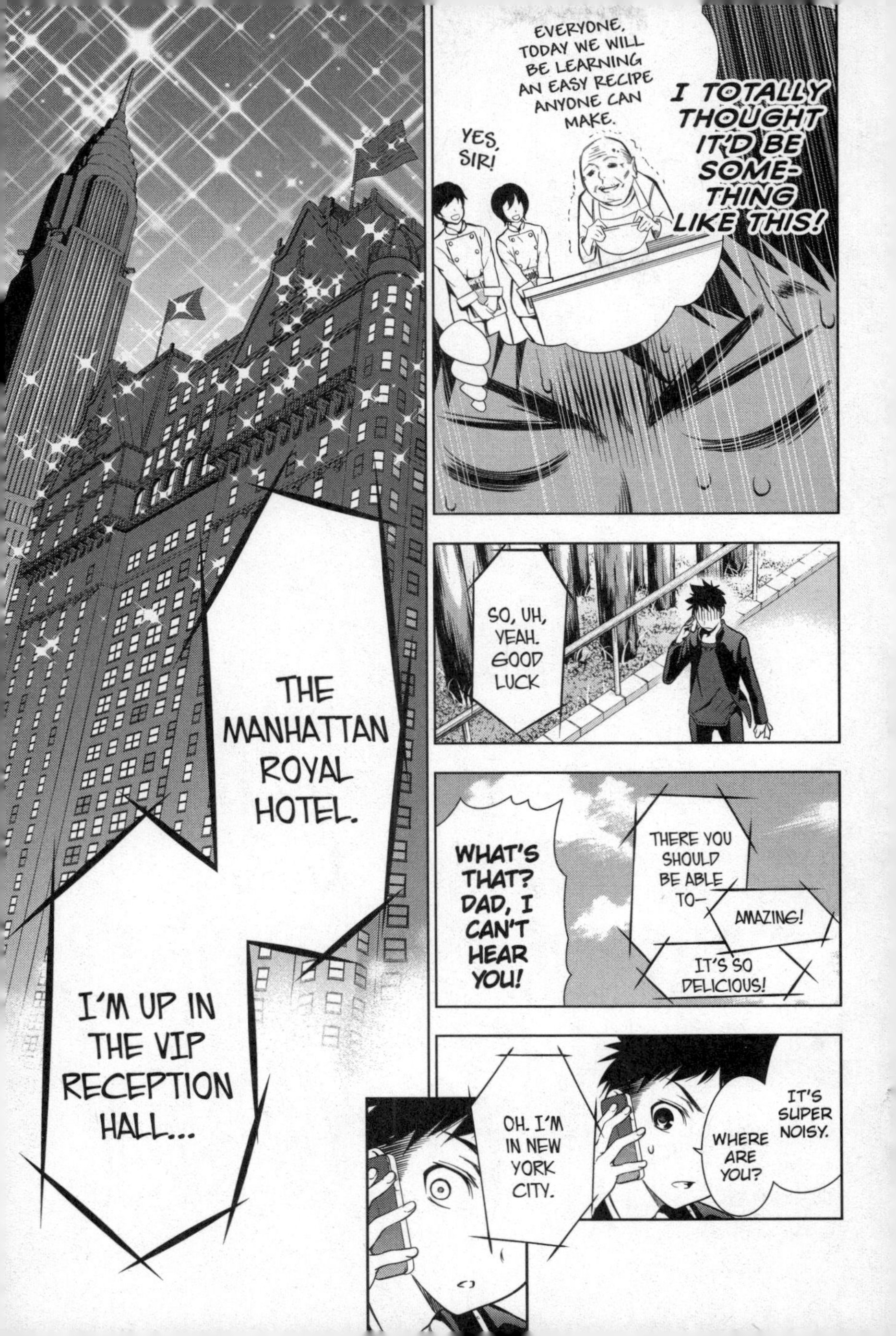
EVERYONE, TODAY WE WILL BE LEARNING AN EASY RECIPE ANYONE CAN MAKE.
YES, SIR!
I TOTALLY THOUGHT IT'D BE SOME-THING LIKE THIS!
SO, UH, YEAH. GOOD LUCK
THERE YOU SHOULD BE ABLE TO—
AMAZING!
IT'S SO DELICIOUS!
WHAT'S THAT? DAD, I CAN'T HEAR YOU!
IT'S SUPER NOISY.
WHERE ARE YOU?
OH. I'M IN NEW YORK CITY.
THE MANHATTAN ROYAL HOTEL.
I'M UP IN THE VIP RECEPTION HALL...

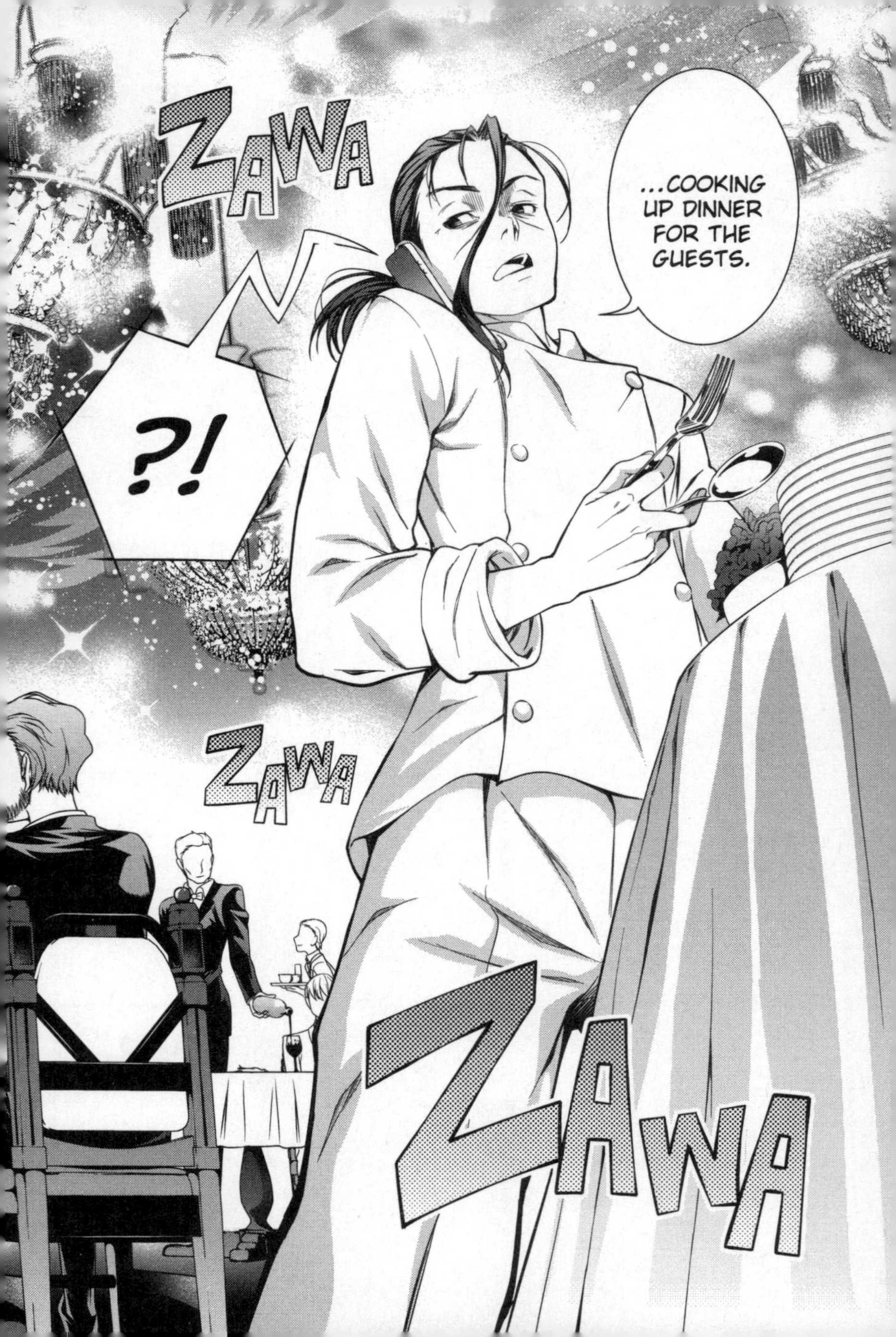
...COOKING UP DINNER FOR THE GUESTS.
ZAWA
?!
ZAWA
ZAWA

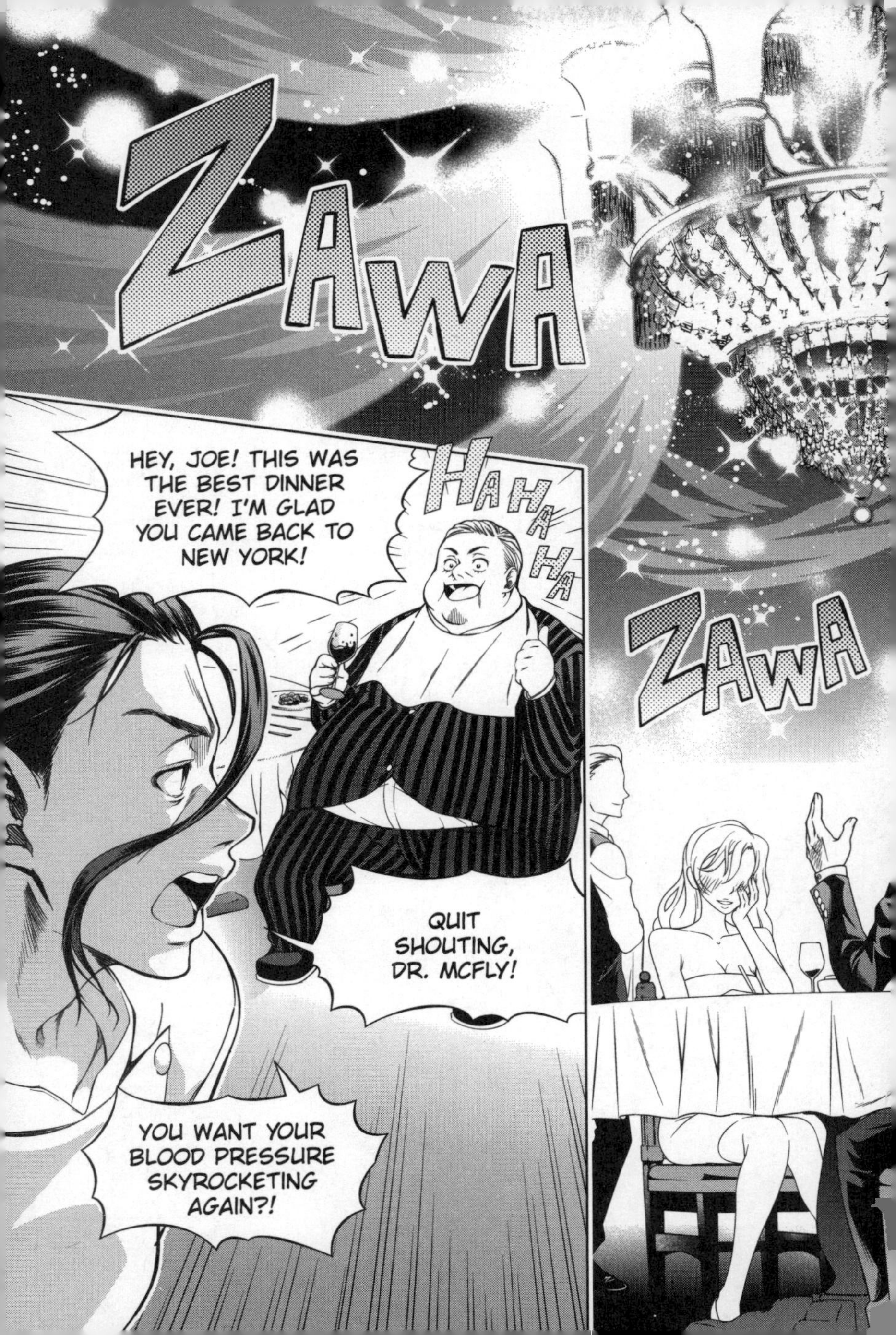
ZAWA
ZAWA
HAHAHAHA
HEY, JOE! THIS WAS THE BEST DINNER EVER! I'M GLAD YOU CAME BACK TO NEW YORK!
QUIT SHOUTING, DR. MCFLY!
YOU WANT YOUR BLOOD PRESSURE SKYROCKETING AGAIN?!

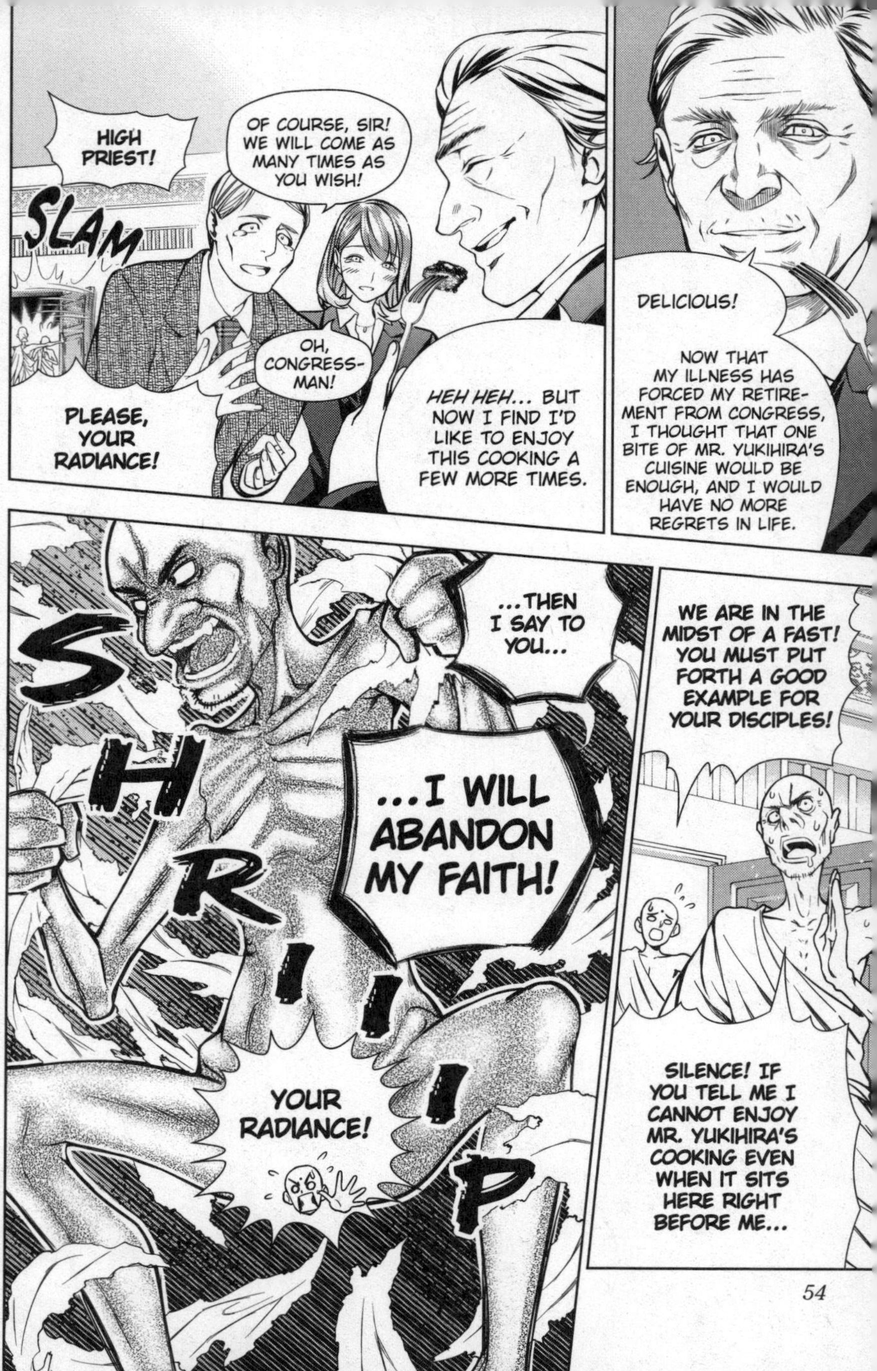
DELICIOUS!
NOW THAT MY ILLNESS HAS FORCED MY RETIREMENT FROM CONGRESS, I THOUGHT THAT ONE BITE OF MR. YUKIHIRA'S CUISINE WOULD BE ENOUGH, AND I WOULD HAVE NO MORE REGRETS IN LIFE.
HEH HEH... BUT NOW I FIND I'D LIKE TO ENJOY THIS COOKING A FEW MORE TIMES.
OF COURSE, SIR! WE WILL COME AS MANY TIMES AS YOU WISH!
OH, CONGRESSMAN!
HIGH PRIEST!
SLAM
PLEASE, YOUR RADIANCE!
WE ARE IN THE MIDST OF A FAST! YOU MUST PUT FORTH A GOOD EXAMPLE FOR YOUR DISCIPLES!
SILENCE! IF YOU TELL ME I CANNOT ENJOY MR. YUKIHIRA'S COOKING EVEN WHEN IT SITS HERE RIGHT BEFORE ME...
...THEN I SAY TO YOU...
...I WILL ABANDON MY FAITH!
SHRIIIP
YOUR RADIANCE!

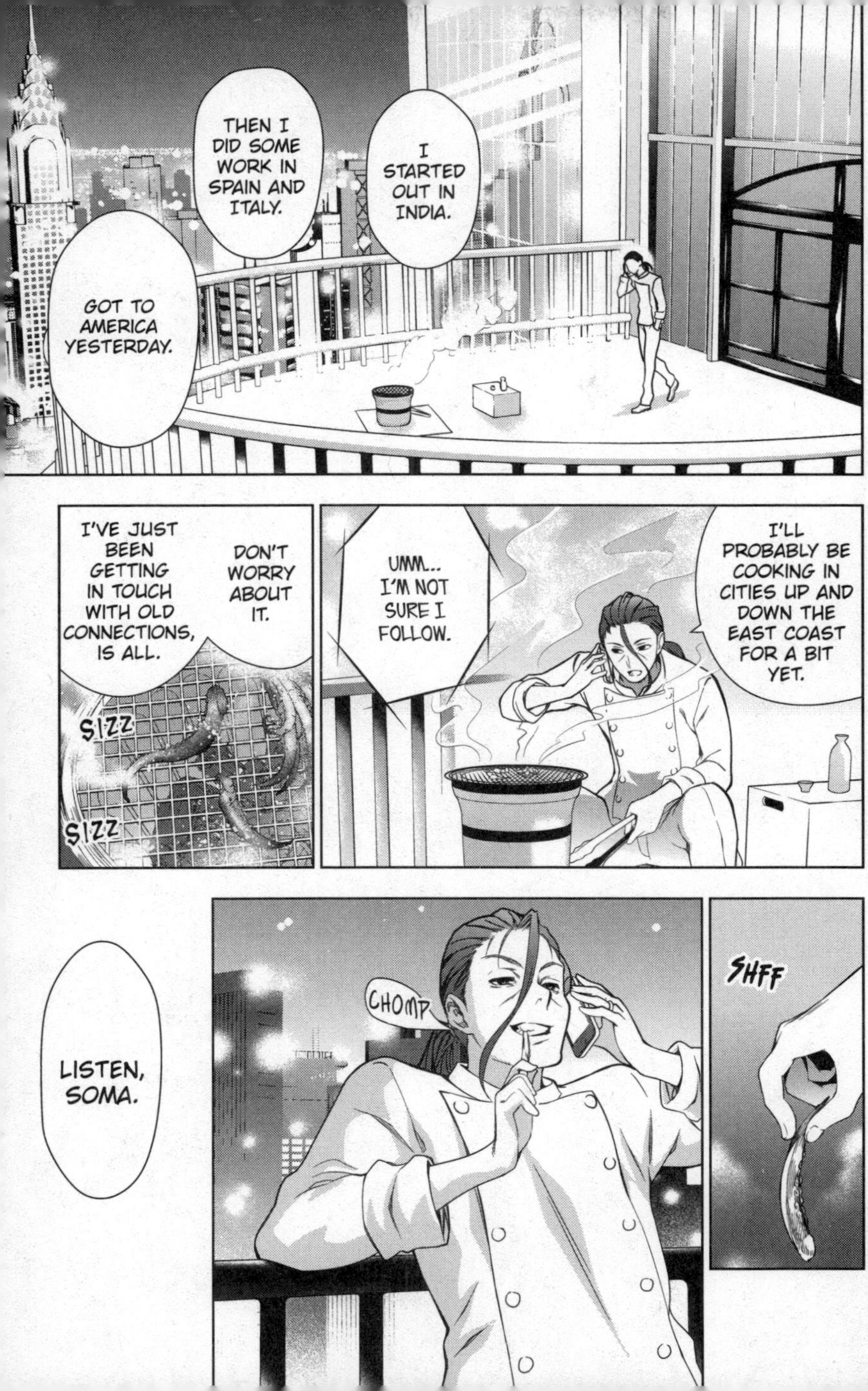
I STARTED OUT IN INDIA.
THEN I DID SOME WORK IN SPAIN AND ITALY.
GOT TO AMERICA YESTERDAY.
I'LL PROBABLY BE COOKING IN CITIES UP AND DOWN THE EAST COAST FOR A BIT YET.
UMM... I'M NOT SURE I FOLLOW.
DON'T WORRY ABOUT IT.
I'VE JUST BEEN GETTING IN TOUCH WITH OLD CONNECTIONS, IS ALL.
SIZZ
SIZZ
SHFF
CHOMP
LISTEN, SOMA.

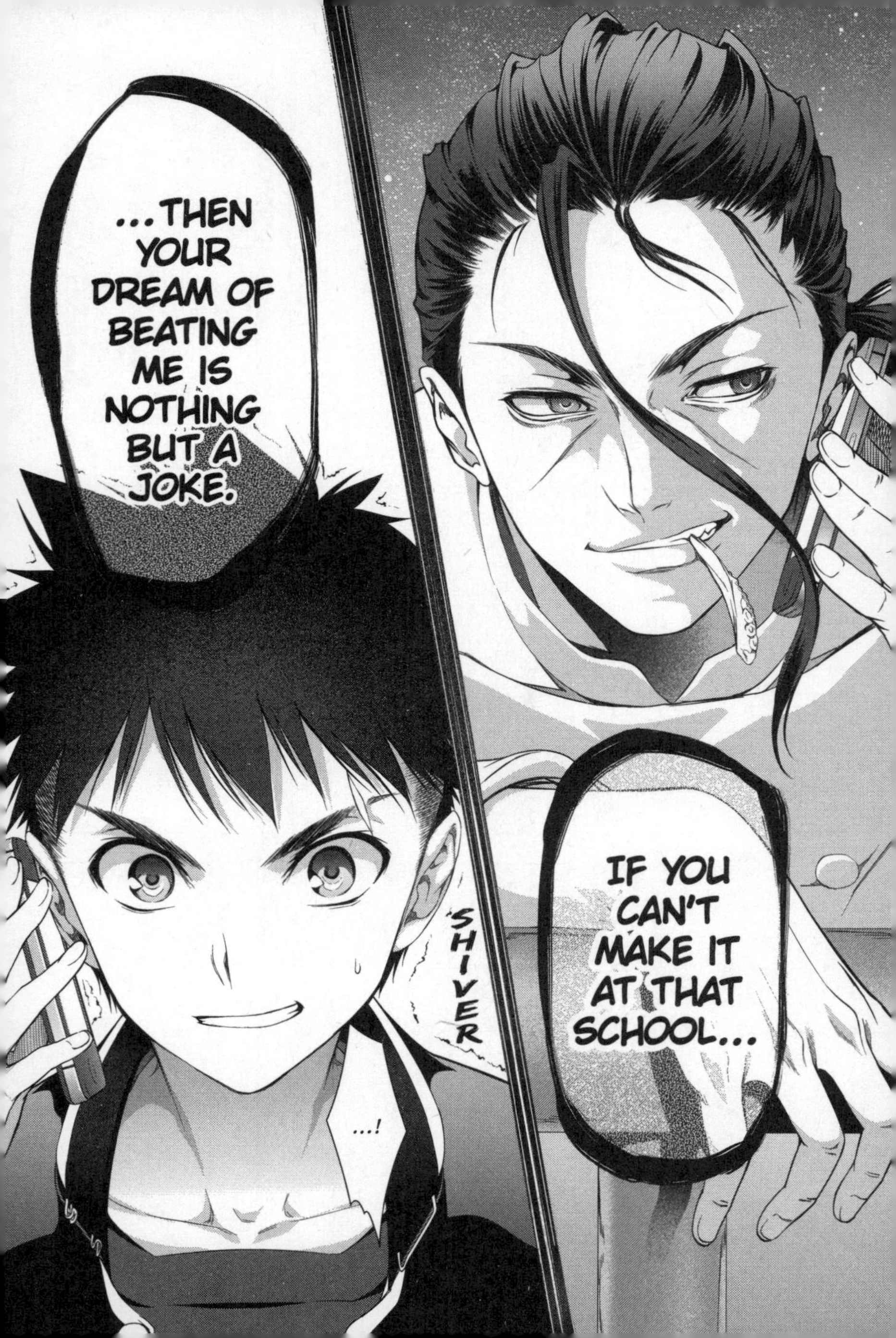
IF YOU CAN'T MAKE IT AT THAT SCHOOL...
...THEN YOUR DREAM OF BEATING ME IS NOTHING BUT A JOKE.
SHIVER
...!

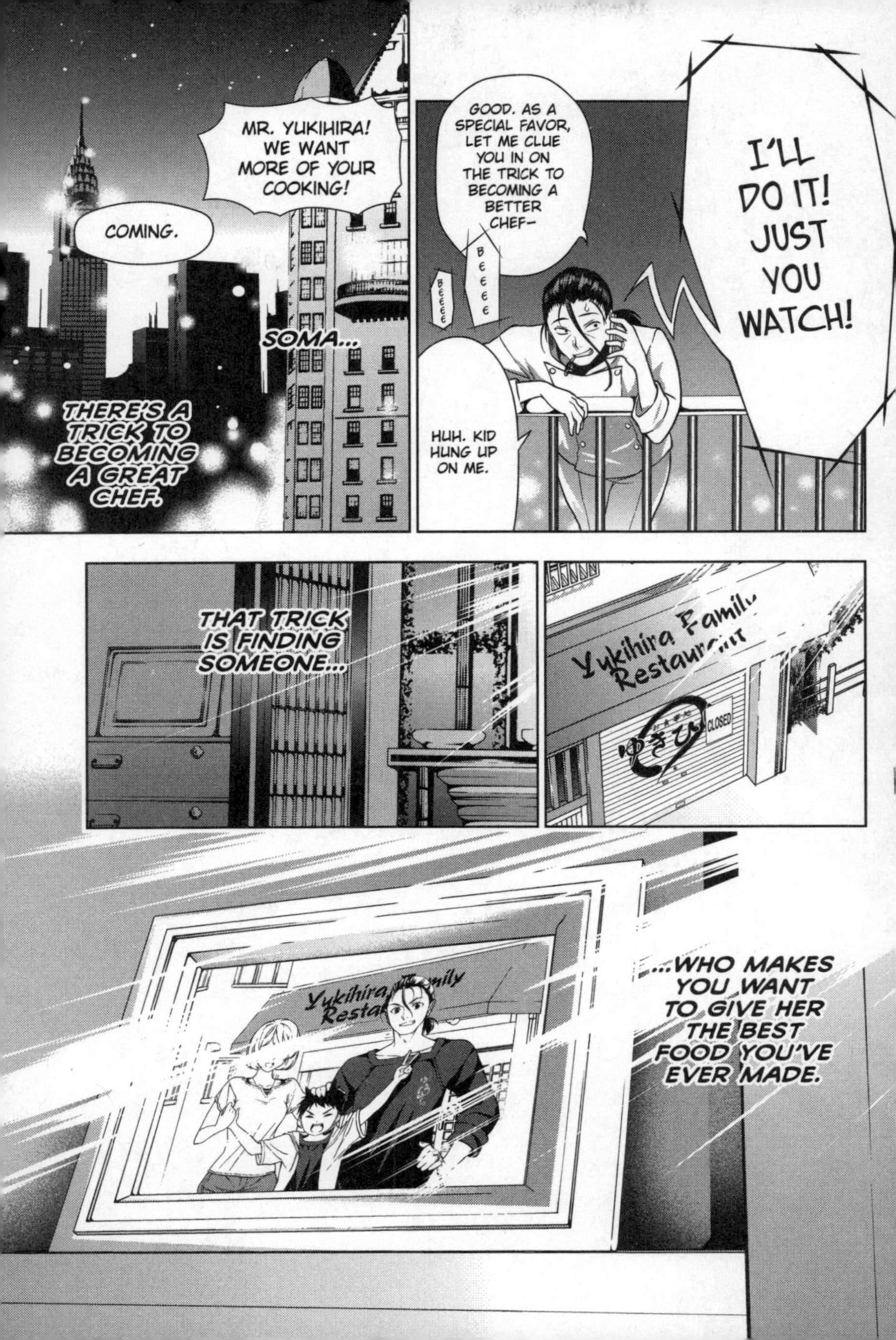
I'LL DO IT! JUST YOU WATCH!
GOOD. AS A SPECIAL FAVOR, LET ME CLUE YOU IN ON THE TRICK TO BECOMING A BETTER CHEF—
BEEEE
BEEEE
HUH. KID HUNG UP ON ME.
MR. YUKIHIRA! WE WANT MORE OF YOUR COOKING!
COMING.
SOMA...
THERE'S A TRICK TO BECOMING A GREAT CHEF.
CLOSED
THAT TRICK IS FINDING SOMEONE...
...WHO MAKES YOU WANT TO GIVE HER THE BEST FOOD YOU'VE EVER MADE.

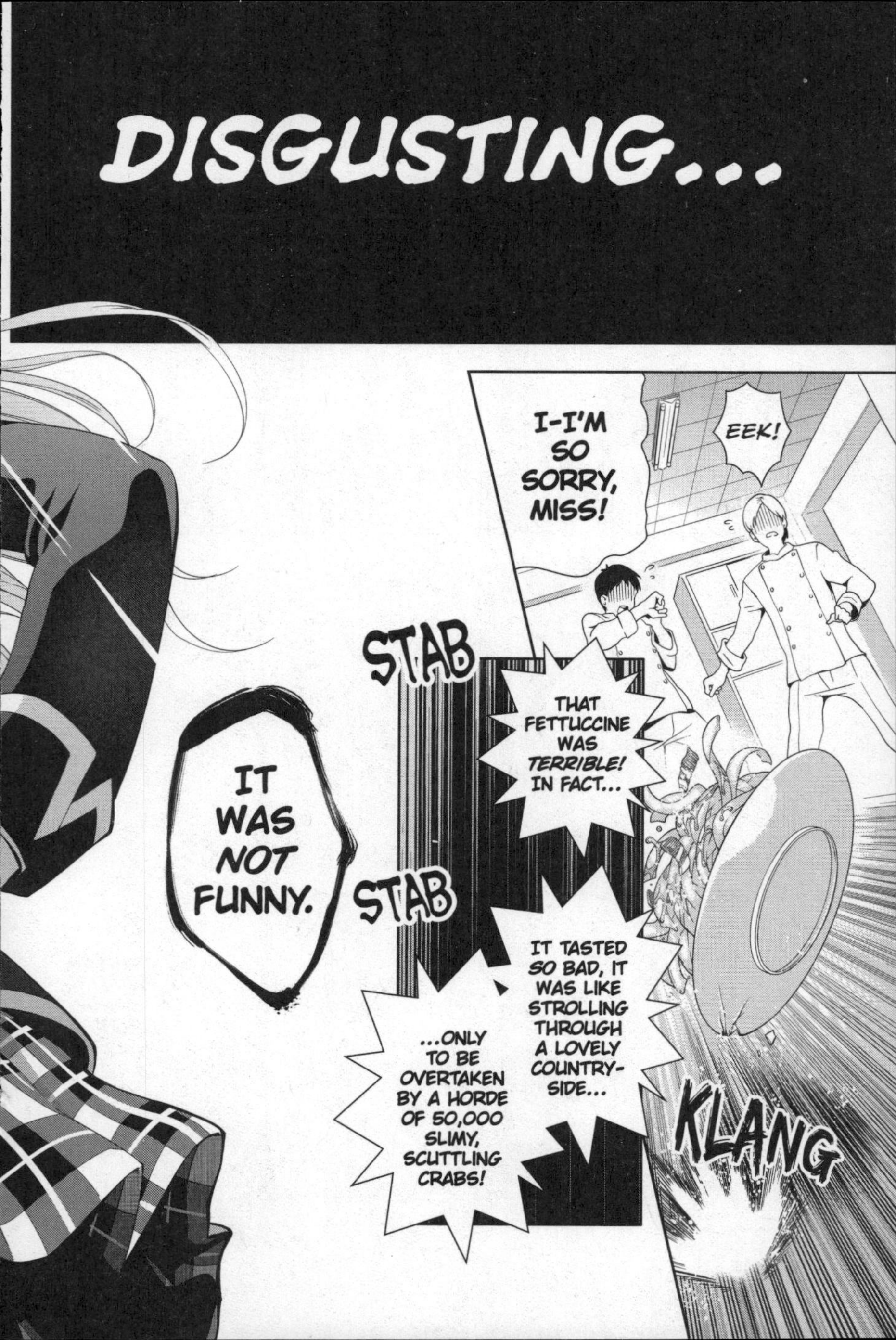
DISGUSTING...
EEK!
I-I'M SO SORRY, MISS!
THAT FETTUCCINE WAS TERRIBLE! IN FACT...
STAB
IT TASTED SO BAD, IT WAS LIKE STROLLING THROUGH A LOVELY COUNTRY-SIDE...
...ONLY TO BE OVERTAKEN BY A HORDE OF 50,000 SLIMY, SCUTTLING CRABS!
KLANG
STAB
IT WAS NOT FUNNY.

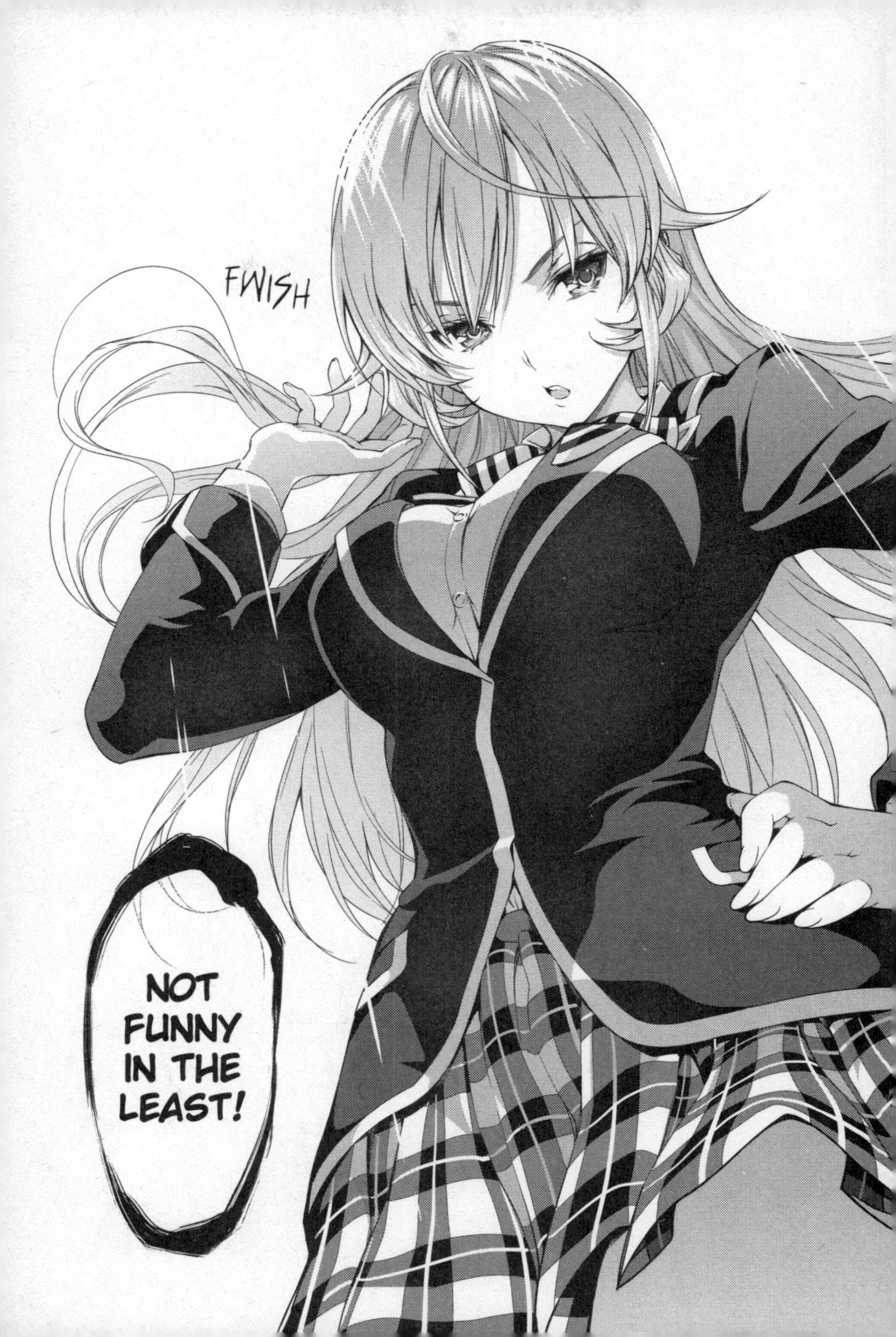
FWISH
NOT FUNNY IN THE LEAST!

Food Wars!
SHOKUGEKI NO SOMA

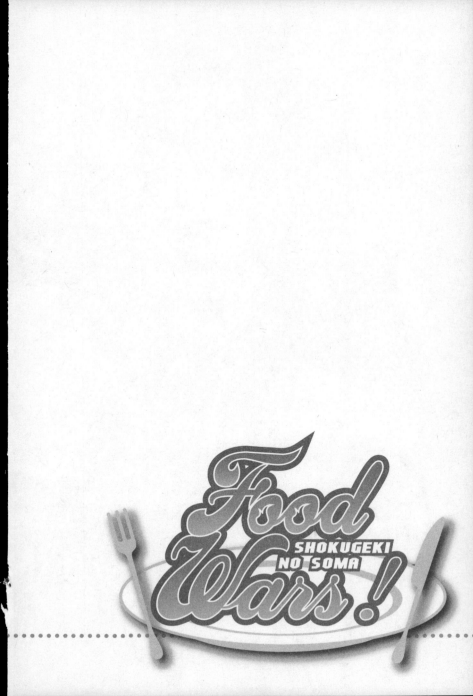

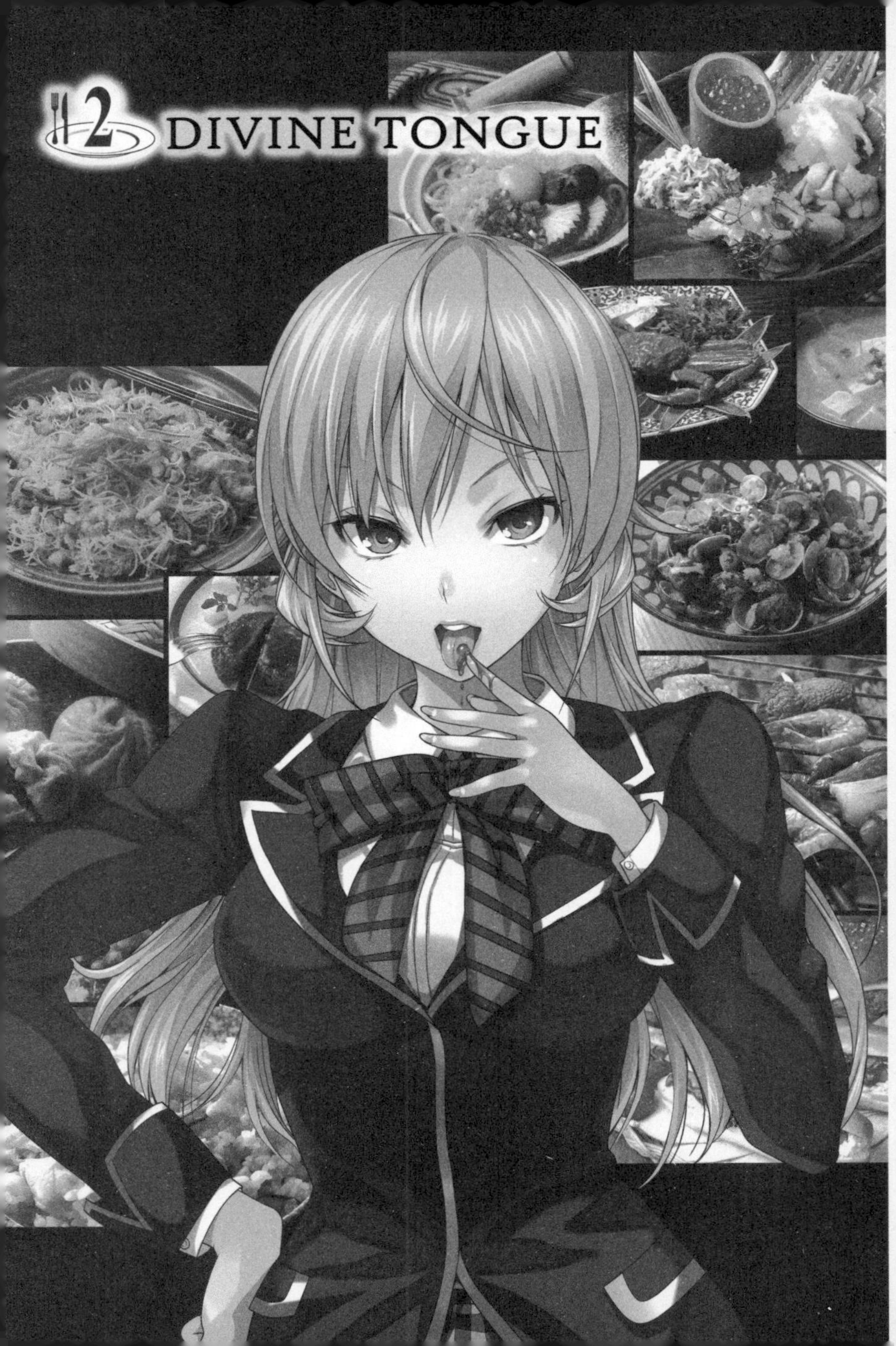
2 DIVINE TONGUE

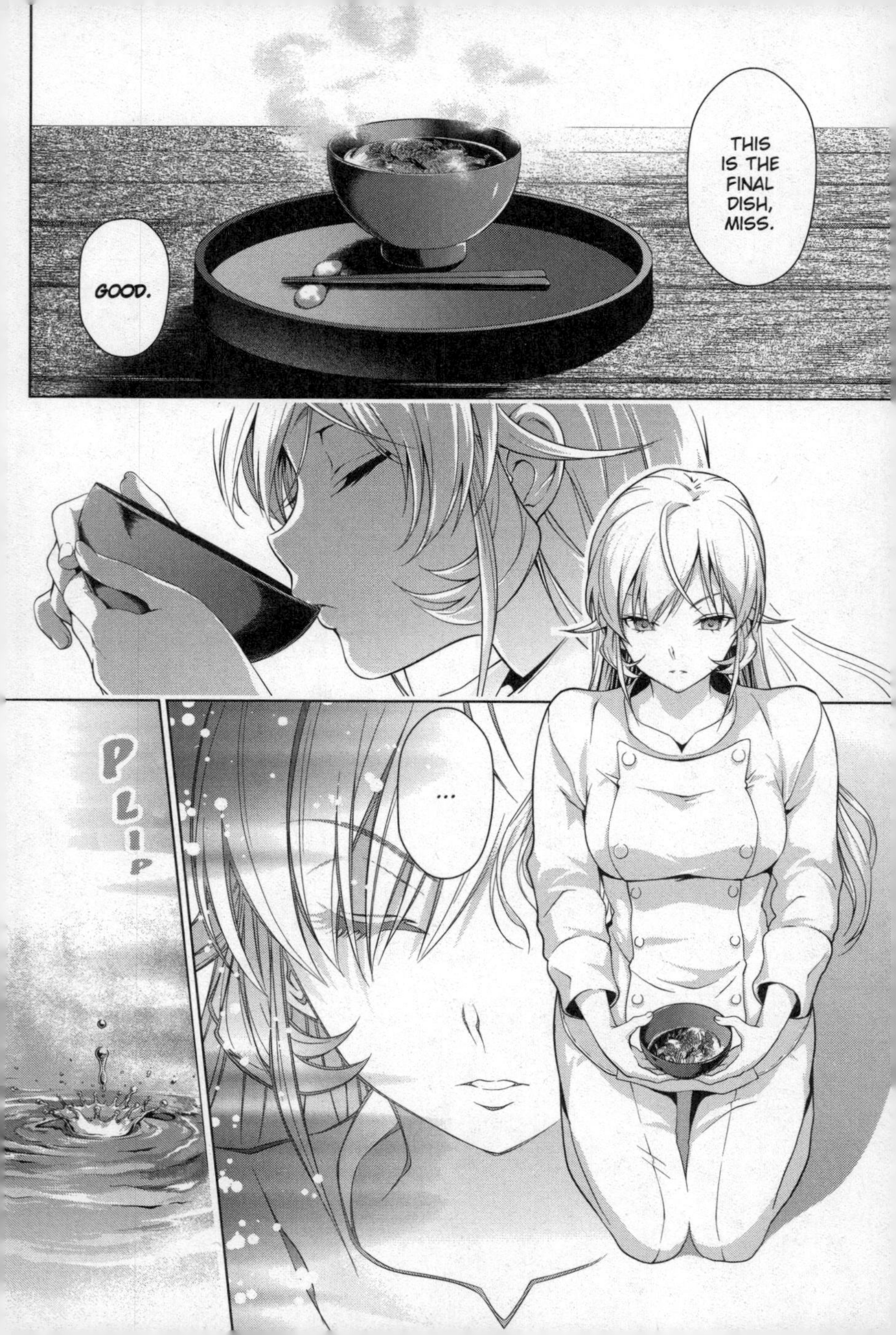
THIS IS THE FINAL DISH, MISS.
GOOD.
...
PLIP

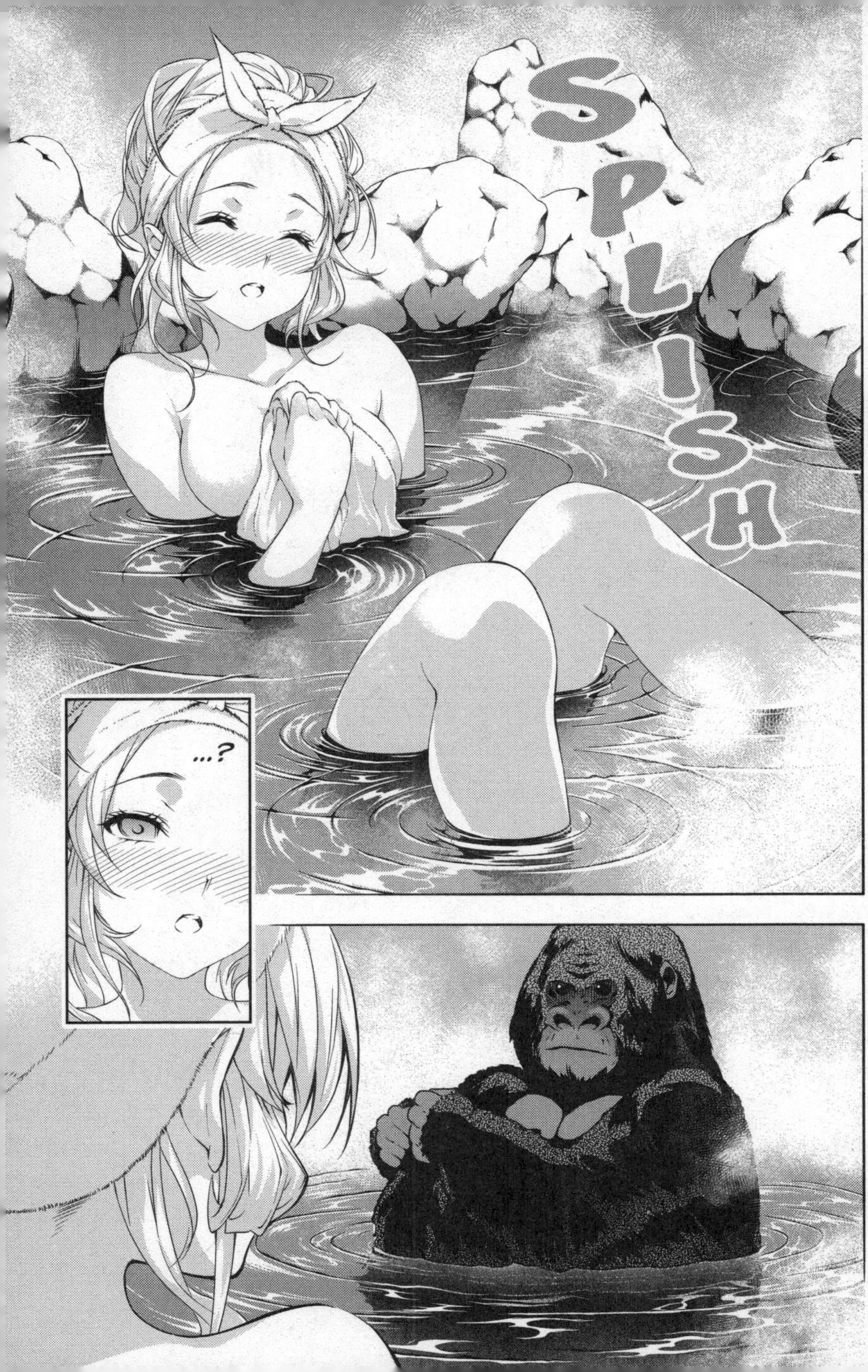
SPLISH
...?

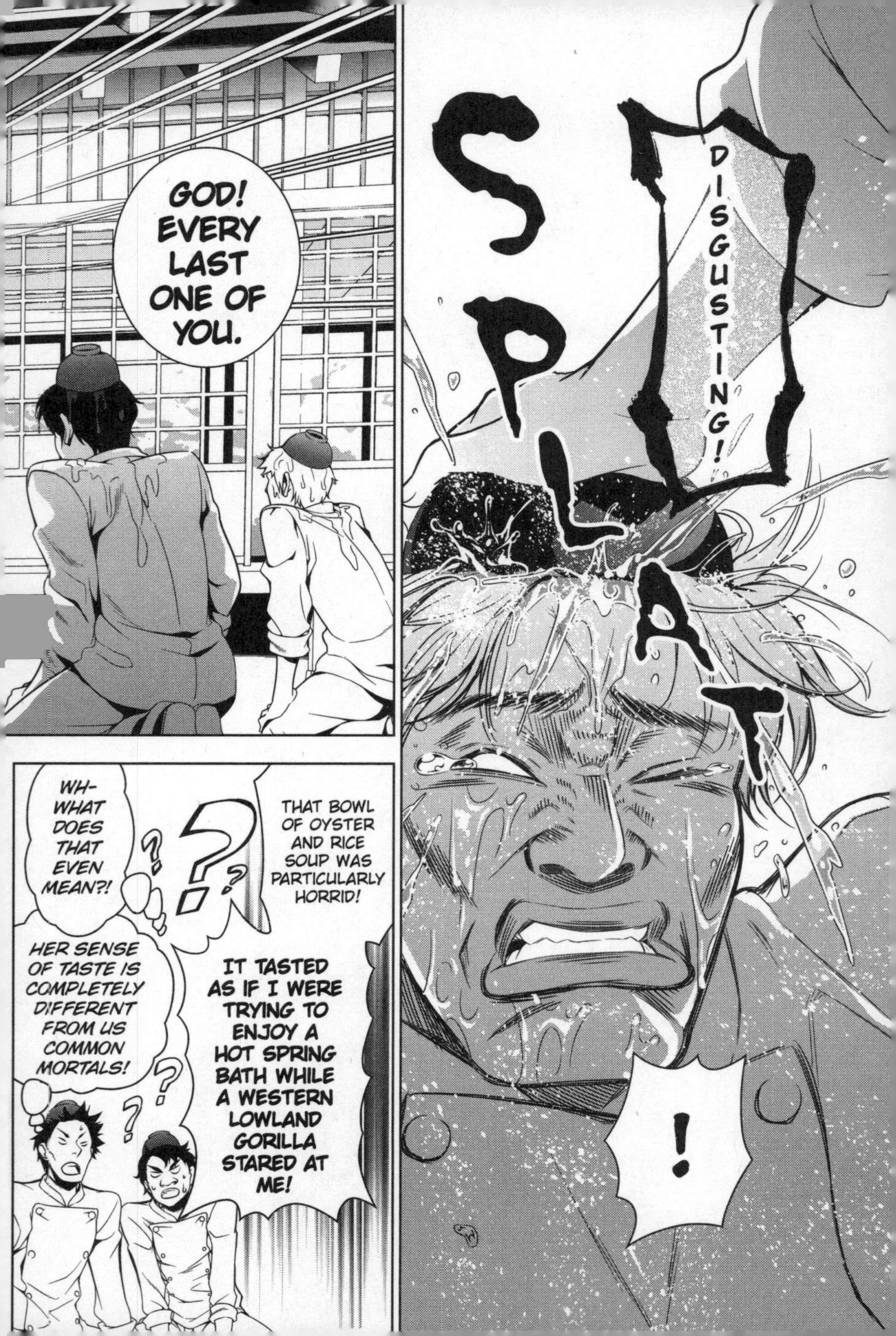
SPLAT
DISGUSTING!
!
GOD! EVERY LAST ONE OF YOU.
THAT BOWL OF OYSTER AND RICE SOUP WAS PARTICULARLY HORRID!
WH-WHAT DOES THAT EVEN MEAN?!
IT TASTED AS IF I WERE TRYING TO ENJOY A HOT SPRING BATH WHILE A WESTERN LOWLAND GORILLA STARED AT ME!
HER SENSE OF TASTE IS COMPLETELY DIFFERENT FROM US COMMON MORTALS!

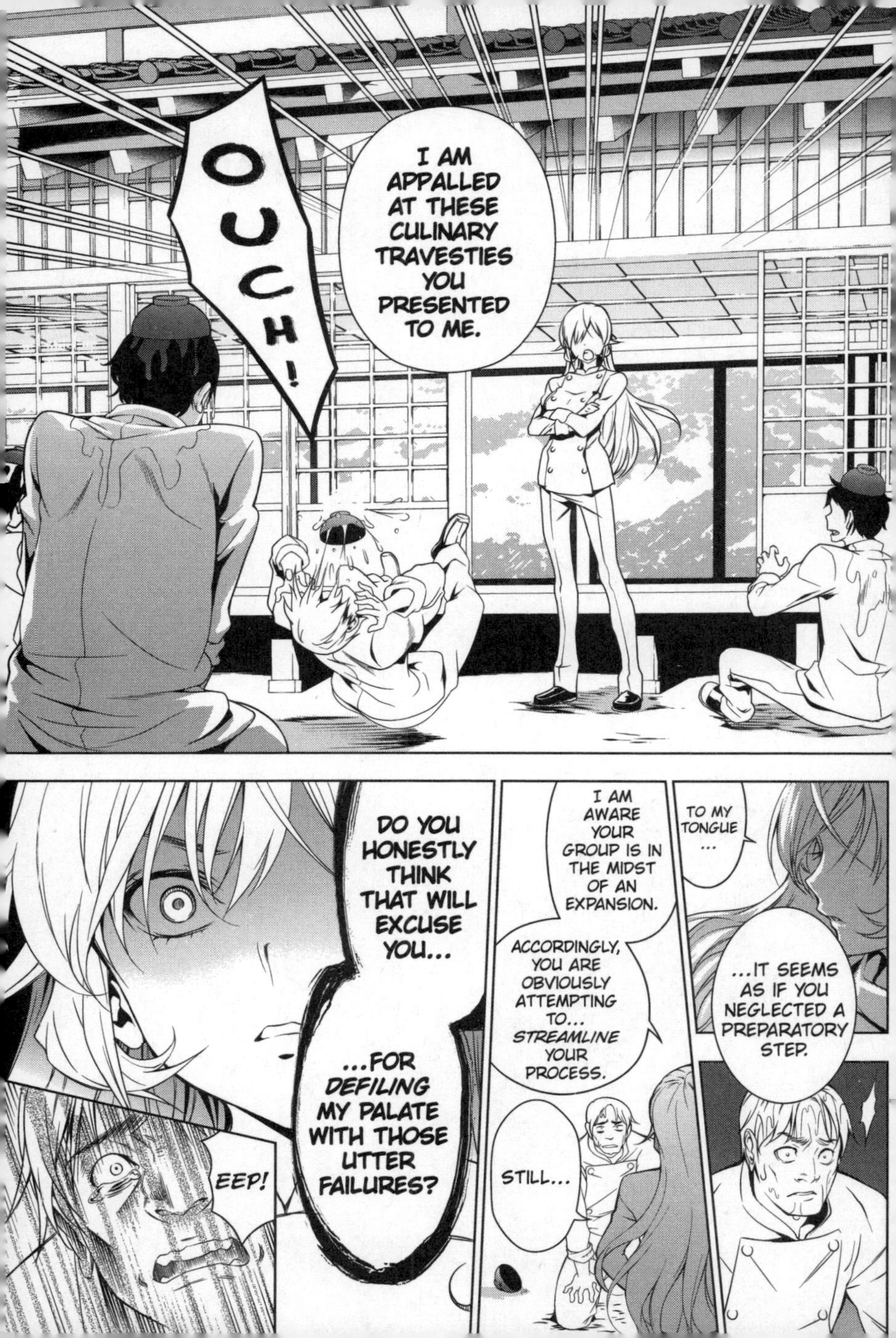
I AM APPALLED AT THESE CULINARY TRAVESTIES YOU PRESENTED TO ME.
OUCH!
TO MY TONGUE...
...IT SEEMS AS IF YOU NEGLECTED A PREPARATORY STEP.
I AM AWARE YOUR GROUP IS IN THE MIDST OF AN EXPANSION.
ACCORDINGLY, YOU ARE OBVIOUSLY ATTEMPTING TO... *STREAMLINE* YOUR PROCESS.
STILL...
DO YOU HONESTLY THINK THAT WILL EXCUSE YOU...
...FOR *DEFILING* MY PALATE WITH THOSE UTTER FAILURES?
EEP!

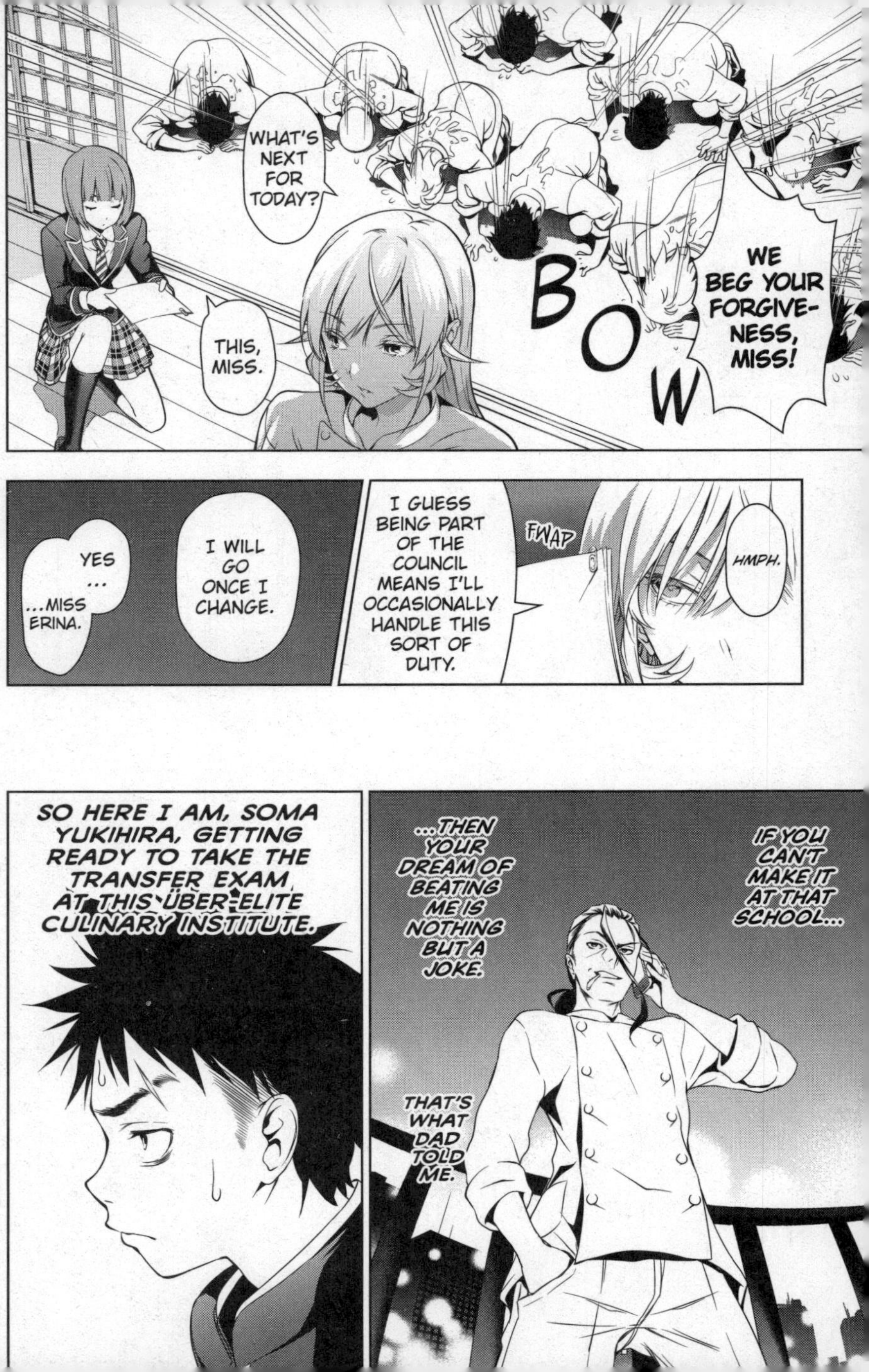
WE BEG YOUR FORGIVE-NESS, MISS!
BOW
WHAT'S NEXT FOR TODAY?
THIS, MISS.
HMPH.
FWAP
I GUESS BEING PART OF THE COUNCIL MEANS I'LL OCCASIONALLY HANDLE THIS SORT OF DUTY.
I WILL GO ONCE I CHANGE.
YES... ...MISS ERINA.
IF YOU CAN'T MAKE IT AT THAT SCHOOL...
...THEN YOUR DREAM OF BEATING ME IS NOTHING BUT A JOKE.
THAT'S WHAT DAD TOLD ME.
SO HERE I AM, SOMA YUKIHIRA, GETTING READY TO TAKE THE TRANSFER EXAM AT THIS ÜBER-ELITE CULINARY INSTITUTE.

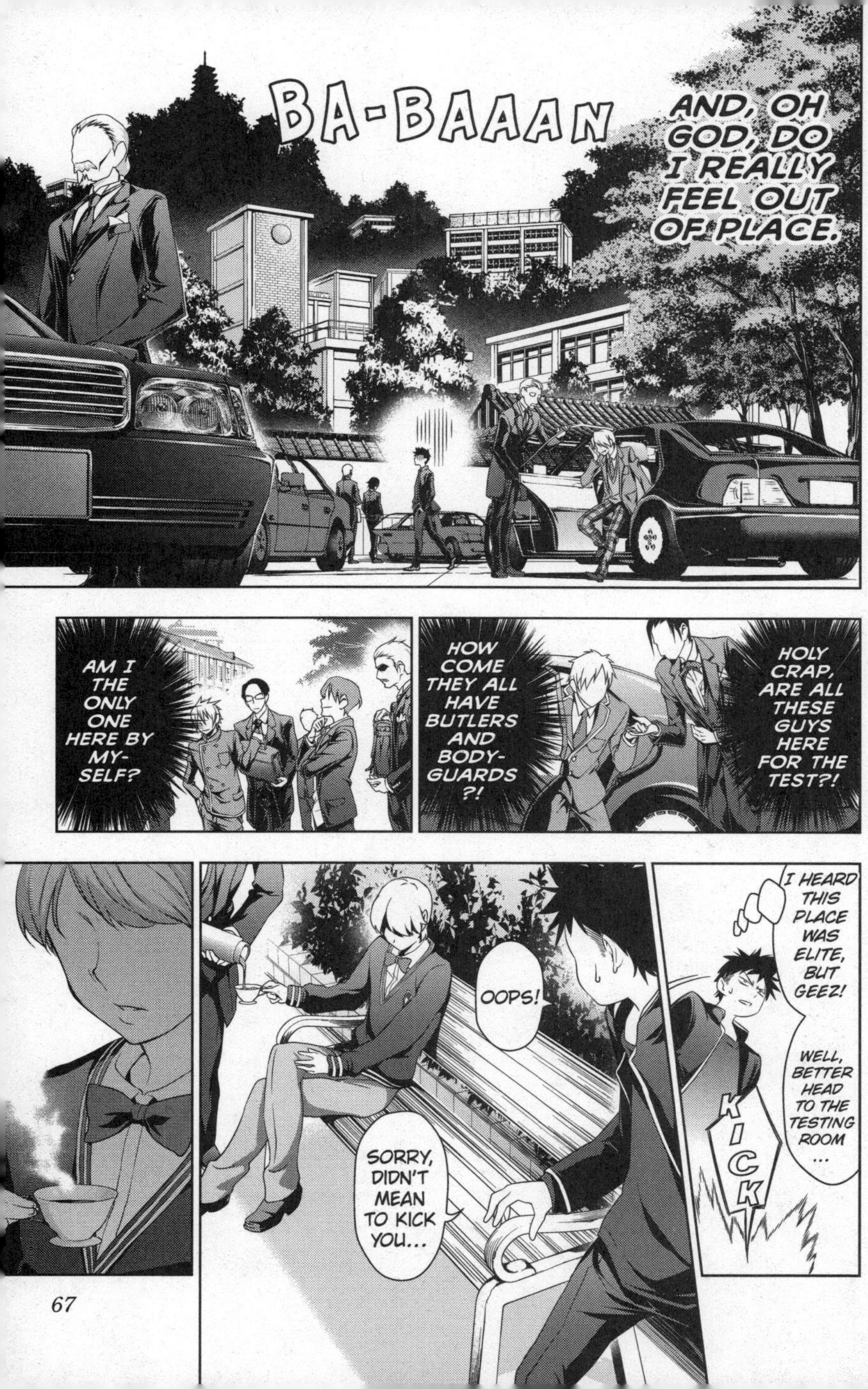

AND, OH GOD, DO I REALLY FEEL OUT OF PLACE.
BA-BAAAN
HOLY CRAP, ARE ALL THESE GUYS HERE FOR THE TEST?!
HOW COME THEY ALL HAVE BUTLERS AND BODY-GUARDS?!
AM I THE ONLY ONE HERE BY MY-SELF?
I HEARD THIS PLACE WAS ELITE, BUT GEEZ!
WELL, BETTER HEAD TO THE TESTING ROOM ...
KICK
OOPS!
SORRY, DIDN'T MEAN TO KICK YOU...

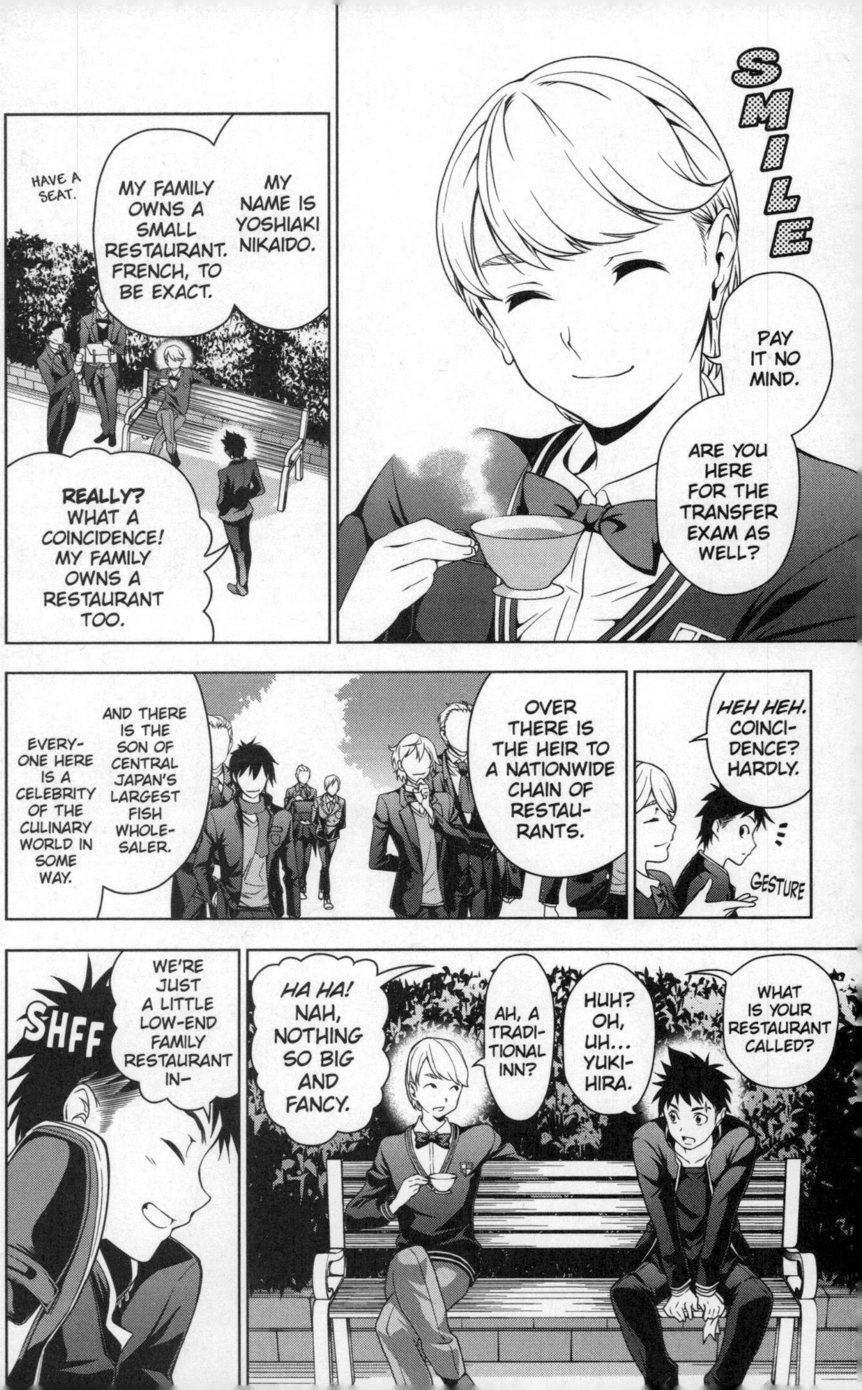
SMILE
PAY IT NO MIND.
ARE YOU HERE FOR THE TRANSFER EXAM AS WELL?
MY NAME IS YOSHIAKI NIKAIDO.
MY FAMILY OWNS A SMALL RESTAURANT. FRENCH, TO BE EXACT.
HAVE A SEAT.
REALLY? WHAT A COINCIDENCE! MY FAMILY OWNS A RESTAURANT TOO.
HEH HEH. COINCIDENCE? HARDLY.
GESTURE
OVER THERE IS THE HEIR TO A NATIONWIDE CHAIN OF RESTAURANTS.
AND THERE IS THE SON OF CENTRAL JAPAN'S LARGEST FISH WHOLESALER.
EVERYONE HERE IS A CELEBRITY OF THE CULINARY WORLD IN SOME WAY.
WHAT IS YOUR RESTAURANT CALLED?
HUH? OH, UH... YUKIHIRA.
AH, A TRADITIONAL INN?
HA HA! NAH, NOTHING SO BIG AND FANCY.
SHFF
WE'RE JUST A LITTLE LOW-END FAMILY RESTAURANT IN-

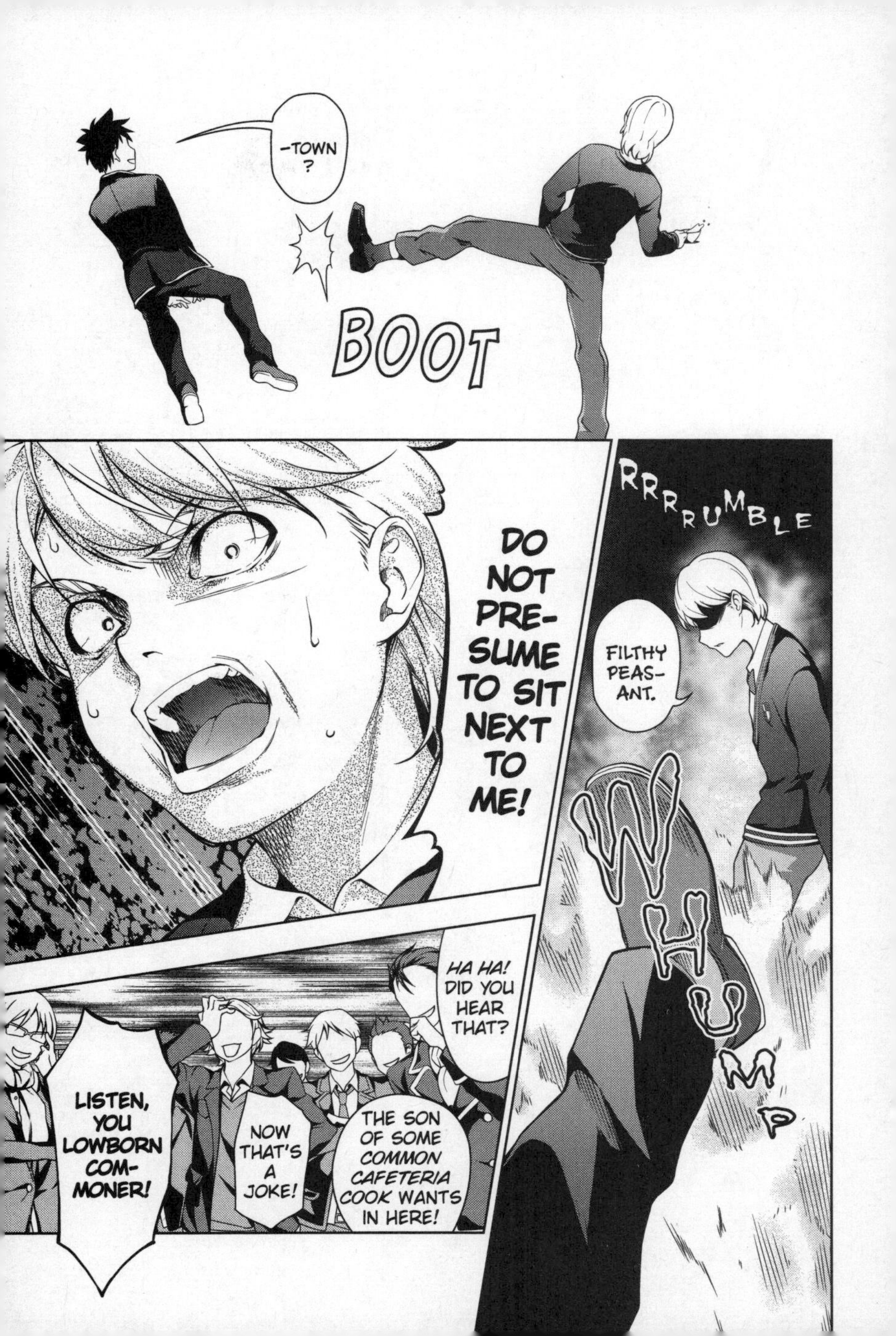
-TOWN ?
BOOT
RRRRUMBLE
FILTHY PEASANT.
WHUMP
DO NOT PRESUME TO SIT NEXT TO ME!
HA HA! DID YOU HEAR THAT?
THE SON OF SOME COMMON CAFETERIA COOK WANTS IN HERE!
NOW THAT'S A JOKE!
LISTEN, YOU LOWBORN COMMONER!

PEASANTS LIKE YOU HAVE NO PLACE HERE.
THIS IS A HOLY GARDEN OF HAUTE CUISINE...
...WHERE ONLY THE UPPER CLASS OF THE CULINARY WORLD IS ALLOWED TO TREAD.
THIS...
...IS THE TOTSUKI SARYO CULINARY INSTITUTE!
A LOWBORN COMMONER LIKE YOU WILL PROBABLY BE REJECTED ON YOUR APPLICATION ALO-GURPH!

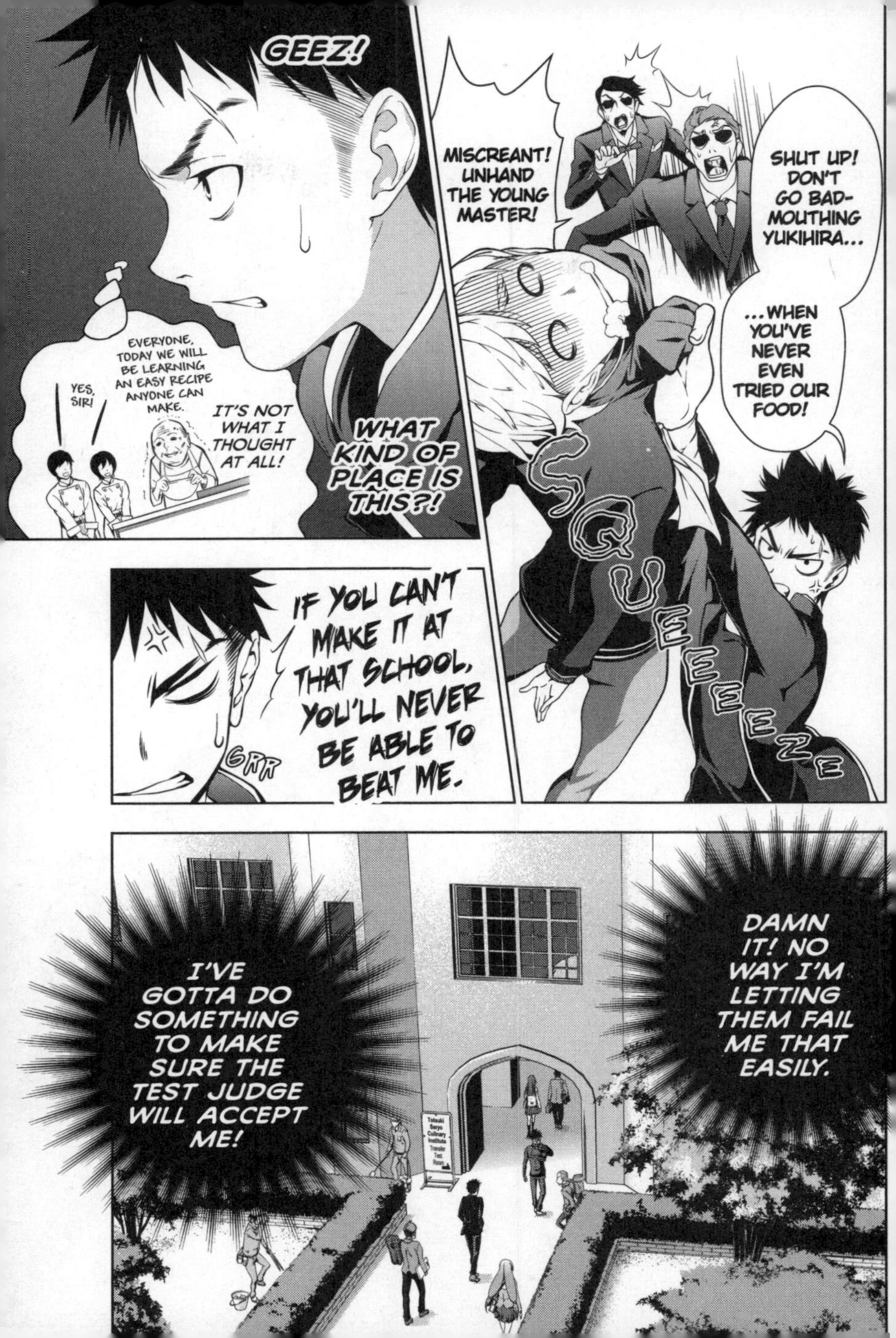
MISCREANT! UNHAND THE YOUNG MASTER!
SHUT UP! DON'T GO BAD-MOUTHING YUKIHIRA...
...WHEN YOU'VE NEVER EVEN TRIED OUR FOOD!
SQUEEEEEZE
GEEZ!
EVERYONE, TODAY WE WILL BE LEARNING AN EASY RECIPE ANYONE CAN MAKE.
YES, SIR!
IT'S NOT WHAT I THOUGHT AT ALL!
WHAT KIND OF PLACE IS THIS?!
IF YOU CAN'T MAKE IT AT THAT SCHOOL, YOU'LL NEVER BE ABLE TO BEAT ME.
GRR
DAMN IT! NO WAY I'M LETTING THEM FAIL ME THAT EASILY.
I'VE GOTTA DO SOMETHING TO MAKE SURE THE TEST JUDGE WILL ACCEPT ME!
Totsuki Saryo Culinary Institute Transfer Test Room

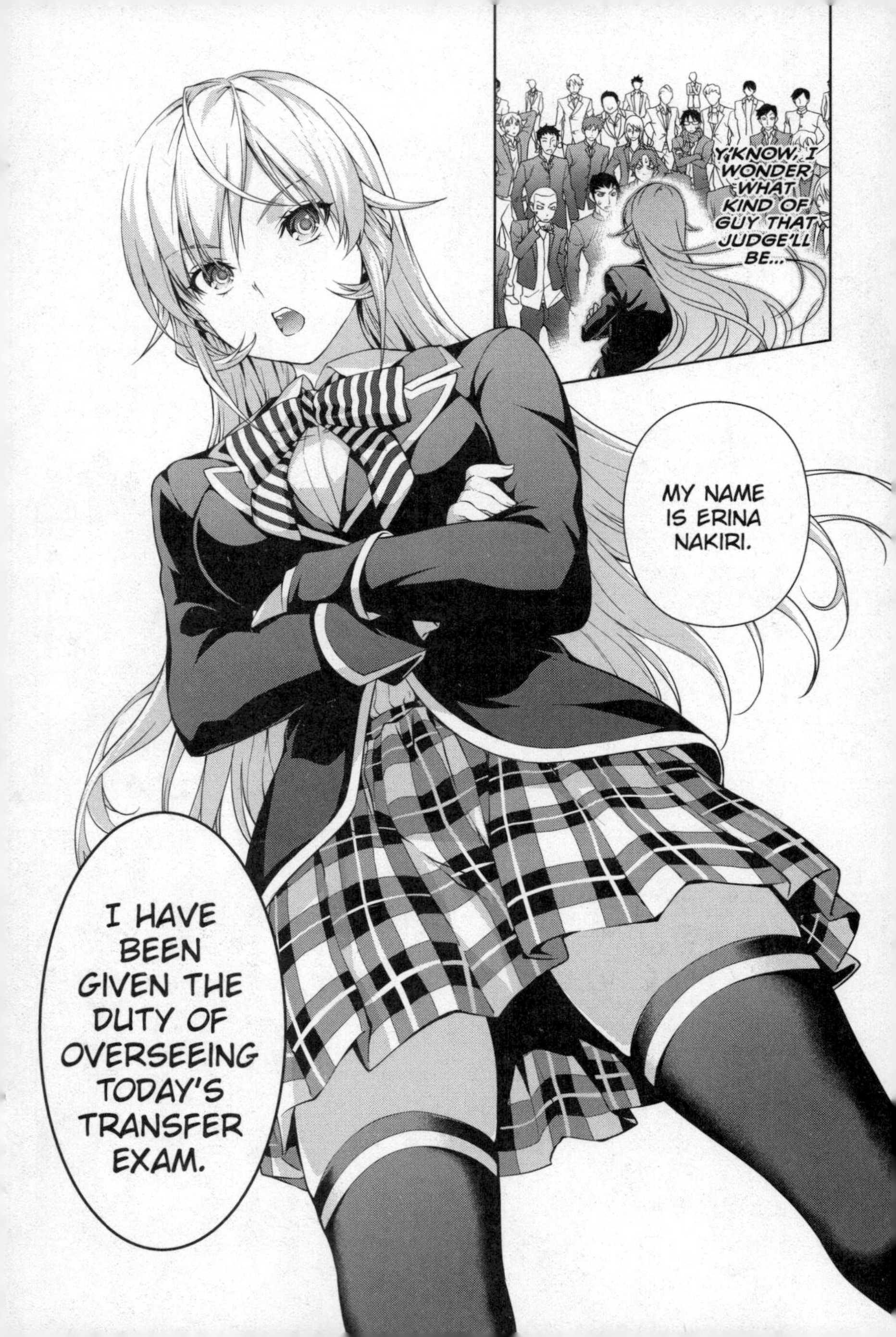
Y'KNOW, I WONDER WHAT KIND OF GUY THAT JUDGE'LL BE...
MY NAME IS ERINA NAKIRI.
I HAVE BEEN GIVEN THE DUTY OF OVERSEEING TODAY'S TRANSFER EXAM.

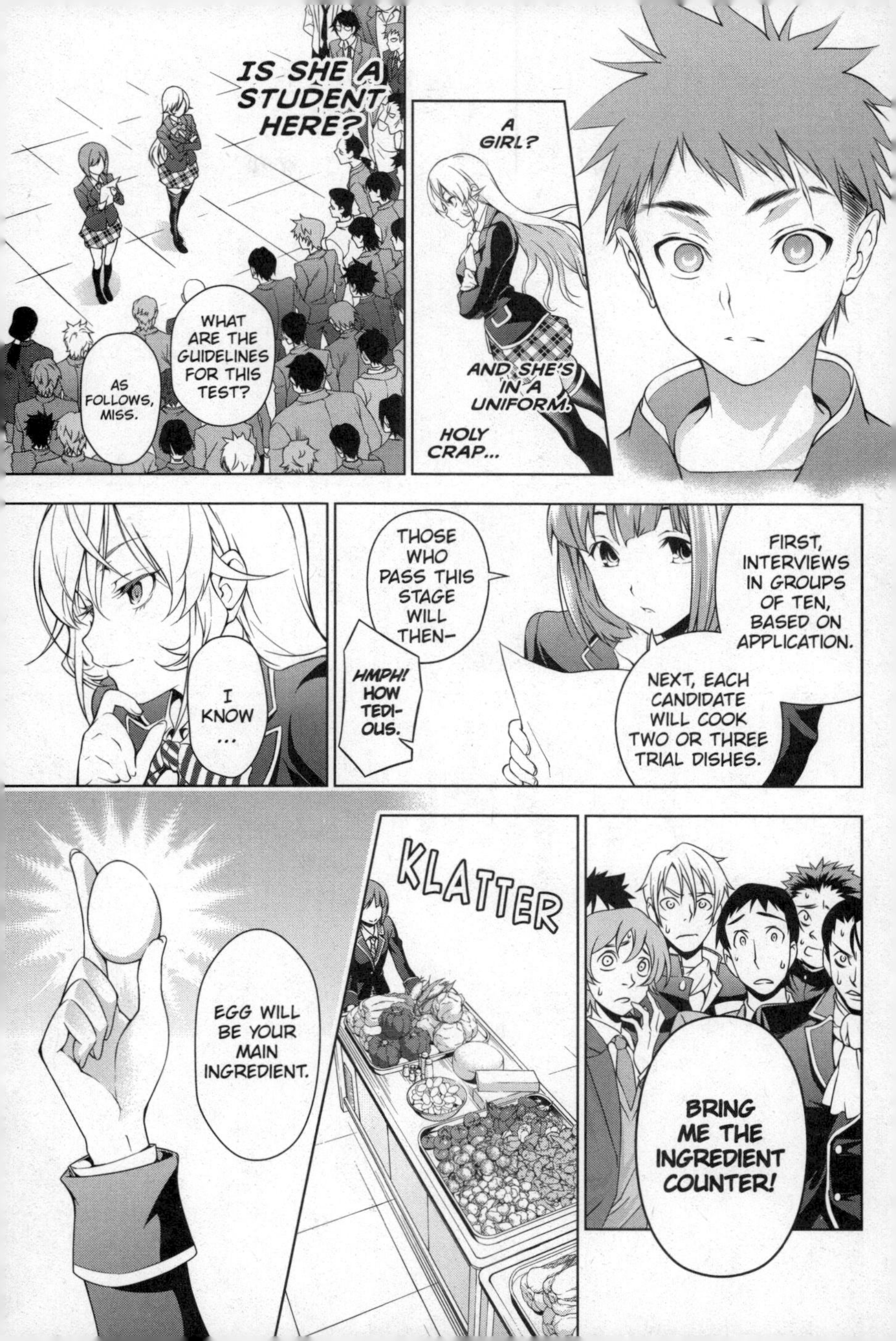
A GIRL?
AND SHE'S IN A UNIFORM.
HOLY CRAP...
IS SHE A STUDENT HERE?
WHAT ARE THE GUIDELINES FOR THIS TEST?
AS FOLLOWS, MISS.
FIRST, INTERVIEWS IN GROUPS OF TEN, BASED ON APPLICATION.
NEXT, EACH CANDIDATE WILL COOK TWO OR THREE TRIAL DISHES.
THOSE WHO PASS THIS STAGE WILL THEN—
HMPH! HOW TEDIOUS.
I KNOW ...
BRING ME THE INGREDIENT COUNTER!
KLATTER
EGG WILL BE YOUR MAIN INGREDIENT.

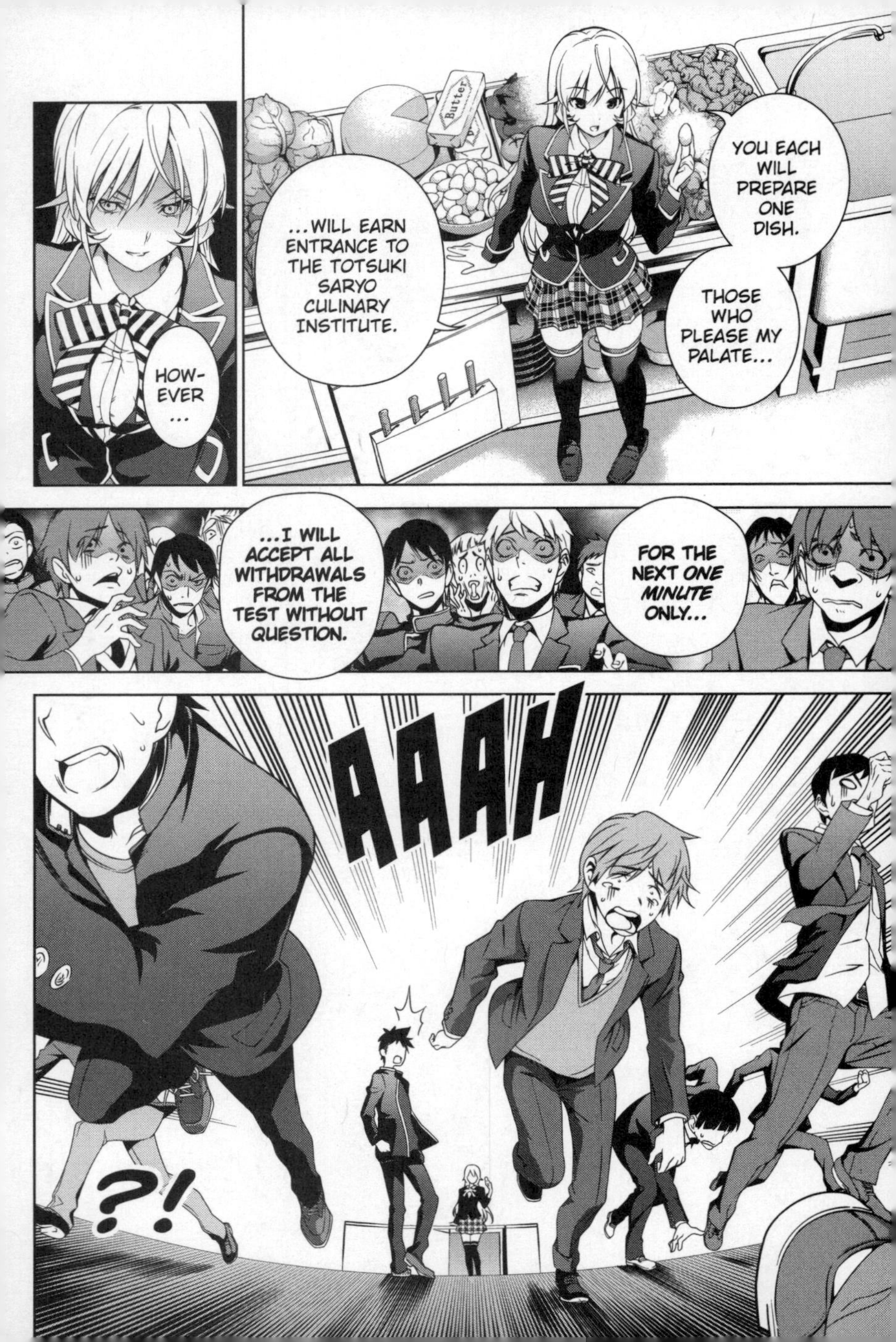

YOU EACH WILL PREPARE ONE DISH.
THOSE WHO PLEASE MY PALATE...
...WILL EARN ENTRANCE TO THE TOTSUKI SARYO CULINARY INSTITUTE.
Butter
HOW-EVER ...
FOR THE NEXT *ONE MINUTE* ONLY...
...I WILL ACCEPT ALL WITHDRAWALS FROM THE TEST WITHOUT QUESTION.
AAAH
?!

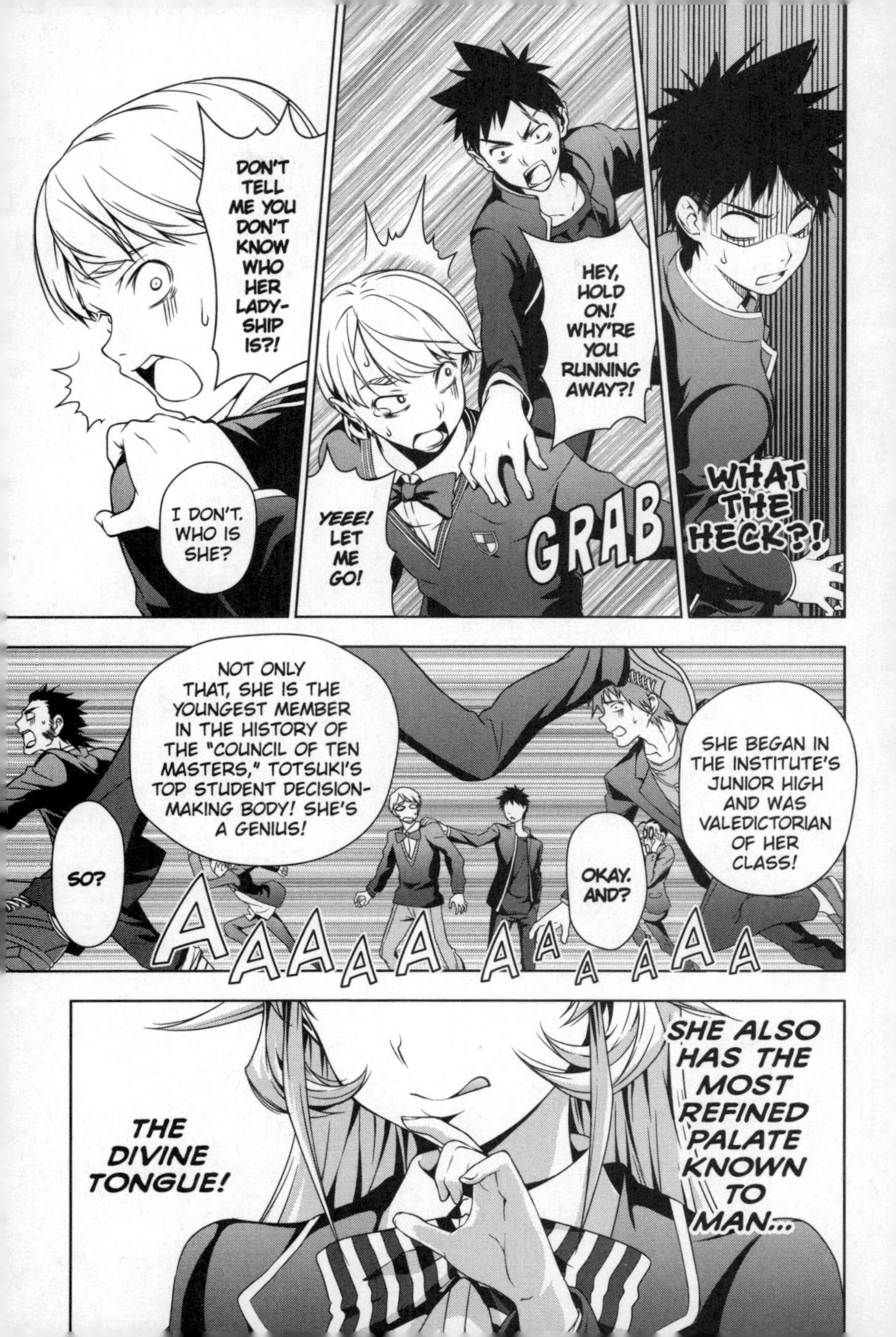
WHAT THE HECK?!
HEY, HOLD ON! WHY'RE YOU RUNNING AWAY?!
GRAB
YEEE! LET ME GO!
DON'T TELL ME YOU DON'T KNOW WHO HER LADYSHIP IS?!
I DON'T. WHO IS SHE?
SHE BEGAN IN THE INSTITUTE'S JUNIOR HIGH AND WAS VALEDICTORIAN OF HER CLASS!
OKAY. AND?
NOT ONLY THAT, SHE IS THE YOUNGEST MEMBER IN THE HISTORY OF THE "COUNCIL OF TEN MASTERS," TOTSUKI'S TOP STUDENT DECISION-MAKING BODY! SHE'S A GENIUS!
SO?
AAAAAAAAAAA
SHE ALSO HAS THE MOST REFINED PALATE KNOWN TO MAN...
THE DIVINE TONGUE!

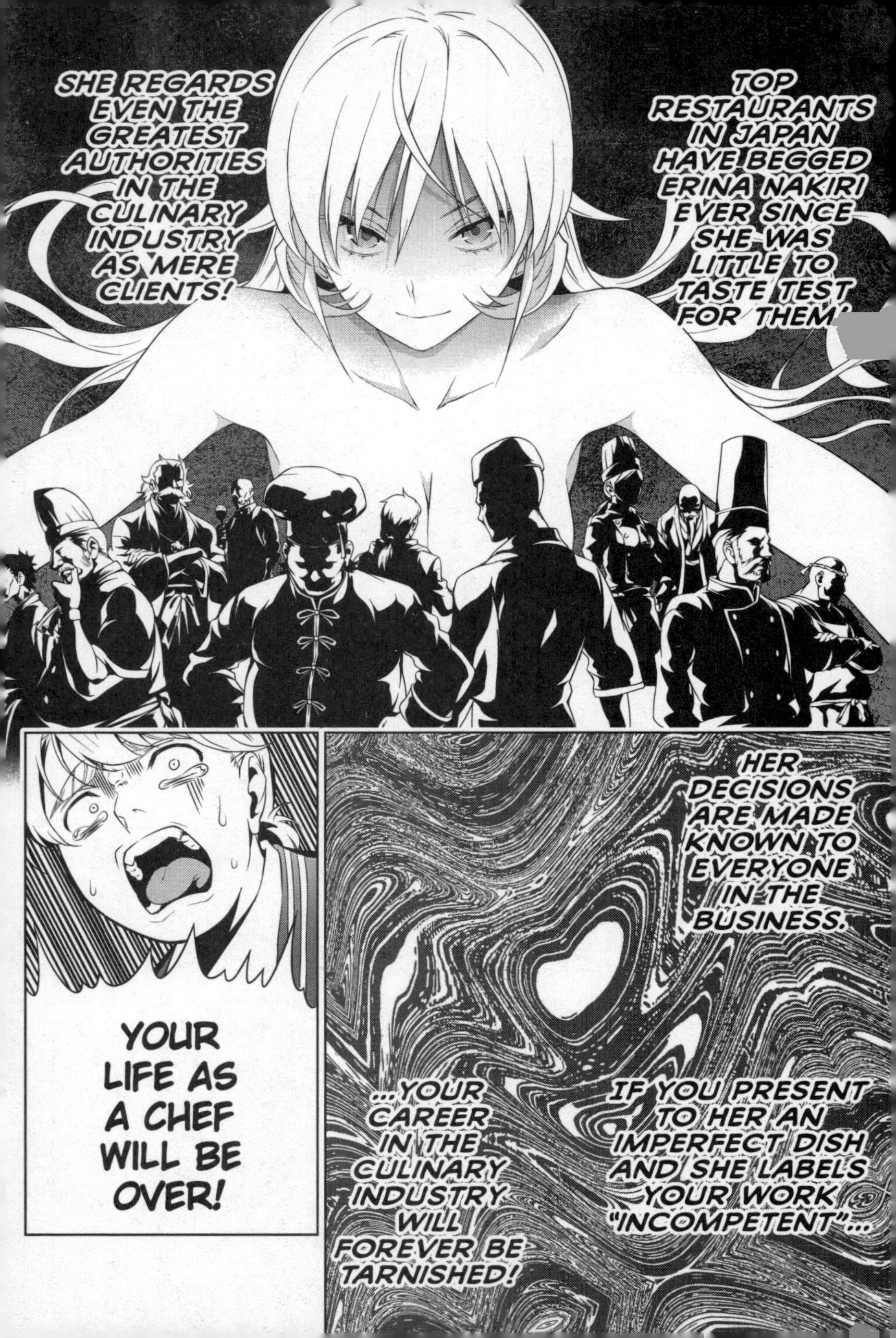
TOP RESTAURANTS IN JAPAN HAVE BEGGED ERINA NAKIRI EVER SINCE SHE WAS LITTLE TO TASTE TEST FOR THEM!
SHE REGARDS EVEN THE GREATEST AUTHORITIES IN THE CULINARY INDUSTRY AS MERE CLIENTS!
HER DECISIONS ARE MADE KNOWN TO EVERYONE IN THE BUSINESS.
IF YOU PRESENT TO HER AN IMPERFECT DISH AND SHE LABELS YOUR WORK "INCOMPETENT"...
...YOUR CAREER IN THE CULINARY INDUSTRY WILL FOREVER BE TARNISHED!
YOUR LIFE AS A CHEF WILL BE OVER!

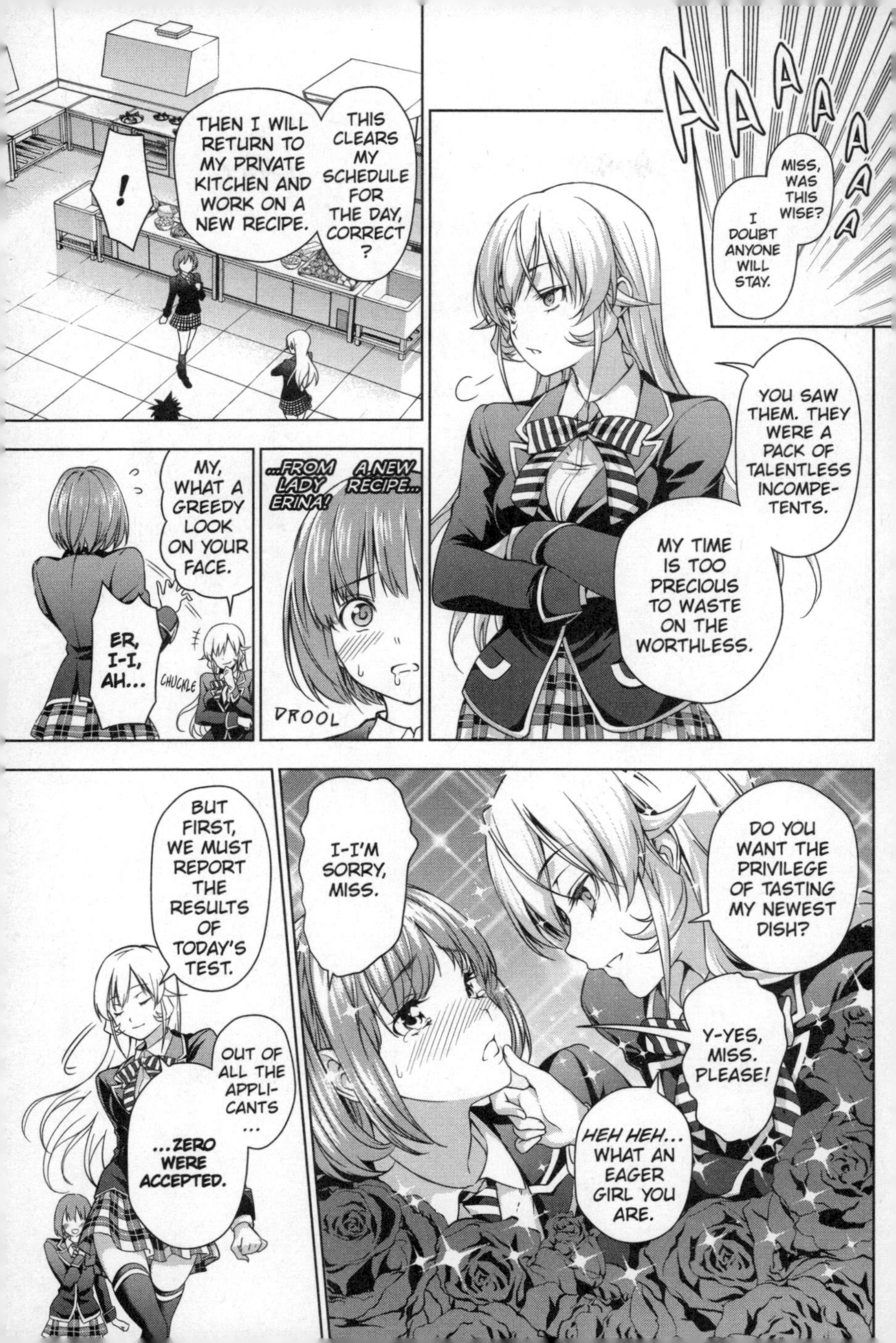
AAAAAAAAA
MISS, WAS THIS WISE?
I DOUBT ANYONE WILL STAY.
YOU SAW THEM. THEY WERE A PACK OF TALENTLESS INCOMPE-TENTS.
MY TIME IS TOO PRECIOUS TO WASTE ON THE WORTHLESS.
THIS CLEARS MY SCHEDULE FOR THE DAY, CORRECT?
THEN I WILL RETURN TO MY PRIVATE KITCHEN AND WORK ON A NEW RECIPE.
!
A NEW RECIPE...
...FROM LADY ERINA!
DROOL
MY, WHAT A GREEDY LOOK ON YOUR FACE.
ER, I-I, AH...
CHUCKLE
I-I'M SORRY, MISS.
DO YOU WANT THE PRIVILEGE OF TASTING MY NEWEST DISH?
Y-YES, MISS. PLEASE!
HEH HEH... WHAT AN EAGER GIRL YOU ARE.
BUT FIRST, WE MUST REPORT THE RESULTS OF TODAY'S TEST.
OUT OF ALL THE APPLI-CANTS...
...ZERO WERE ACCEPTED.

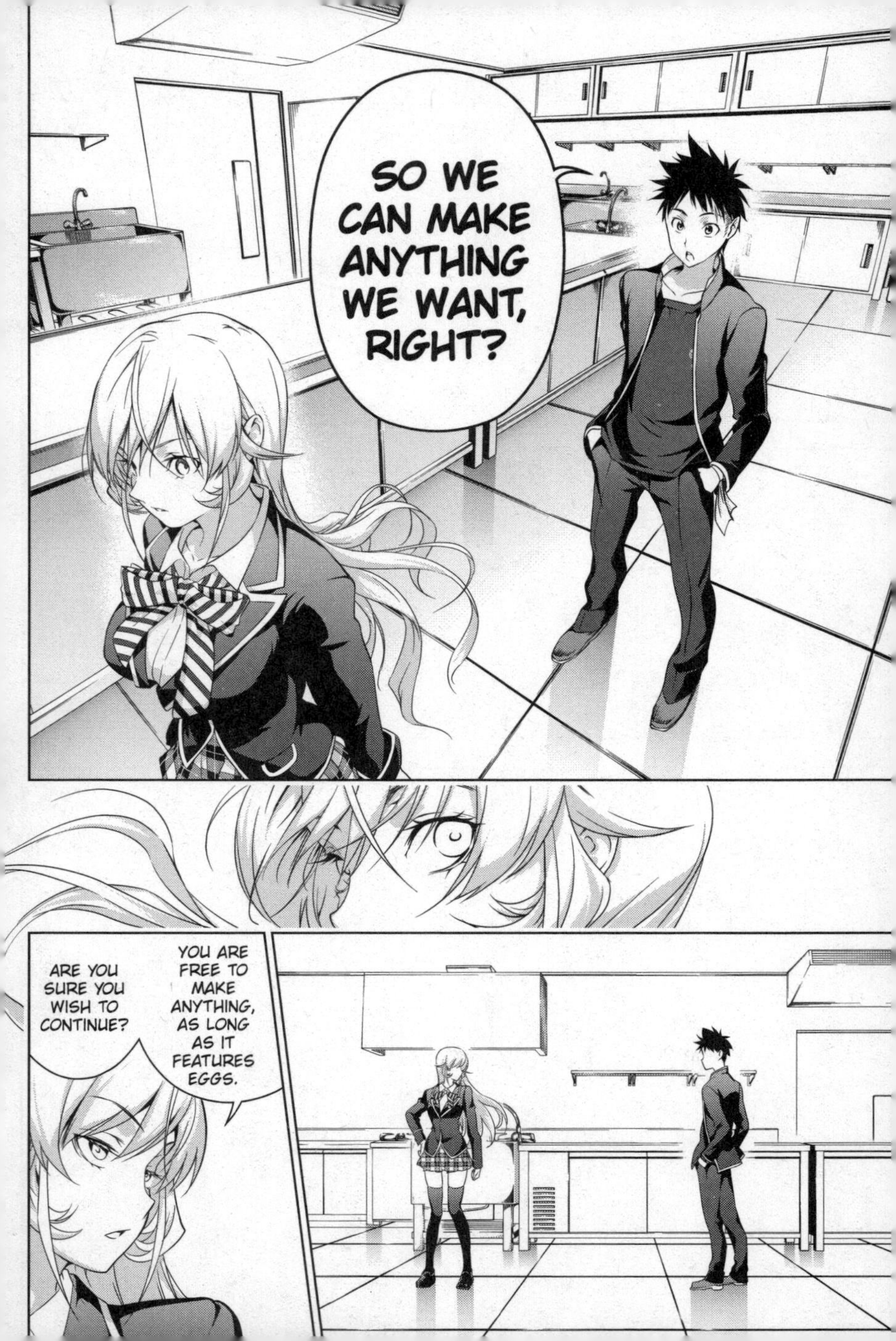
SO WE CAN MAKE ANYTHING WE WANT, RIGHT?
YOU ARE FREE TO MAKE ANYTHING, AS LONG AS IT FEATURES EGGS.
ARE YOU SURE YOU WISH TO CONTINUE?

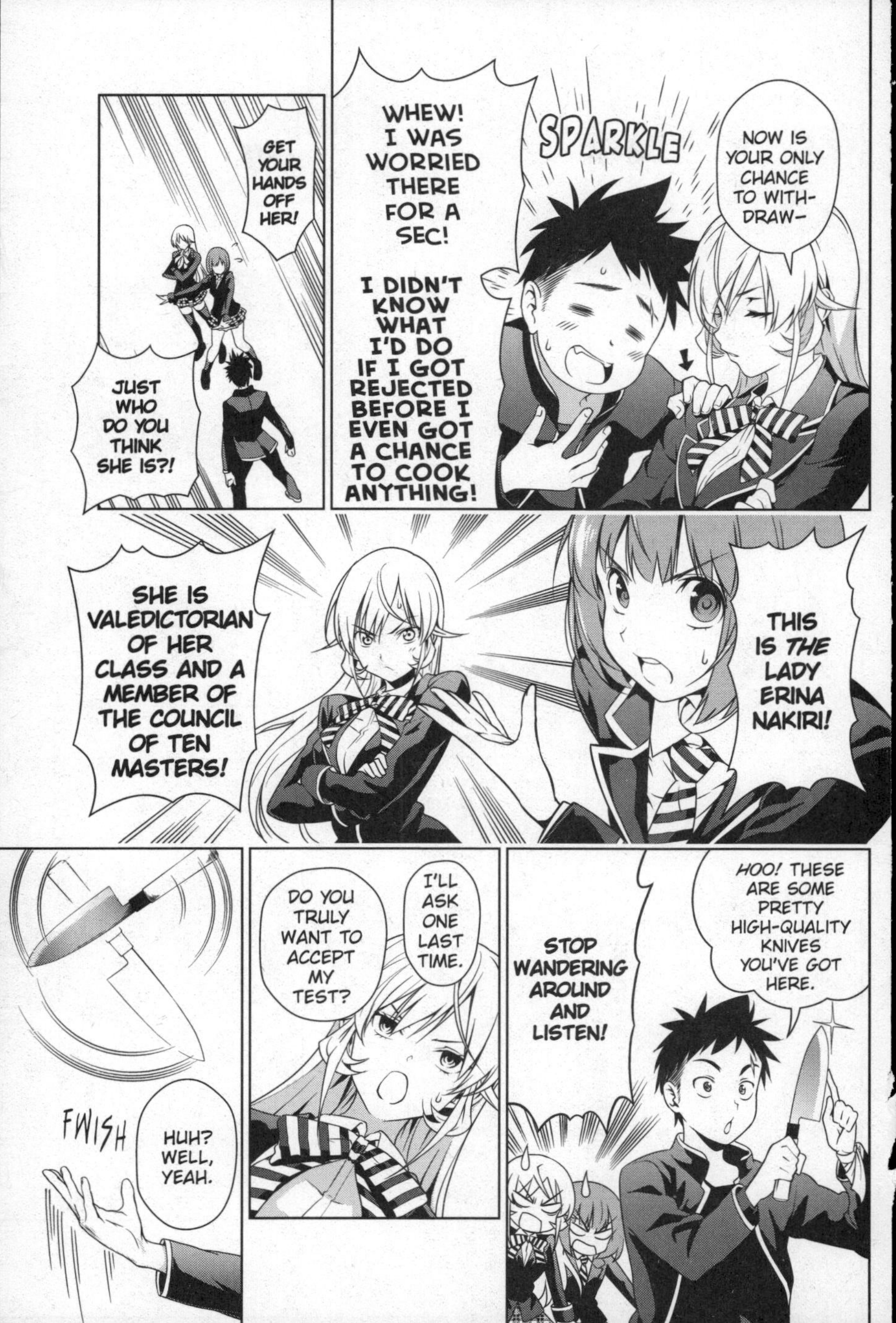
NOW IS YOUR ONLY CHANCE TO WITH-DRAW—
SPARKLE
WHEW! I WAS WORRIED THERE FOR A SEC!
I DIDN'T KNOW WHAT I'D DO IF I GOT REJECTED BEFORE I EVEN GOT A CHANCE TO COOK ANYTHING!
GET YOUR HANDS OFF HER!
JUST WHO DO YOU THINK SHE IS?!
THIS IS *THE* LADY ERINA NAKIRI!
SHE IS VALEDICTORIAN OF HER CLASS AND A MEMBER OF THE COUNCIL OF TEN MASTERS!
HOO! THESE ARE SOME PRETTY HIGH-QUALITY KNIVES YOU'VE GOT HERE.
STOP WANDERING AROUND AND LISTEN!
I'LL ASK ONE LAST TIME.
DO YOU TRULY WANT TO ACCEPT MY TEST?
FWISH
HUH? WELL, YEAH.

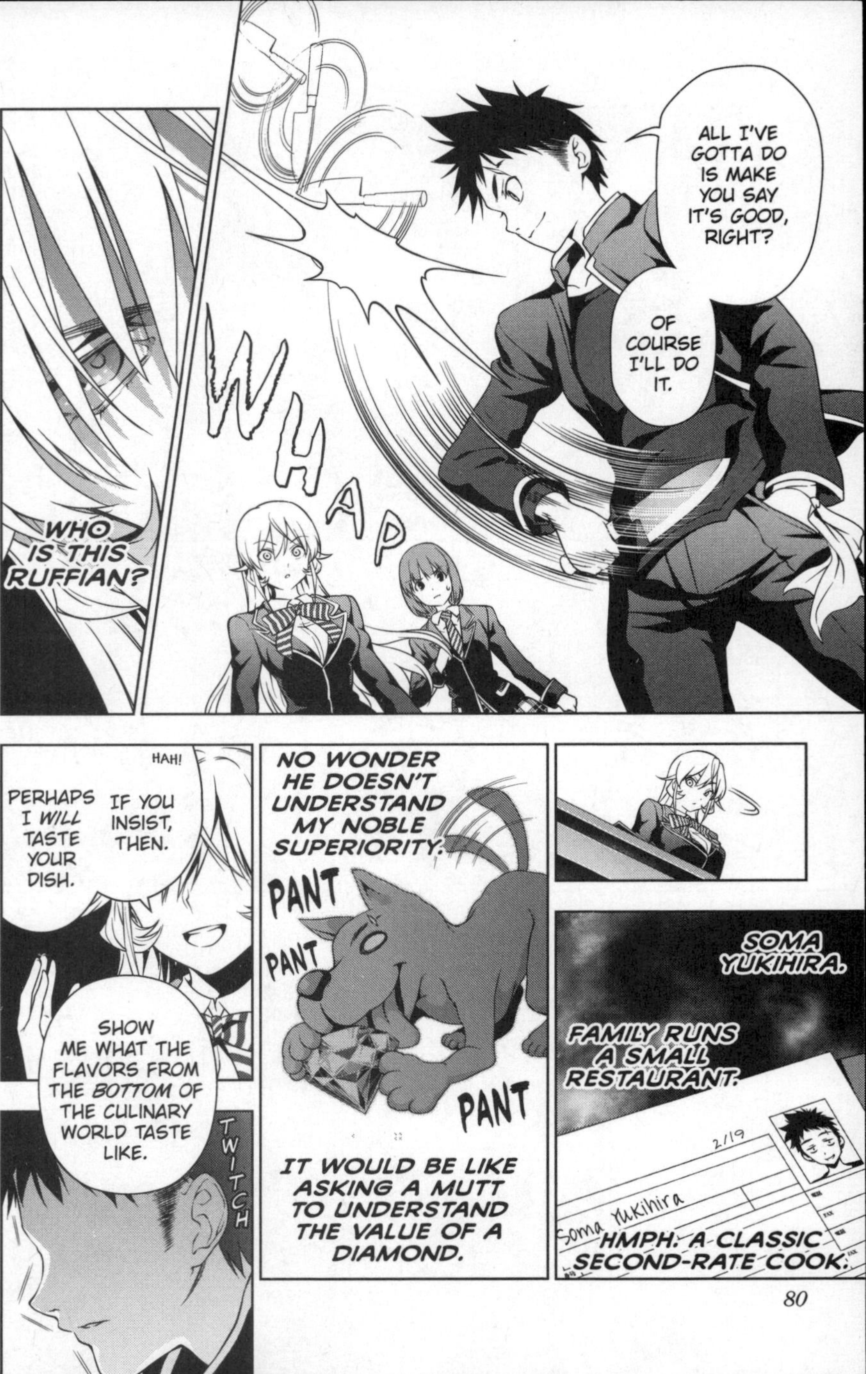
ALL I'VE GOTTA DO IS MAKE YOU SAY IT'S GOOD, RIGHT?
OF COURSE I'LL DO IT.
WHAP
WHO IS THIS RUFFIAN?
SOMA YUKIHIRA.
FAMILY RUNS A SMALL RESTAURANT.
2/19
Soma Yukihira
HMPH. A CLASSIC SECOND-RATE COOK.
NO WONDER HE DOESN'T UNDERSTAND MY NOBLE SUPERIORITY.
PANT
PANT
PANT
IT WOULD BE LIKE ASKING A MUTT TO UNDERSTAND THE VALUE OF A DIAMOND.
HAH!
IF YOU INSIST, THEN.
PERHAPS I *WILL* TASTE YOUR DISH.
SHOW ME WHAT THE FLAVORS FROM THE *BOTTOM* OF THE CULINARY WORLD TASTE LIKE.
TWITCH

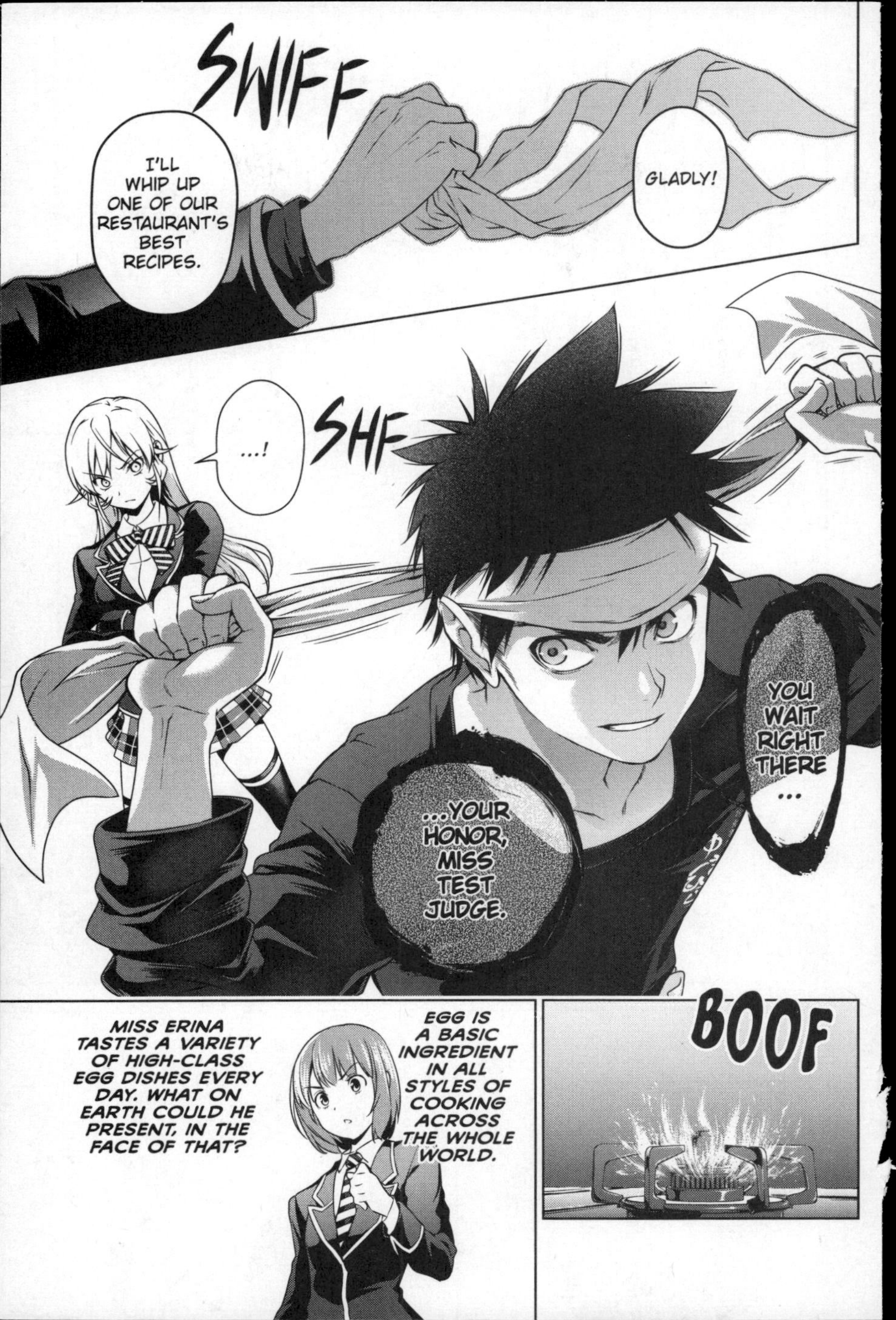
GLADLY!
SWIFF
I'LL WHIP UP ONE OF OUR RESTAURANT'S BEST RECIPES.
YOU WAIT RIGHT THERE...
...YOUR HONOR, MISS TEST JUDGE.
SHF
...!
BOOF
EGG IS A BASIC INGREDIENT IN ALL STYLES OF COOKING ACROSS THE WHOLE WORLD.
MISS ERINA TASTES A VARIETY OF HIGH-CLASS EGG DISHES EVERY DAY. WHAT ON EARTH COULD HE PRESENT, IN THE FACE OF THAT?

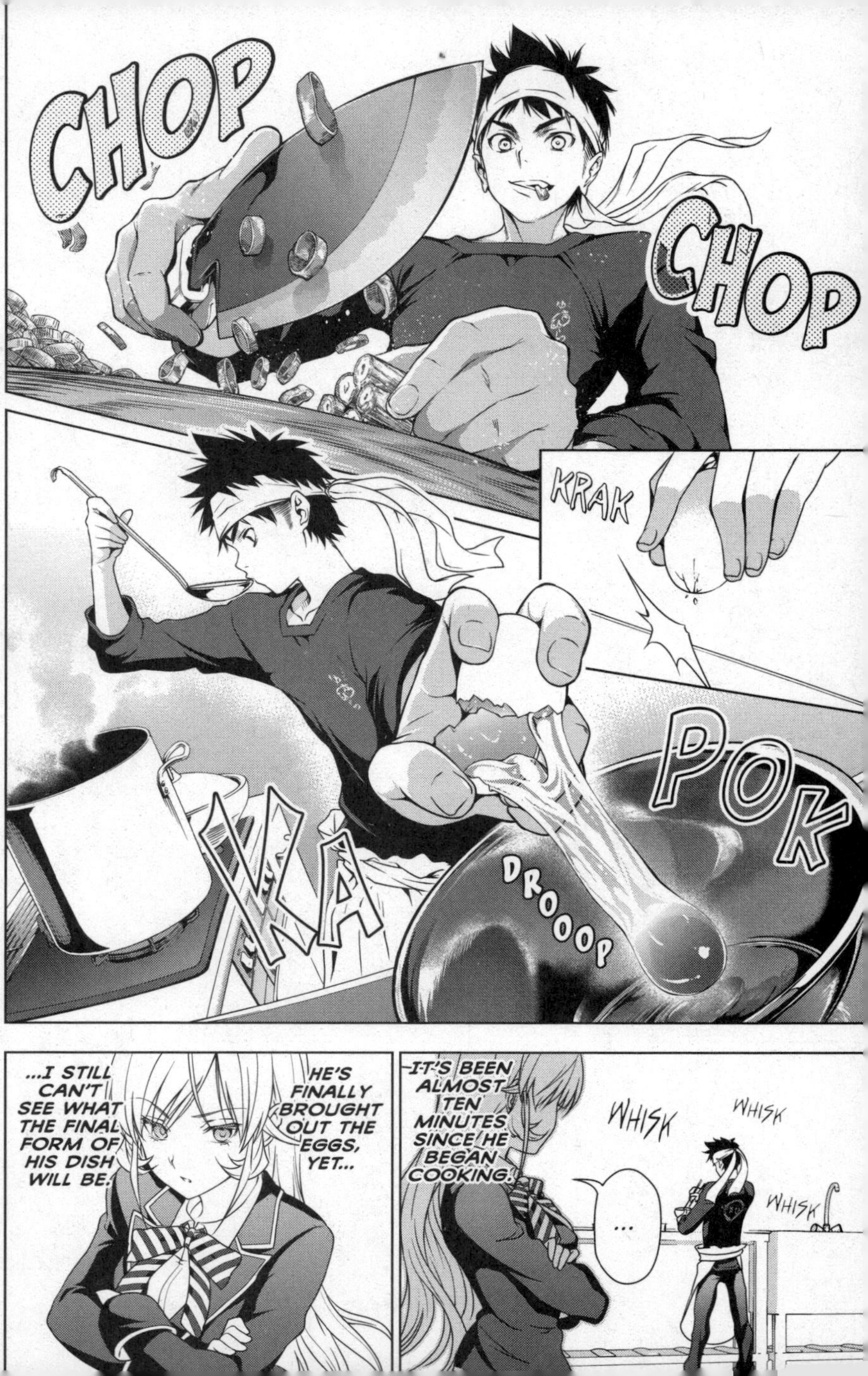
CHOP
CHOP
KRAK
POK
DROOOP
KA
IT'S BEEN ALMOST TEN MINUTES SINCE HE BEGAN COOKING.
WHISK
WHISK
WHISK
...
HE'S FINALLY BROUGHT OUT THE EGGS, YET...
...I STILL CAN'T SEE WHAT THE FINAL FORM OF HIS DISH WILL BE.

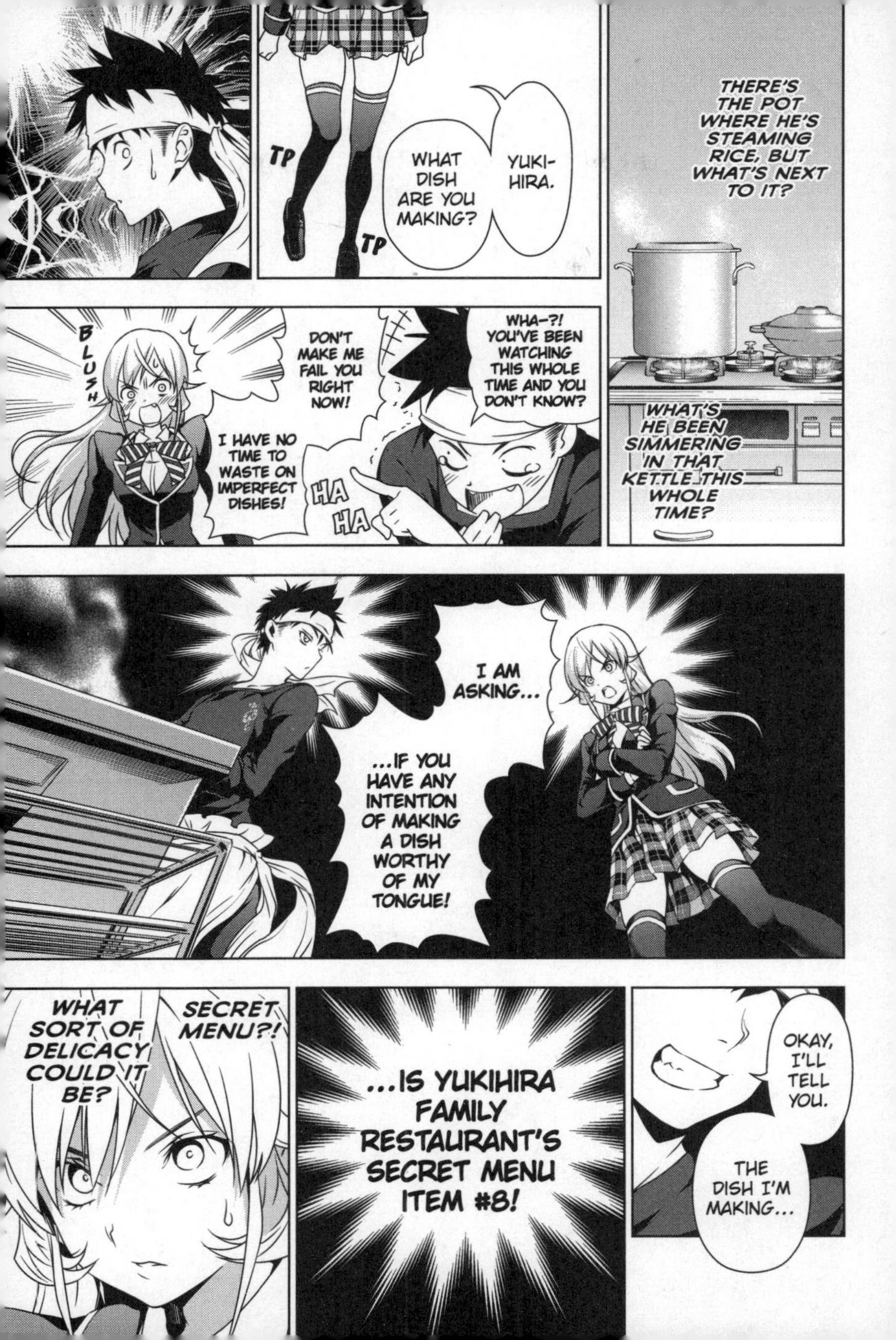
THERE'S THE POT WHERE HE'S STEAMING RICE, BUT WHAT'S NEXT TO IT?
WHAT'S HE BEEN SIMMERING IN THAT KETTLE THIS WHOLE TIME?
YUKI-HIRA.
WHAT DISH ARE YOU MAKING?
TP
TP
WHA-?! YOU'VE BEEN WATCHING THIS WHOLE TIME AND YOU DON'T KNOW?
HA
HA
DON'T MAKE ME FAIL YOU RIGHT NOW!
I HAVE NO TIME TO WASTE ON IMPERFECT DISHES!
BLUSH
I AM ASKING...
...IF YOU HAVE ANY INTENTION OF MAKING A DISH WORTHY OF MY TONGUE!
OKAY, I'LL TELL YOU.
THE DISH I'M MAKING...
...IS YUKIHIRA FAMILY RESTAURANT'S SECRET MENU ITEM #8!
SECRET MENU?!
WHAT SORT OF DELICACY COULD IT BE?

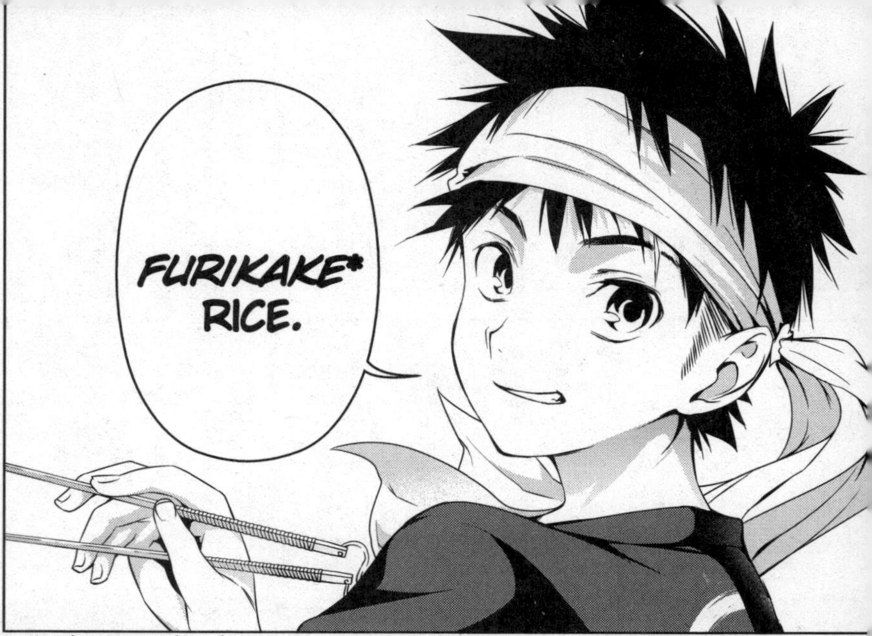
FURIKAKE* RICE.

*SEAWEED, SESAME SEEDS, AND OTHER SEASONINGS SPRINKLED OVER RICE. OFTEN SOLD IN INEXPENSIVE PACKETS.

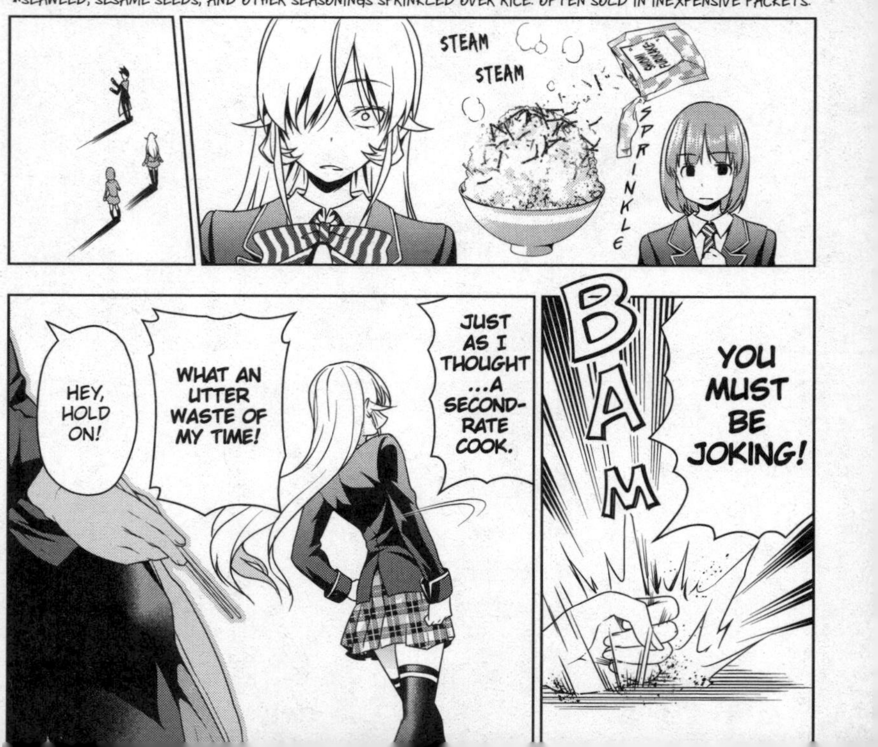
STEAM
STEAM
SPRINKLE
BAM
YOU MUST BE JOKING!
JUST AS I THOUGHT ...A SECOND-RATE COOK.
WHAT AN UTTER WASTE OF MY TIME!
HEY, HOLD ON!

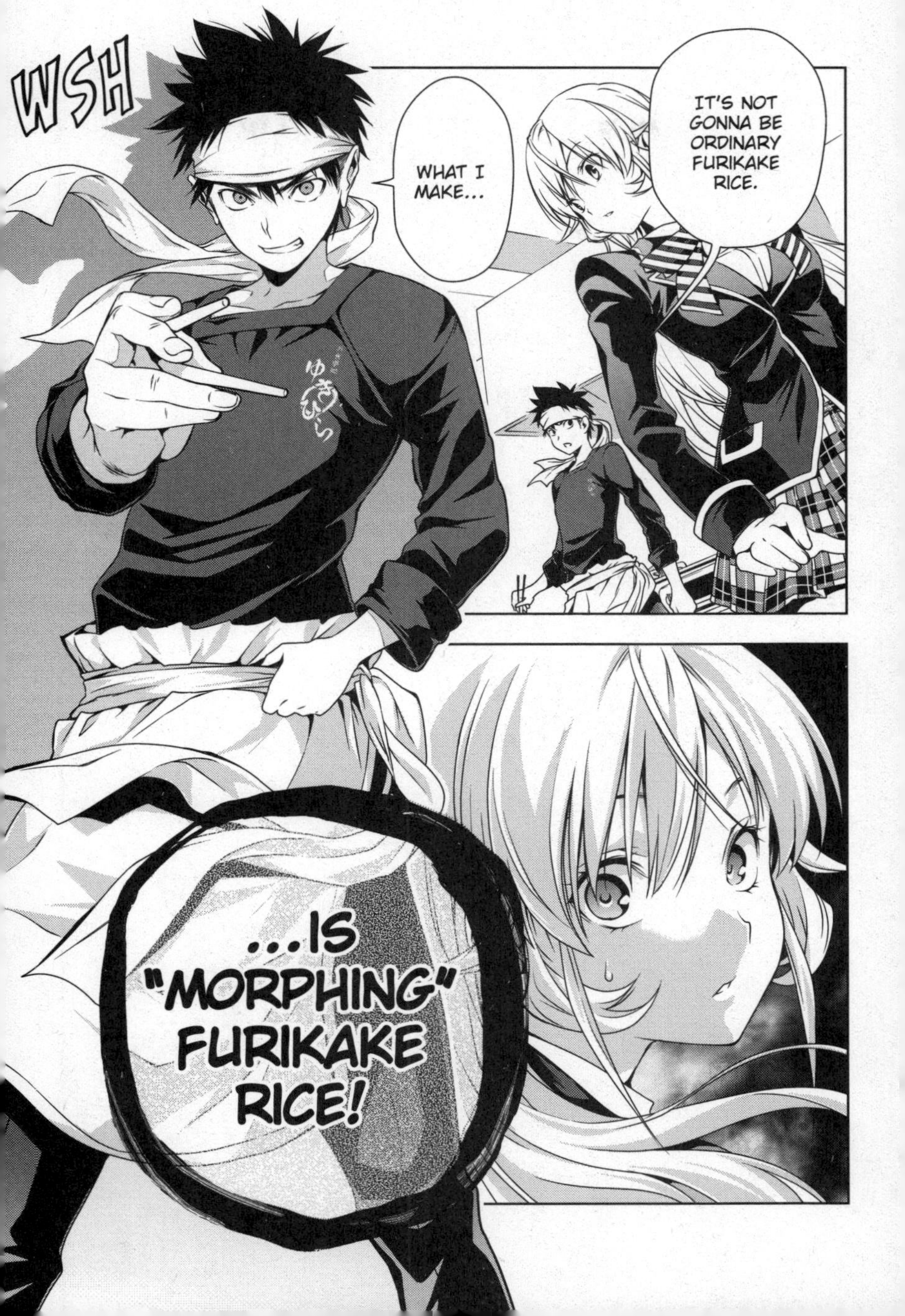
IT'S NOT GONNA BE ORDINARY FURIKAKE RICE.
WHAT I MAKE...
WSH
..."MORPHING" FURIKAKE RICE!

Food Wars!
SHOKUGEKI NO SOMA

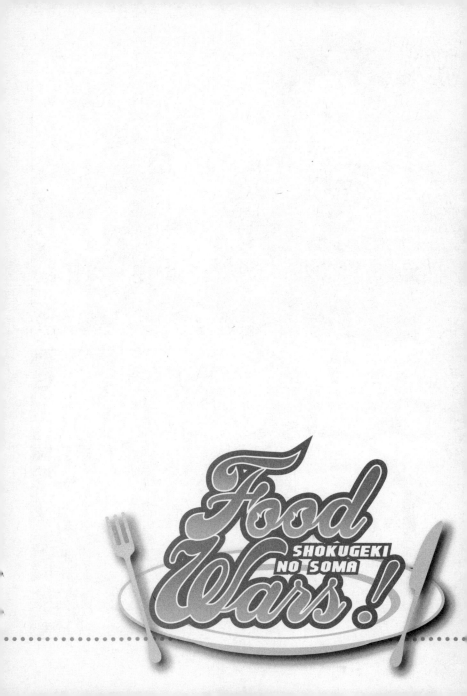

3 "MORPHING" FURIKAKE

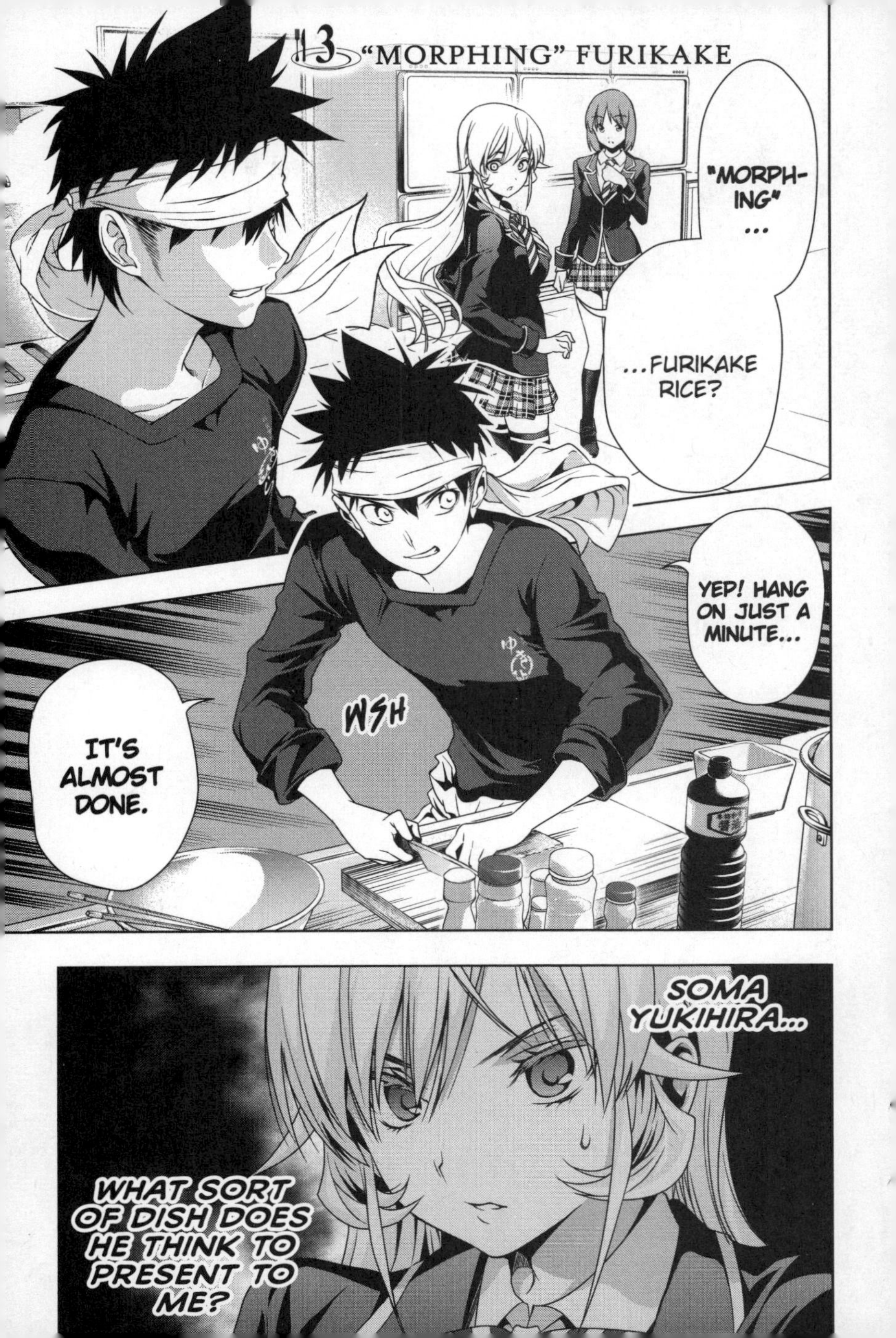
"MORPHING" ...
...FURIKAKE RICE?
YEP! HANG ON JUST A MINUTE...
WSH
IT'S ALMOST DONE.
SOMA YUKIHIRA...
WHAT SORT OF DISH DOES HE THINK TO PRESENT TO ME?

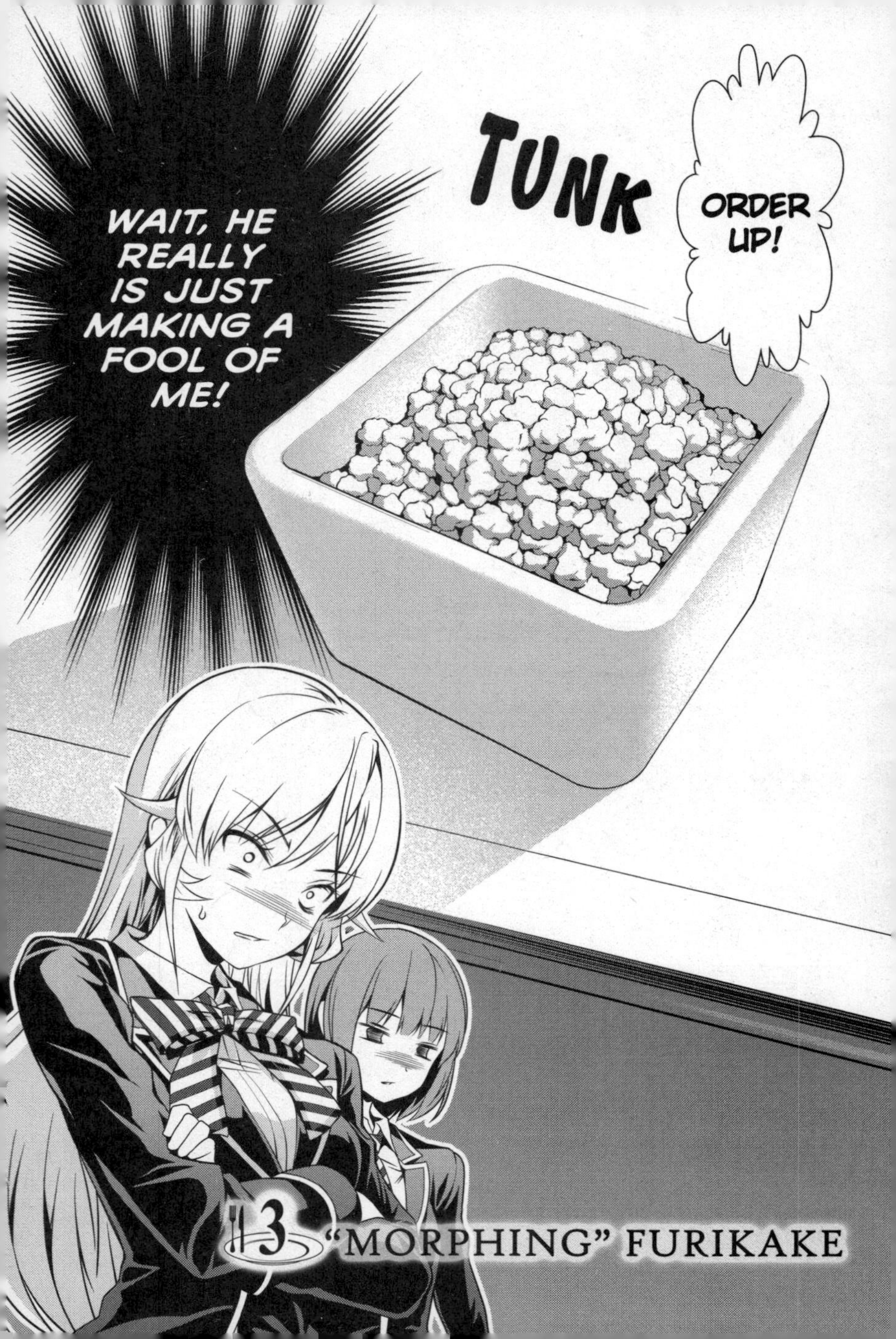
TUNK
ORDER UP!
WAIT, HE REALLY IS JUST MAKING A FOOL OF ME!

3 "MORPHING" FURIKAKE

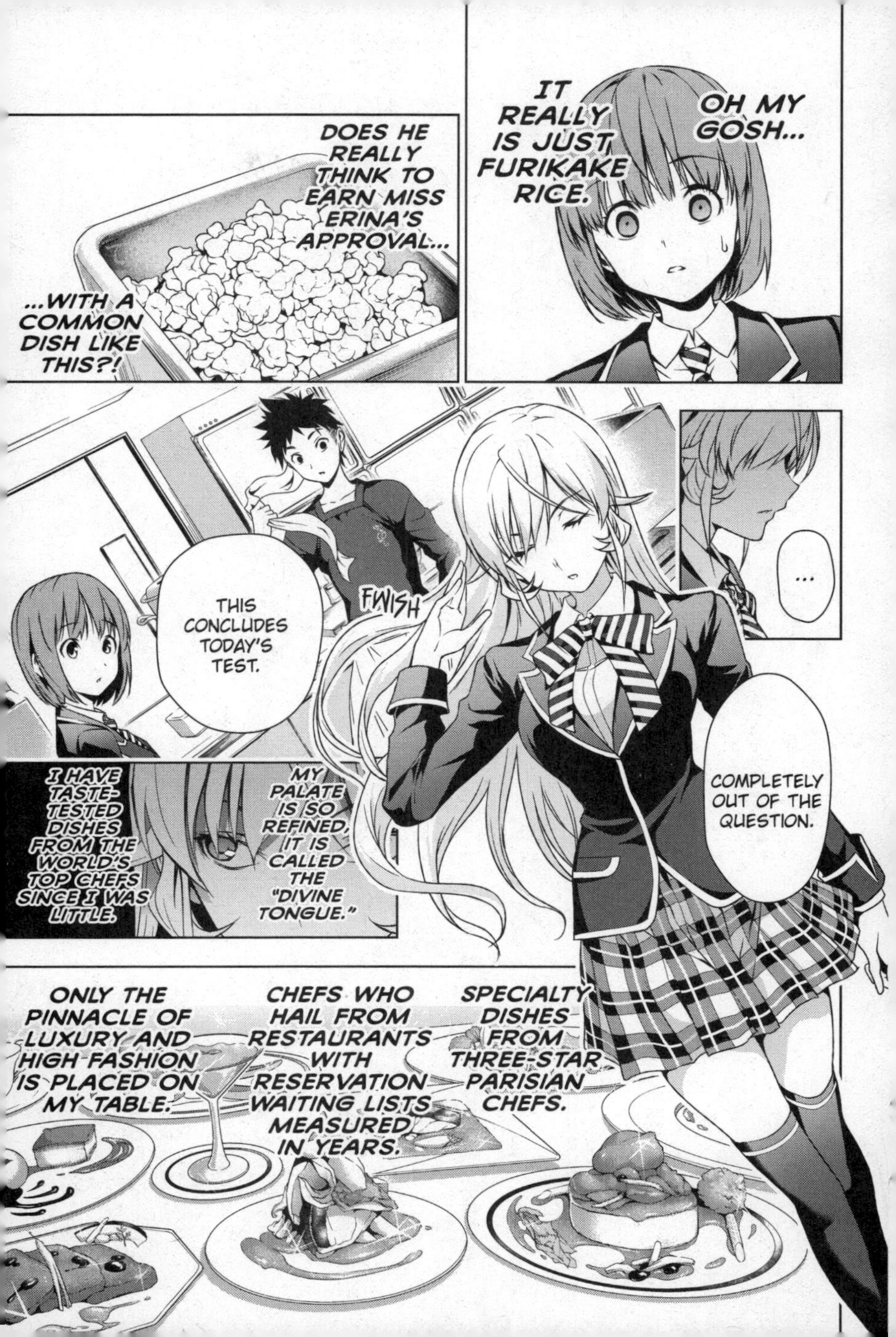

OH MY GOSH...
IT REALLY IS JUST FURIKAKE RICE.
DOES HE REALLY THINK TO EARN MISS ERINA'S APPROVAL...
...WITH A COMMON DISH LIKE THIS?!
...
THIS CONCLUDES TODAY'S TEST.
FWISH
COMPLETELY OUT OF THE QUESTION.
MY PALATE IS SO REFINED, IT IS CALLED THE "DIVINE TONGUE."
I HAVE TASTE-TESTED DISHES FROM THE WORLD'S TOP CHEFS SINCE I WAS LITTLE.
SPECIALTY DISHES FROM THREE-STAR PARISIAN CHEFS.
CHEFS WHO HAIL FROM RESTAURANTS WITH RESERVATION WAITING LISTS MEASURED IN YEARS.
ONLY THE PINNACLE OF LUXURY AND HIGH FASHION IS PLACED ON MY TABLE.

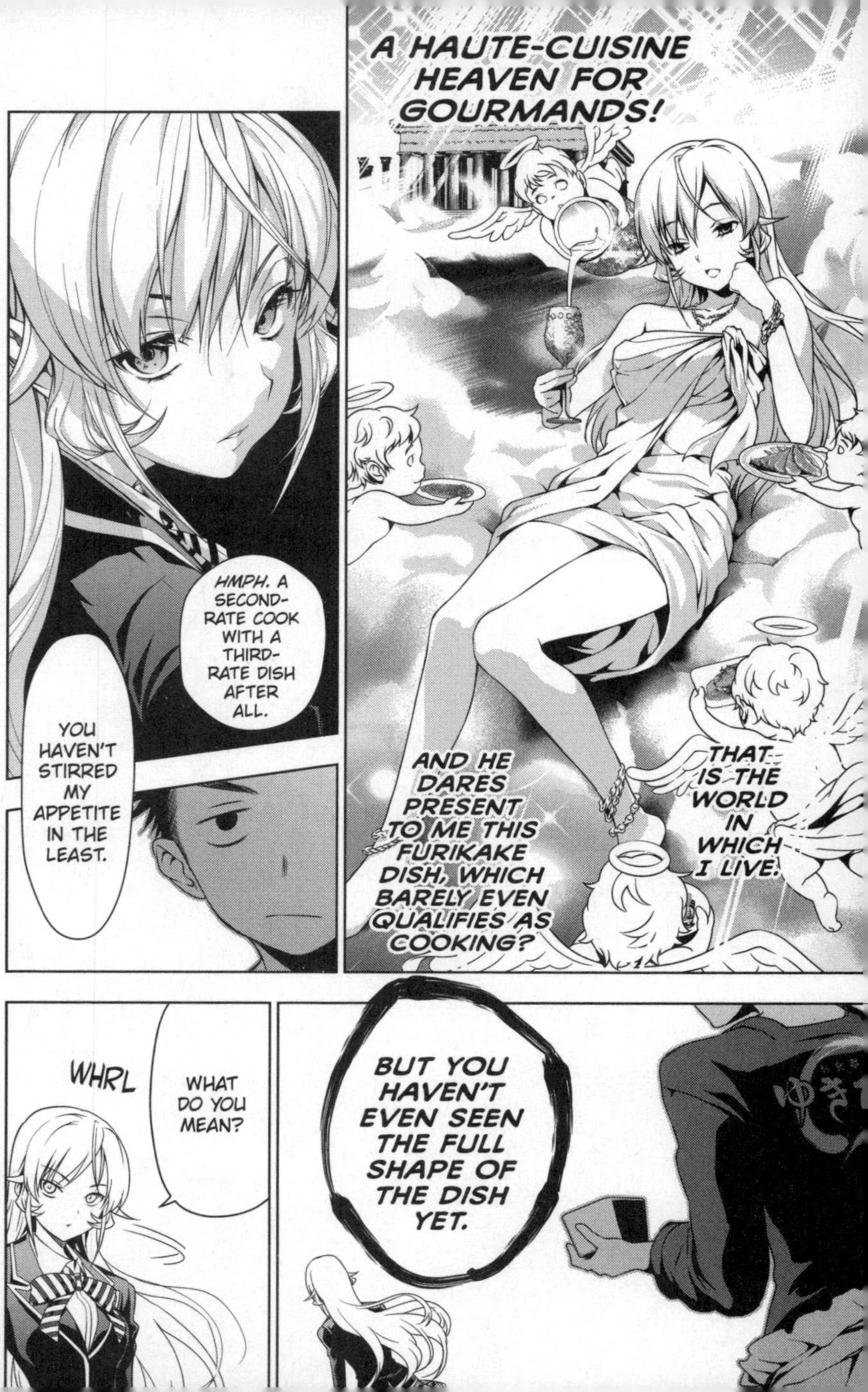
A HAUTE-CUISINE HEAVEN FOR GOURMANDS!
THAT IS THE WORLD IN WHICH I LIVE.
AND HE DARES PRESENT TO ME THIS FURIKAKE DISH, WHICH BARELY EVEN QUALIFIES AS COOKING?
HMPH. A SECOND-RATE COOK WITH A THIRD-RATE DISH AFTER ALL.
YOU HAVEN'T STIRRED MY APPETITE IN THE LEAST.
BUT YOU HAVEN'T EVEN SEEN THE FULL SHAPE OF THE DISH YET.
WHAT DO YOU MEAN?
WHRL

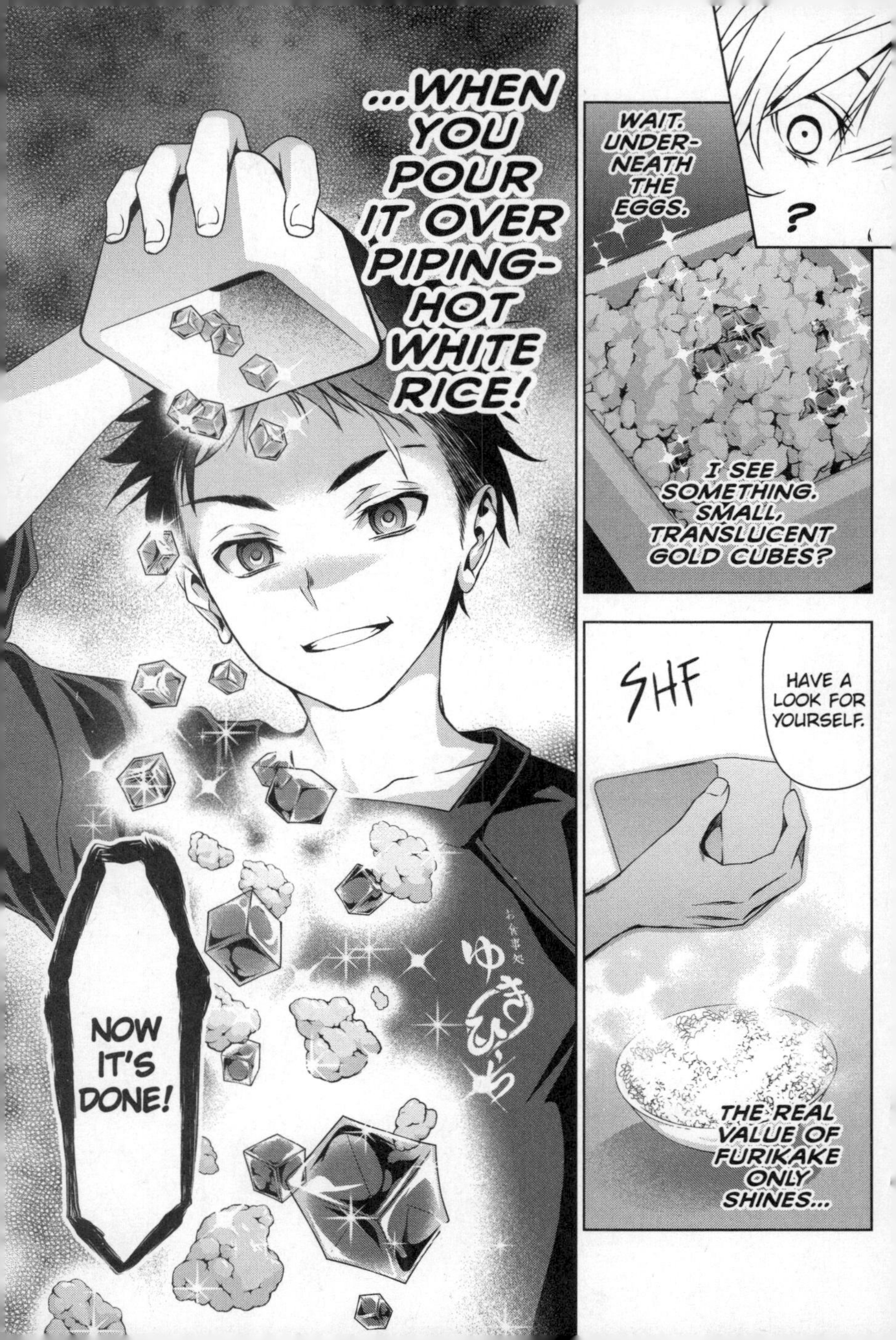
?
WAIT. UNDER-NEATH THE EGGS.
I SEE SOMETHING. SMALL, TRANSLUCENT GOLD CUBES?
HAVE A LOOK FOR YOURSELF.
SHF
THE REAL VALUE OF FURIKAKE ONLY SHINES...
...WHEN YOU POUR IT OVER PIPING-HOT WHITE RICE!
お食事処
ゆきひら
NOW IT'S DONE!

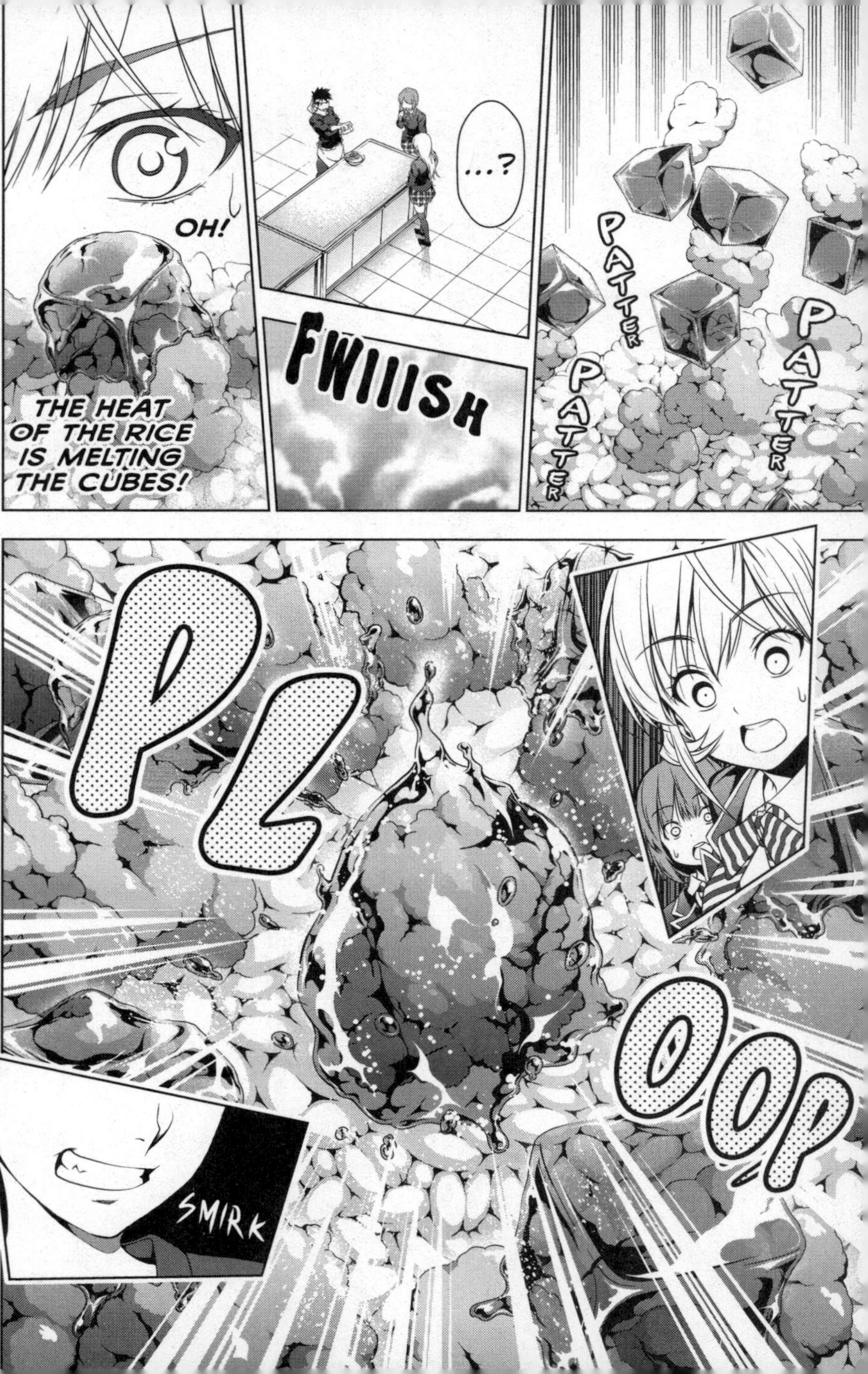
PATTER PATTER
PATTER PATTER
...?
FWIIISH
OH!
THE HEAT OF THE RICE IS MELTING THE CUBES!
PLOOOP
SMIRK

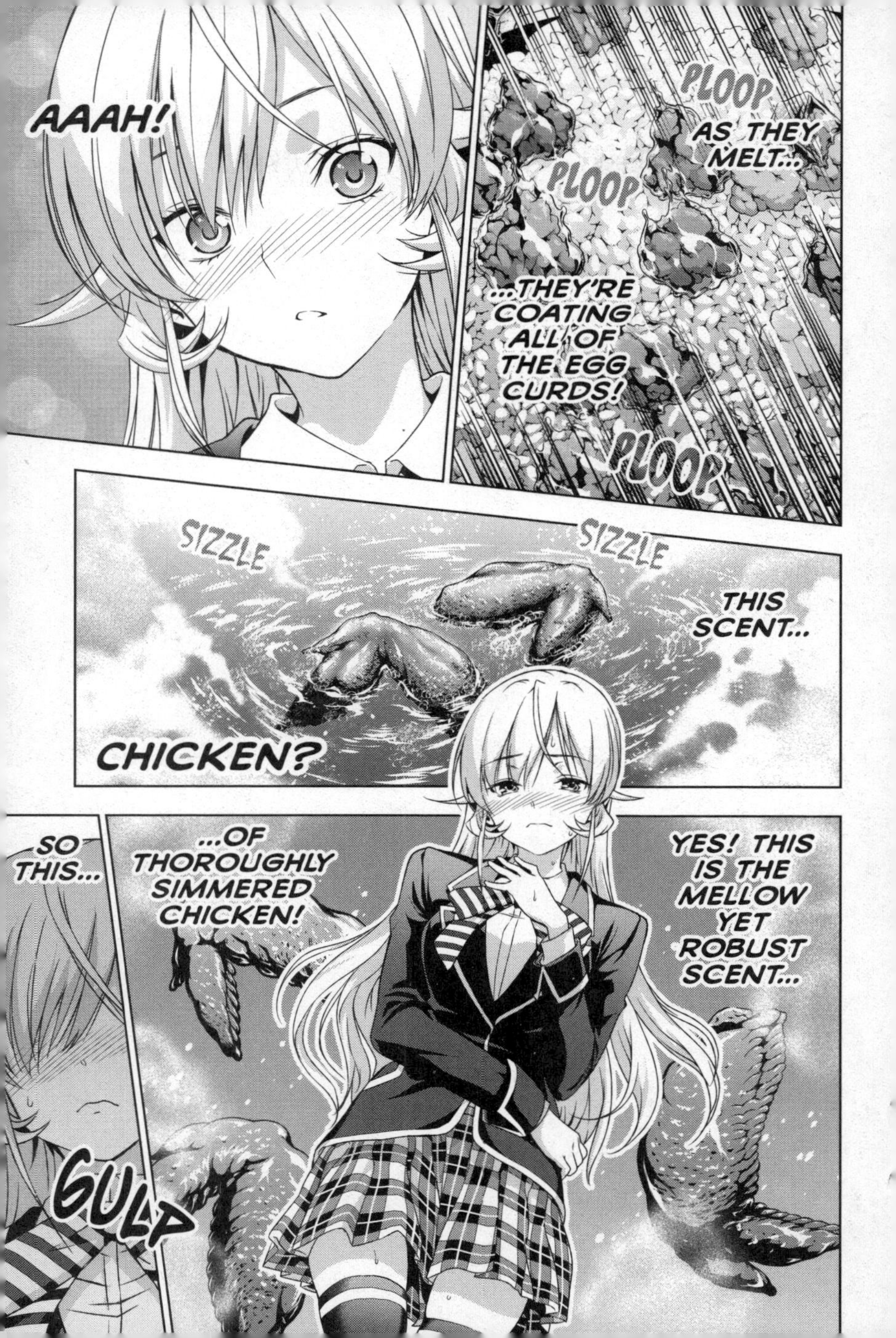
PLOOP
AS THEY MELT...
PLOOP
...THEY'RE COATING ALL OF THE EGG CURDS!
PLOOP
AAAH!
SIZZLE
SIZZLE
THIS SCENT...
CHICKEN?
YES! THIS IS THE MELLOW YET ROBUST SCENT...
...OF THOROUGHLY SIMMERED CHICKEN!
SO THIS...
GULP

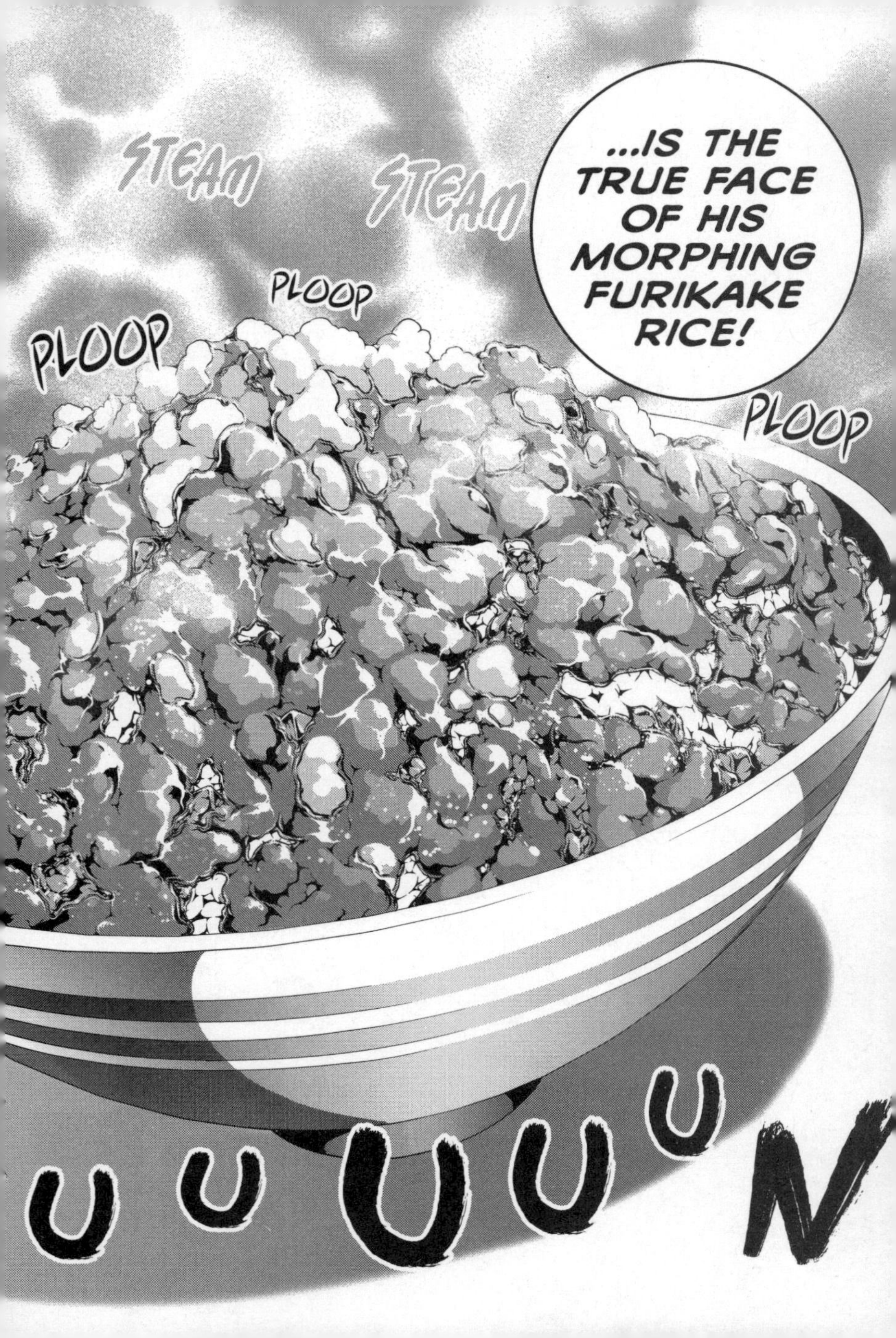

...IS THE TRUE FACE OF HIS MORPHING FURIKAKE RICE!
STEAM
STEAM
PLOOP
PLOOP
PLOOP
UUUUUUN

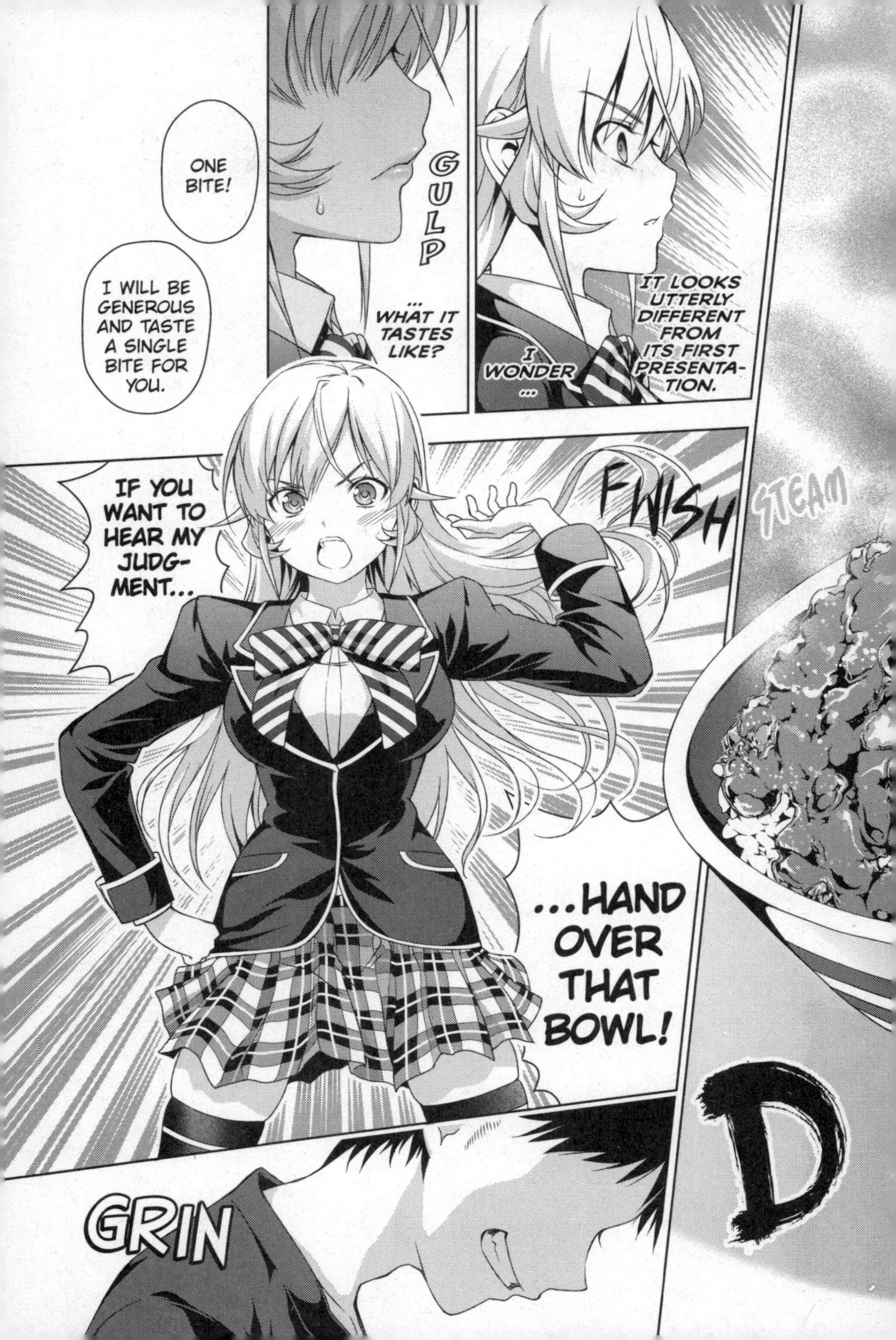
IT LOOKS UTTERLY DIFFERENT FROM ITS FIRST PRESENTATION.
I WONDER...
GULP
...WHAT IT TASTES LIKE?
ONE BITE!
I WILL BE GENEROUS AND TASTE A SINGLE BITE FOR YOU.
STEAM
FWISH
IF YOU WANT TO HEAR MY JUDGMENT...
...HAND OVER THAT BOWL!
D
GRIN

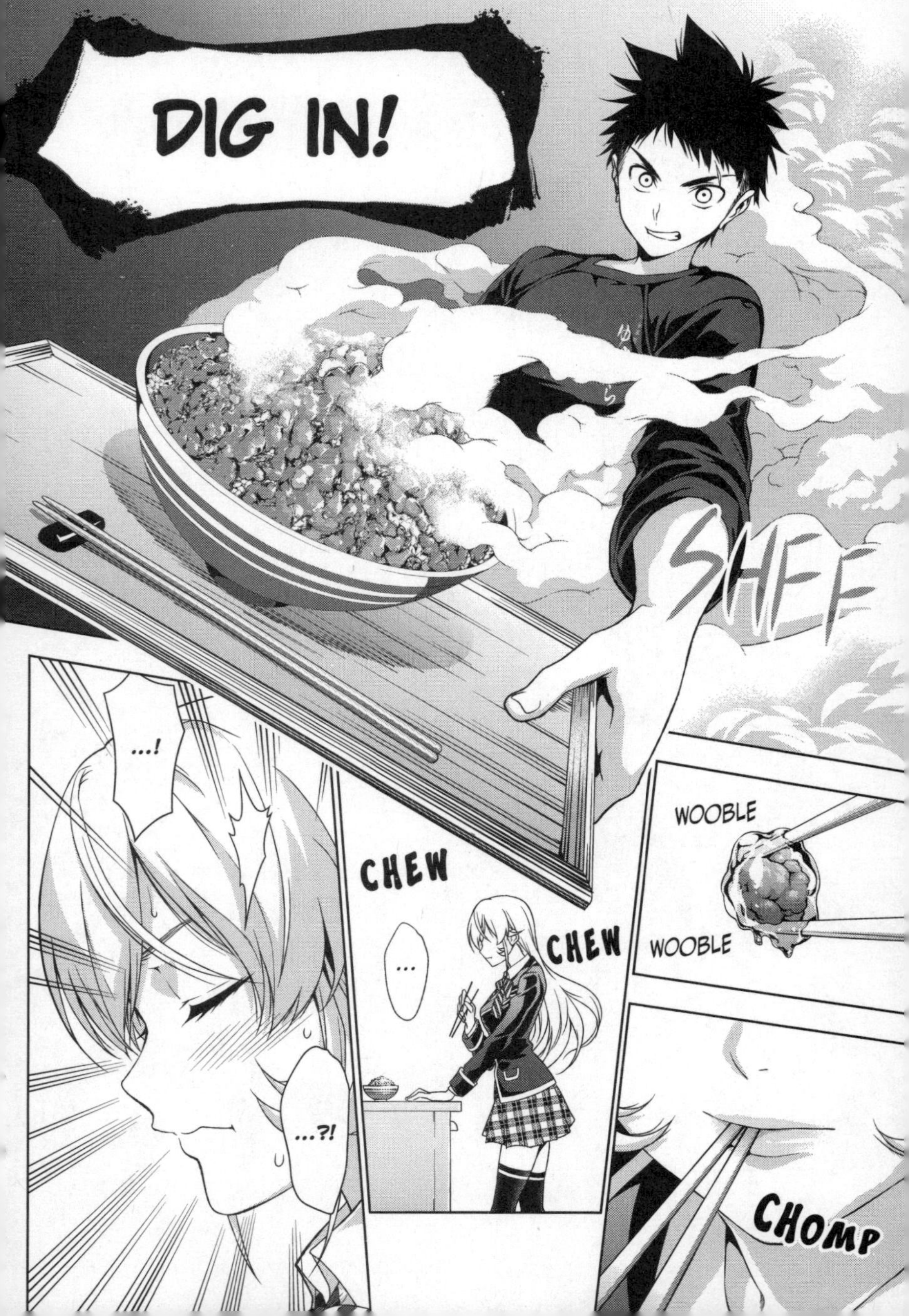
DIG IN!
SHFF
WOOBLE
WOOBLE
CHOMP
CHEW
CHEW
...
...!
...?!

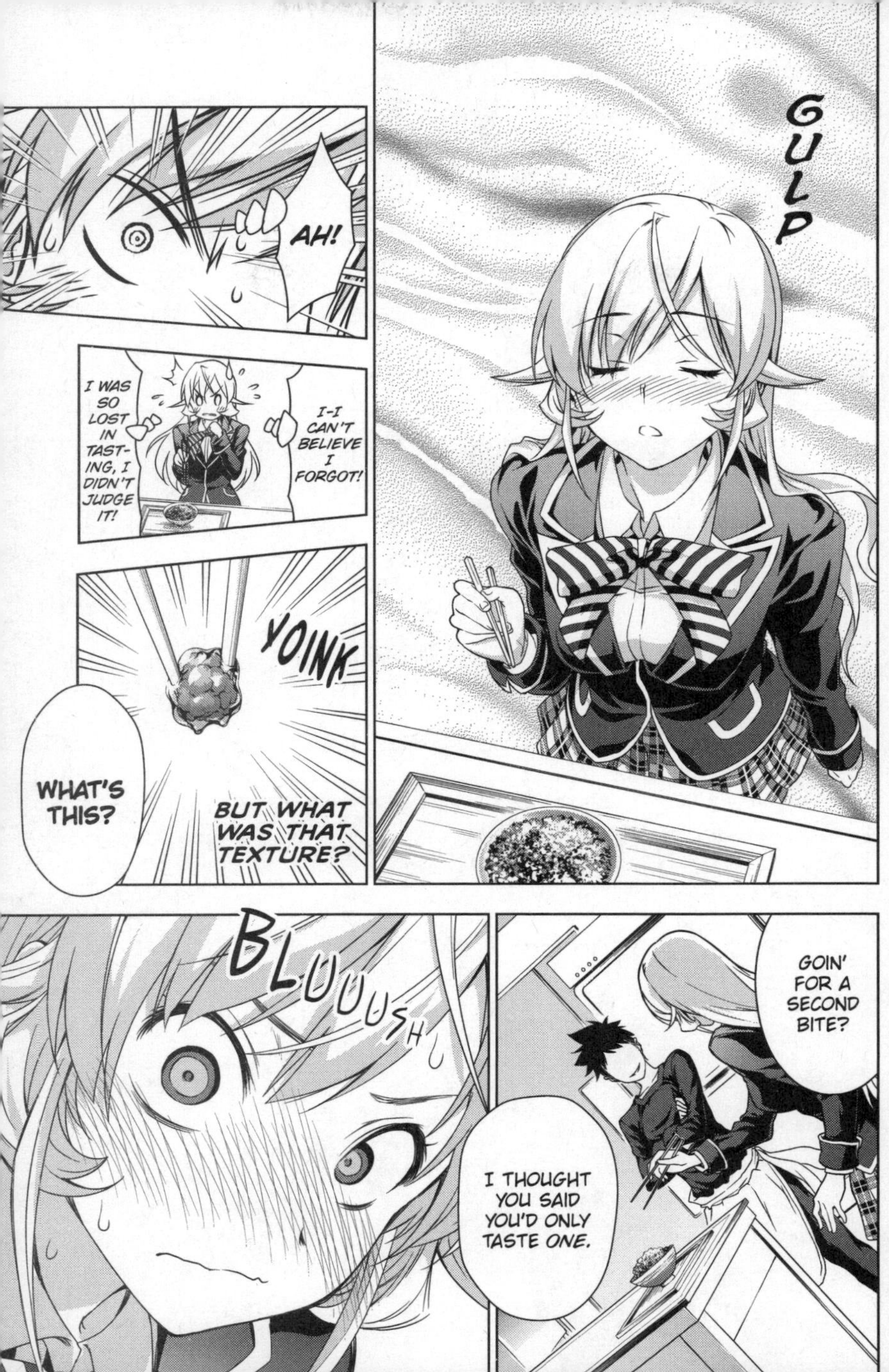
GULP
AH!
I-I CAN'T BELIEVE I FORGOT!
I WAS SO LOST IN TASTING, I DIDN'T JUDGE IT!
YOINK
WHAT'S THIS?
BUT WHAT WAS THAT TEXTURE?
GOIN' FOR A SECOND BITE?
I THOUGHT YOU SAID YOU'D ONLY TASTE ONE.
BLUUUSH

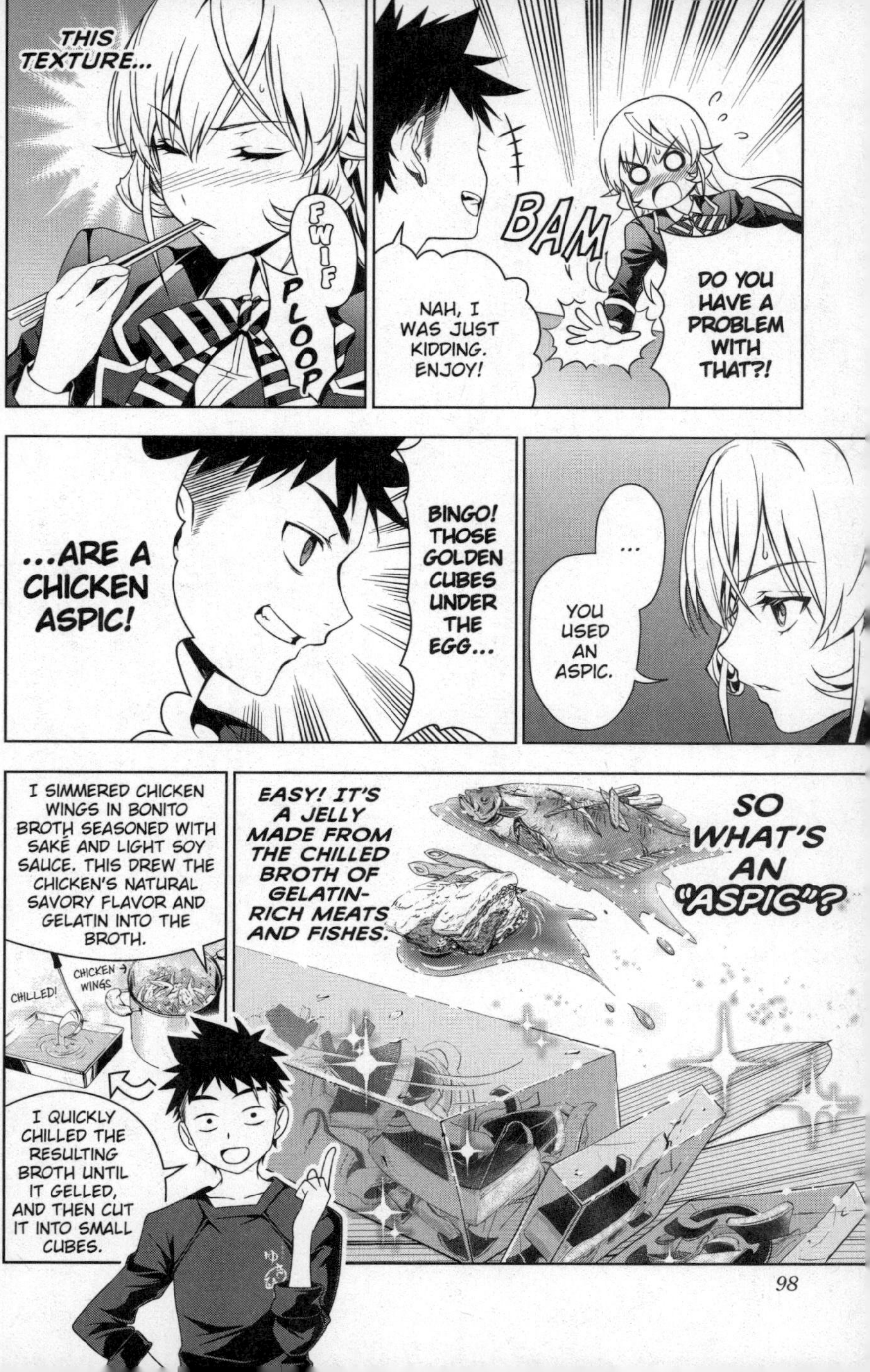
BAM
DO YOU HAVE A PROBLEM WITH THAT?!
NAH, I WAS JUST KIDDING. ENJOY!
THIS TEXTURE...
FWIF
PLOOP
...
YOU USED AN ASPIC.
BINGO! THOSE GOLDEN CUBES UNDER THE EGG...
...ARE A CHICKEN ASPIC!
SO WHAT'S AN "ASPIC"?
EASY! IT'S A JELLY MADE FROM THE CHILLED BROTH OF GELATIN-RICH MEATS AND FISHES.
I SIMMERED CHICKEN WINGS IN BONITO BROTH SEASONED WITH SAKÉ AND LIGHT SOY SAUCE. THIS DREW THE CHICKEN'S NATURAL SAVORY FLAVOR AND GELATIN INTO THE BROTH.
CHICKEN WINGS
CHILLED!
I QUICKLY CHILLED THE RESULTING BROTH UNTIL IT GELLED, AND THEN CUT IT INTO SMALL CUBES.

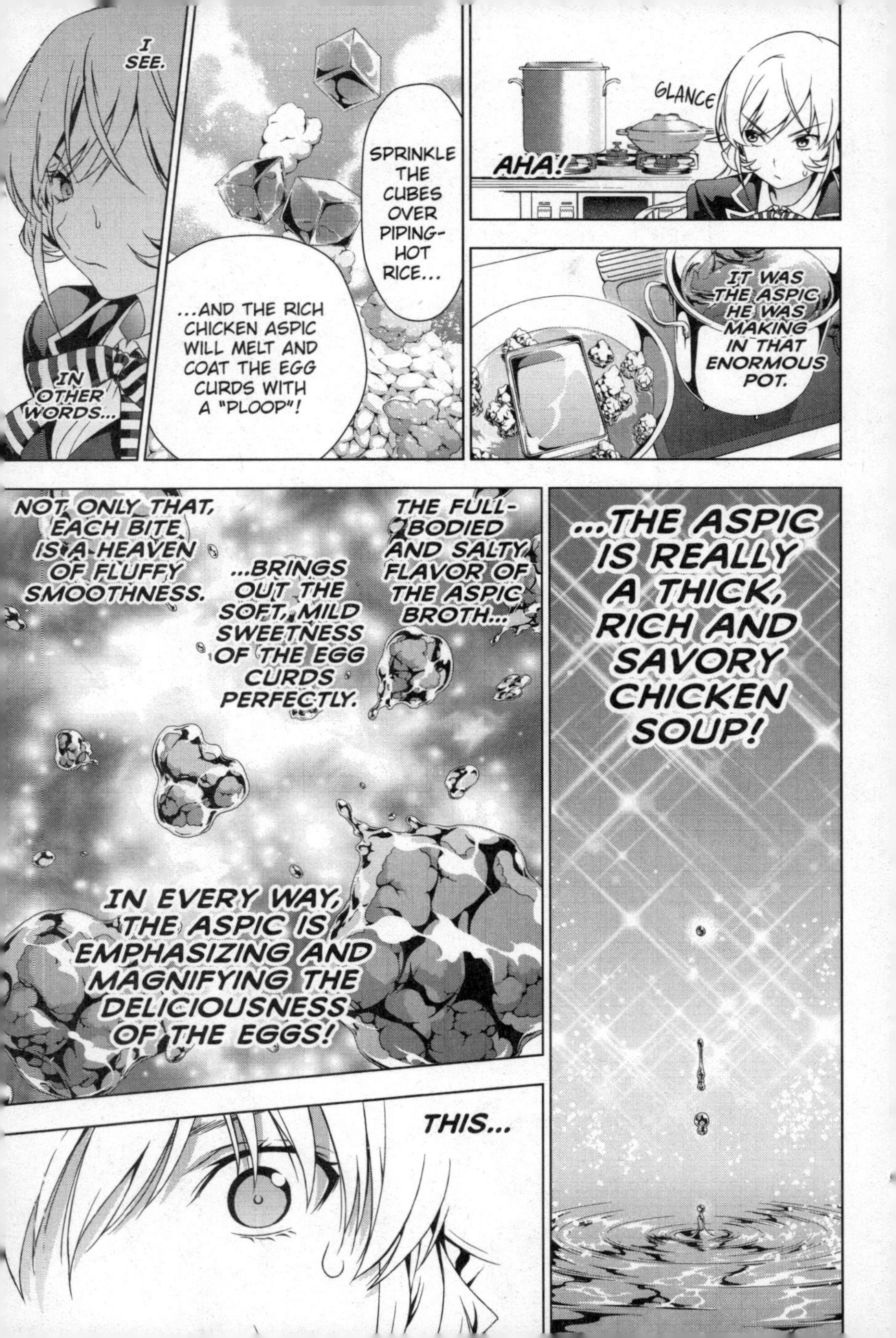
GLANCE
AHA!
IT WAS THE ASPIC HE WAS MAKING IN THAT ENORMOUS POT.
SPRINKLE THE CUBES OVER PIPING-HOT RICE...
...AND THE RICH CHICKEN ASPIC WILL MELT AND COAT THE EGG CURDS WITH A "PLOOP"!
I SEE.
IN OTHER WORDS...
...THE ASPIC IS REALLY A THICK, RICH AND SAVORY CHICKEN SOUP!
THE FULL-BODIED AND SALTY FLAVOR OF THE ASPIC BROTH...
...BRINGS OUT THE SOFT, MILD SWEETNESS OF THE EGG CURDS PERFECTLY.
NOT ONLY THAT, EACH BITE IS A HEAVEN OF FLUFFY SMOOTHNESS.
IN EVERY WAY, THE ASPIC IS EMPHASIZING AND MAGNIFYING THE DELICIOUSNESS OF THE EGGS!
THIS...

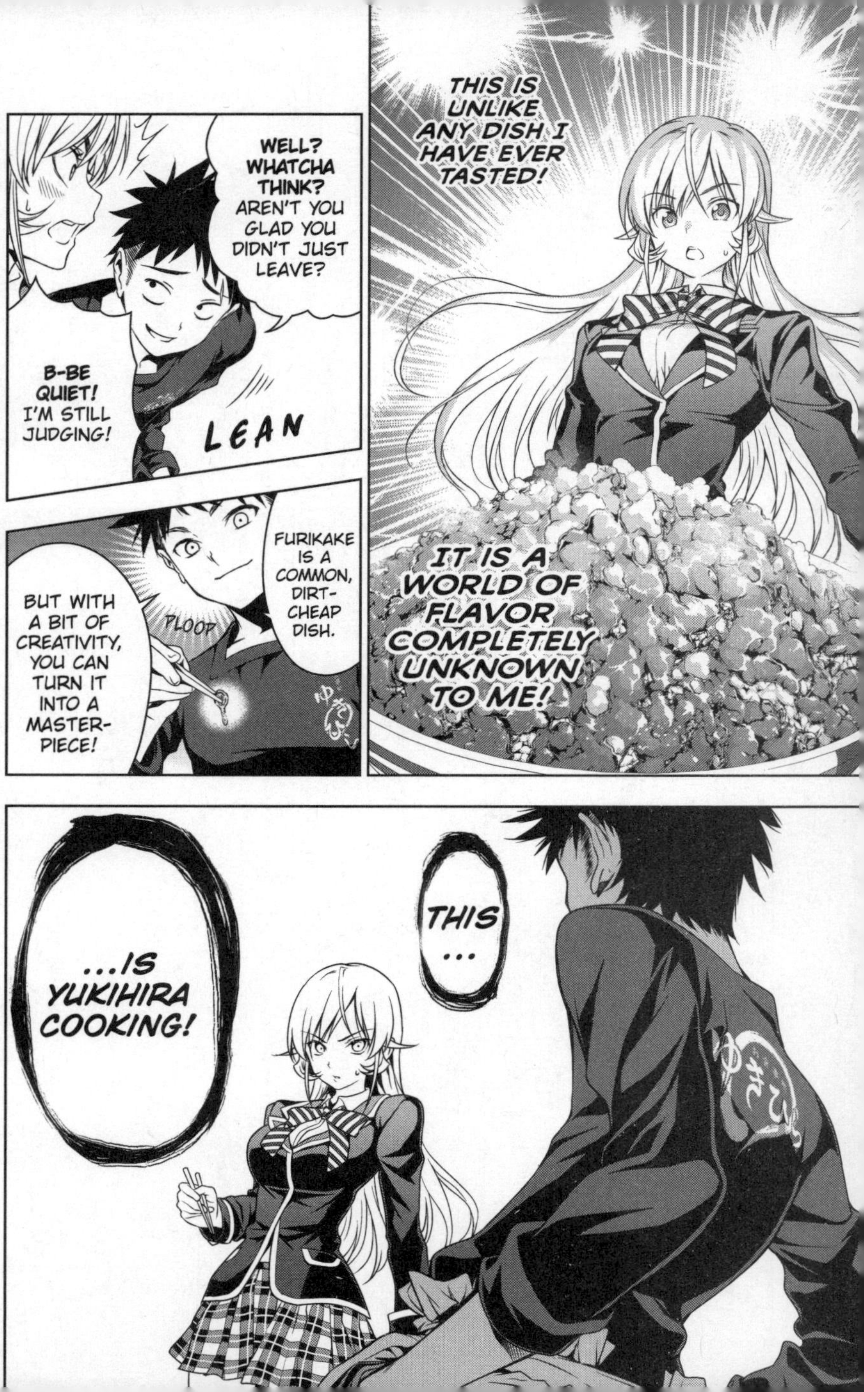
THIS IS UNLIKE ANY DISH I HAVE EVER TASTED!
IT IS A WORLD OF FLAVOR COMPLETELY UNKNOWN TO ME!
WELL? WHATCHA THINK? AREN'T YOU GLAD YOU DIDN'T JUST LEAVE?
B-BE QUIET! I'M STILL JUDGING!
LEAN
FURIKAKE IS A COMMON, DIRT-CHEAP DISH.
PLOOP
BUT WITH A BIT OF CREATIVITY, YOU CAN TURN IT INTO A MASTER-PIECE!
THIS...
...IS YUKIHIRA COOKING!

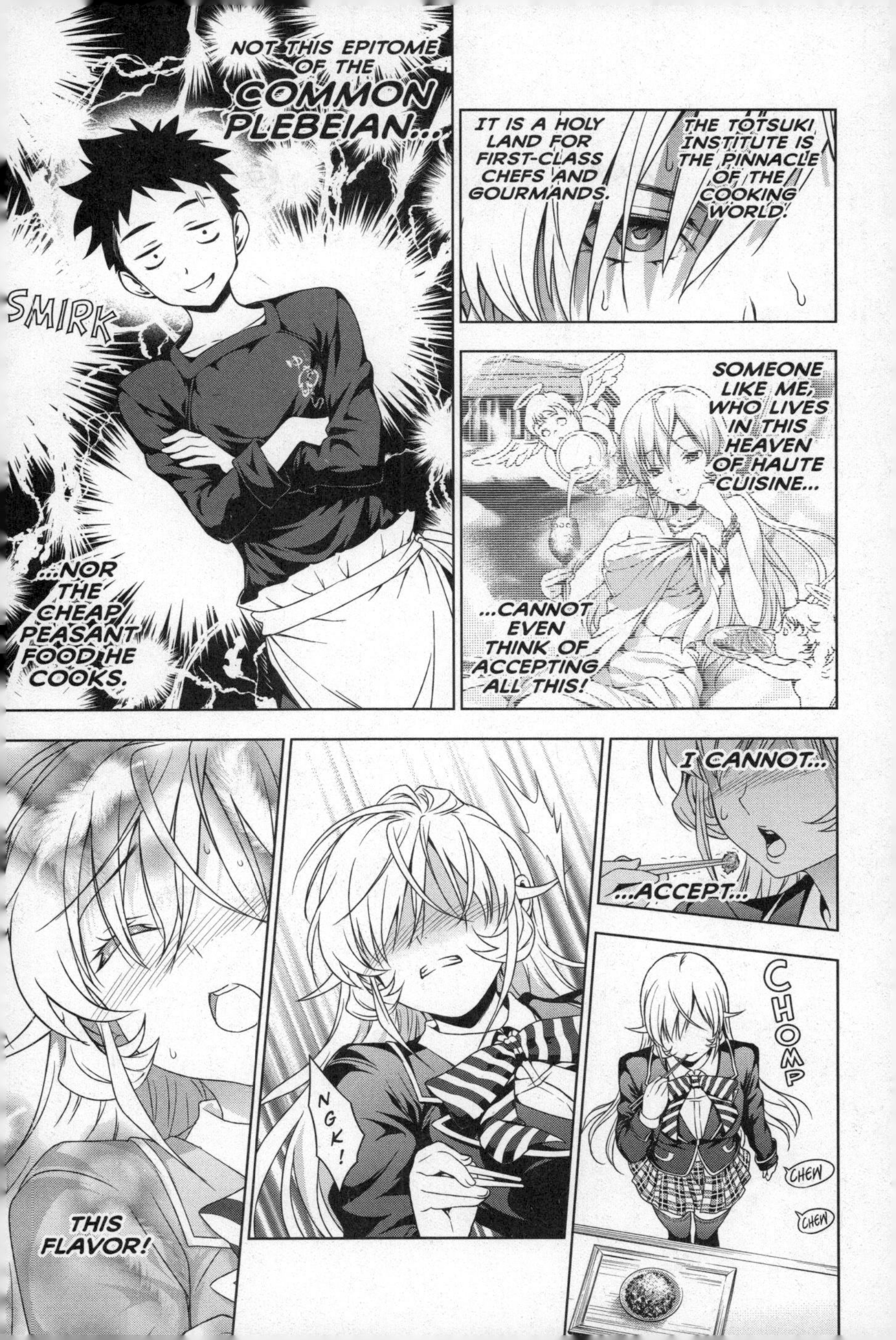
THE TOTSUKI INSTITUTE IS THE PINNACLE OF THE COOKING WORLD!
IT IS A HOLY LAND FOR FIRST-CLASS CHEFS AND GOURMANDS.
SOMEONE LIKE ME, WHO LIVES IN THIS HEAVEN OF HAUTE CUISINE...
...CANNOT EVEN THINK OF ACCEPTING ALL THIS!
NOT THIS EPITOME OF THE COMMON PLEBEIAN...
SMIRK
...NOR THE CHEAP PEASANT FOOD HE COOKS.
I CANNOT...
...ACCEPT...
CHOMP
CHEW
CHEW
NGK!
THIS FLAVOR!

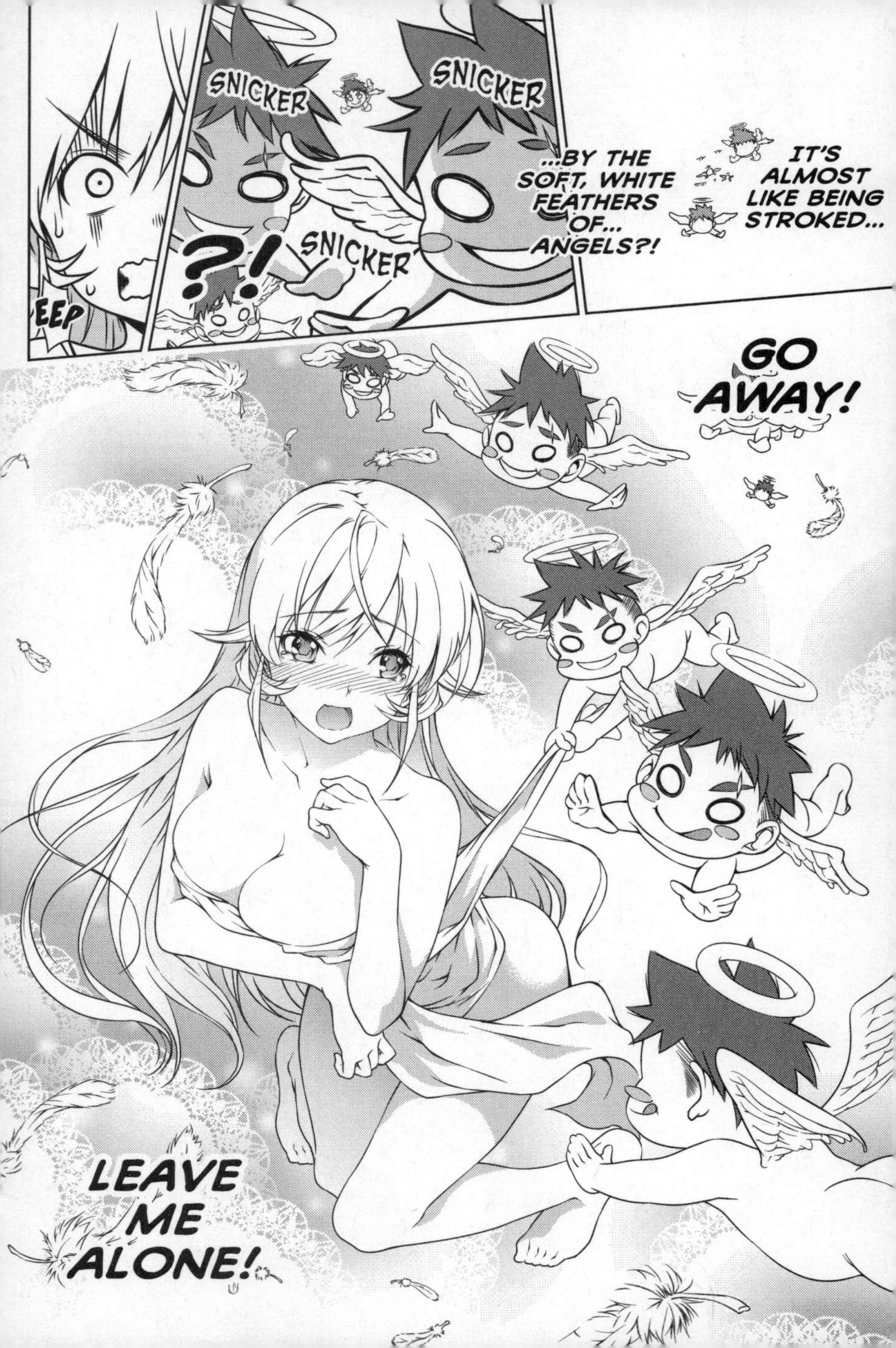
IT'S ALMOST LIKE BEING STROKED...
...BY THE SOFT, WHITE FEATHERS OF... ANGELS?!
SNICKER
SNICKER
SNICKER
?!
EEP
GO AWAY!
LEAVE ME ALONE!

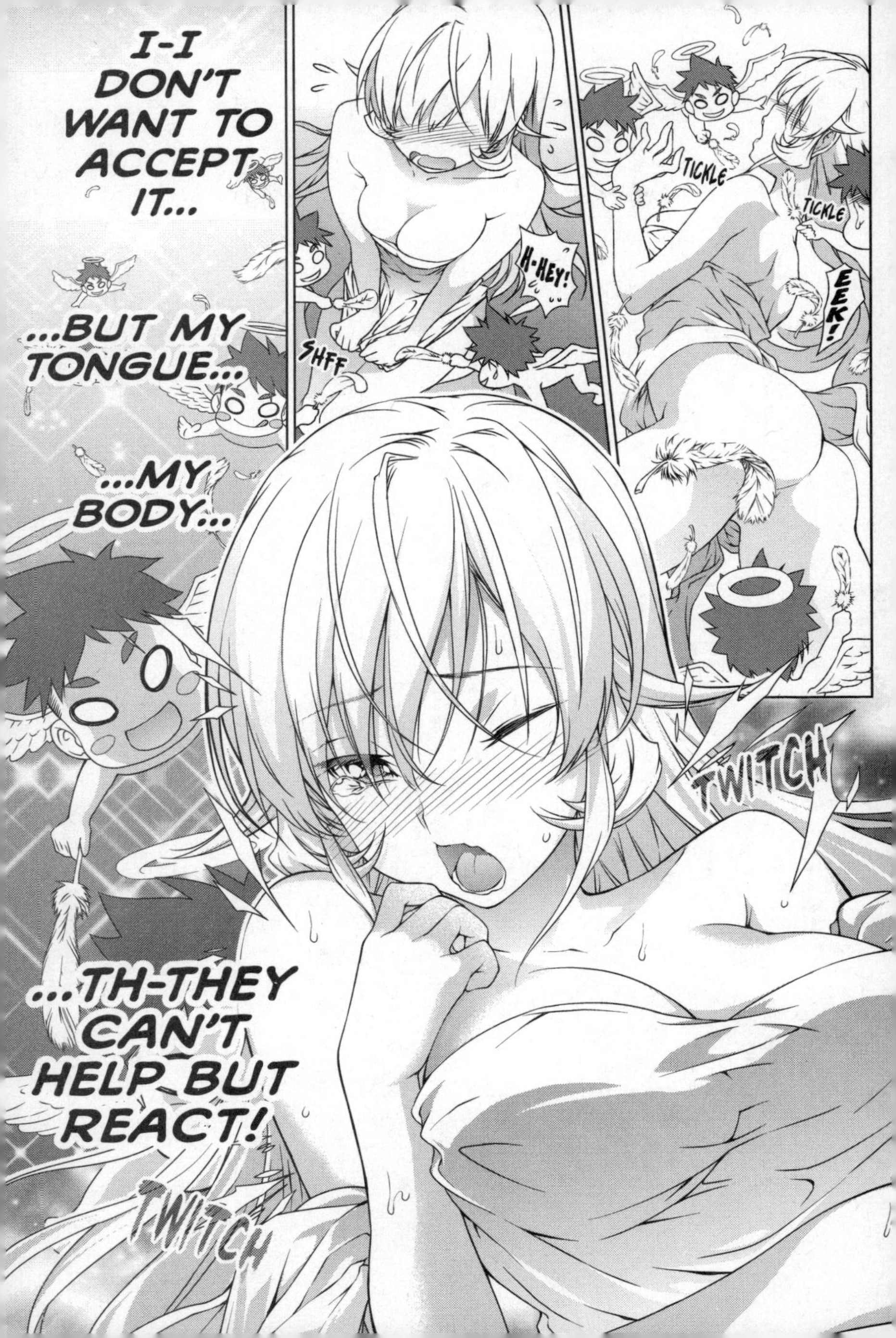
TICKLE
TICKLE
EEK!
H-HEY!
SHFF
I-I DON'T WANT TO ACCEPT IT...
...BUT MY TONGUE...
...MY BODY...
...TH-THEY CAN'T HELP BUT REACT!
TWITCH
TWITCH

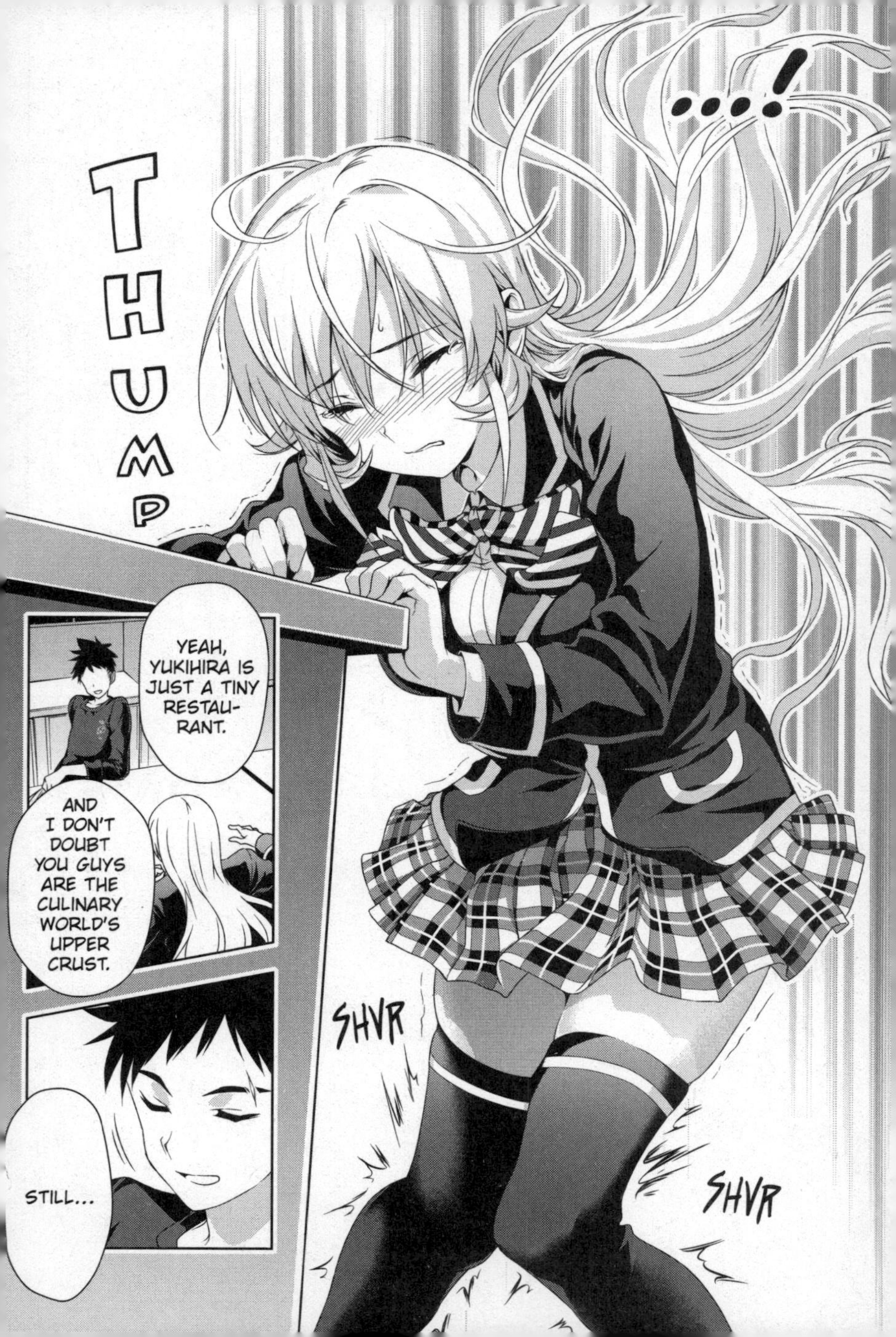
...!
THUMP
SHVR
SHVR
YEAH, YUKIHIRA IS JUST A TINY RESTAU-RANT.
AND I DON'T DOUBT YOU GUYS ARE THE CULINARY WORLD'S UPPER CRUST.
STILL...

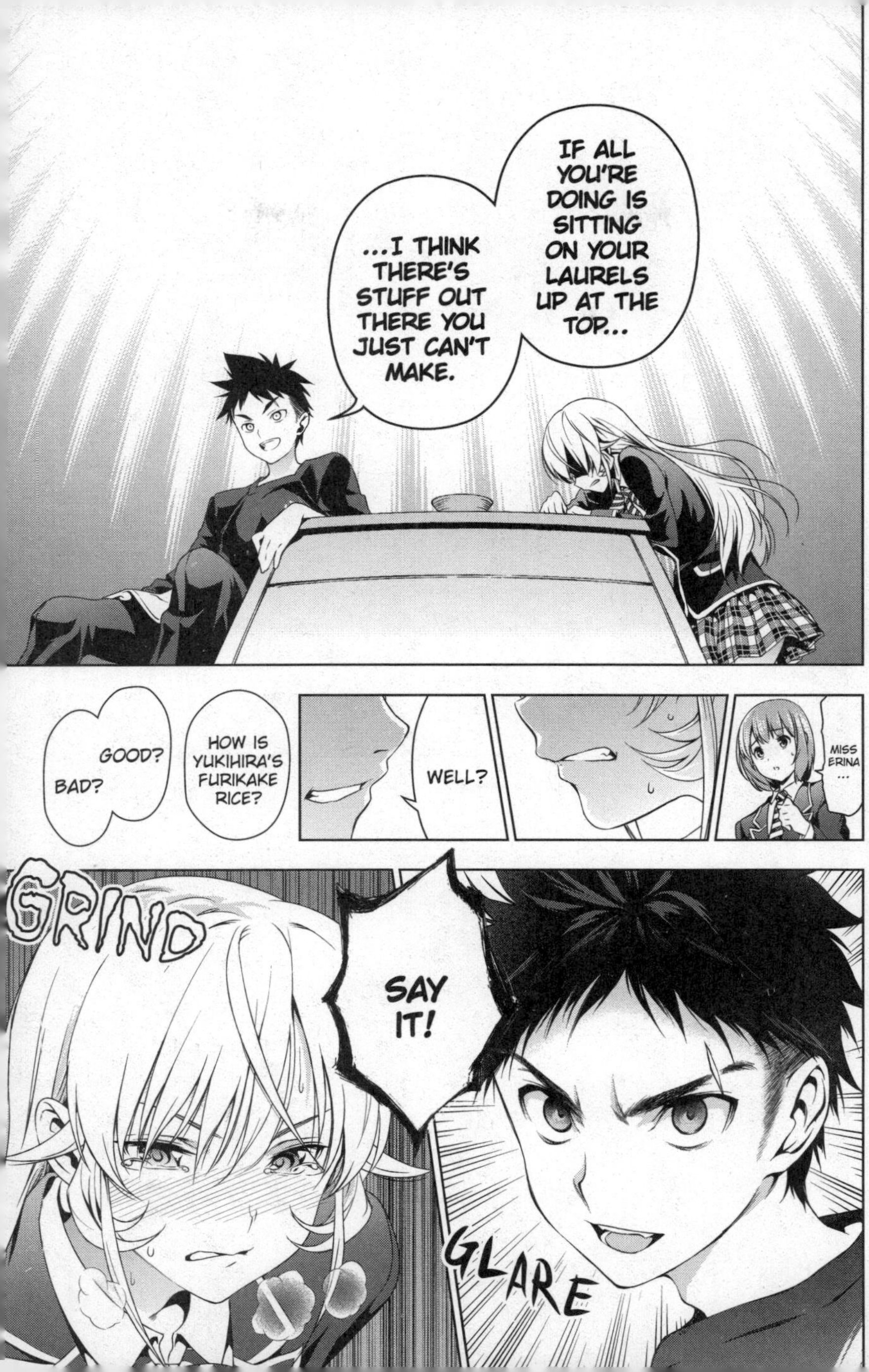
IF ALL YOU'RE DOING IS SITTING ON YOUR LAURELS UP AT THE TOP...
...I THINK THERE'S STUFF OUT THERE YOU JUST CAN'T MAKE.
MISS ERINA ...
WELL?
HOW IS YUKIHIRA'S FURIKAKE RICE?
GOOD? BAD?
SAY IT!
GRIND
GLARE

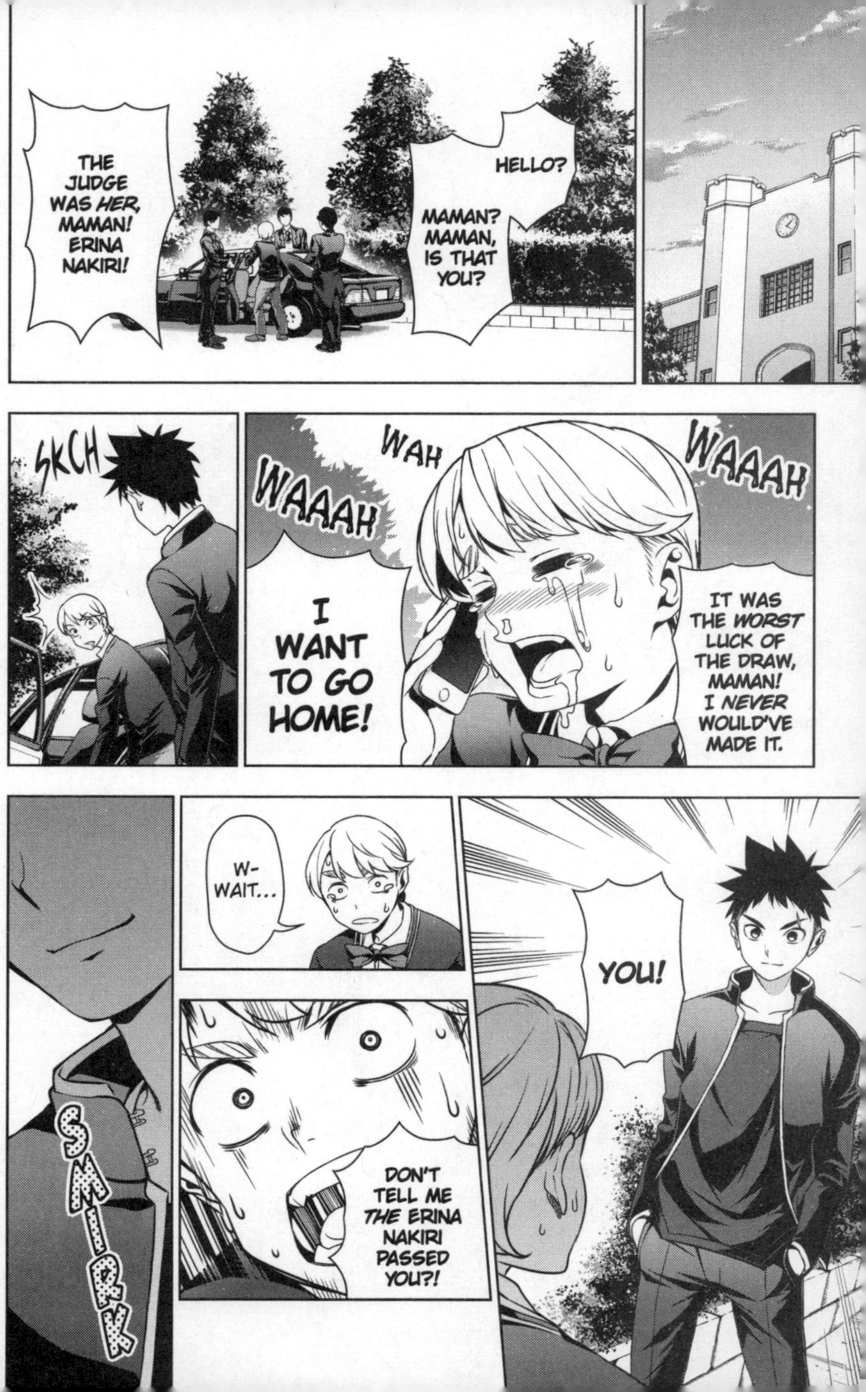
HELLO?
MAMAN? MAMAN, IS THAT YOU?
THE JUDGE WAS HER, MAMAN! ERINA NAKIRI!
WAAAAH
WAH
IT WAS THE WORST LUCK OF THE DRAW, MAMAN! I NEVER WOULD'VE MADE IT.
WAAAAH
I WANT TO GO HOME!
SKCH
YOU!
W- WAIT...
DON'T TELL ME THE ERINA NAKIRI PASSED YOU?!
SMIRK

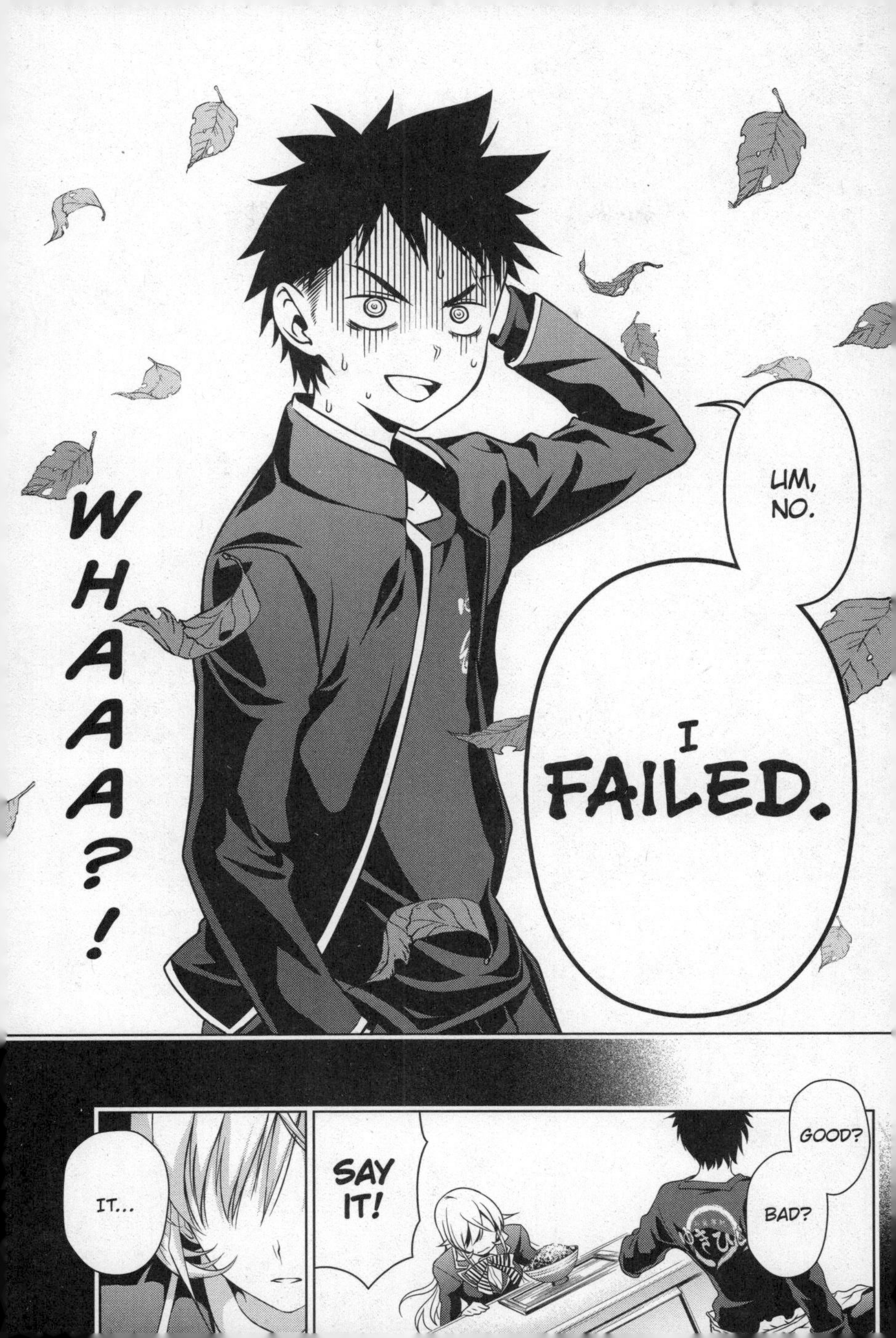
UM, NO.
I FAILED.
WHAAAA?!
GOOD?
BAD?
SAY IT!
IT...

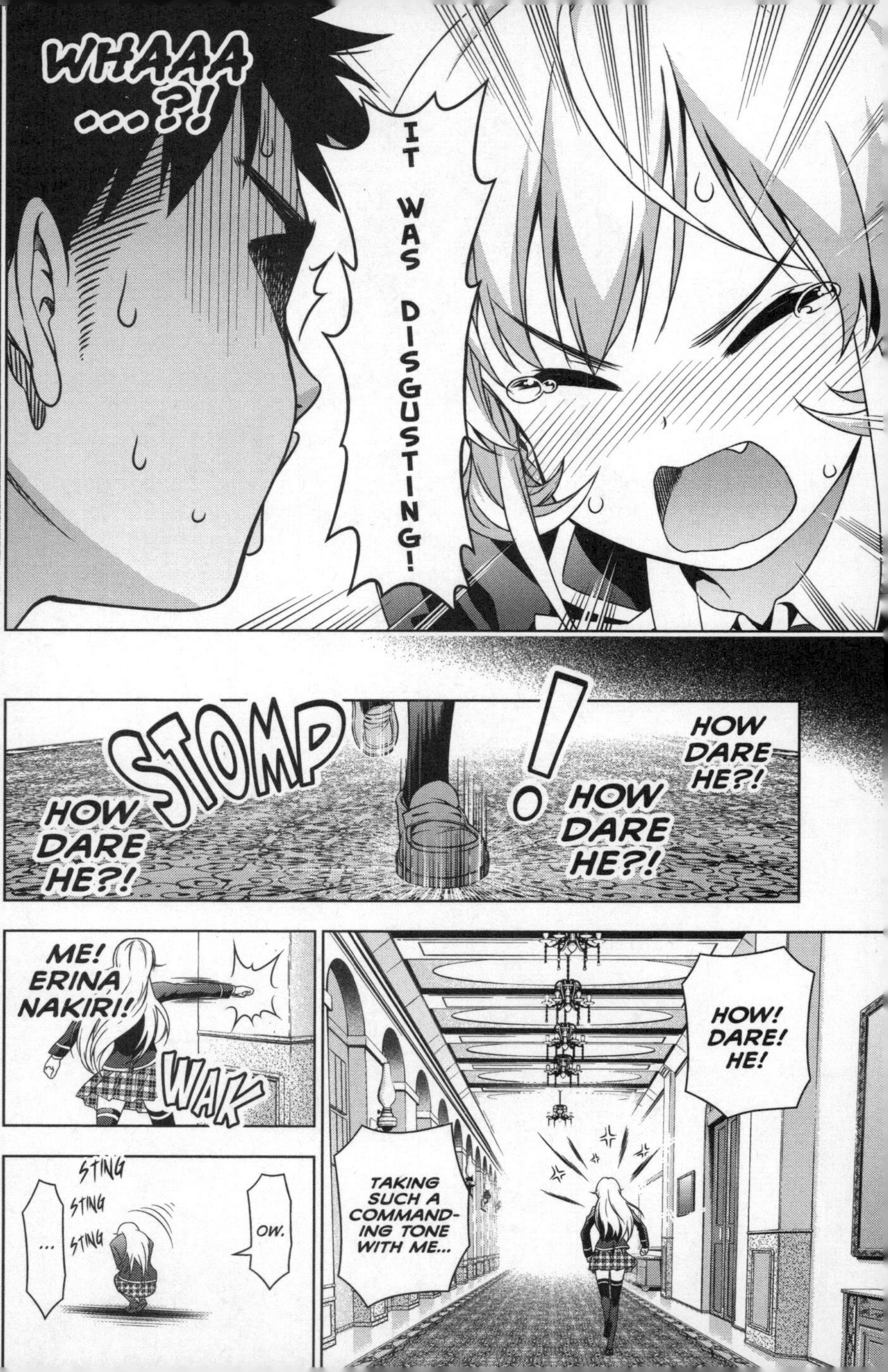
IT WAS DISGUSTING!
WHAAA ...?!
HOW DARE HE?!
HOW DARE HE?!
!
STOMP
HOW DARE HE?!
HOW! DARE! HE!
TAKING SUCH A COMMAND-ING TONE WITH ME...
ME! ERINA NAKIRI!
WAK
OW.
STING
STING
STING
...

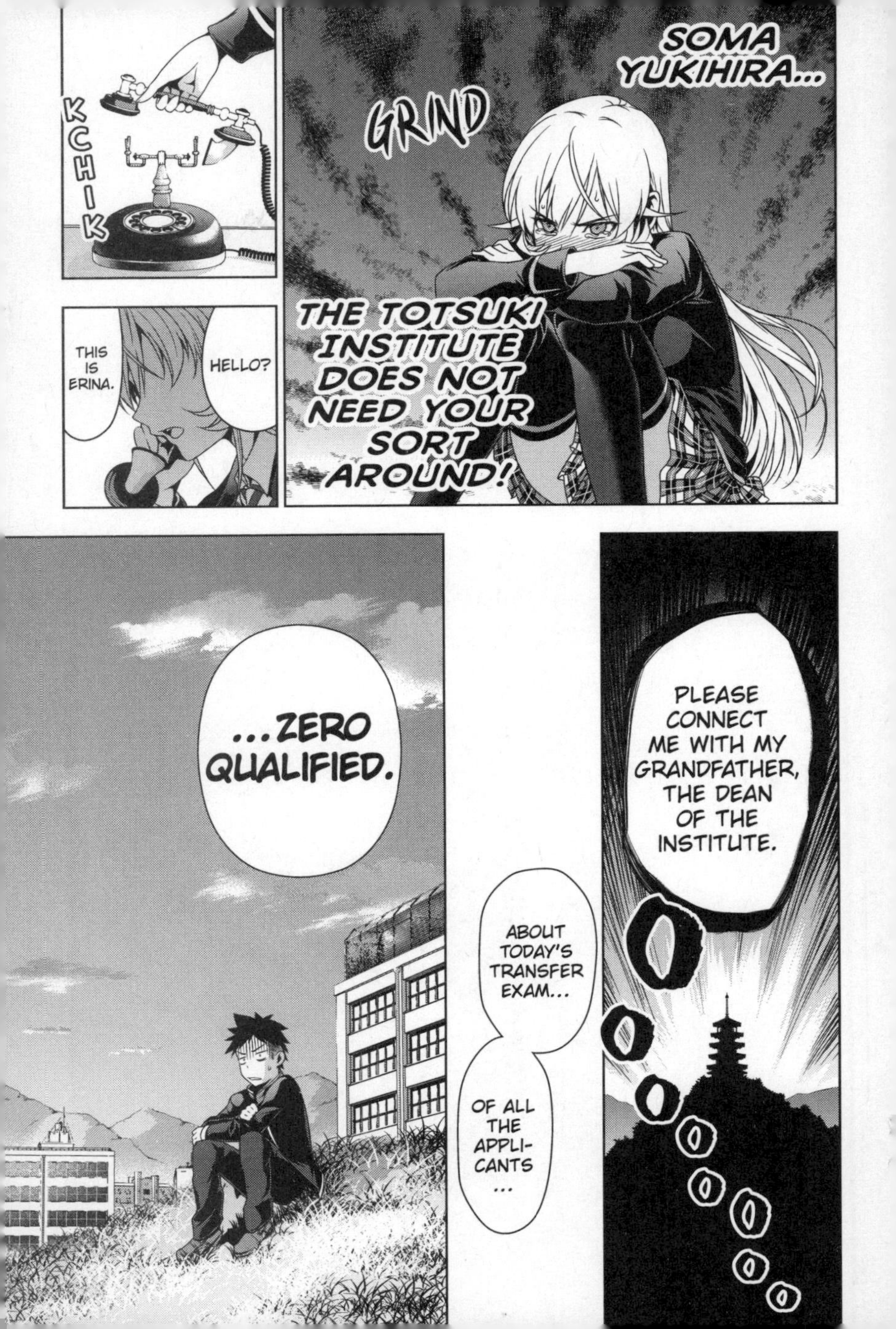
SOMA YUKIHIRA...
GRND
THE TOTSUKI INSTITUTE DOES NOT NEED YOUR SORT AROUND!
KCHIK
HELLO?
THIS IS ERINA.
PLEASE CONNECT ME WITH MY GRANDFATHER, THE DEAN OF THE INSTITUTE.
ABOUT TODAY'S TRANSFER EXAM...
OF ALL THE APPLICANTS...
...ZERO QUALIFIED.

Food Wars!
SHOKUGEKI NO SOMA

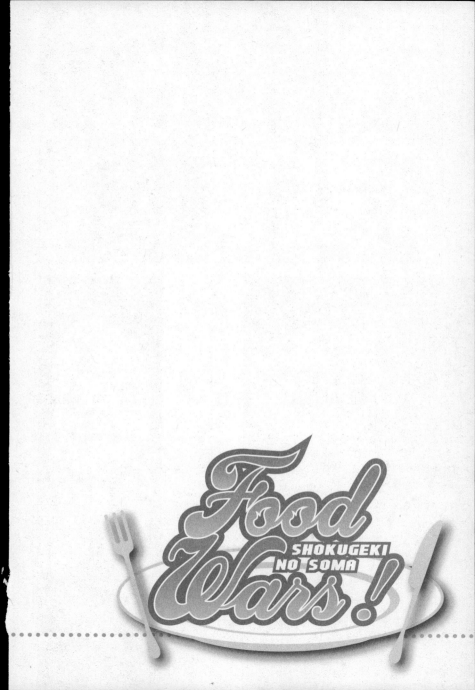

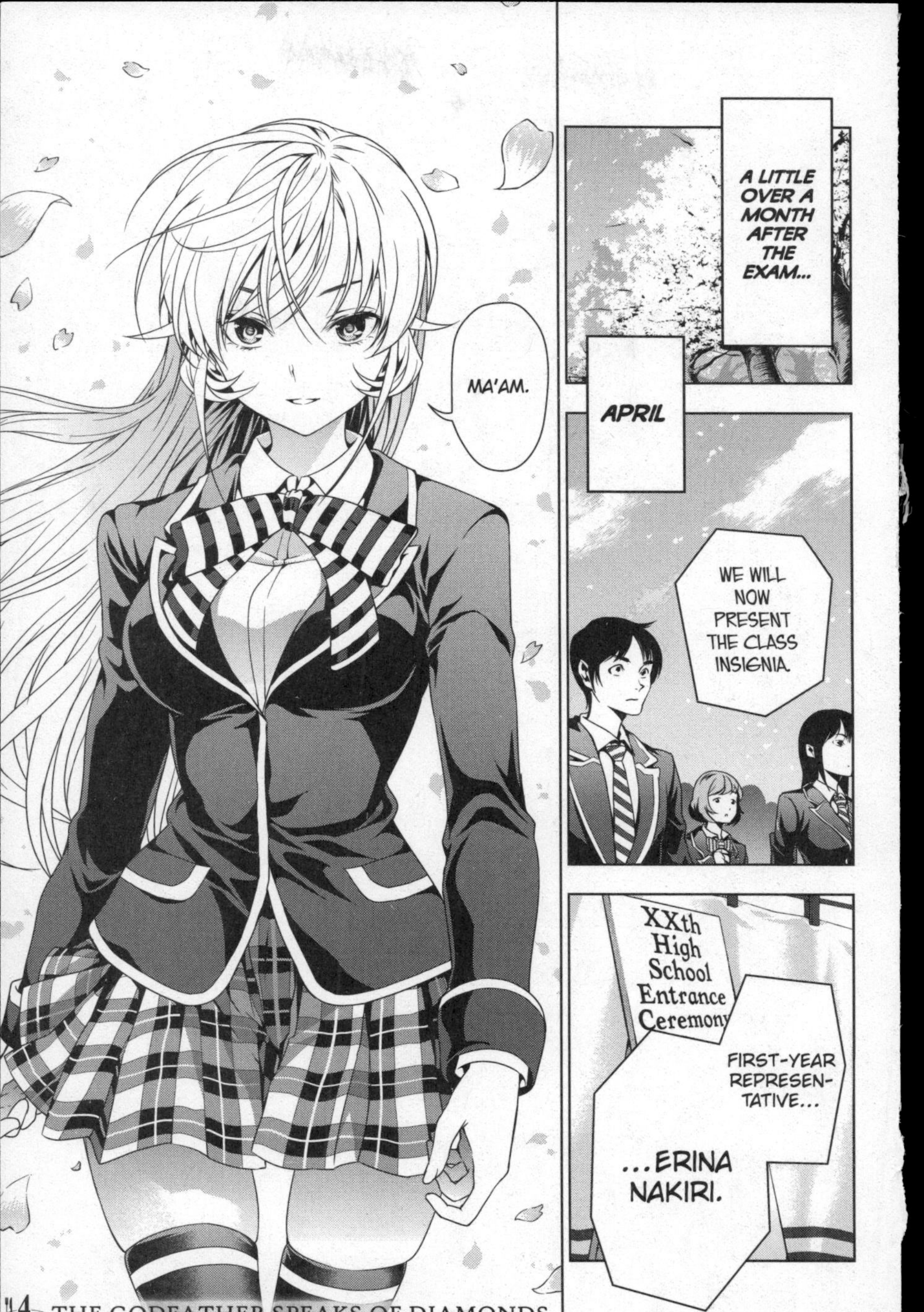
A LITTLE OVER A MONTH AFTER THE EXAM...
APRIL
WE WILL NOW PRESENT THE CLASS INSIGNIA.
XXth High School Entrance Ceremony
FIRST-YEAR REPRESENTATIVE...
...ERINA NAKIRI.
MA'AM.

14 THE GODFATHER SPEAKS OF DIAMONDS

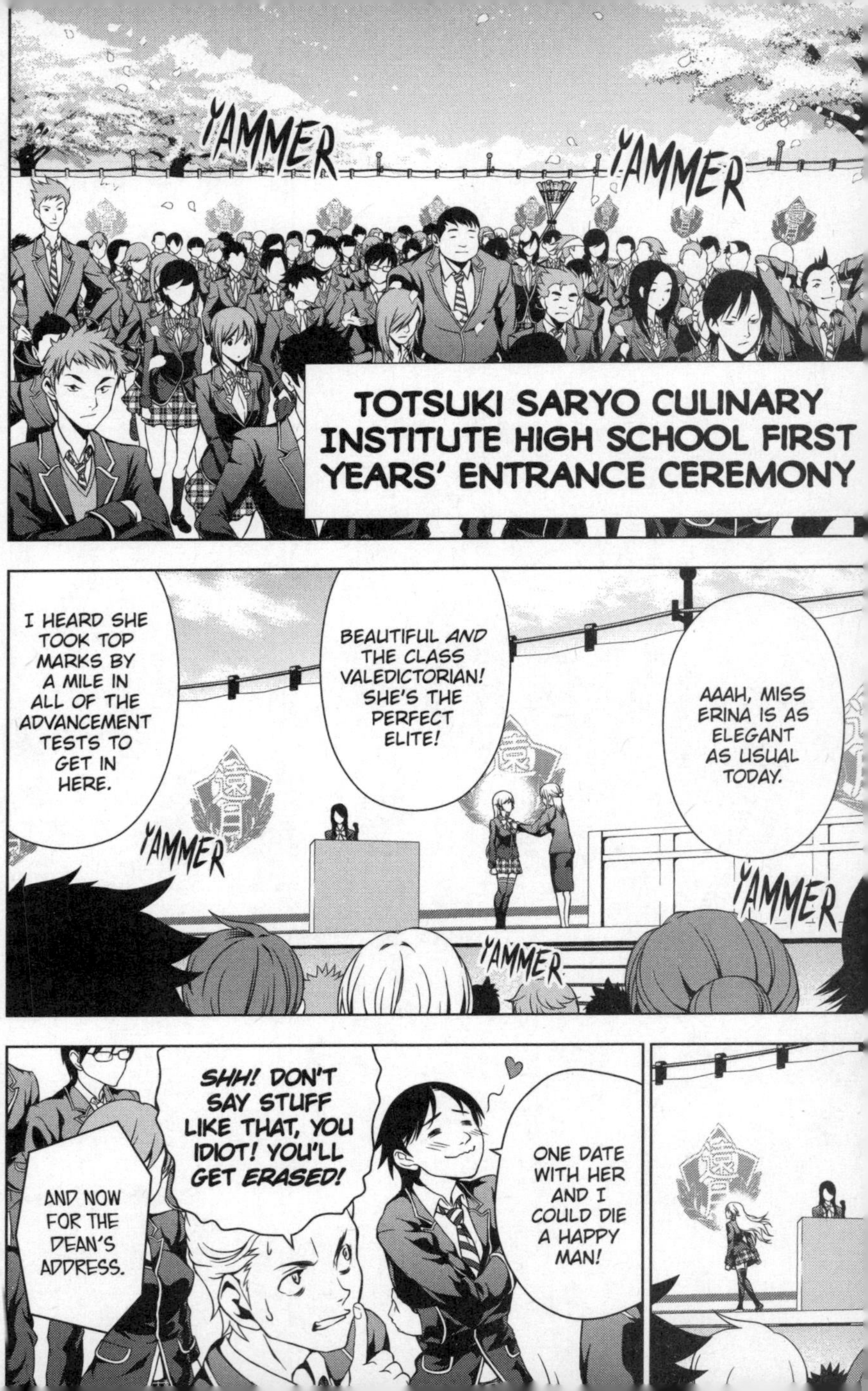
YAMMER
YAMMER
TOTSUKI SARYO CULINARY INSTITUTE HIGH SCHOOL FIRST YEARS' ENTRANCE CEREMONY
AAAH, MISS ERINA IS AS ELEGANT AS USUAL TODAY.
BEAUTIFUL AND THE CLASS VALEDICTORIAN! SHE'S THE PERFECT ELITE!
I HEARD SHE TOOK TOP MARKS BY A MILE IN ALL OF THE ADVANCEMENT TESTS TO GET IN HERE.
YAMMER
YAMMER
YAMMER
ONE DATE WITH HER AND I COULD DIE A HAPPY MAN!
SHH! DON'T SAY STUFF LIKE THAT, YOU IDIOT! YOU'LL GET ERASED!
AND NOW FOR THE DEAN'S ADDRESS.

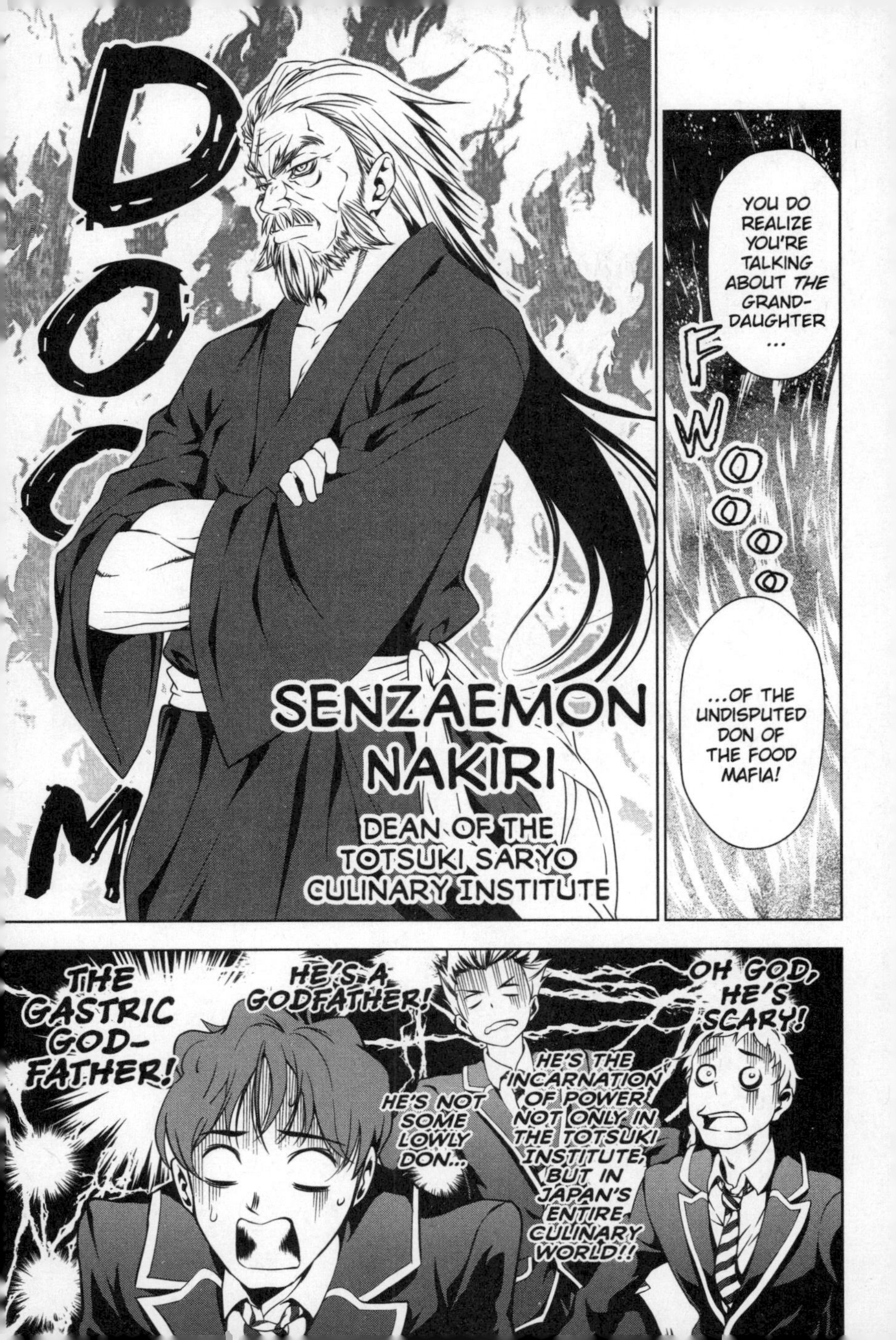
YOU DO REALIZE YOU'RE TALKING ABOUT *THE* GRAND-DAUGHTER...
FWOOOO
...OF THE UNDISPUTED DON OF THE FOOD MAFIA!
DOOM
SENZAEMON NAKIRI
DEAN OF THE TOTSUKI SARYO CULINARY INSTITUTE
OH GOD, HE'S SCARY!
HE'S A GODFATHER!
THE GASTRIC GOD-FATHER!
HE'S THE INCARNATION OF POWER NOT ONLY IN THE TOTSUKI INSTITUTE, BUT IN JAPAN'S ENTIRE CULINARY WORLD!!
HE'S NOT SOME LOWLY DON...

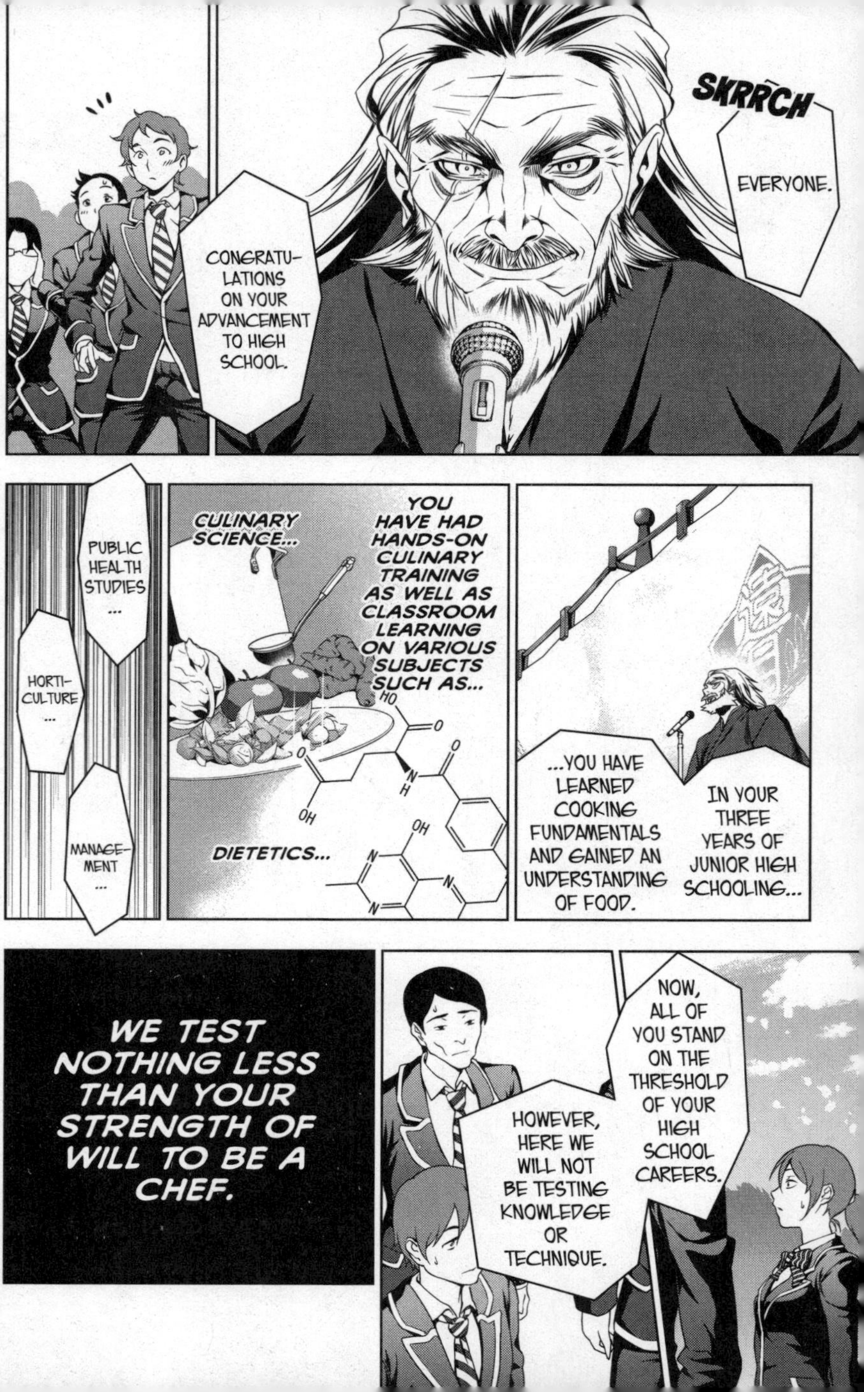
SKRRCH
EVERYONE.
CONGRATULATIONS ON YOUR ADVANCEMENT TO HIGH SCHOOL.
IN YOUR THREE YEARS OF JUNIOR HIGH SCHOOLING...
...YOU HAVE LEARNED COOKING FUNDAMENTALS AND GAINED AN UNDERSTANDING OF FOOD.
YOU HAVE HAD HANDS-ON CULINARY TRAINING AS WELL AS CLASSROOM LEARNING ON VARIOUS SUBJECTS SUCH AS...
CULINARY SCIENCE...
DIETETICS...
PUBLIC HEALTH STUDIES...
HORTICULTURE...
MANAGEMENT...
NOW, ALL OF YOU STAND ON THE THRESHOLD OF YOUR HIGH SCHOOL CAREERS.
HOWEVER, HERE WE WILL NOT BE TESTING KNOWLEDGE OR TECHNIQUE.
WE TEST NOTHING LESS THAN YOUR STRENGTH OF WILL TO BE A CHEF.

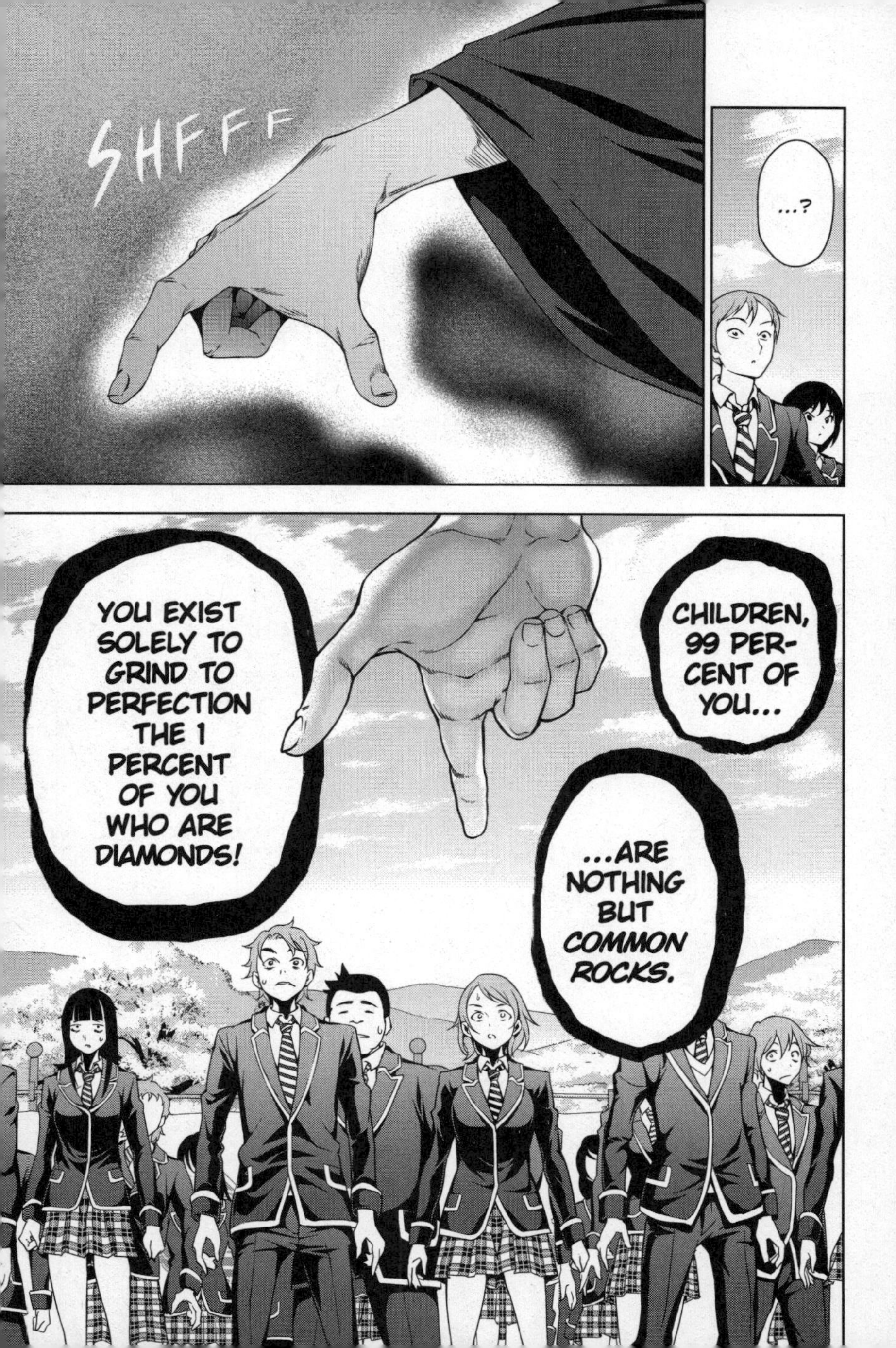
...?
SHFFF
CHILDREN, 99 PER-CENT OF YOU...
...ARE NOTHING BUT COMMON ROCKS.
YOU EXIST SOLELY TO GRIND TO PERFECTION THE 1 PERCENT OF YOU WHO ARE DIAMONDS!

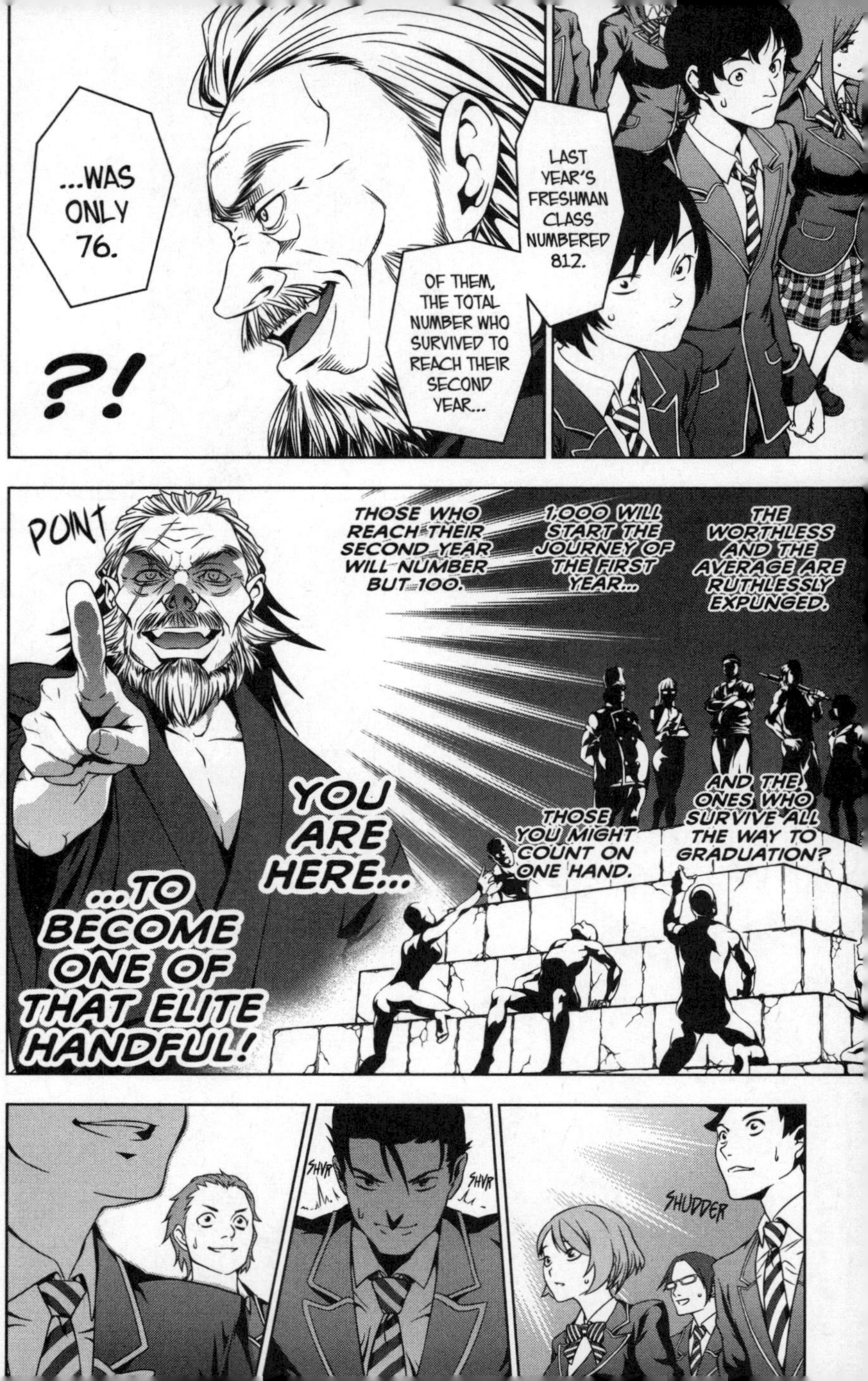
LAST YEAR'S FRESHMAN CLASS NUMBERED 812.
OF THEM, THE TOTAL NUMBER WHO SURVIVED TO REACH THEIR SECOND YEAR...
...WAS ONLY 76.
?!
THE WORTHLESS AND THE AVERAGE ARE RUTHLESSLY EXPUNGED.
1,000 WILL START THE JOURNEY OF THE FIRST YEAR...
THOSE WHO REACH THEIR SECOND YEAR WILL NUMBER BUT 100.
AND THE ONES WHO SURVIVE ALL THE WAY TO GRADUATION?
THOSE YOU MIGHT COUNT ON ONE HAND.
POINT
YOU ARE HERE...
...TO BECOME ONE OF THAT ELITE HANDFUL!
SHUDDER
SHVR
SHVR

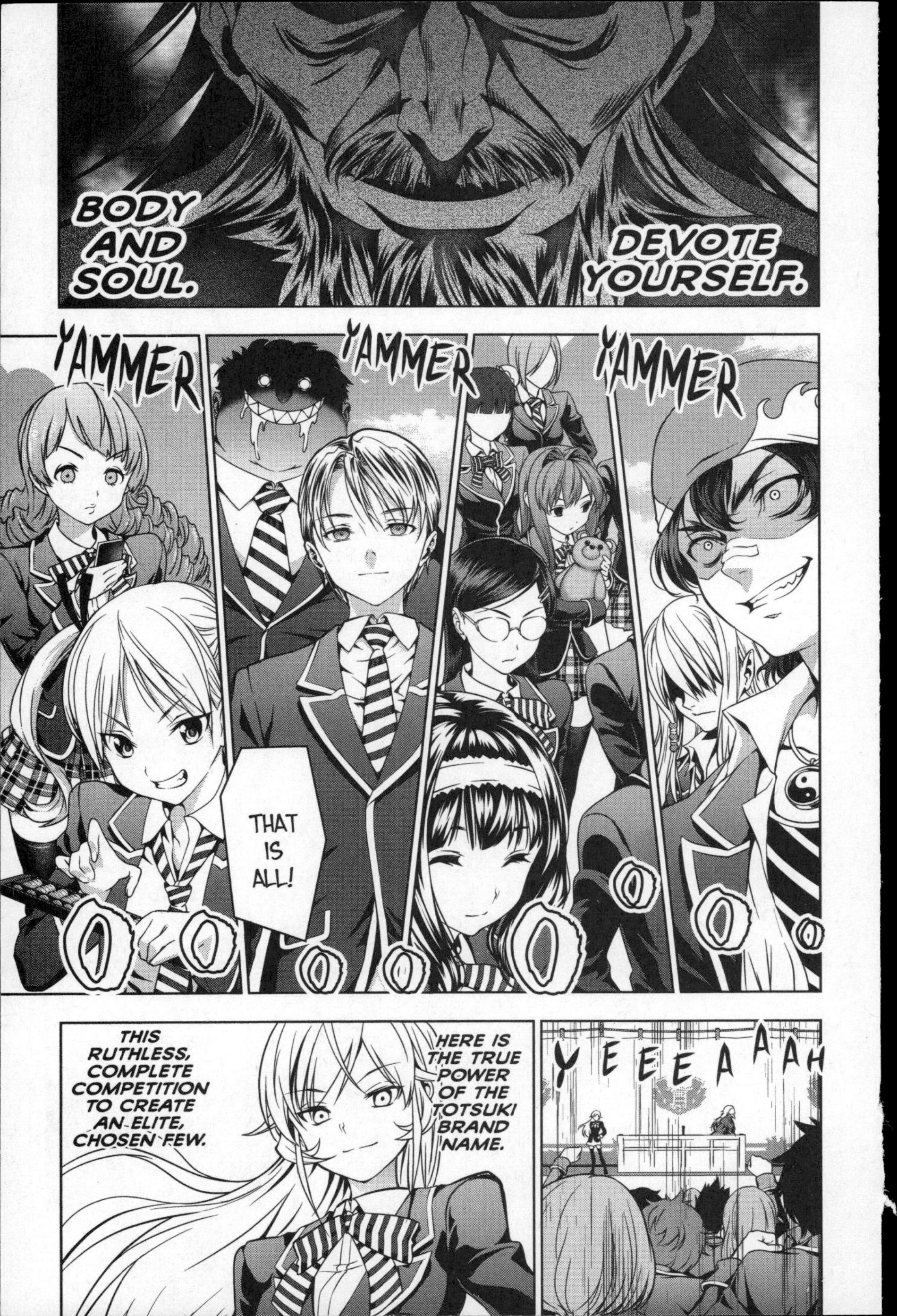
DEVOTE YOURSELF.
BODY AND SOUL.
YAMMER
YAMMER
YAMMER
THAT IS ALL!
YEEEAAAH
HERE IS THE TRUE POWER OF THE TOTSUKI BRAND NAME.
THIS RUTHLESS, COMPLETE COMPETITION TO CREATE AN ELITE, CHOSEN FEW.

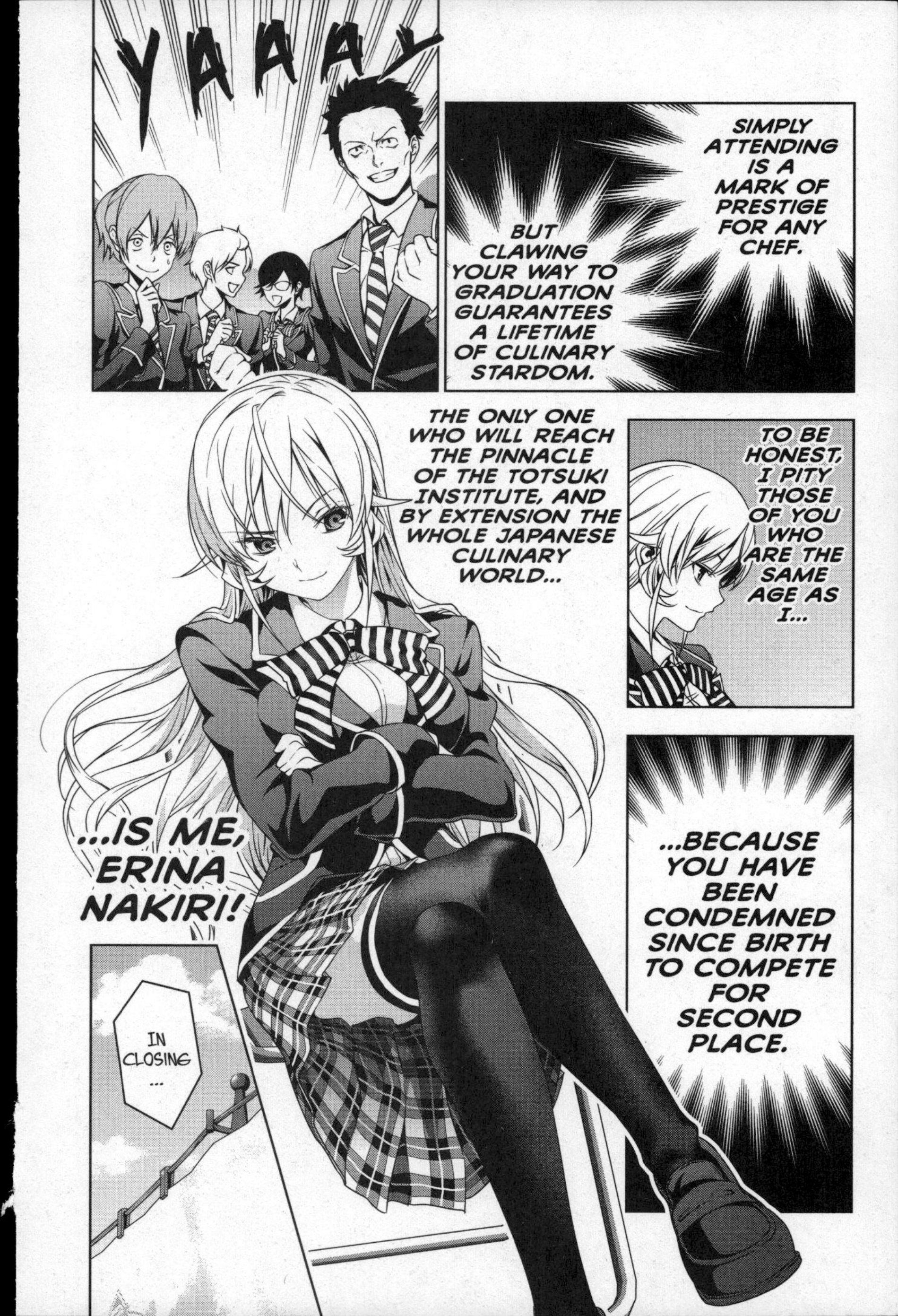
SIMPLY ATTENDING IS A MARK OF PRESTIGE FOR ANY CHEF.
BUT CLAWING YOUR WAY TO GRADUATION GUARANTEES A LIFETIME OF CULINARY STARDOM.
YAAAY
TO BE HONEST, I PITY THOSE OF YOU WHO ARE THE SAME AGE AS I...
...BECAUSE YOU HAVE BEEN CONDEMNED SINCE BIRTH TO COMPETE FOR SECOND PLACE.
THE ONLY ONE WHO WILL REACH THE PINNACLE OF THE TOTSUKI INSTITUTE, AND BY EXTENSION THE WHOLE JAPANESE CULINARY WORLD...
...IS ME, ERINA NAKIRI!
IN CLOSING ...

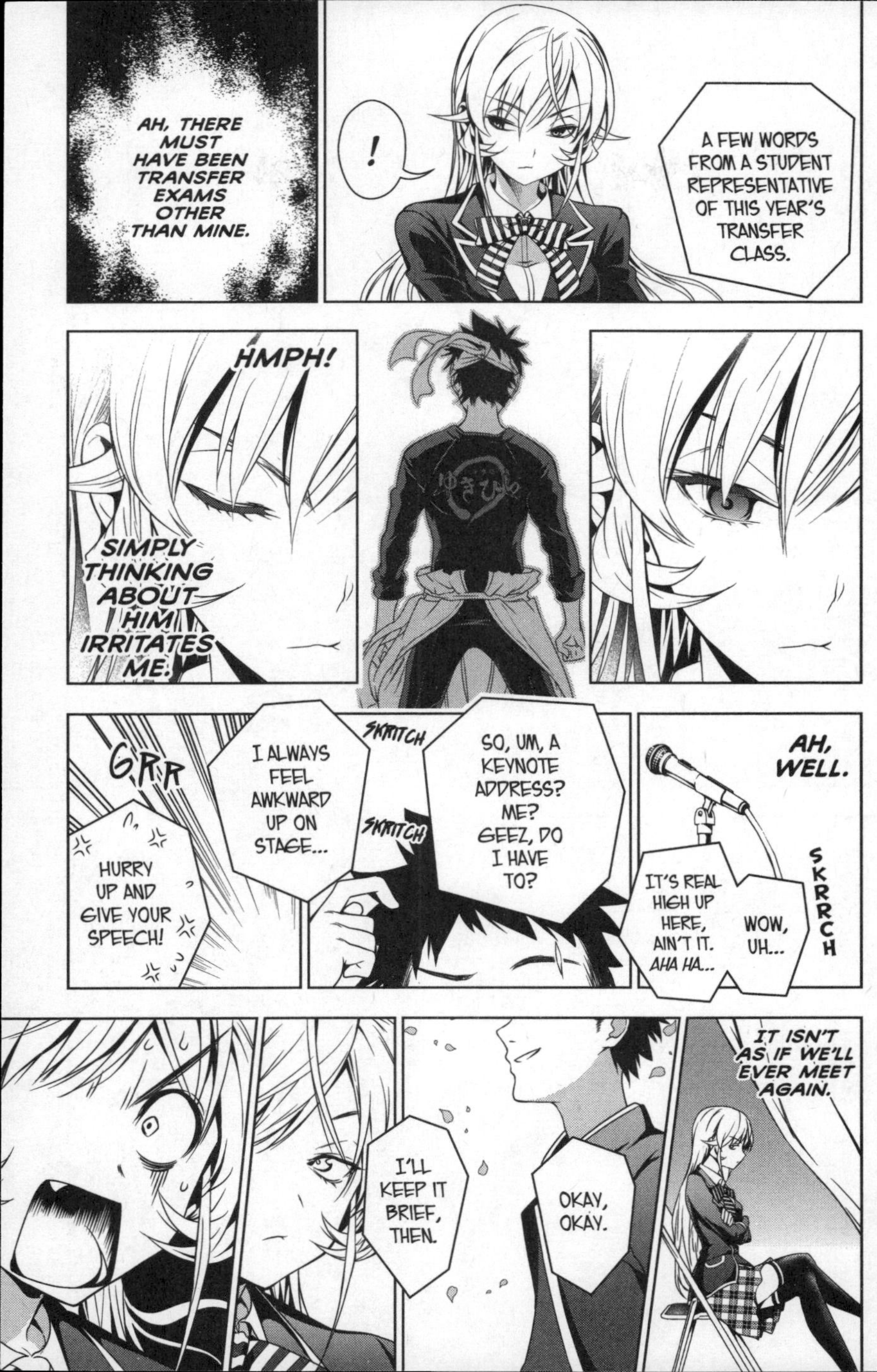
A FEW WORDS FROM A STUDENT REPRESENTATIVE OF THIS YEAR'S TRANSFER CLASS.
!
AH, THERE MUST HAVE BEEN TRANSFER EXAMS OTHER THAN MINE.
HMPH!
SIMPLY THINKING ABOUT HIM IRRITATES ME.
AH, WELL.
SKRRCH
WOW, UH...
IT'S REAL HIGH UP HERE, AIN'T IT. AHA HA...
SO, UM, A KEYNOTE ADDRESS? ME? GEEZ, DO I HAVE TO?
SKRITCH
SKRITCH
I ALWAYS FEEL AWKWARD UP ON STAGE...
GRR
HURRY UP AND GIVE YOUR SPEECH!
IT ISN'T AS IF WE'LL EVER MEET AGAIN.
OKAY, OKAY.
I'LL KEEP IT BRIEF, THEN.

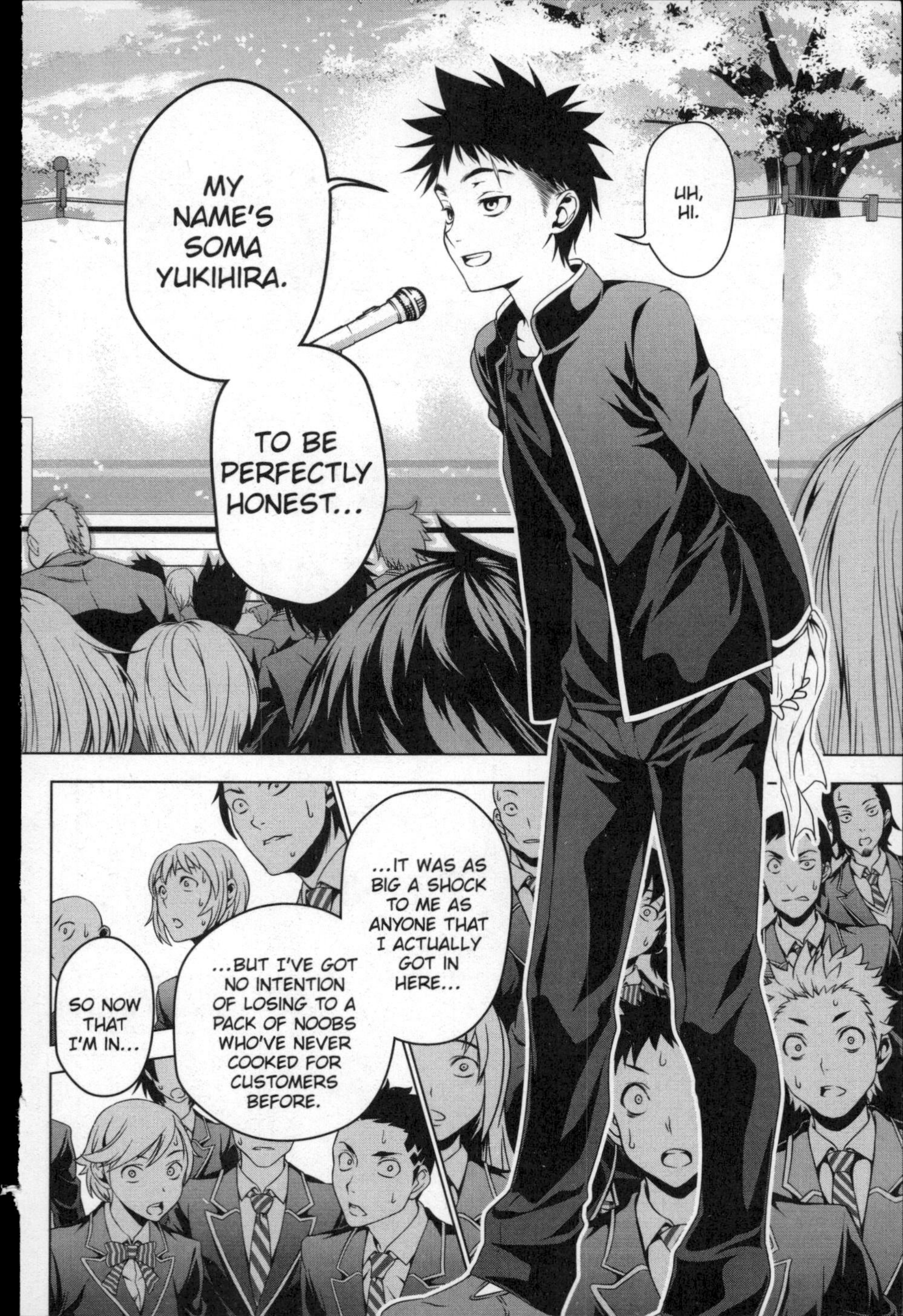
UH, HI.
MY NAME'S SOMA YUKIHIRA.
TO BE PERFECTLY HONEST...
...IT WAS AS BIG A SHOCK TO ME AS ANYONE THAT I ACTUALLY GOT IN HERE...
...BUT I'VE GOT NO INTENTION OF LOSING TO A PACK OF NOOBS WHO'VE NEVER COOKED FOR CUSTOMERS BEFORE.
SO NOW THAT I'M IN...

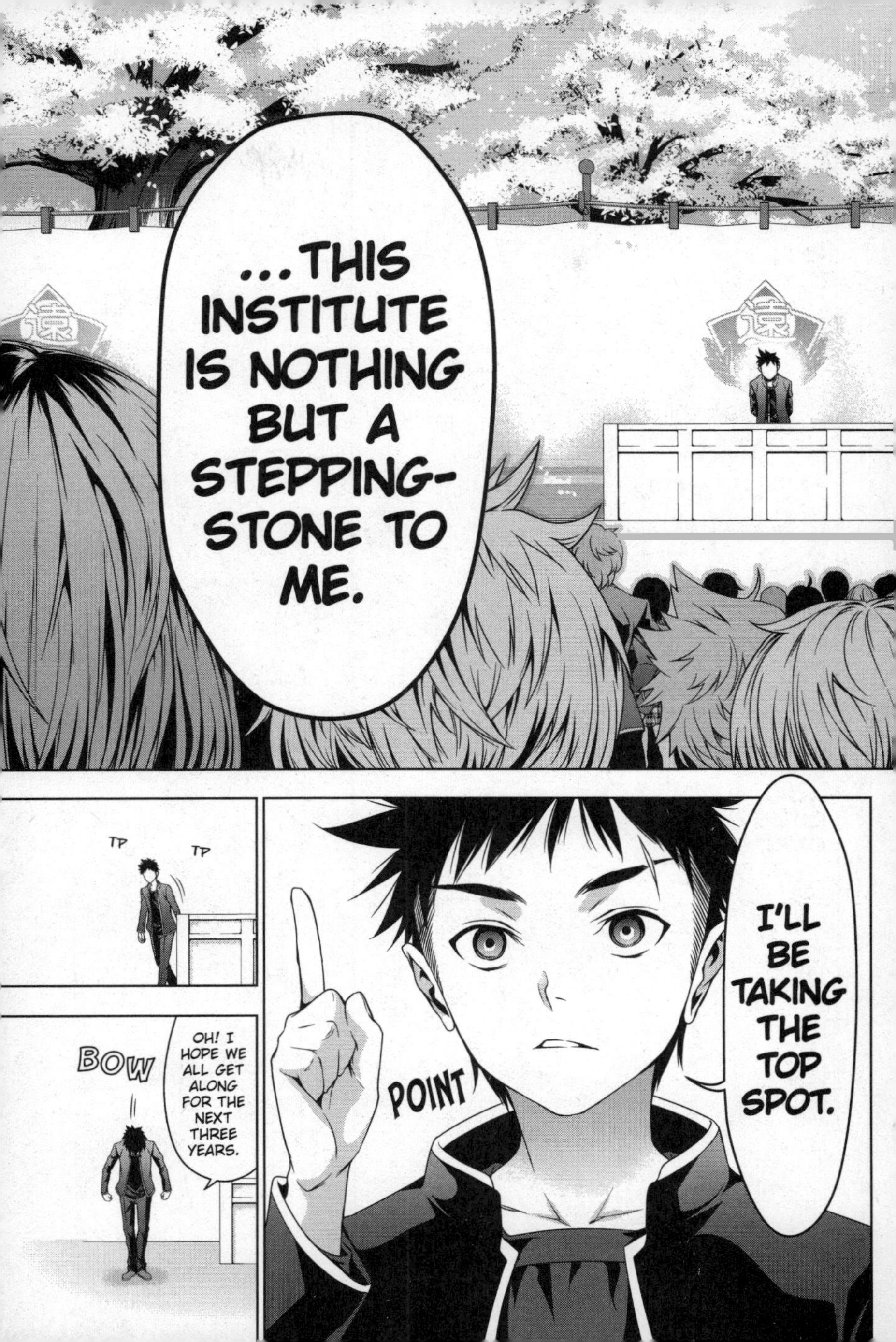
...THIS INSTITUTE IS NOTHING BUT A STEPPING-STONE TO ME.
I'LL BE TAKING THE TOP SPOT.
POINT
TP TP
BOW
OH! I HOPE WE ALL GET ALONG FOR THE NEXT THREE YEARS.

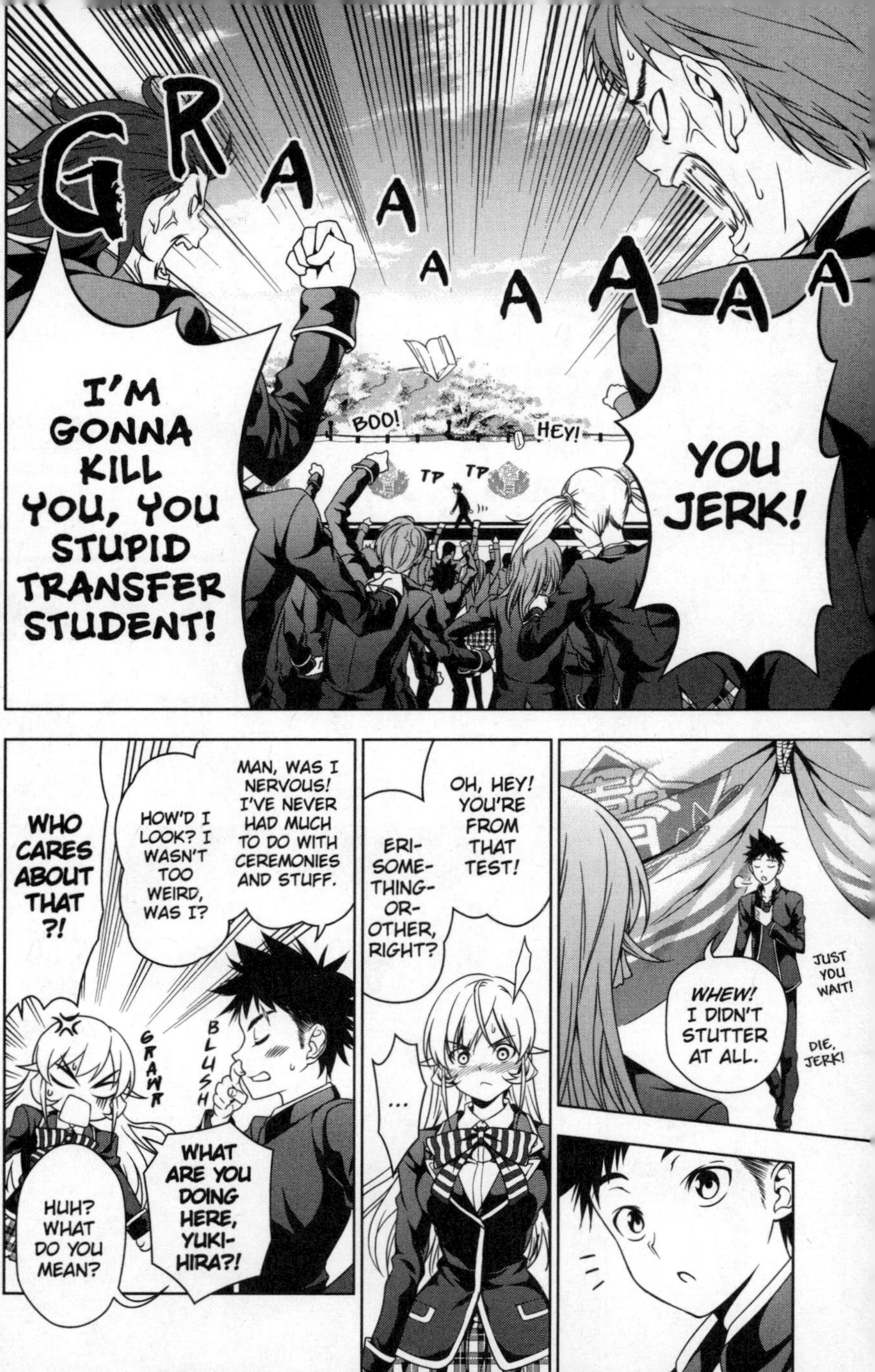
GRAAAAAAAA
YOU JERK!
HEY!
TP TP
BOO!
I'M GONNA KILL YOU, YOU STUPID TRANSFER STUDENT!
JUST YOU WAIT!
WHEW! I DIDN'T STUTTER AT ALL.
DIE, JERK!
OH, HEY! YOU'RE FROM THAT TEST!
ERI-SOMETHING-OR-OTHER, RIGHT?
...
MAN, WAS I NERVOUS! I'VE NEVER HAD MUCH TO DO WITH CEREMONIES AND STUFF.
HOW'D I LOOK? I WASN'T TOO WEIRD, WAS I?
WHO CARES ABOUT THAT?!
BLUSH
GRAWR
WHAT ARE YOU DOING HERE, YUKIHIRA?!
HUH? WHAT DO YOU MEAN?

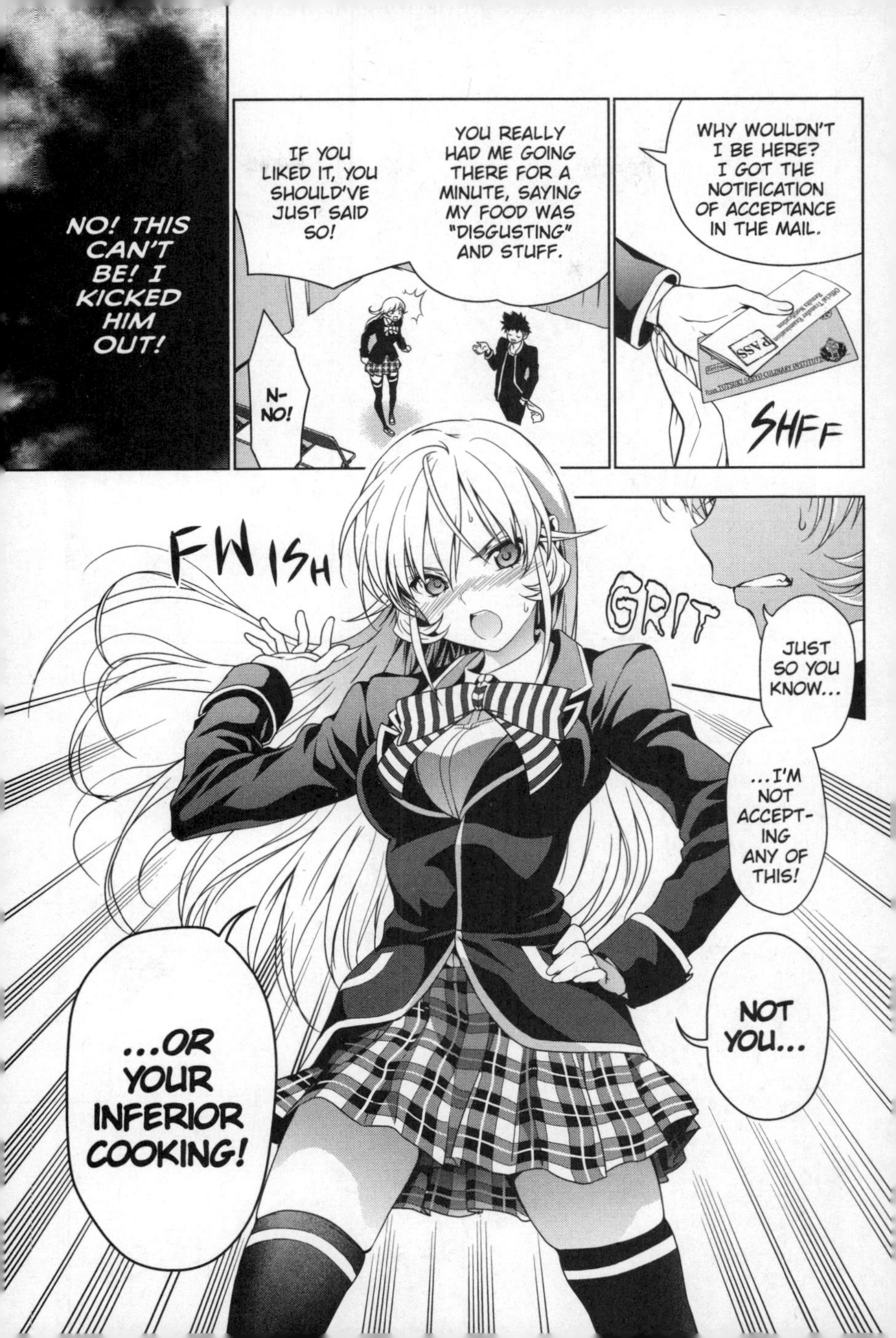
WHY WOULDN'T I BE HERE? I GOT THE NOTIFICATION OF ACCEPTANCE IN THE MAIL.
SHFF
YOU REALLY HAD ME GOING THERE FOR A MINUTE, SAYING MY FOOD WAS "DISGUSTING" AND STUFF.
IF YOU LIKED IT, YOU SHOULD'VE JUST SAID SO!
N-NO!
NO! THIS CAN'T BE! I KICKED HIM OUT!
GRIT
JUST SO YOU KNOW...
...I'M NOT ACCEPT-ING ANY OF THIS!
NOT YOU...
...OR YOUR INFERIOR COOKING!
FWISH

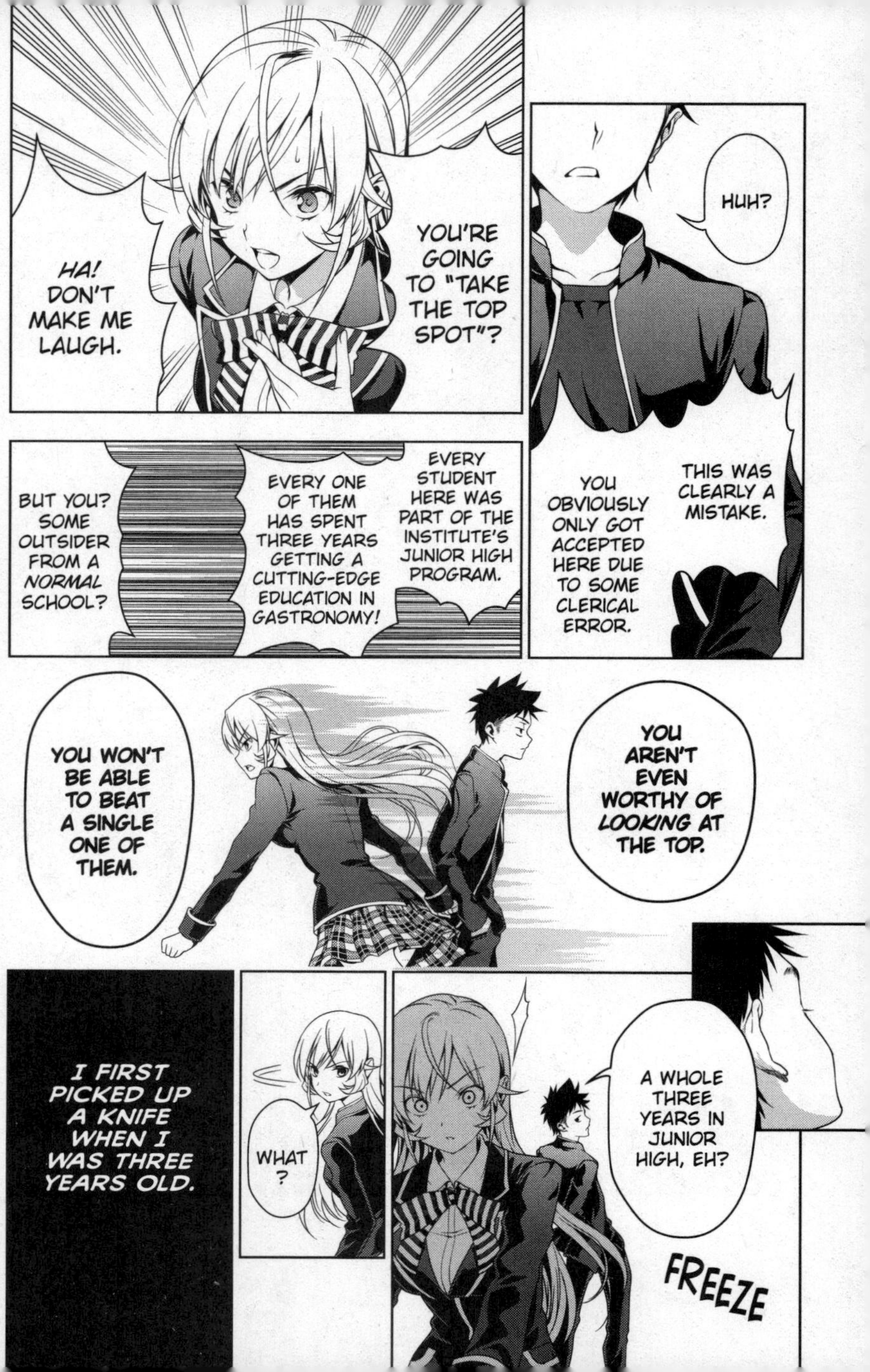
HUH?
THIS WAS CLEARLY A MISTAKE.
YOU OBVIOUSLY ONLY GOT ACCEPTED HERE DUE TO SOME CLERICAL ERROR.
YOU'RE GOING TO "TAKE THE TOP SPOT"?
HA! DON'T MAKE ME LAUGH.
EVERY STUDENT HERE WAS PART OF THE INSTITUTE'S JUNIOR HIGH PROGRAM.
EVERY ONE OF THEM HAS SPENT THREE YEARS GETTING A CUTTING-EDGE EDUCATION IN GASTRONOMY!
BUT YOU? SOME OUTSIDER FROM A NORMAL SCHOOL?
YOU AREN'T EVEN WORTHY OF LOOKING AT THE TOP.
YOU WON'T BE ABLE TO BEAT A SINGLE ONE OF THEM.
A WHOLE THREE YEARS IN JUNIOR HIGH, EH?
FREEZE
WHAT?
I FIRST PICKED UP A KNIFE WHEN I WAS THREE YEARS OLD.

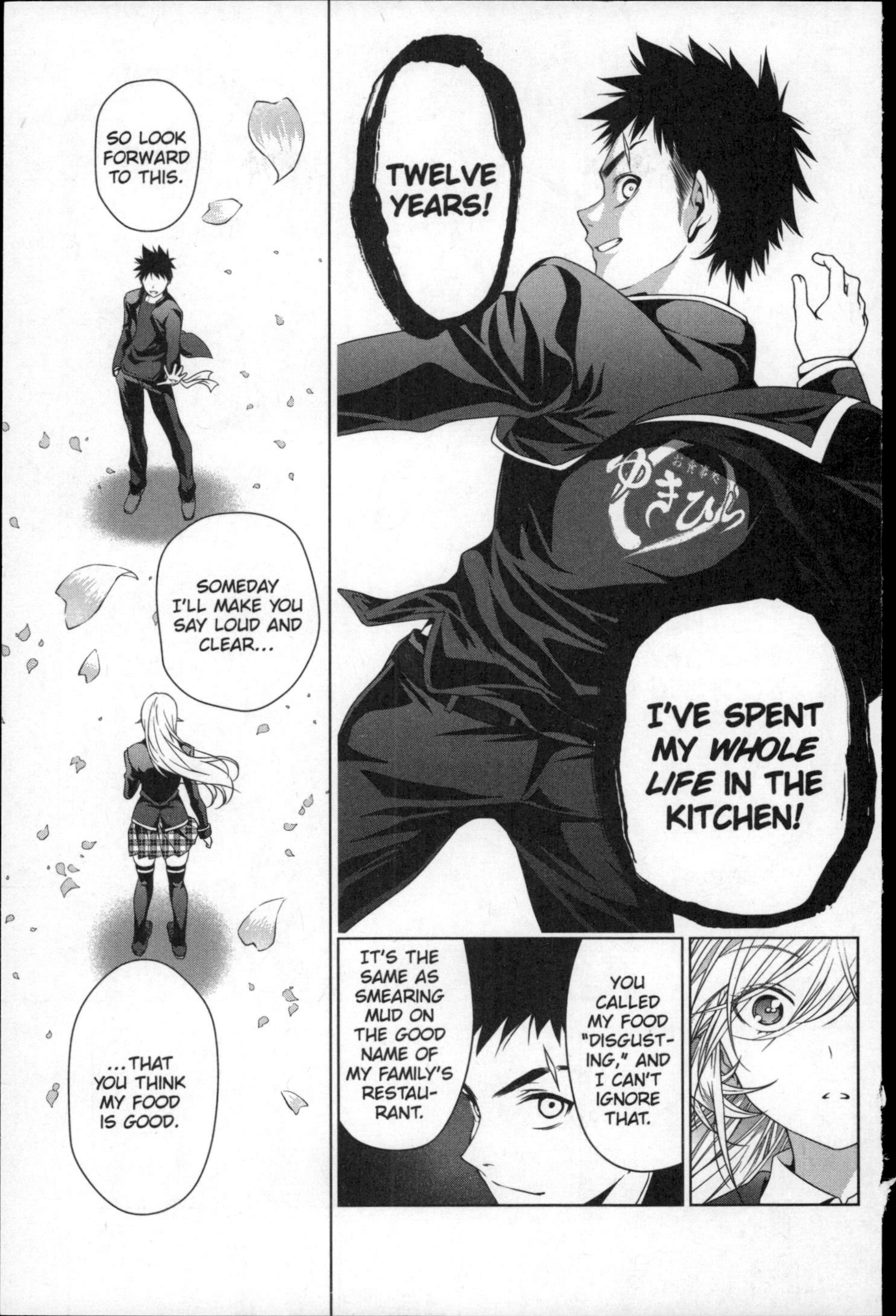
TWELVE YEARS!
ゆきひら
I'VE SPENT MY *WHOLE LIFE* IN THE KITCHEN!
YOU CALLED MY FOOD "DISGUSTING," AND I CAN'T IGNORE THAT.
IT'S THE SAME AS SMEARING MUD ON THE GOOD NAME OF MY FAMILY'S RESTAURANT.
SO LOOK FORWARD TO THIS.
SOMEDAY I'LL MAKE YOU SAY LOUD AND CLEAR...
...THAT YOU THINK MY FOOD IS GOOD.

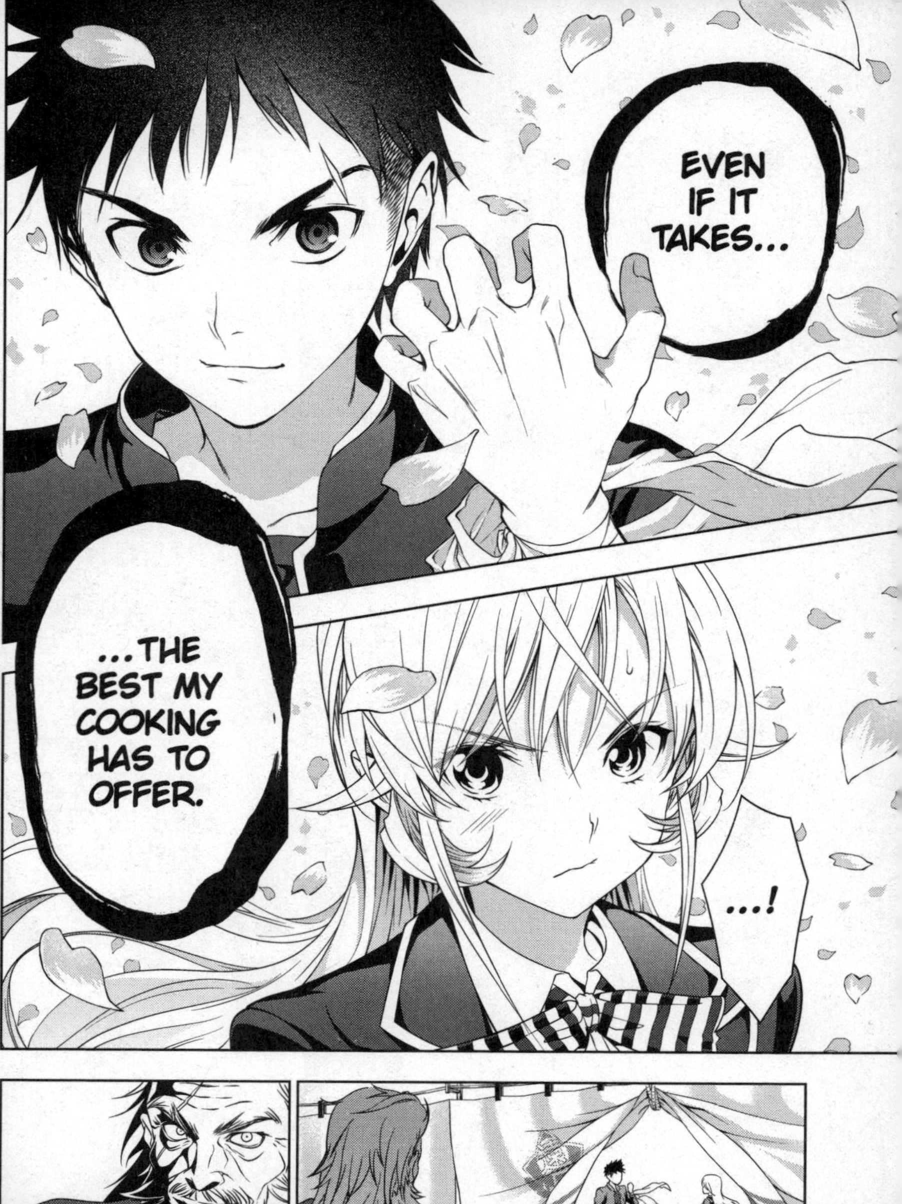
EVEN IF IT TAKES...
...THE BEST MY COOKING HAS TO OFFER.
...!

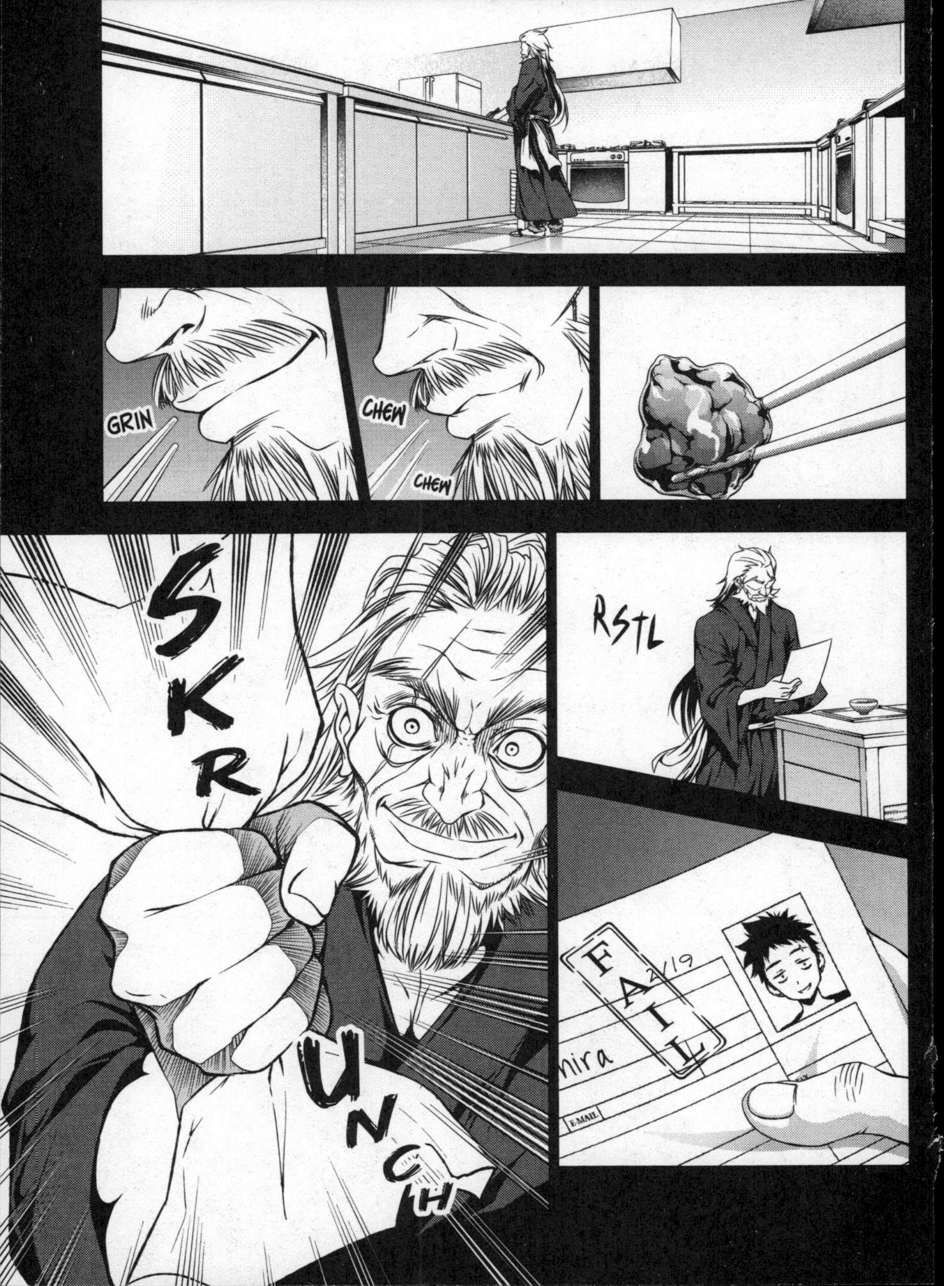
CHEW
CHEW
GRIN
RSTL
FAIL
2/19
nira
E-MAIL
SKRUNCH

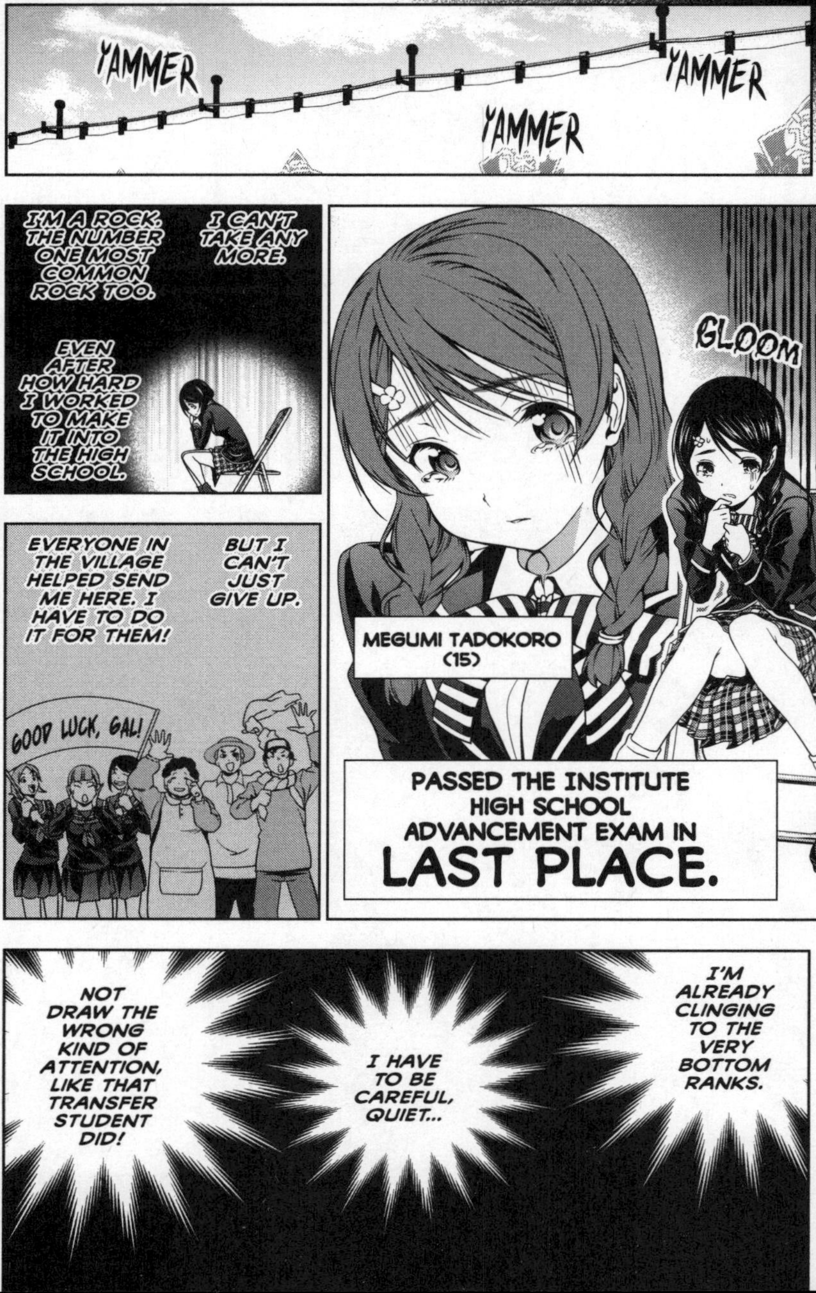
YAMMER
YAMMER
YAMMER
GLOOM
MEGUMI TADOKORO (15)
PASSED THE INSTITUTE HIGH SCHOOL ADVANCEMENT EXAM IN LAST PLACE.
I CAN'T TAKE ANY MORE.
I'M A ROCK. THE NUMBER ONE MOST COMMON ROCK TOO.
EVEN AFTER HOW HARD I WORKED TO MAKE IT INTO THE HIGH SCHOOL.
BUT I CAN'T JUST GIVE UP.
EVERYONE IN THE VILLAGE HELPED SEND ME HERE. I HAVE TO DO IT FOR THEM!
GOOD LUCK, GAL!
I'M ALREADY CLINGING TO THE VERY BOTTOM RANKS.
I HAVE TO BE CAREFUL, QUIET...
NOT DRAW THE WRONG KIND OF ATTENTION, LIKE THAT TRANSFER STUDENT DID!

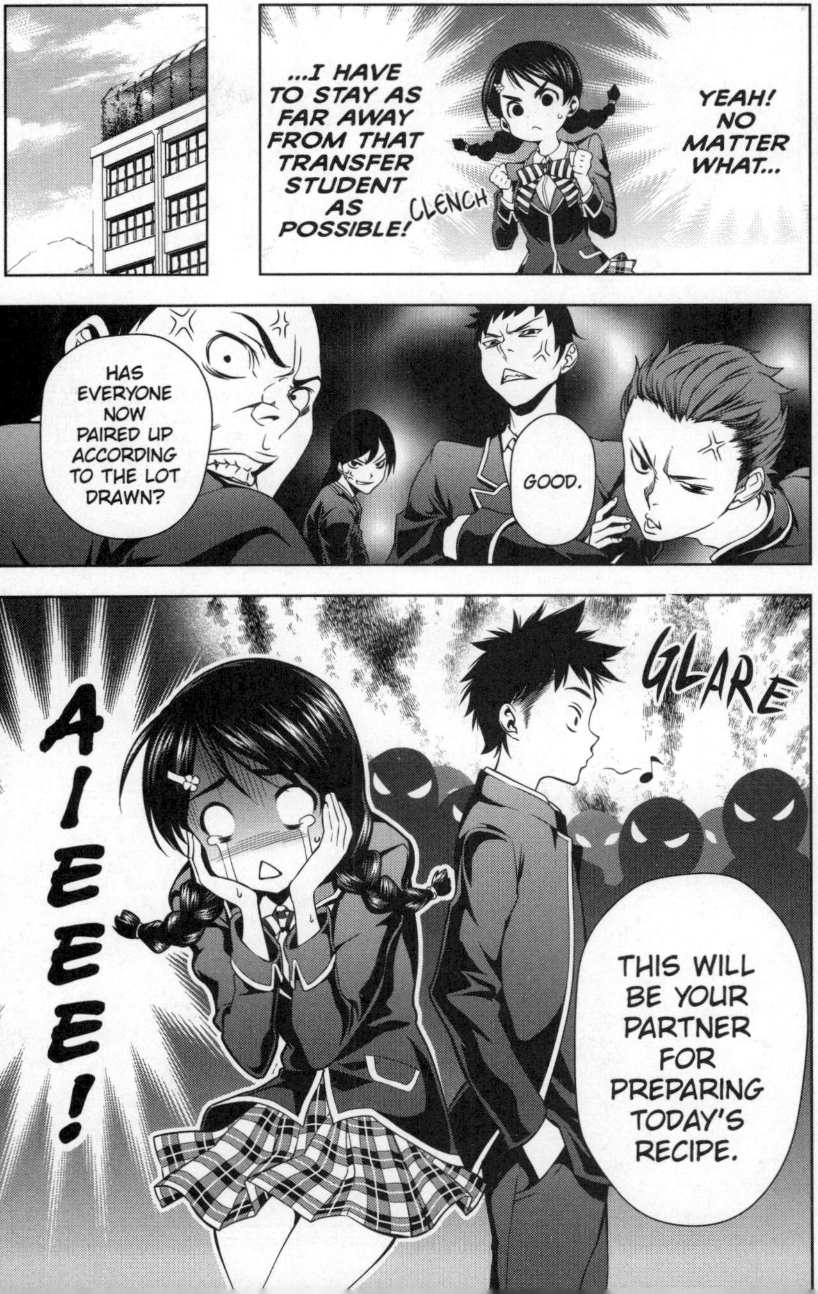
YEAH! NO MATTER WHAT...
...I HAVE TO STAY AS FAR AWAY FROM THAT TRANSFER STUDENT AS POSSIBLE!
CLENCH
HAS EVERYONE NOW PAIRED UP ACCORDING TO THE LOT DRAWN?
GOOD.
GLARE
THIS WILL BE YOUR PARTNER FOR PREPARING TODAY'S RECIPE.
AIEEEE!

Yukihira Style

ASPIC & EGG CURDS FURIKAKE RICE ~PRACTICAL RECIPE~

HERE'S HOW TO MAKE "MORPHING" FURIKAKE RICE, WITH THE CHICKEN ADDED!

ARTIST: YUTO TSUKUDA

INGREDIENTS (2-3 SERVINGS)

7 CHICKEN WINGS

1 TABLESPOON SESAME OIL

(A)
1 TEASPOON GRATED GINGER
700 CC BONITO BROTH
1 TABLESPOON EACH SAKÉ, SUGAR, MIRIN
50 CC LIGHT SOY SAUCE

4 EGGS

DICED SPRING ONION

(B)
1 TABLESPOON SUGAR
A PINCH OF SALT

1. HEAT SESAME OIL IN FRYING PAN AND SAUTÉ CHICKEN WINGS UNTIL GOLDEN BROWN ON BOTH SIDES.

2. PUT ITEMS FROM (1) AND (A) INTO A POT AND TURN ON HIGH UNTIL IT BOILS. SKIM SCUM OFF TOP. REDUCE HEAT TO LOW AND SIMMER UNTIL BROTH IS REDUCED BY HALF.

3. POUR BROTH INTO A CONTAINER TO COOL. ONCE COOLED, PLACE IN REFRIGERATOR TO CHILL AND HARDEN. DEBONE CHICKEN WINGS AND CUT INTO STRIPS.

4. MAKE THE EGG CURDS. CRACK EGGS INTO BOWL, ADD (B), AND WHISK. POUR INTO FRYING PAN ON LOW HEAT, STIRRING RAPIDLY TO CREATE THE CURDS. ONCE DONE, MOVE TO PLATE.

5. ONCE (3) HARDENS, REMOVE FROM CONTAINER AND CUT INTO 1 CM X 1 CM SQUARES.

6. POUR ASPIC, EGG CURDS, AND CHICKEN STRIPS OVER HOT RICE. SPRINKLE WITH DICED SPRING ONION AND ENJOY!

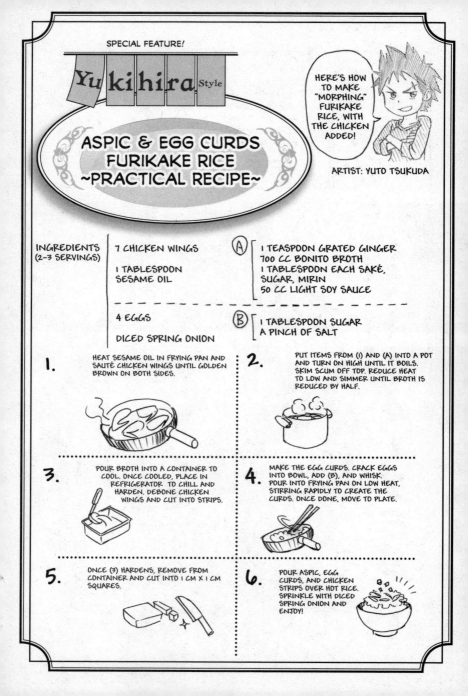

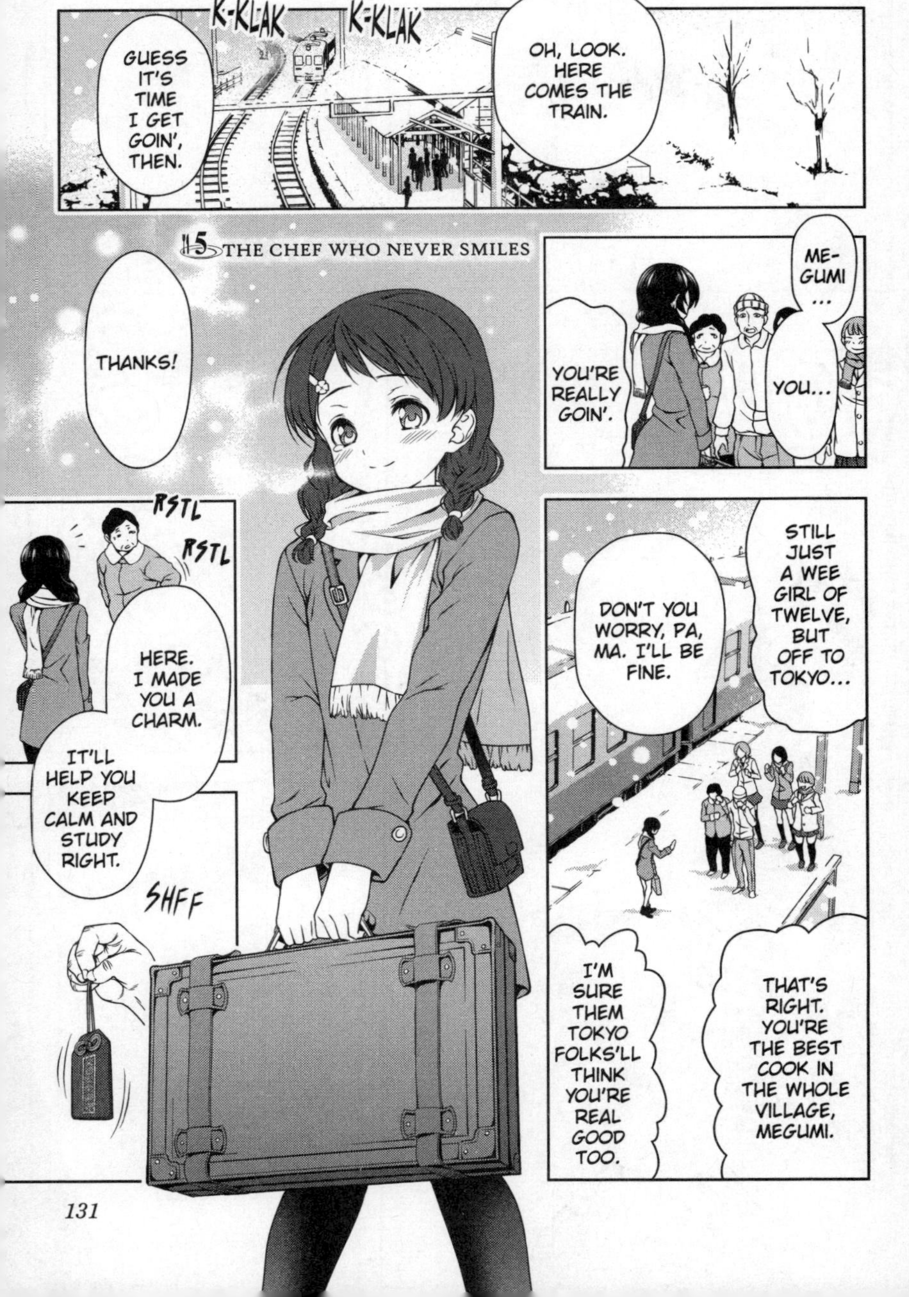
K-KLAK
K-KLAK
OH, LOOK. HERE COMES THE TRAIN.
GUESS IT'S TIME I GET GOIN', THEN.
15 THE CHEF WHO NEVER SMILES
ME-GUMI ...
YOU...
YOU'RE REALLY GOIN'.
STILL JUST A WEE GIRL OF TWELVE, BUT OFF TO TOKYO...
DON'T YOU WORRY, PA, MA. I'LL BE FINE.
THAT'S RIGHT. YOU'RE THE BEST COOK IN THE WHOLE VILLAGE, MEGUMI.
I'M SURE THEM TOKYO FOLKS'LL THINK YOU'RE REAL GOOD TOO.
RSTL
RSTL
HERE. I MADE YOU A CHARM.
IT'LL HELP YOU KEEP CALM AND STUDY RIGHT.
SHFF
THANKS!

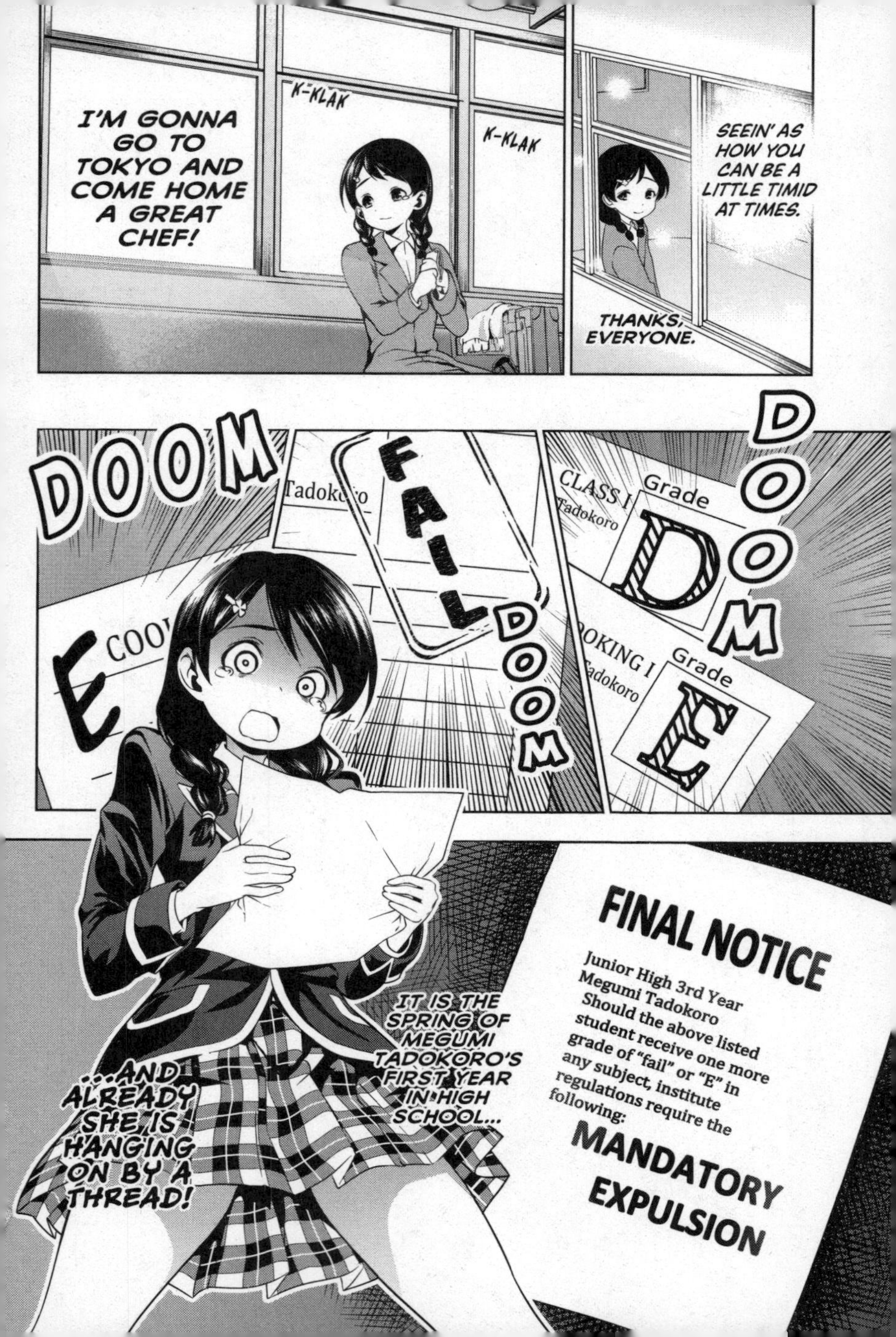

SEEIN' AS HOW YOU CAN BE A LITTLE TIMID AT TIMES.
THANKS, EVERYONE.
K-KLAK
K-KLAK
I'M GONNA GO TO TOKYO AND COME HOME A GREAT CHEF!
DOOM
CLASS I
Tadokoro
Grade
D
DOOM
OOKING I
Tadokoro
Grade
E
FAIL
Tadokoro
DOOM
E
DOOM
FINAL NOTICE
Junior High 3rd Year
Megumi Tadokoro
Should the above listed student receive one more grade of "fail" or "E" in any subject, institute regulations require the following:
MANDATORY EXPULSION
IT IS THE SPRING OF MEGUMI TADOKORO'S FIRST YEAR IN HIGH SCHOOL...
...AND ALREADY SHE IS HANGING ON BY A THREAD!

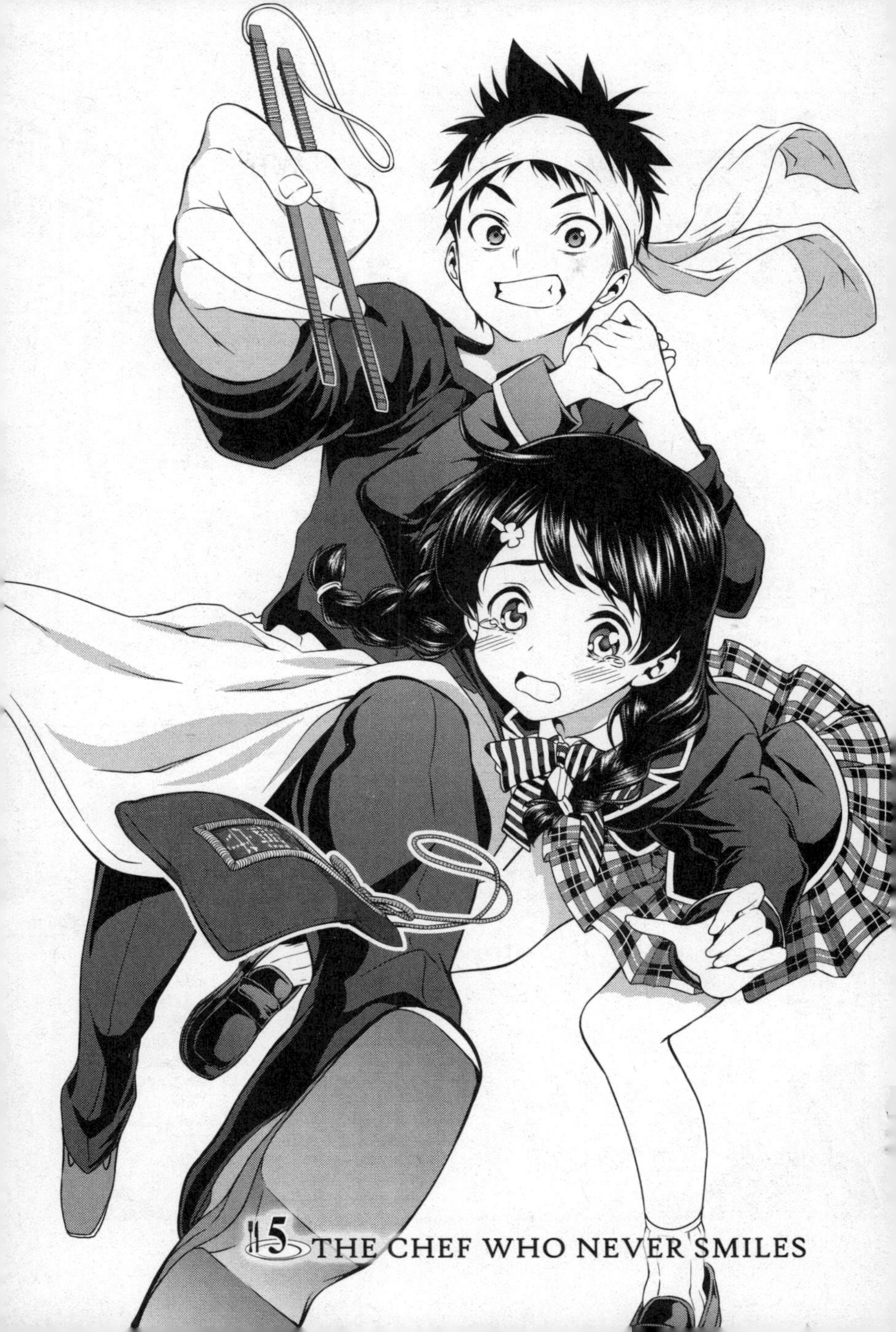

5 THE CHEF WHO NEVER SMILES

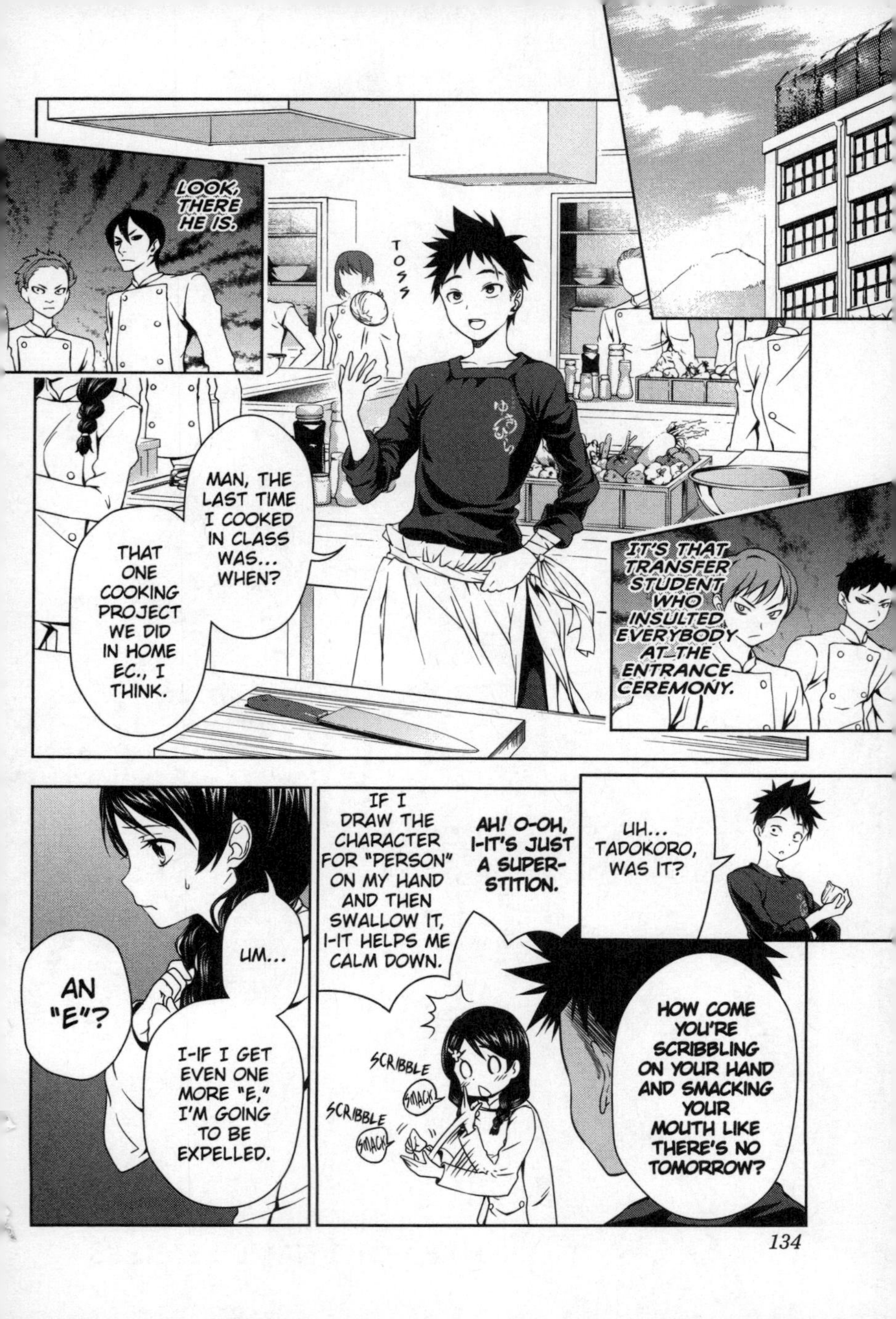
LOOK, THERE HE IS.
TOSS
IT'S THAT TRANSFER STUDENT WHO INSULTED EVERYBODY AT THE ENTRANCE CEREMONY.
MAN, THE LAST TIME I COOKED IN CLASS WAS... WHEN?
THAT ONE COOKING PROJECT WE DID IN HOME EC., I THINK.
UH... TADOKORO, WAS IT?
HOW COME YOU'RE SCRIBBLING ON YOUR HAND AND SMACKING YOUR MOUTH LIKE THERE'S NO TOMORROW?
AH! O-OH, I-IT'S JUST A SUPER-STITION.
IF I DRAW THE CHARACTER FOR "PERSON" ON MY HAND AND THEN SWALLOW IT, I-IT HELPS ME CALM DOWN.
SCRIBBLE
SMACK
SCRIBBLE
SMACK
UM...
I-IF I GET EVEN ONE MORE "E," I'M GOING TO BE EXPELLED.
AN "E"?

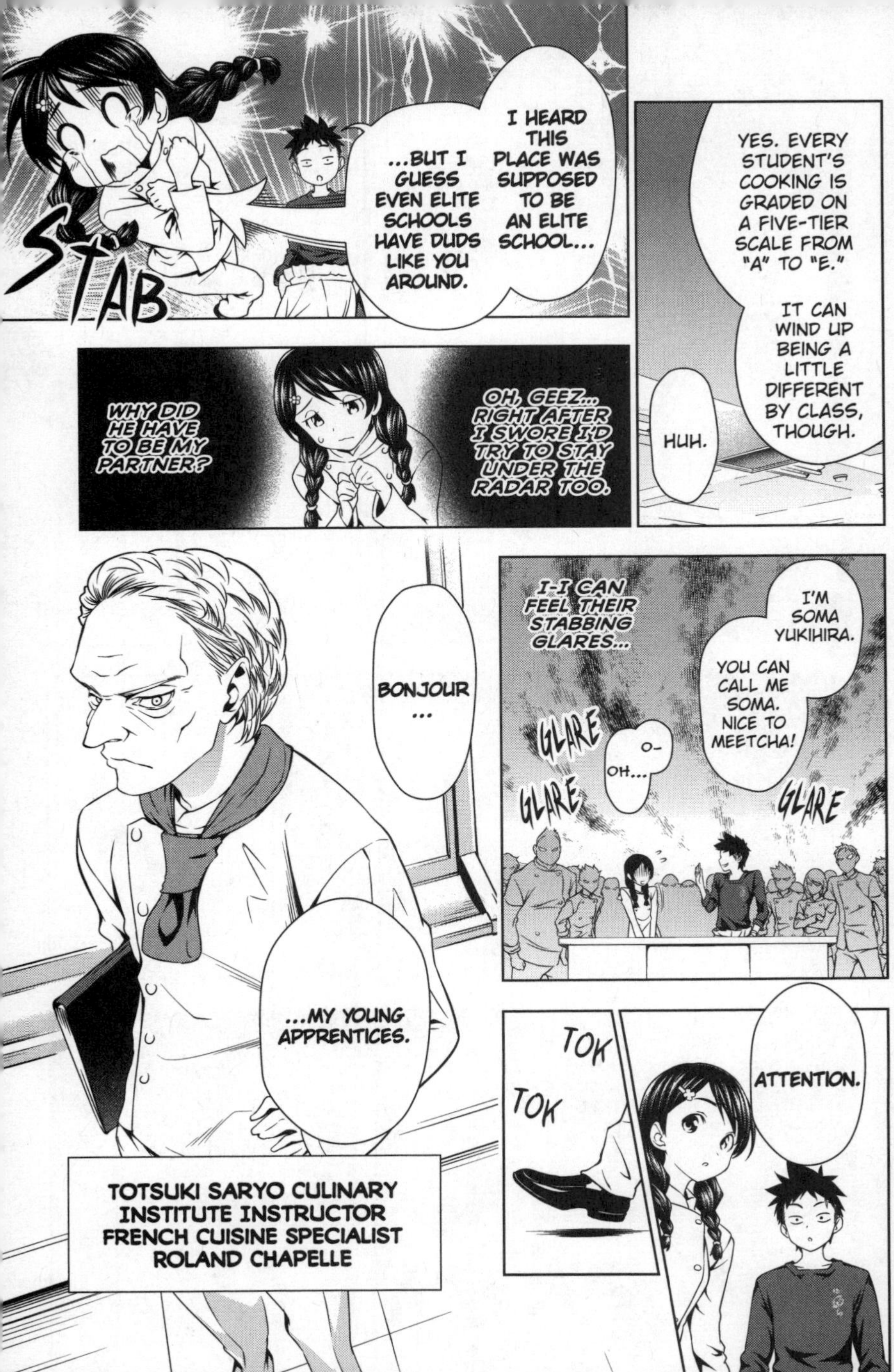
YES. EVERY STUDENT'S COOKING IS GRADED ON A FIVE-TIER SCALE FROM "A" TO "E."
IT CAN WIND UP BEING A LITTLE DIFFERENT BY CLASS, THOUGH.
HUH.
I HEARD THIS PLACE WAS SUPPOSED TO BE AN ELITE SCHOOL...
...BUT I GUESS EVEN ELITE SCHOOLS HAVE DUDS LIKE YOU AROUND.
STAB
OH, GEEZ... RIGHT AFTER I SWORE I'D TRY TO STAY UNDER THE RADAR TOO.
WHY DID HE HAVE TO BE MY PARTNER?
I'M SOMA YUKIHIRA.
YOU CAN CALL ME SOMA. NICE TO MEETCHA!
I-I CAN FEEL THEIR STABBING GLARES...
O- OH...
GLARE
GLARE
GLARE
ATTENTION.
TOK
TOK
BONJOUR...
...MY YOUNG APPRENTICES.
TOTSUKI SARYO CULINARY INSTITUTE INSTRUCTOR FRENCH CUISINE SPECIALIST ROLAND CHAPELLE

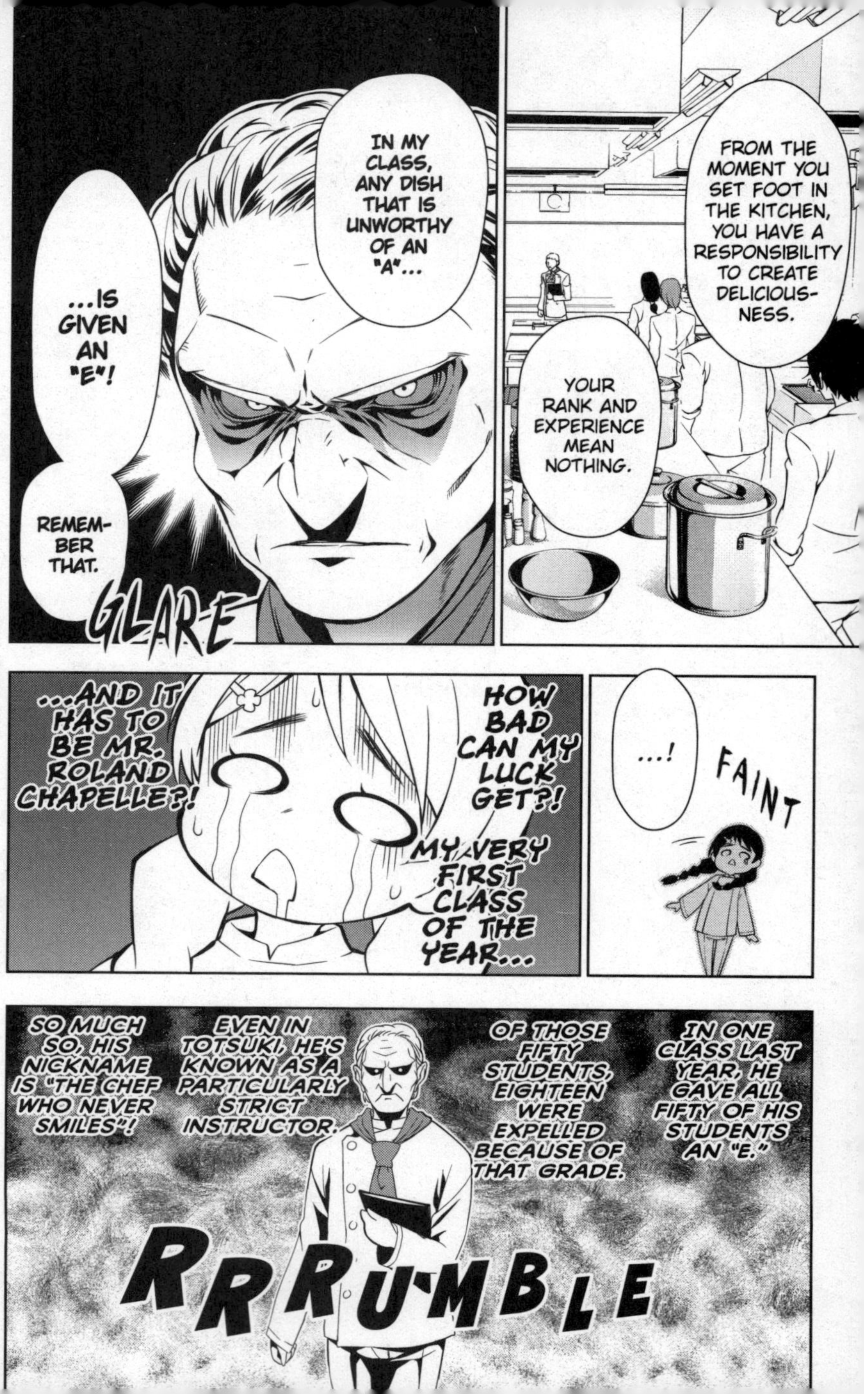
FROM THE MOMENT YOU SET FOOT IN THE KITCHEN, YOU HAVE A RESPONSIBILITY TO CREATE DELICIOUS-NESS.
YOUR RANK AND EXPERIENCE MEAN NOTHING.
IN MY CLASS, ANY DISH THAT IS UNWORTHY OF AN "A"...
...IS GIVEN AN "E"!
REMEM-BER THAT.
GLARE
...!
FAINT
HOW BAD CAN MY LUCK GET?!
...AND IT HAS TO BE MR. ROLAND CHAPELLE?!
MY VERY FIRST CLASS OF THE YEAR...
IN ONE CLASS LAST YEAR, HE GAVE ALL FIFTY OF HIS STUDENTS AN "E."
OF THOSE FIFTY STUDENTS, EIGHTEEN WERE EXPELLED BECAUSE OF THAT GRADE.
EVEN IN TOTSUKI, HE'S KNOWN AS A PARTICULARLY STRICT INSTRUCTOR.
SO MUCH SO, HIS NICKNAME IS "THE CHEF WHO NEVER SMILES"!
RRRUMBLE

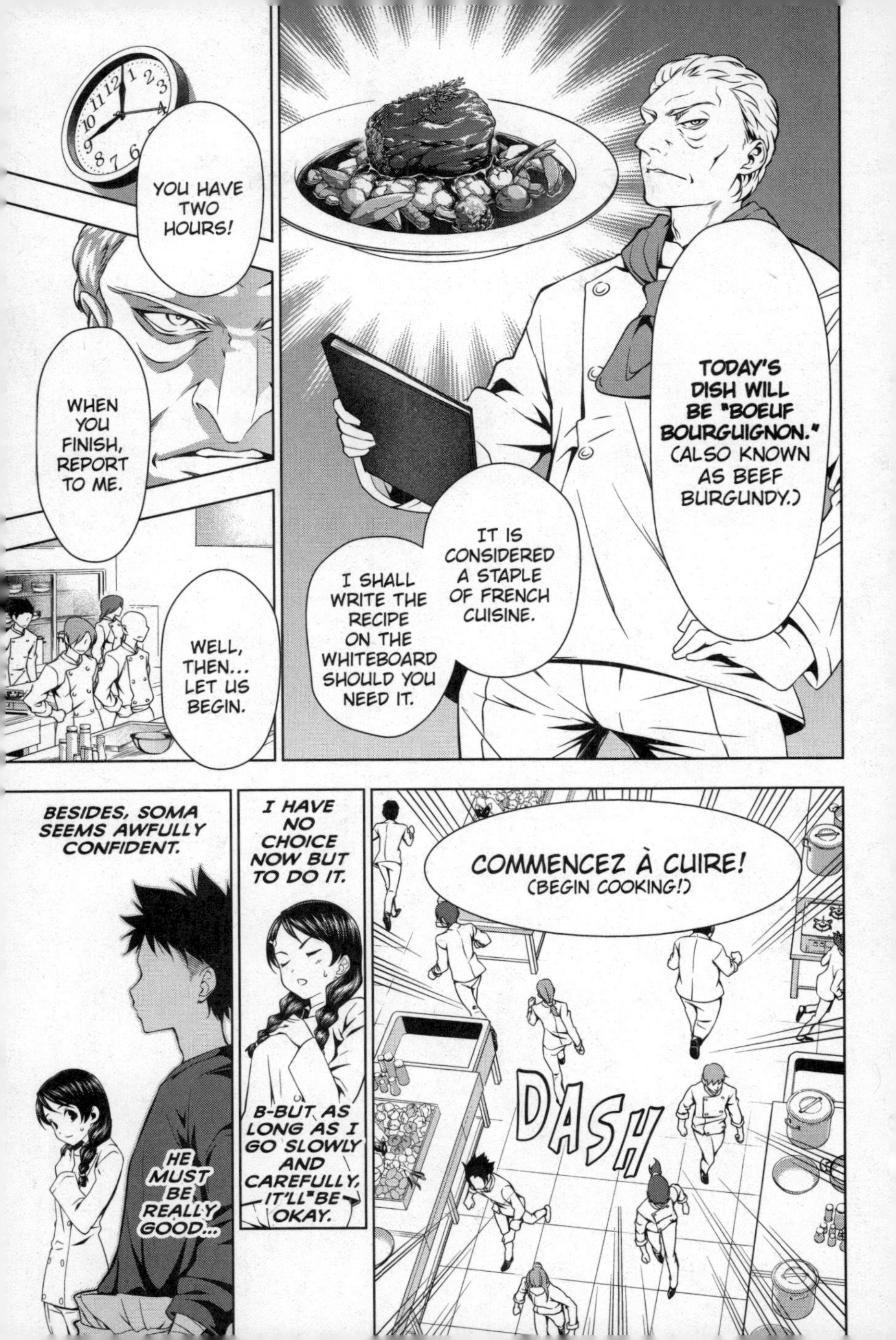
TODAY'S DISH WILL BE "BOEUF BOURGUIGNON." (ALSO KNOWN AS BEEF BURGUNDY.)
IT IS CONSIDERED A STAPLE OF FRENCH CUISINE.
I SHALL WRITE THE RECIPE ON THE WHITEBOARD SHOULD YOU NEED IT.
YOU HAVE TWO HOURS!
WHEN YOU FINISH, REPORT TO ME.
WELL, THEN... LET US BEGIN.
COMMENCEZ À CUIRE! (BEGIN COOKING!)
DASH
I HAVE NO CHOICE NOW BUT TO DO IT.
B-BUT AS LONG AS I GO SLOWLY AND CAREFULLY, IT'LL BE OKAY.
BESIDES, SOMA SEEMS AWFULLY CONFIDENT.
HE MUST BE REALLY GOOD...

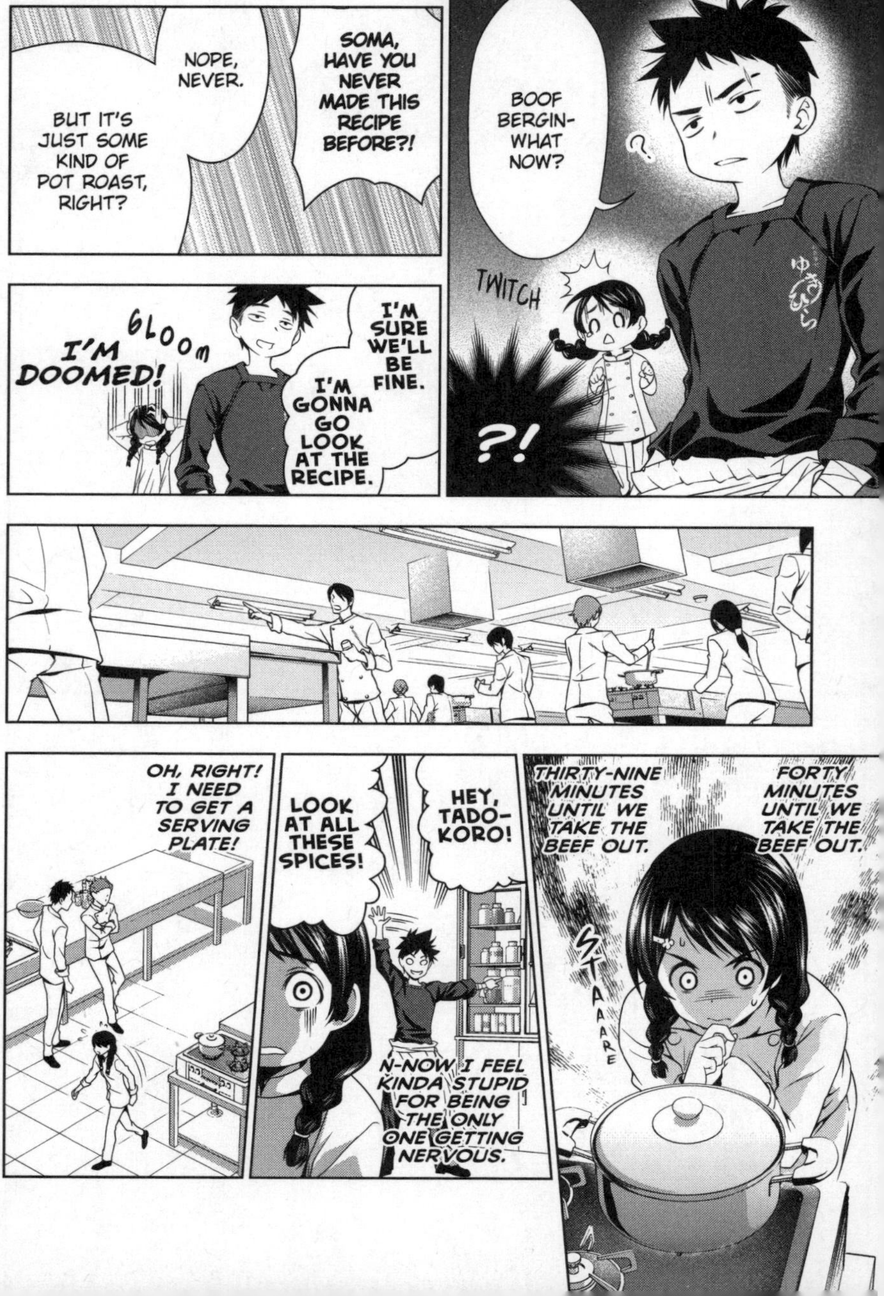
BOOF BERGIN-WHAT NOW?
?
TWITCH
?!
SOMA, HAVE YOU NEVER MADE THIS RECIPE BEFORE?!
NOPE, NEVER.
BUT IT'S JUST SOME KIND OF POT ROAST, RIGHT?
I'M SURE WE'LL BE FINE.
I'M GONNA GO LOOK AT THE RECIPE.
GLOOM
I'M DOOMED!
FORTY MINUTES UNTIL WE TAKE THE BEEF OUT.
THIRTY-NINE MINUTES UNTIL WE TAKE THE BEEF OUT.
STAAARE
HEY, TADOKORO!
LOOK AT ALL THESE SPICES!
N-NOW I FEEL KINDA STUPID FOR BEING THE ONLY ONE GETTING NERVOUS.
OH, RIGHT! I NEED TO GET A SERVING PLATE!

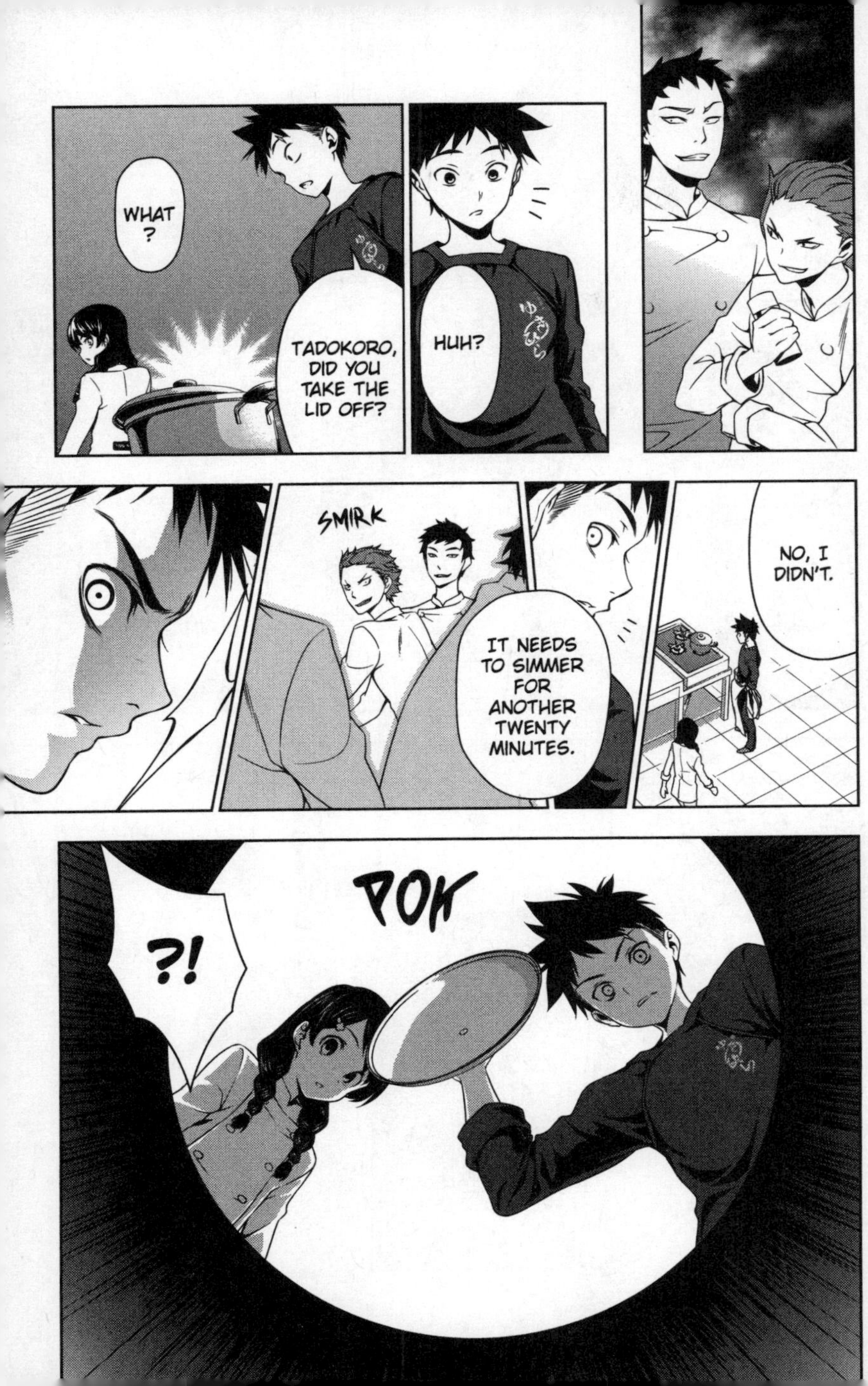
HUH?
TADOKORO, DID YOU TAKE THE LID OFF?
WHAT?
NO, I DIDN'T.
IT NEEDS TO SIMMER FOR ANOTHER TWENTY MINUTES.
SMIRK
POK
?!

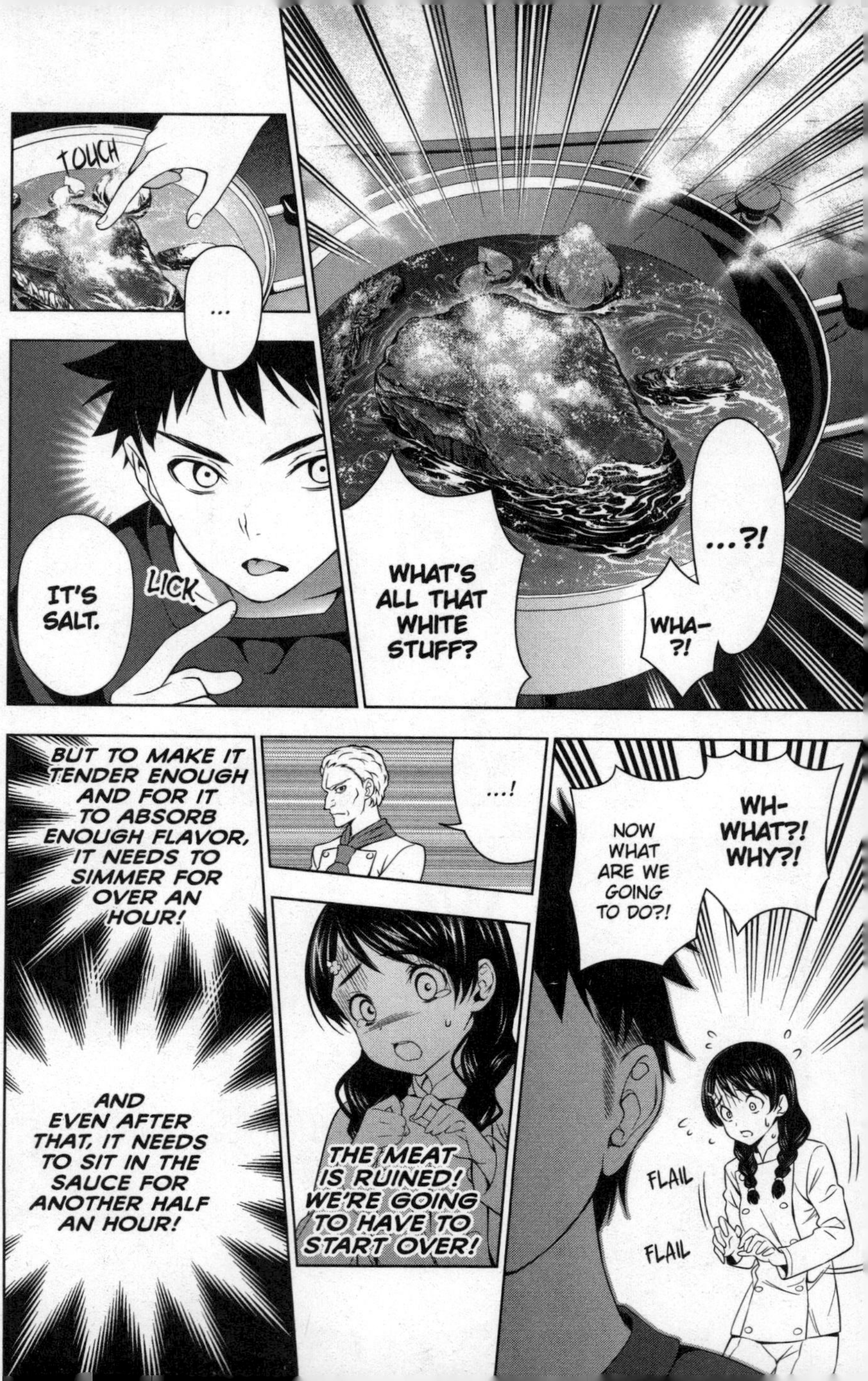
...?!
WHA- ?!
WHAT'S ALL THAT WHITE STUFF?
TOUCH
...
LICK
IT'S SALT.
WH- WHAT?! WHY?!
NOW WHAT ARE WE GOING TO DO?!
FLAIL
FLAIL
...!
THE MEAT IS RUINED! WE'RE GOING TO HAVE TO START OVER!
BUT TO MAKE IT TENDER ENOUGH AND FOR IT TO ABSORB ENOUGH FLAVOR, IT NEEDS TO SIMMER FOR OVER AN HOUR!
AND EVEN AFTER THAT, IT NEEDS TO SIT IN THE SAUCE FOR ANOTHER HALF AN HOUR!

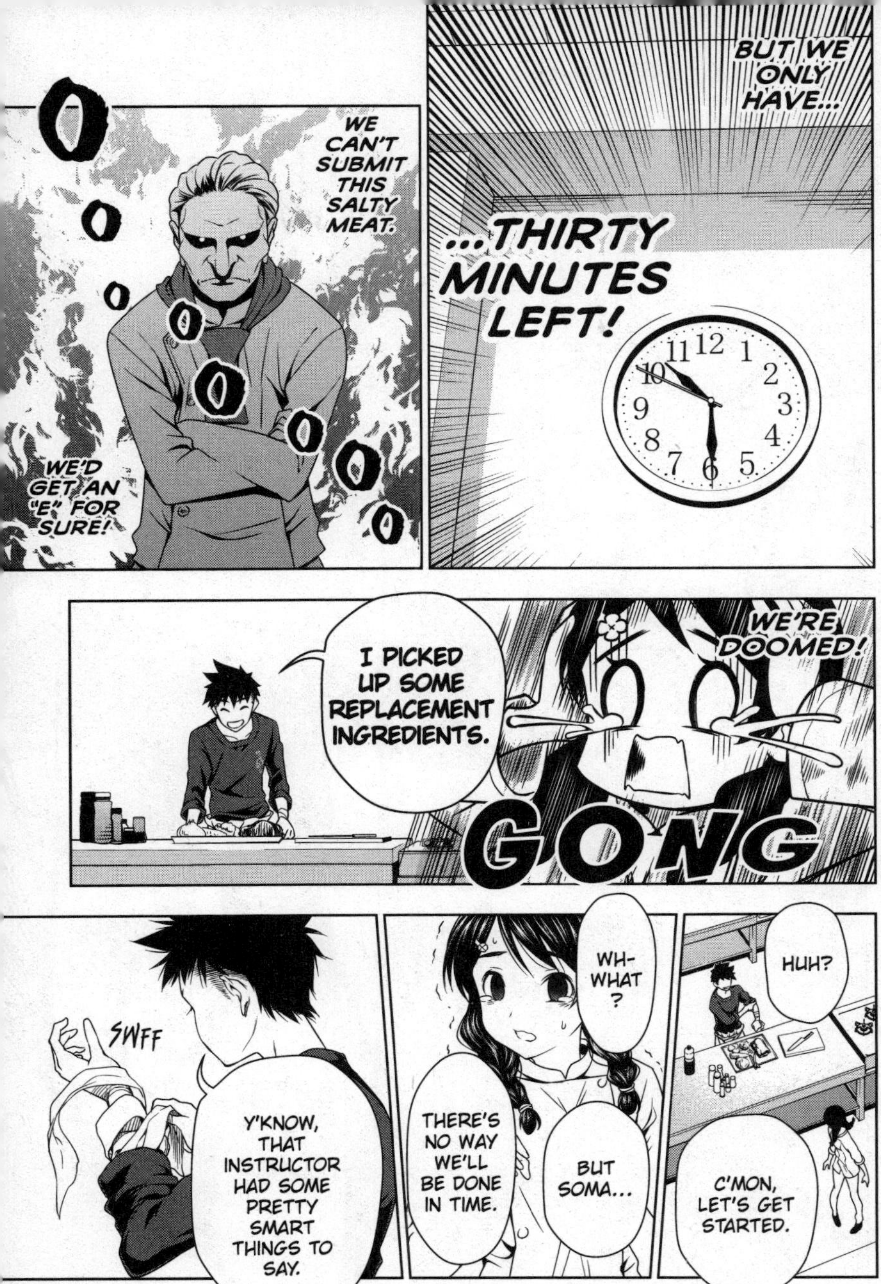
BUT WE ONLY HAVE...
...THIRTY MINUTES LEFT!
WE CAN'T SUBMIT THIS SALTY MEAT.
WE'D GET AN "E" FOR SURE!
WE'RE DOOMED!
GONG
I PICKED UP SOME REPLACEMENT INGREDIENTS.
HUH?
C'MON, LET'S GET STARTED.
WH-WHAT?
BUT SOMA...
THERE'S NO WAY WE'LL BE DONE IN TIME.
SWFF
Y'KNOW, THAT INSTRUCTOR HAD SOME PRETTY SMART THINGS TO SAY.

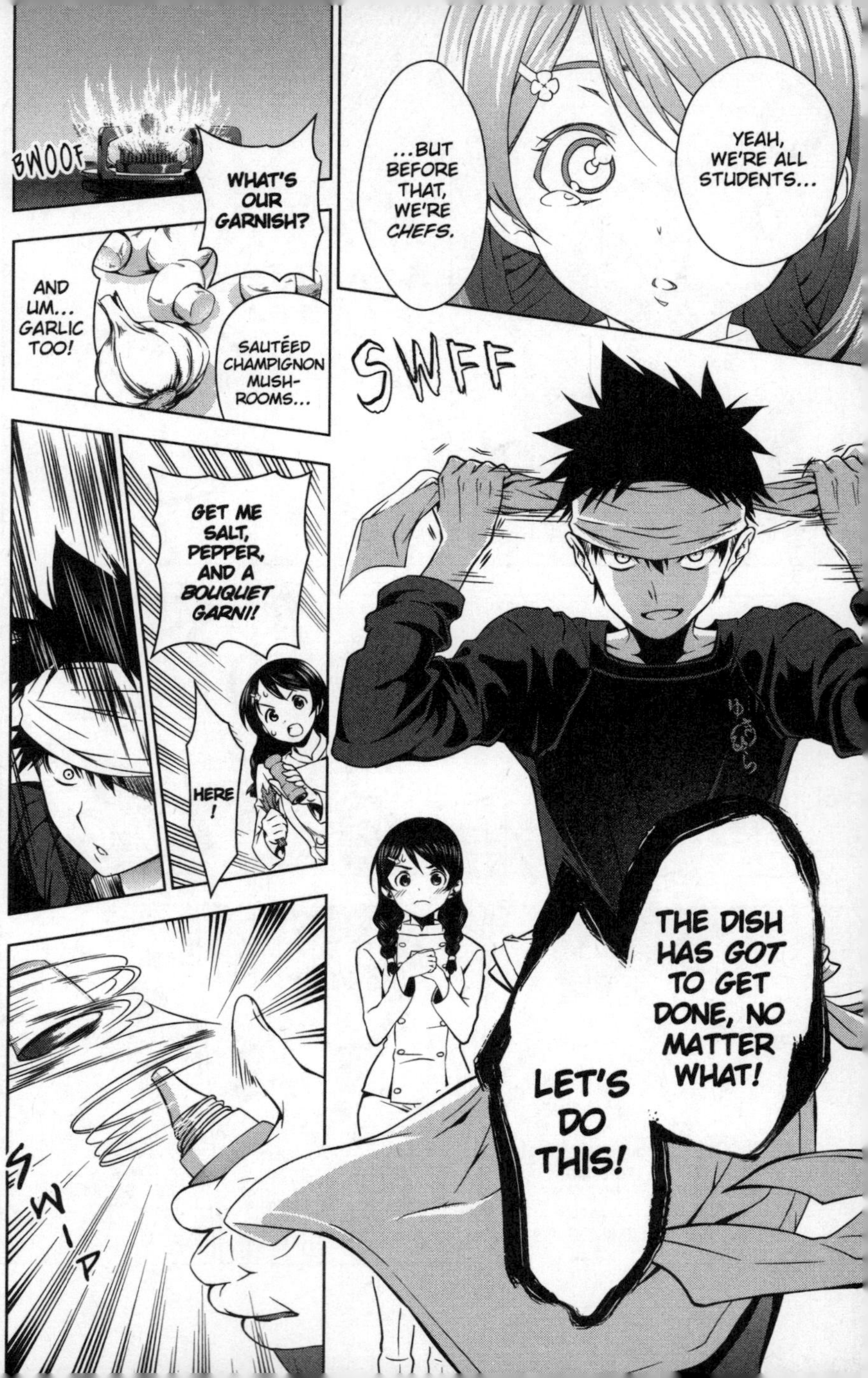
YEAH, WE'RE ALL STUDENTS...
...BUT BEFORE THAT, WE'RE *CHEFS.*
SWFF
THE DISH HAS *GOT* TO GET DONE, NO MATTER WHAT!
LET'S DO THIS!
BWOOF
WHAT'S OUR GARNISH?
SAUTÉED CHAMPIGNON MUSH-ROOMS...
AND UM... GARLIC TOO!
GET ME SALT, PEPPER, AND A *BOUQUET GARNI!!*
HERE!
SWIP

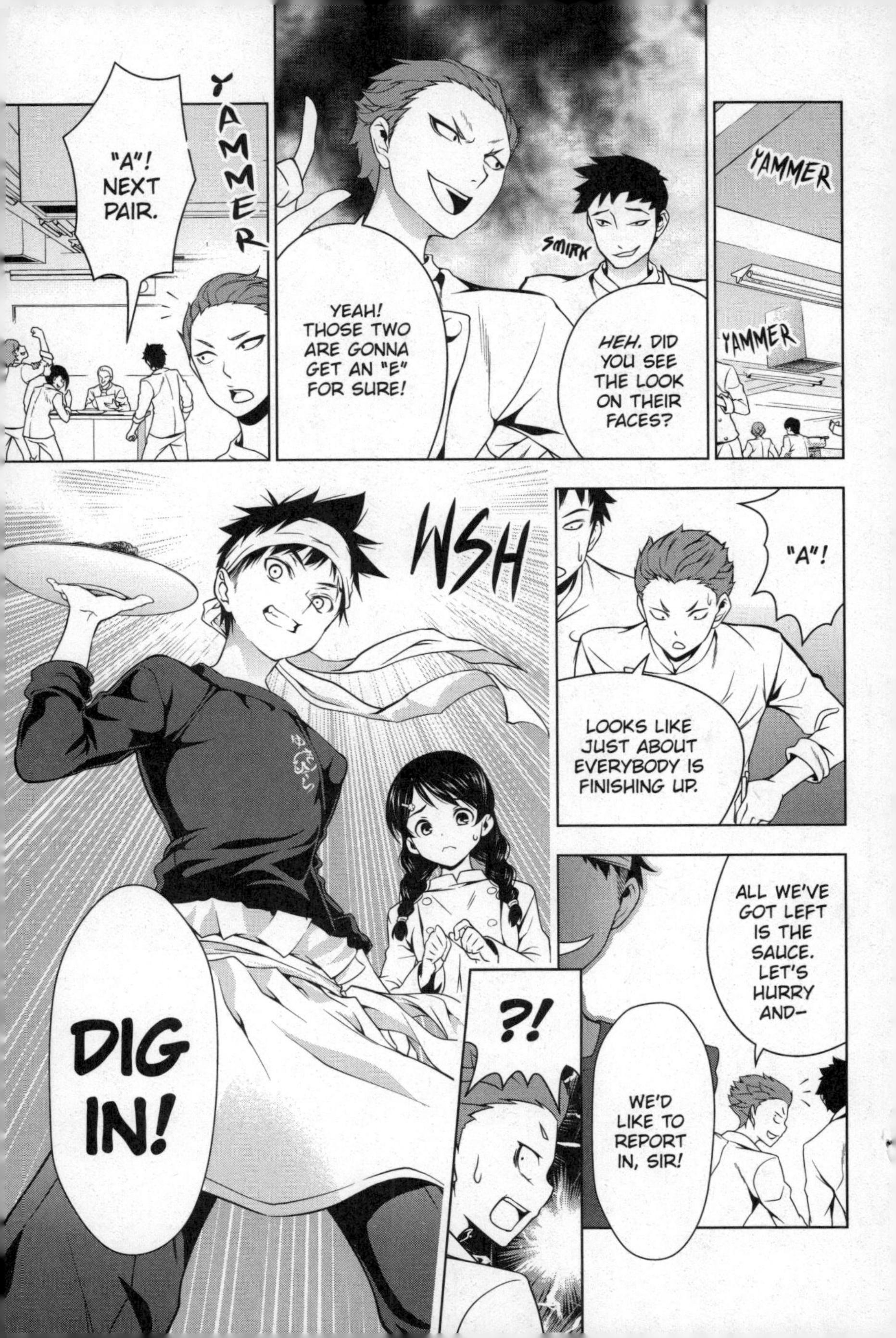
YAMMER
YAMMER
SMIRK
HEH. DID YOU SEE THE LOOK ON THEIR FACES?
YEAH! THOSE TWO ARE GONNA GET AN "E" FOR SURE!
YAMMER
"A"! NEXT PAIR.
"A"!
LOOKS LIKE JUST ABOUT EVERYBODY IS FINISHING UP.
ALL WE'VE GOT LEFT IS THE SAUCE. LET'S HURRY AND-
WE'D LIKE TO REPORT IN, SIR!
?!
WSH
DIG IN!

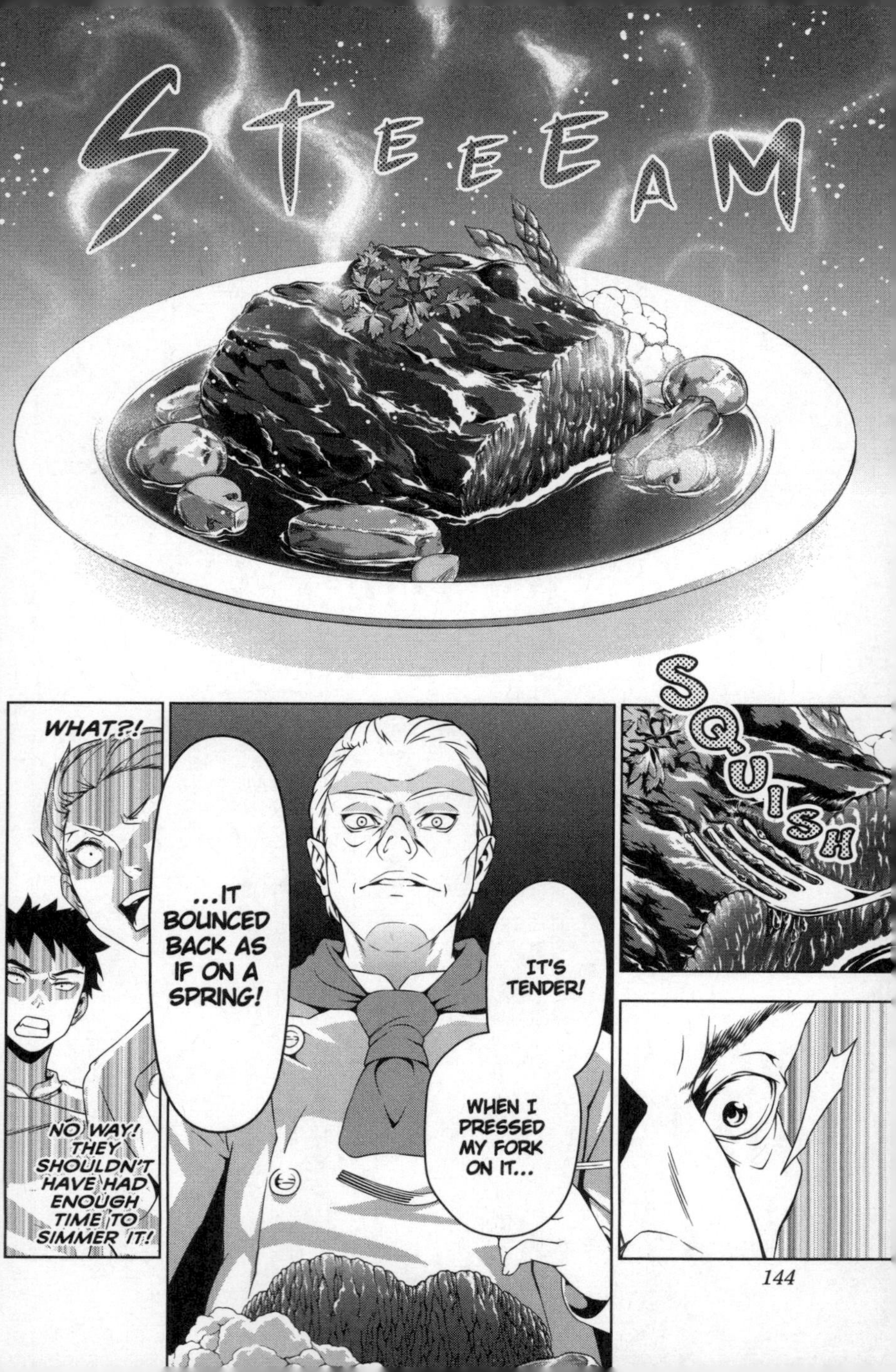
STEEEAM
SQUISH
IT'S TENDER!
WHEN I PRESSED MY FORK ON IT...
...IT BOUNCED BACK AS IF ON A SPRING!
WHAT?!
NO WAY! THEY SHOULDN'T HAVE HAD ENOUGH TIME TO SIMMER IT!

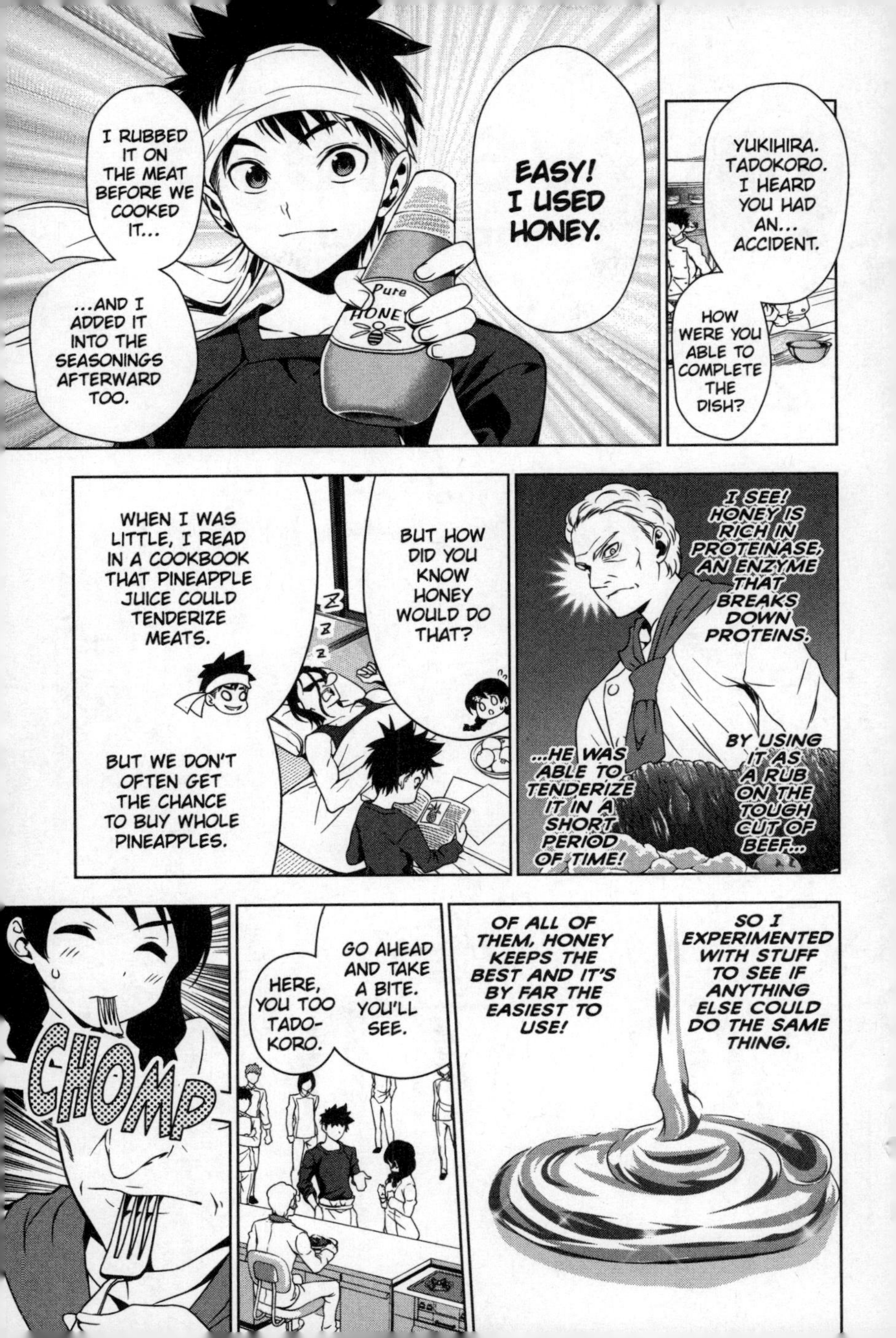
YUKIHIRA. TADOKORO. I HEARD YOU HAD AN... ACCIDENT.
HOW WERE YOU ABLE TO COMPLETE THE DISH?
EASY! I USED HONEY.
Pure HONEY
I RUBBED IT ON THE MEAT BEFORE WE COOKED IT...
...AND I ADDED IT INTO THE SEASONINGS AFTERWARD TOO.
I SEE! HONEY IS RICH IN PROTEINASE, AN ENZYME THAT BREAKS DOWN PROTEINS.
BY USING IT AS A RUB ON THE TOUGH CUT OF BEEF...
...HE WAS ABLE TO TENDERIZE IT IN A SHORT PERIOD OF TIME!
BUT HOW DID YOU KNOW HONEY WOULD DO THAT?
WHEN I WAS LITTLE, I READ IN A COOKBOOK THAT PINEAPPLE JUICE COULD TENDERIZE MEATS.
BUT WE DON'T OFTEN GET THE CHANCE TO BUY WHOLE PINEAPPLES.
SO I EXPERIMENTED WITH STUFF TO SEE IF ANYTHING ELSE COULD DO THE SAME THING.
OF ALL OF THEM, HONEY KEEPS THE BEST AND IT'S BY FAR THE EASIEST TO USE!
GO AHEAD AND TAKE A BITE. YOU'LL SEE.
HERE, YOU TOO TADOKORO.
CHOMP

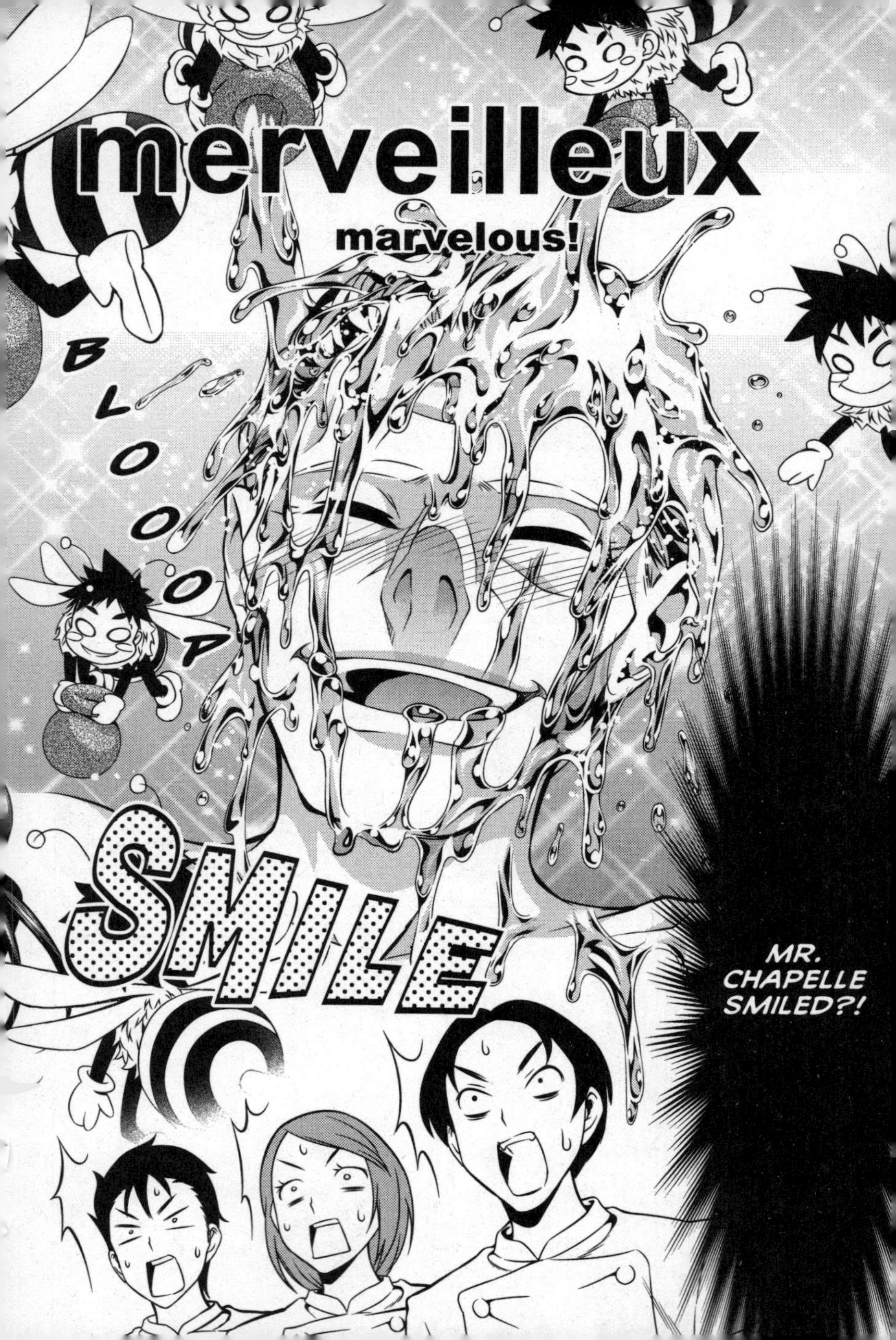
merveilleux
marvelous!
BLOOOOP
SMILE
MR. CHAPELLE SMILED?!

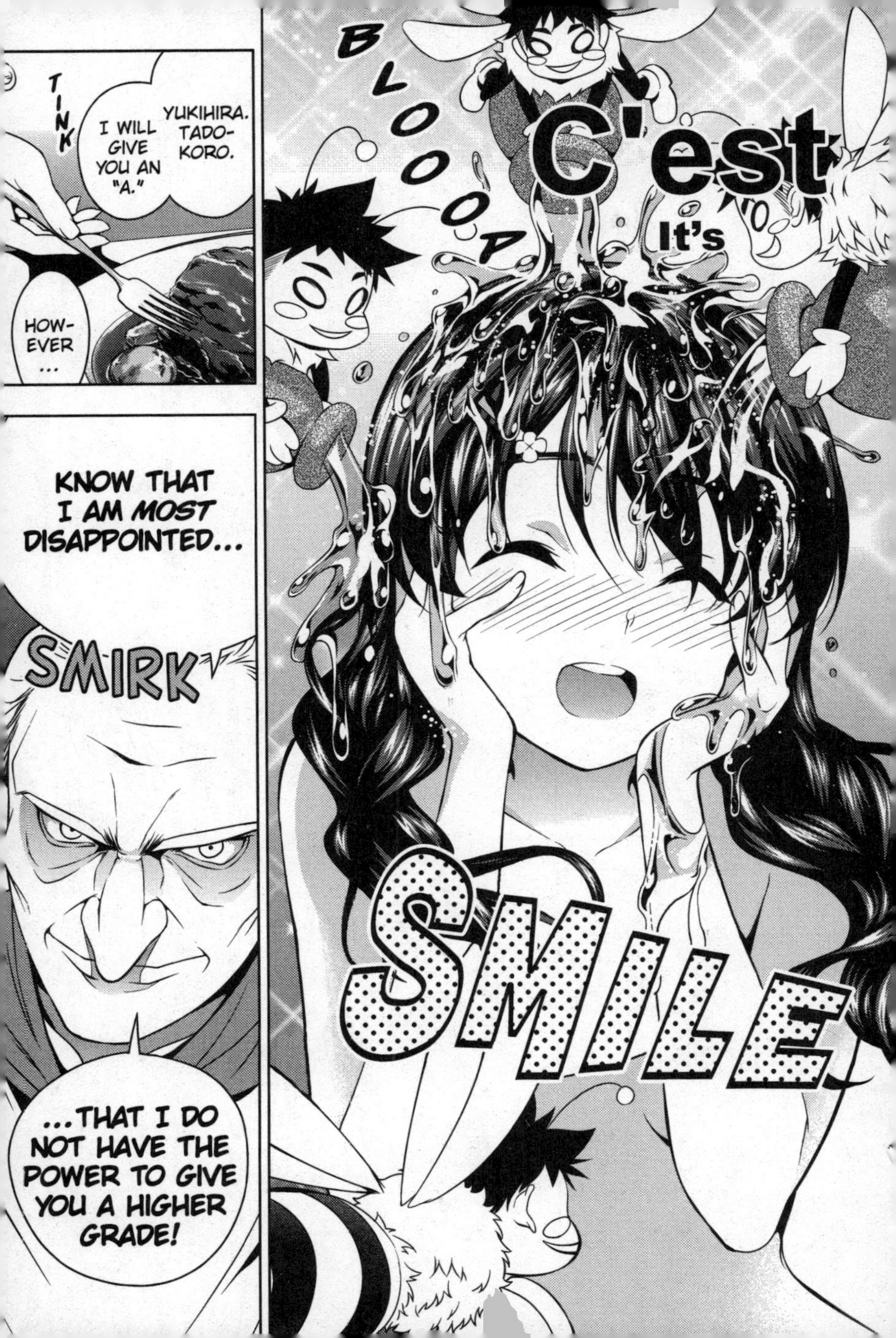
C'est
It's
BLOOOP
SMILE
YUKIHIRA. TADOKORO.
I WILL GIVE YOU AN "A."
TINK
HOWEVER...
KNOW THAT I AM *MOST* DISAPPOINTED...
SMIRK
...THAT I DO NOT HAVE THE POWER TO GIVE YOU A HIGHER GRADE!

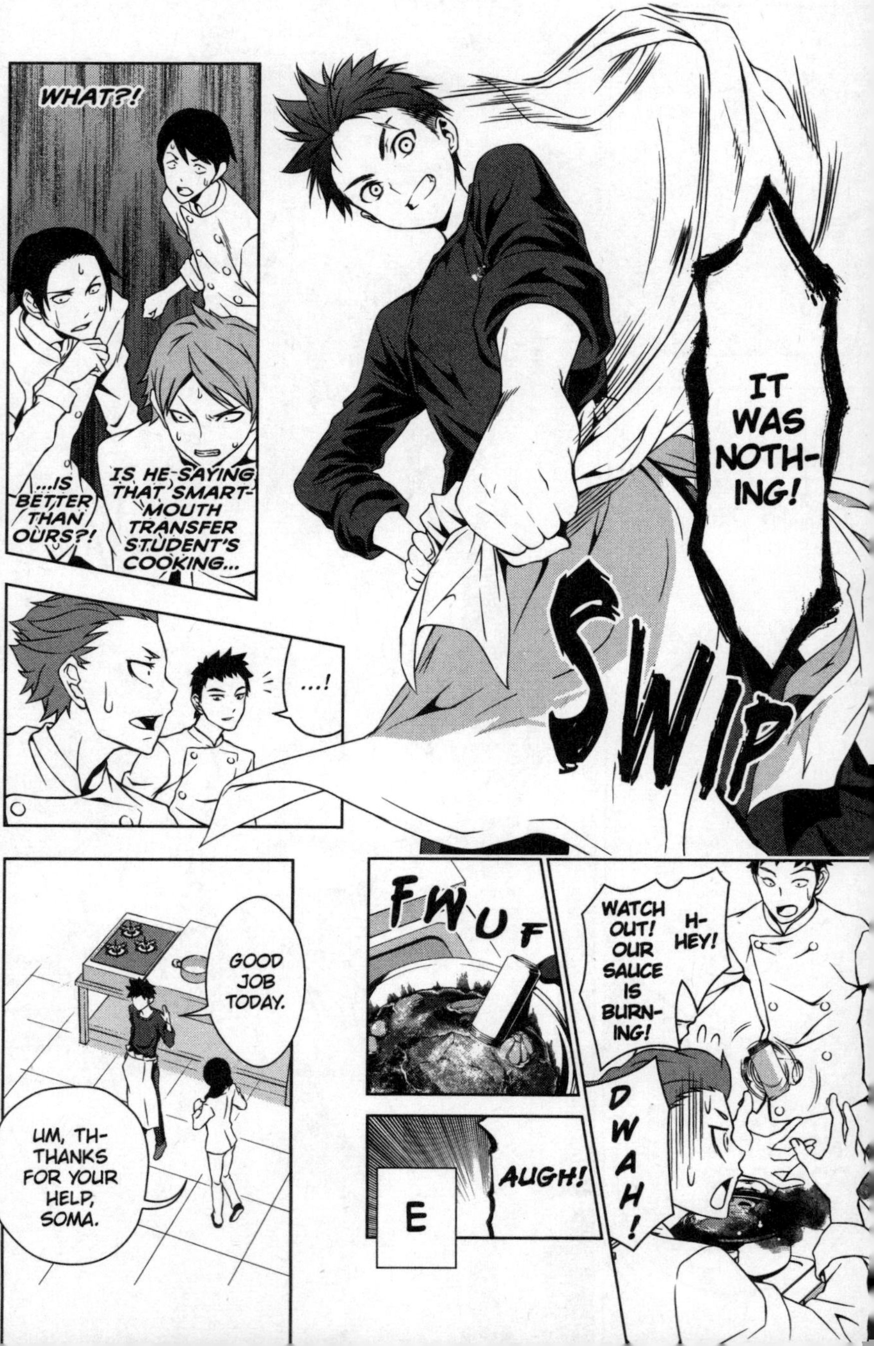
IT WAS NOTHING!
SWIP
WHAT?!
IS HE SAYING THAT SMART-MOUTH TRANSFER STUDENT'S COOKING...
...IS BETTER THAN OURS?!
...!
H-HEY!
WATCH OUT! OUR SAUCE IS BURNING!
DWAH!
FWUF
AUGH!
E
GOOD JOB TODAY.
UM, TH-THANKS FOR YOUR HELP, SOMA.

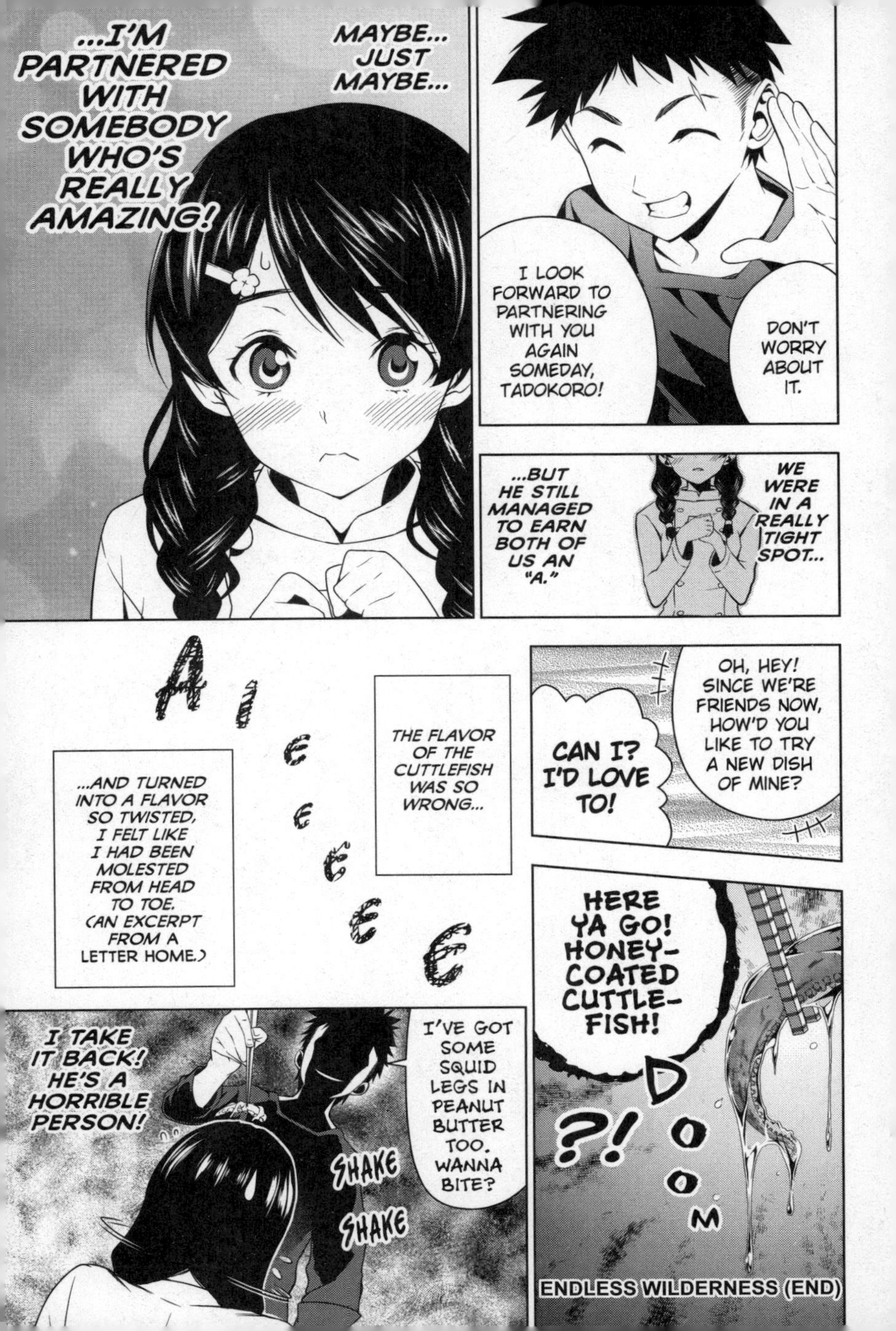
DON'T WORRY ABOUT IT.
I LOOK FORWARD TO PARTNERING WITH YOU AGAIN SOMEDAY, TADOKORO!
WE WERE IN A REALLY TIGHT SPOT...
...BUT HE STILL MANAGED TO EARN BOTH OF US AN "A."
MAYBE... JUST MAYBE...
...I'M PARTNERED WITH SOMEBODY WHO'S REALLY AMAZING!
OH, HEY! SINCE WE'RE FRIENDS NOW, HOW'D YOU LIKE TO TRY A NEW DISH OF MINE?
CAN I? I'D LOVE TO!
HERE YA GO! HONEY-COATED CUTTLE-FISH!
?!
DOOOM
ENDLESS WILDERNESS (END)
AIEEEEE
THE FLAVOR OF THE CUTTLEFISH WAS SO WRONG...
...AND TURNED INTO A FLAVOR SO TWISTED, I FELT LIKE I HAD BEEN MOLESTED FROM HEAD TO TOE. (AN EXCERPT FROM A LETTER HOME.)
I'VE GOT SOME SQUID LEGS IN PEANUT BUTTER TOO. WANNA BITE?
SHAKE
SHAKE
I TAKE IT BACK! HE'S A HORRIBLE PERSON!

ON THE NEXT PAGE, THE ONE-SHOT VERSION OF *FOOD WARS!: SHOKUGEKI NO SOMA* BEGINS. THIS VERSION ORIGINALLY RAN IN THE *JUMP NEXT!* 2012 SPRING EDITION. THINK OF IT AS THE PROTOTYPE TO TODAY'S *FOOD WARS.* I HOPE YOU ENJOY SPOTTING THE LITTLE DIFFERENCES IN THE CHARACTERS AND SETTINGS IN THIS OLDER VERSION. DIG IN!

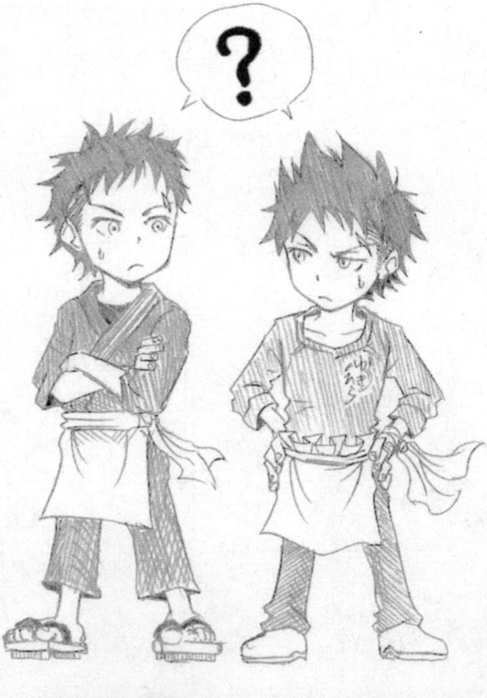
?

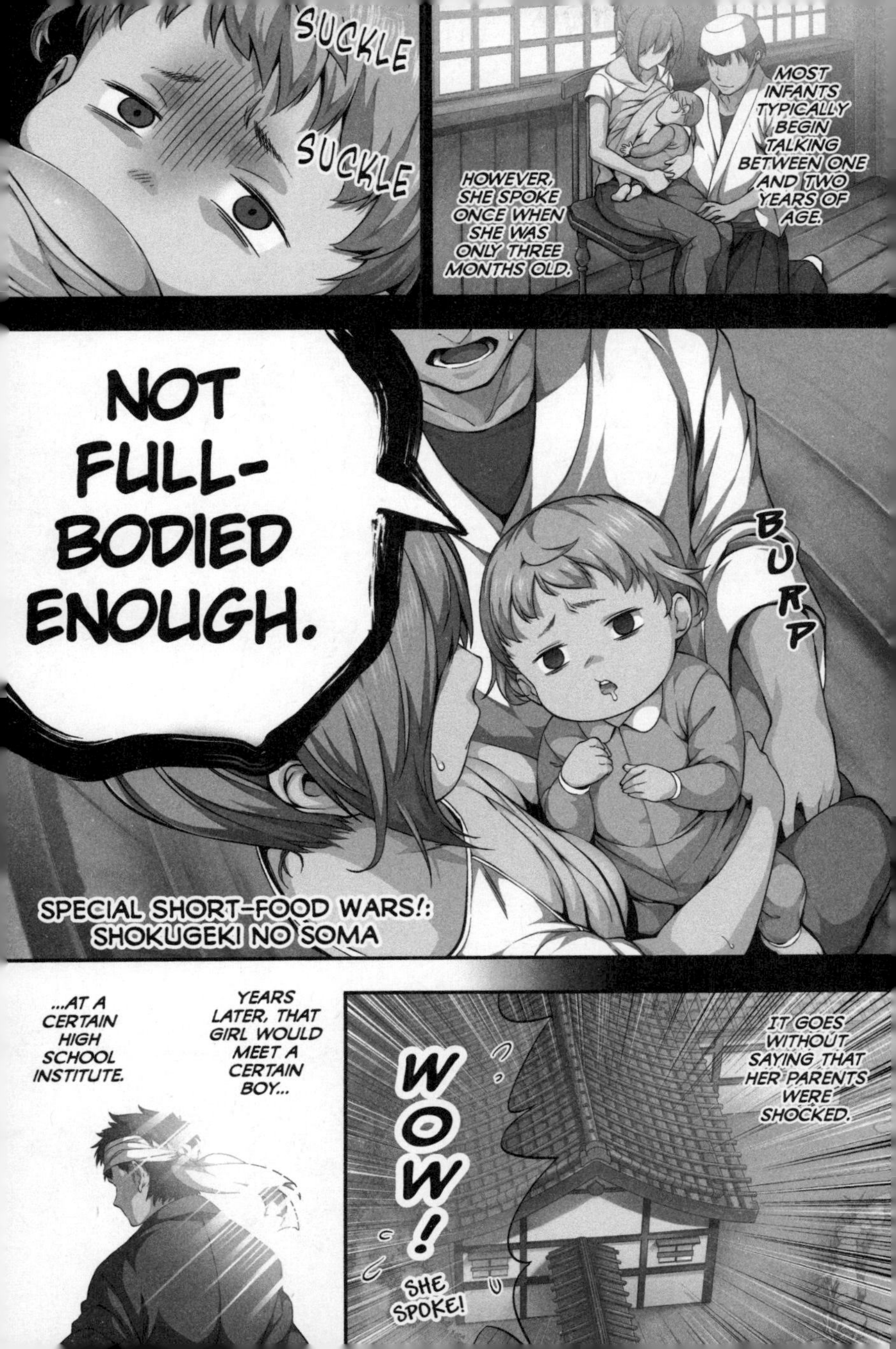

MOST INFANTS TYPICALLY BEGIN TALKING BETWEEN ONE AND TWO YEARS OF AGE.
HOWEVER, SHE SPOKE ONCE WHEN SHE WAS ONLY THREE MONTHS OLD.
SUCKLE
SUCKLE
BURP
NOT FULL-BODIED ENOUGH.
SPECIAL SHORT–FOOD WARS!: SHOKUGEKI NO SOMA
IT GOES WITHOUT SAYING THAT HER PARENTS WERE SHOCKED.
WOW!
SHE SPOKE!
YEARS LATER, THAT GIRL WOULD MEET A CERTAIN BOY...
...AT A CERTAIN HIGH SCHOOL INSTITUTE.

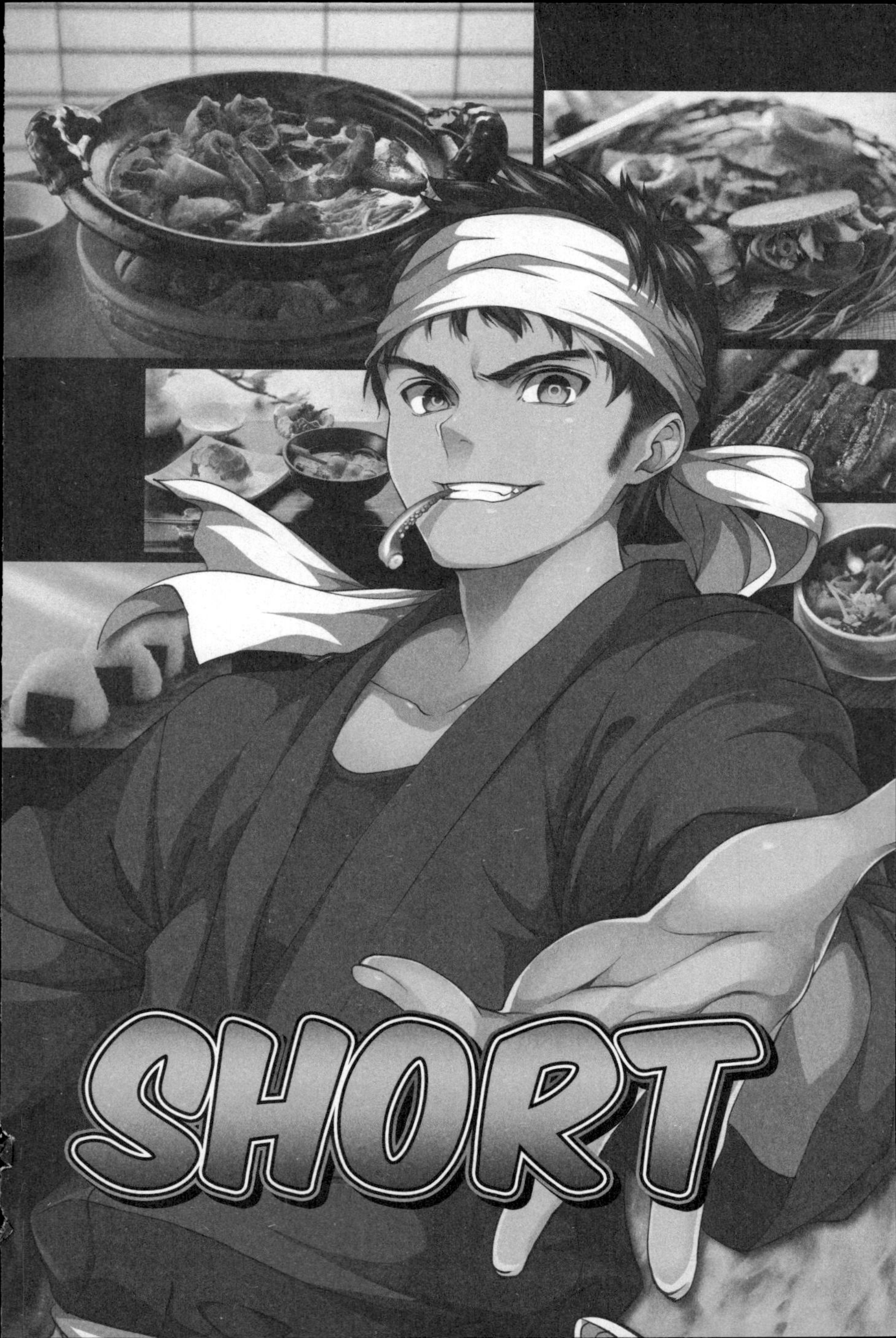
SHORT

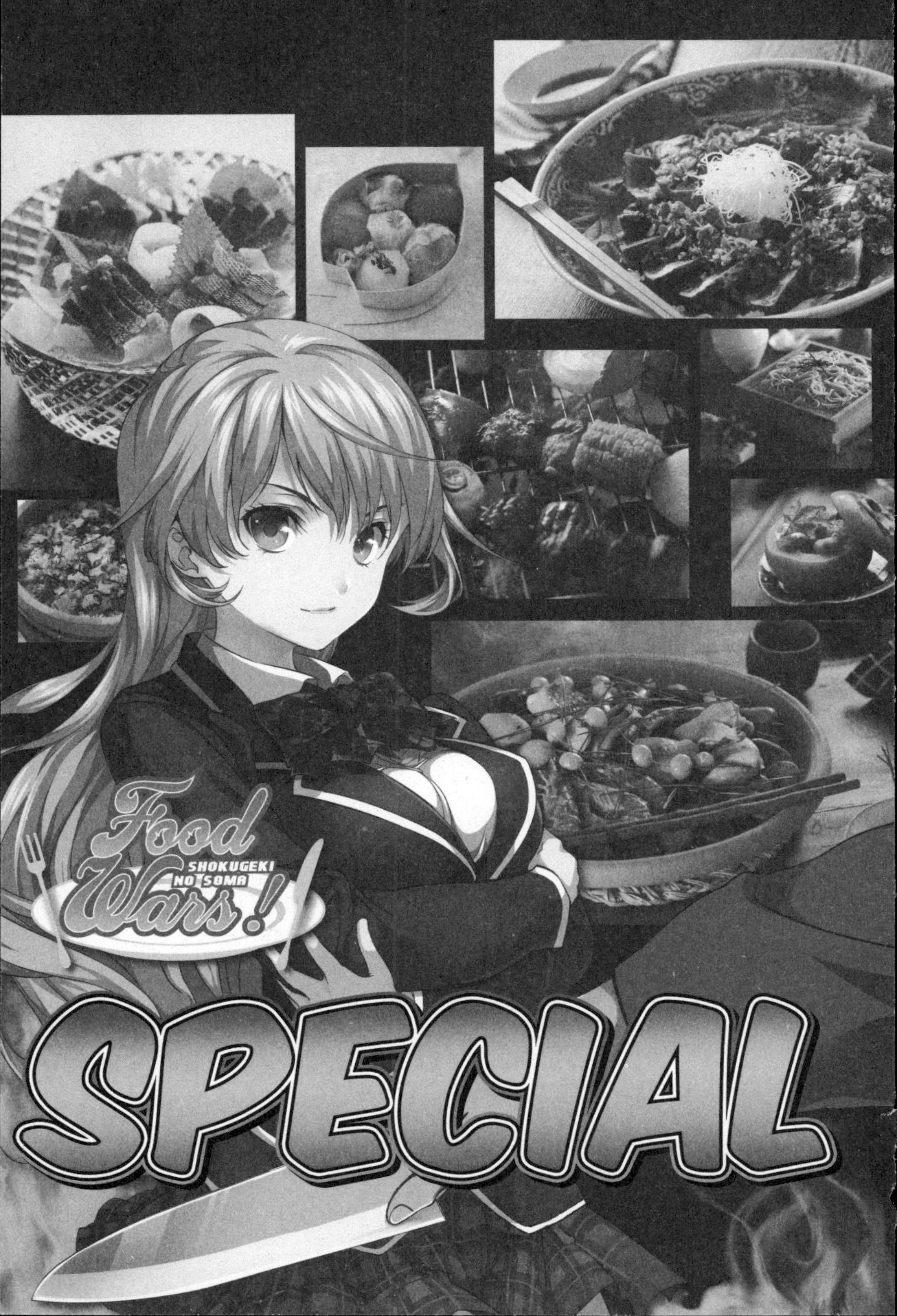
Food Wars!
SHOKUGEKI NO SOMA
SPECIAL

Food Wars!

SHOKUGEKI NO SOMA

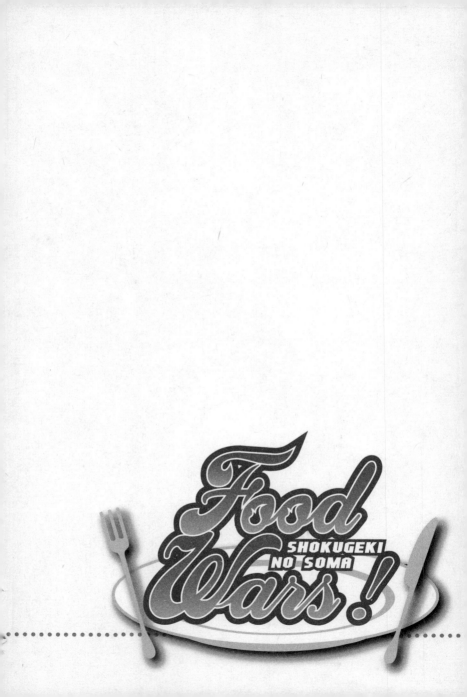

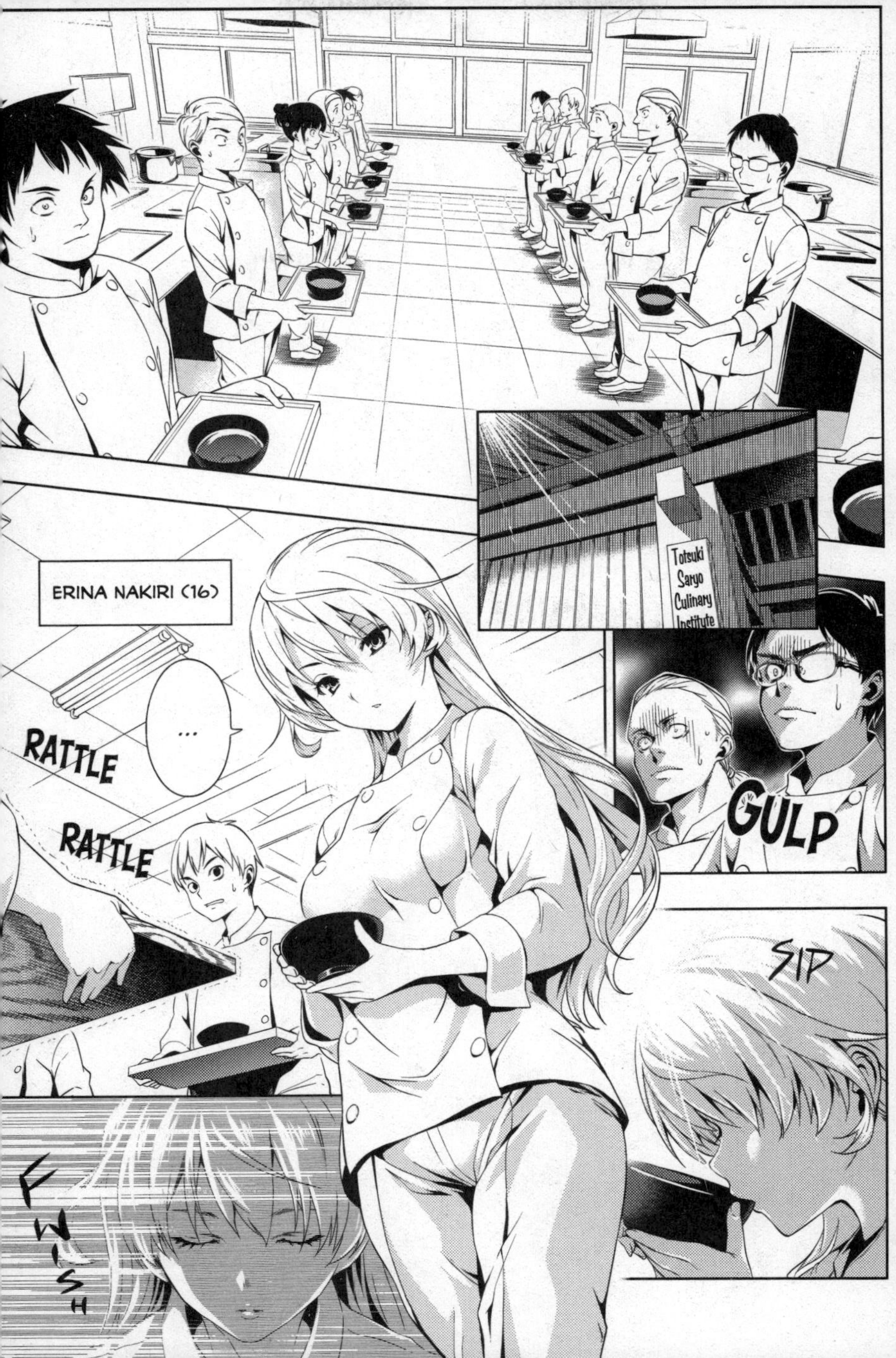

Totsuki Saryo Culinary Institute
GULP
SIP
ERINA NAKIRI (16)
...
RATTLE
RATTLE
FWISH

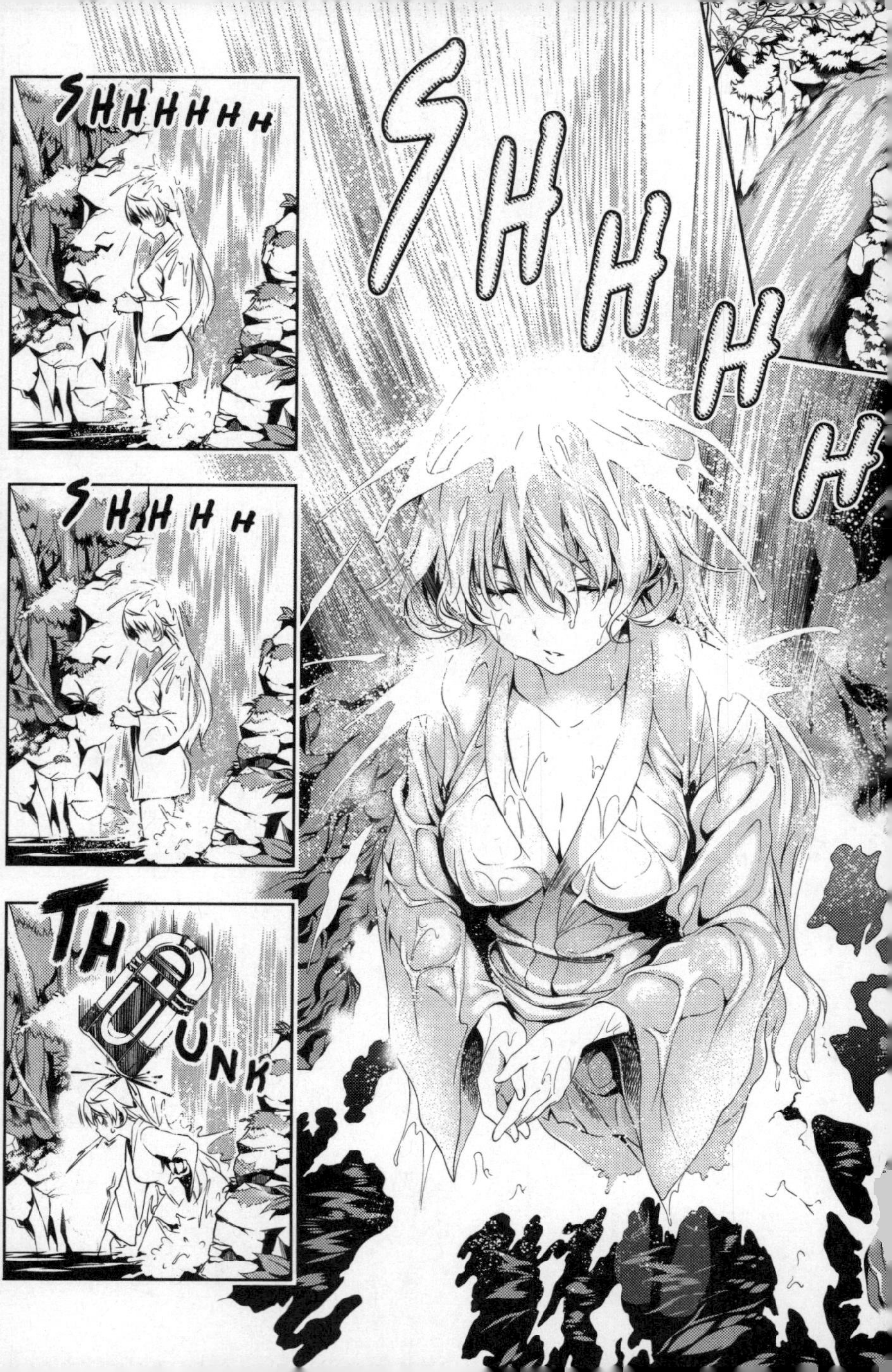
SHHHHHH
SHHHHHHH
SHHHHH
THUNK

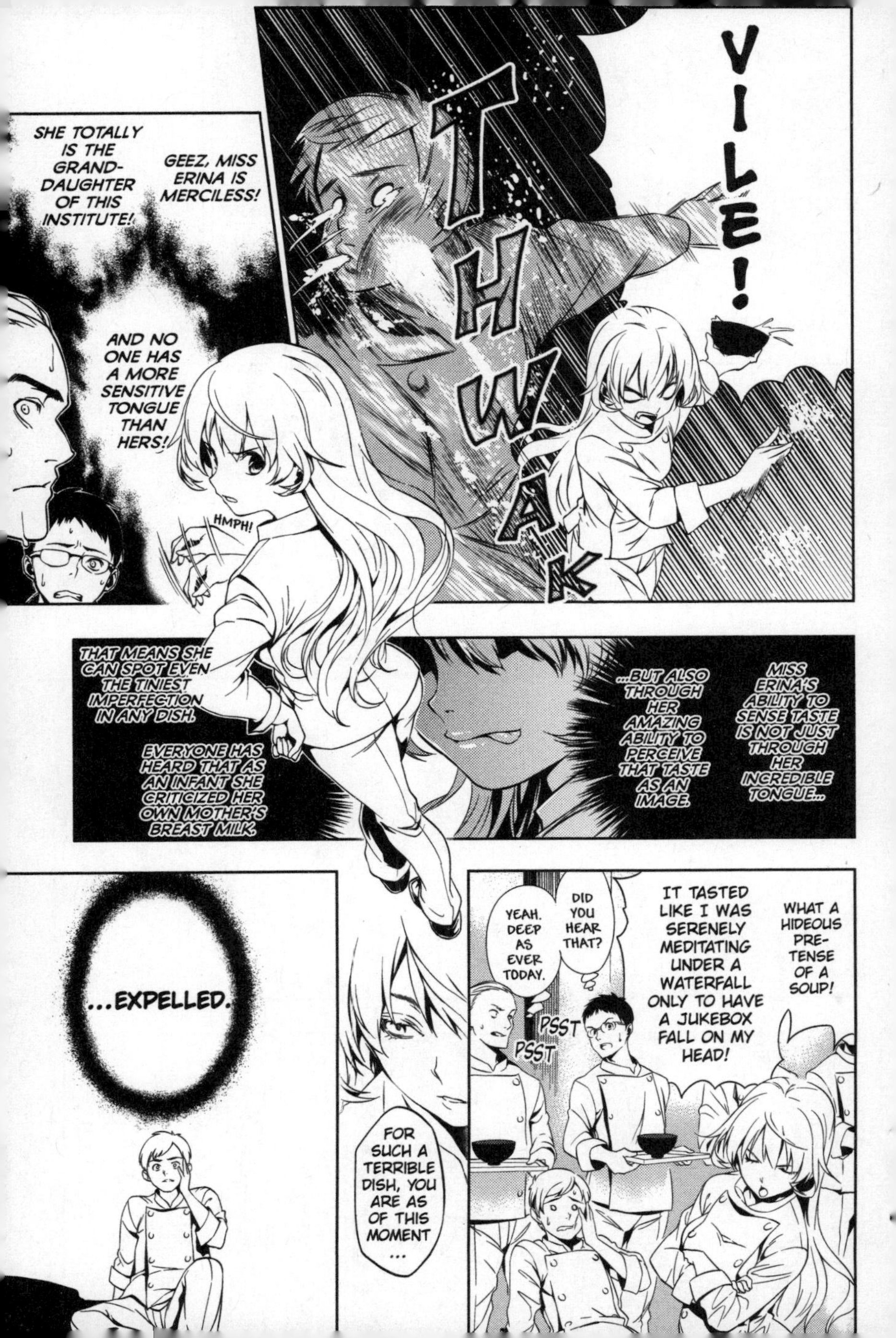
VILE!
THWAK
GEEZ, MISS ERINA IS MERCILESS!
SHE TOTALLY IS THE GRAND-DAUGHTER OF THIS INSTITUTE!
AND NO ONE HAS A MORE SENSITIVE TONGUE THAN HERS!
HMPH!
MISS ERINA'S ABILITY TO SENSE TASTE IS NOT JUST THROUGH HER INCREDIBLE TONGUE...
...BUT ALSO THROUGH HER AMAZING ABILITY TO PERCEIVE THAT TASTE AS AN IMAGE.
THAT MEANS SHE CAN SPOT EVEN THE TINIEST IMPERFECTION IN ANY DISH.
EVERYONE HAS HEARD THAT AS AN INFANT SHE CRITICIZED HER OWN MOTHER'S BREAST MILK.
WHAT A HIDEOUS PRE-TENSE OF A SOUP!
IT TASTED LIKE I WAS SERENELY MEDITATING UNDER A WATERFALL ONLY TO HAVE A JUKEBOX FALL ON MY HEAD!
DID YOU HEAR THAT?
YEAH. DEEP AS EVER TODAY.
PSST
PSST
FOR SUCH A TERRIBLE DISH, YOU ARE AS OF THIS MOMENT ...
...EXPELLED.

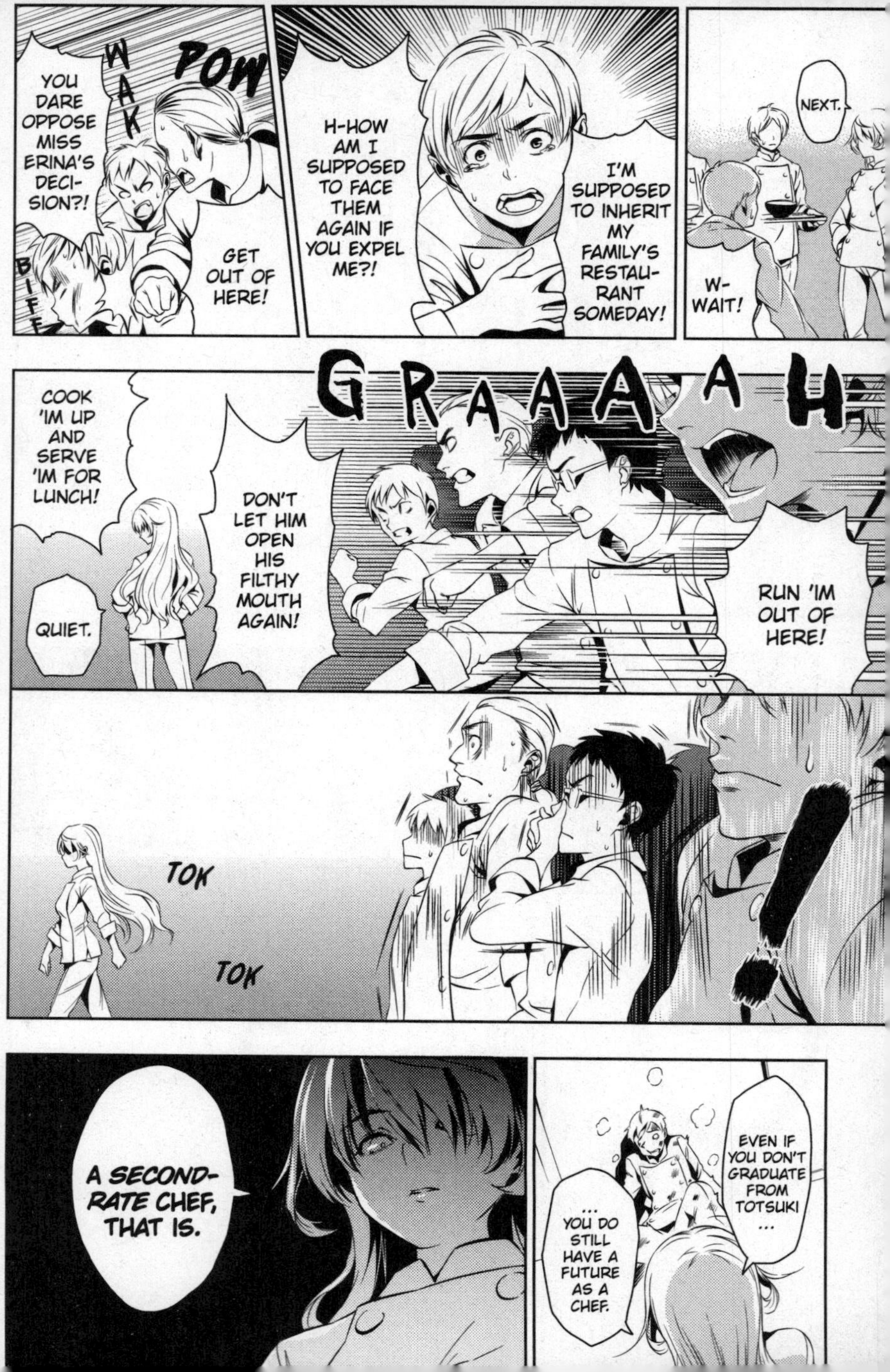
NEXT.
W-WAIT!
I'M SUPPOSED TO INHERIT MY FAMILY'S RESTAURANT SOMEDAY!
H-HOW AM I SUPPOSED TO FACE THEM AGAIN IF YOU EXPEL ME?!
POW
WAK
YOU DARE OPPOSE MISS ERINA'S DECISION?!
GET OUT OF HERE!
BIFF
GRAAAAH
RUN 'IM OUT OF HERE!
DON'T LET HIM OPEN HIS FILTHY MOUTH AGAIN!
COOK 'IM UP AND SERVE 'IM FOR LUNCH!
QUIET.
TOK
TOK
EVEN IF YOU DON'T GRADUATE FROM TOTSUKI...
...YOU DO STILL HAVE A FUTURE AS A CHEF.
A SECOND-RATE CHEF, THAT IS.

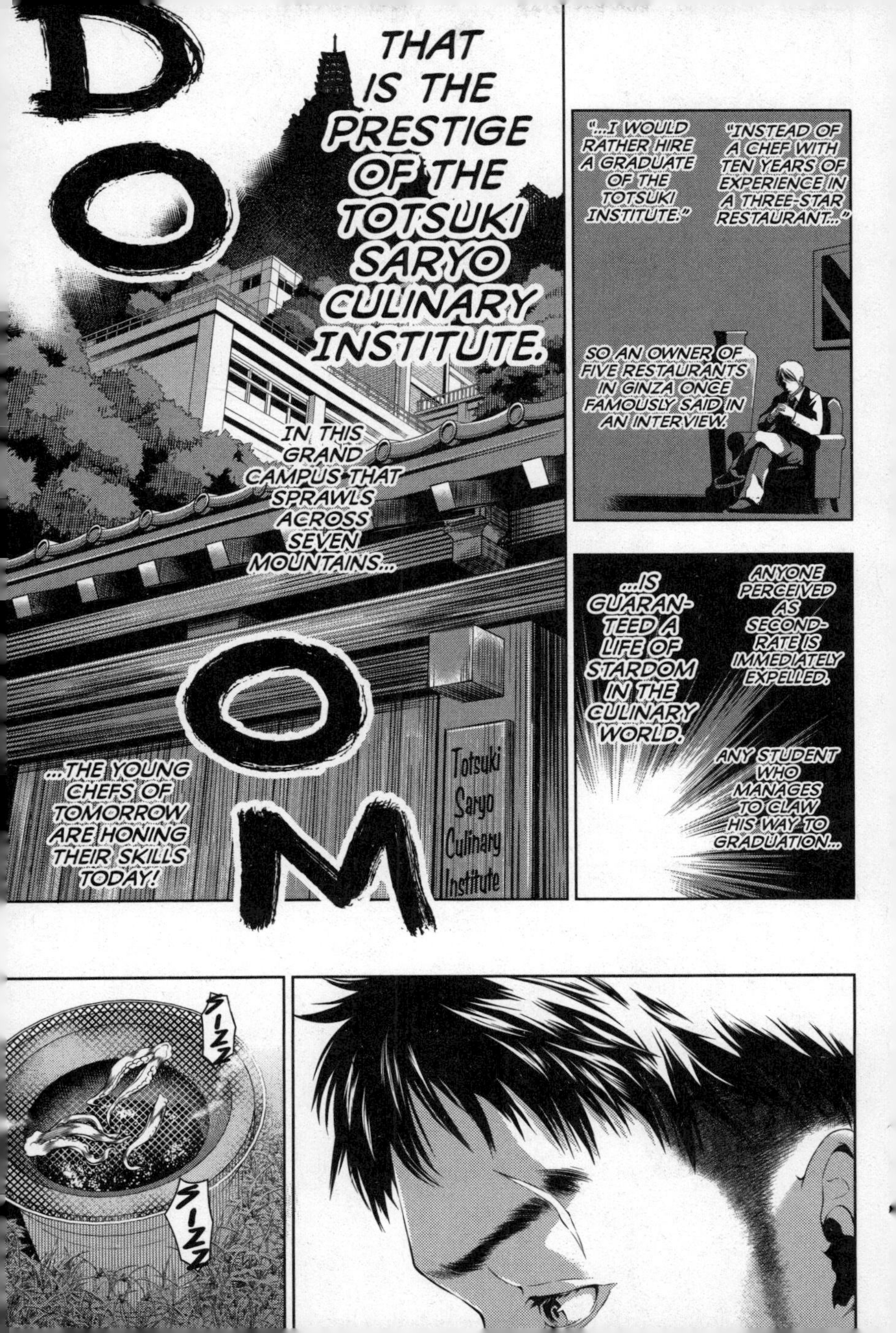
"INSTEAD OF A CHEF WITH TEN YEARS OF EXPERIENCE IN A THREE-STAR RESTAURANT..."
"...I WOULD RATHER HIRE A GRADUATE OF THE TOTSUKI INSTITUTE."
SO AN OWNER OF FIVE RESTAURANTS IN GINZA ONCE FAMOUSLY SAID IN AN INTERVIEW.
ANYONE PERCEIVED AS SECOND-RATE IS IMMEDIATELY EXPELLED.
ANY STUDENT WHO MANAGES TO CLAW HIS WAY TO GRADUATION...
...IS GUARAN-TEED A LIFE OF STARDOM IN THE CULINARY WORLD.
THAT IS THE PRESTIGE OF THE TOTSUKI SARYO CULINARY INSTITUTE.
DOOM
IN THIS GRAND CAMPUS THAT SPRAWLS ACROSS SEVEN MOUNTAINS...
...THE YOUNG CHEFS OF TOMORROW ARE HONING THEIR SKILLS TODAY!
Totsuki Saryo Culinary Institute
SIZZ
SIZZ

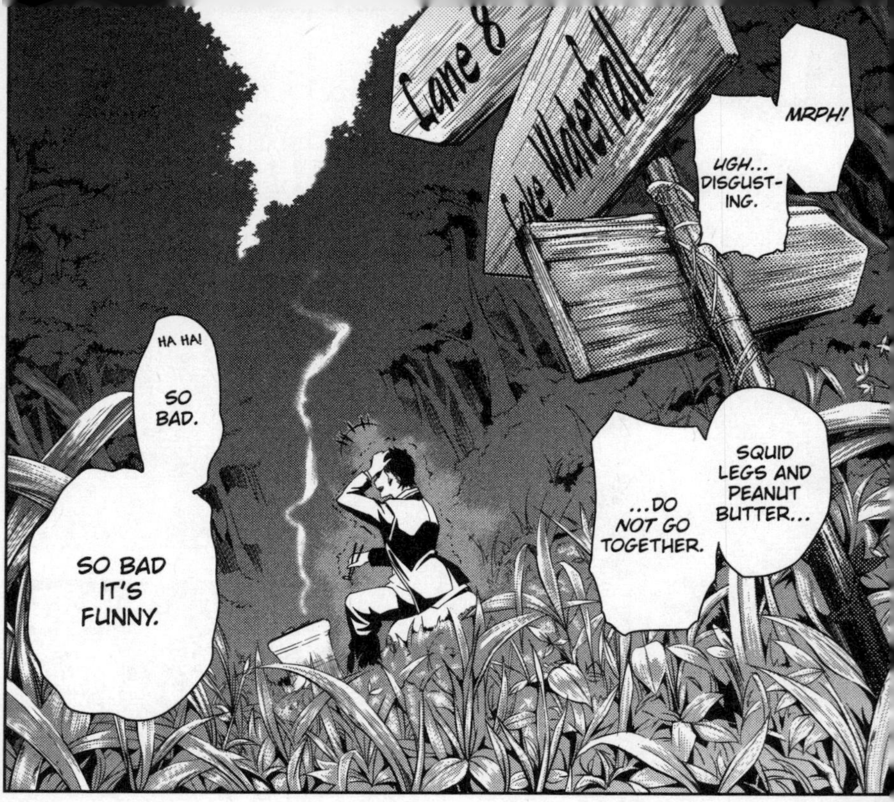
Lane 8
MRPH!
UGH... DISGUST-ING.
SQUID LEGS AND PEANUT BUTTER...
...DO NOT GO TOGETHER.
HA HA!
SO BAD.
SO BAD IT'S FUNNY.

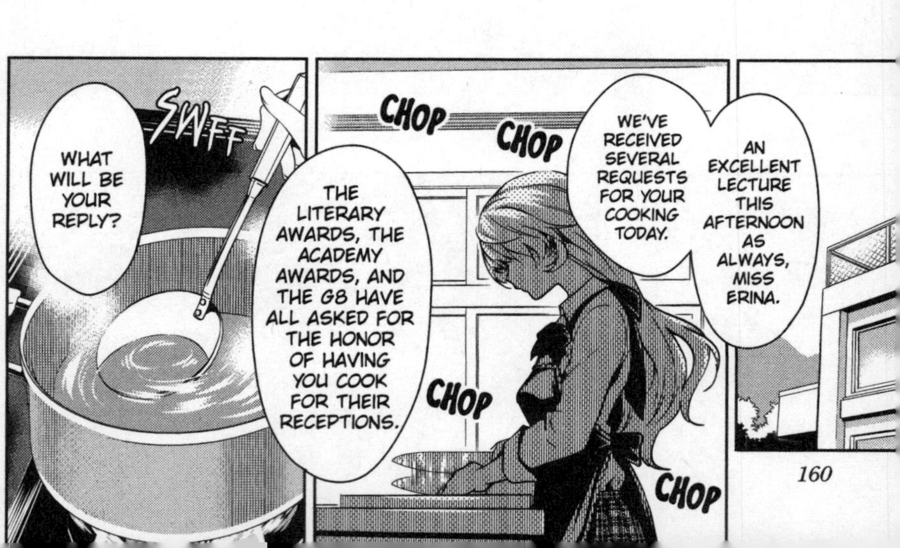
AN EXCELLENT LECTURE THIS AFTERNOON AS ALWAYS, MISS ERINA.
WE'VE RECEIVED SEVERAL REQUESTS FOR YOUR COOKING TODAY.
CHOP
CHOP
CHOP
CHOP
THE LITERARY AWARDS, THE ACADEMY AWARDS, AND THE G8 HAVE ALL ASKED FOR THE HONOR OF HAVING YOU COOK FOR THEIR RECEPTIONS.
SWFF
WHAT WILL BE YOUR REPLY?

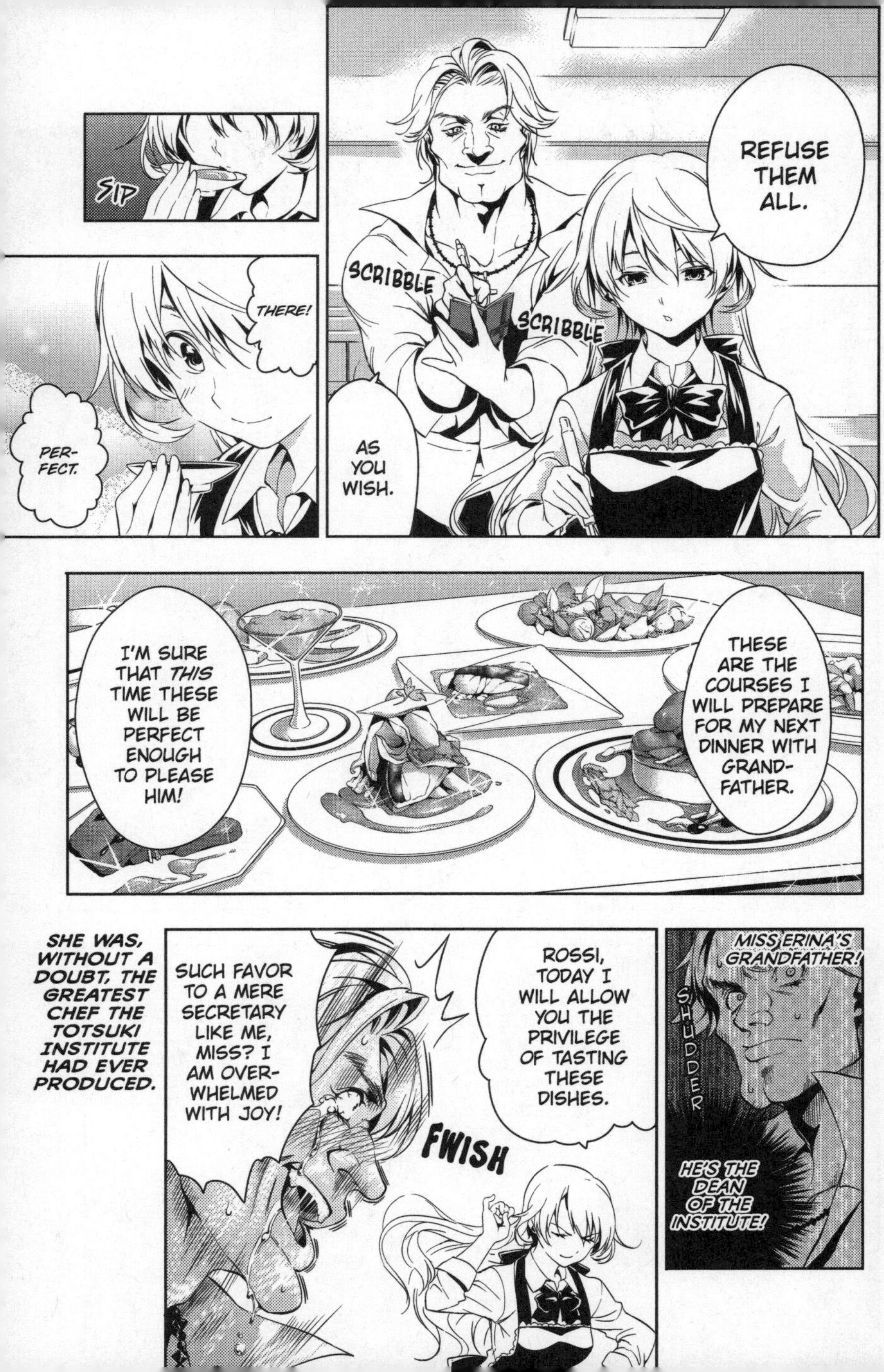
REFUSE THEM ALL.
SCRIBBLE
SCRIBBLE
AS YOU WISH.
SIP
THERE!
PER-FECT.
THESE ARE THE COURSES I WILL PREPARE FOR MY NEXT DINNER WITH GRAND-FATHER.
I'M SURE THAT *THIS* TIME THESE WILL BE PERFECT ENOUGH TO PLEASE HIM!
MISS ERINA'S GRANDFATHER!
SHUDDER
HE'S THE DEAN OF THE INSTITUTE!
ROSSI, TODAY I WILL ALLOW YOU THE PRIVILEGE OF TASTING THESE DISHES.
SUCH FAVOR TO A MERE SECRETARY LIKE ME, MISS? I AM OVER-WHELMED WITH JOY!
FWISH
SHE WAS, WITHOUT A DOUBT, THE GREATEST CHEF THE TOTSUKI INSTITUTE HAD EVER PRODUCED.

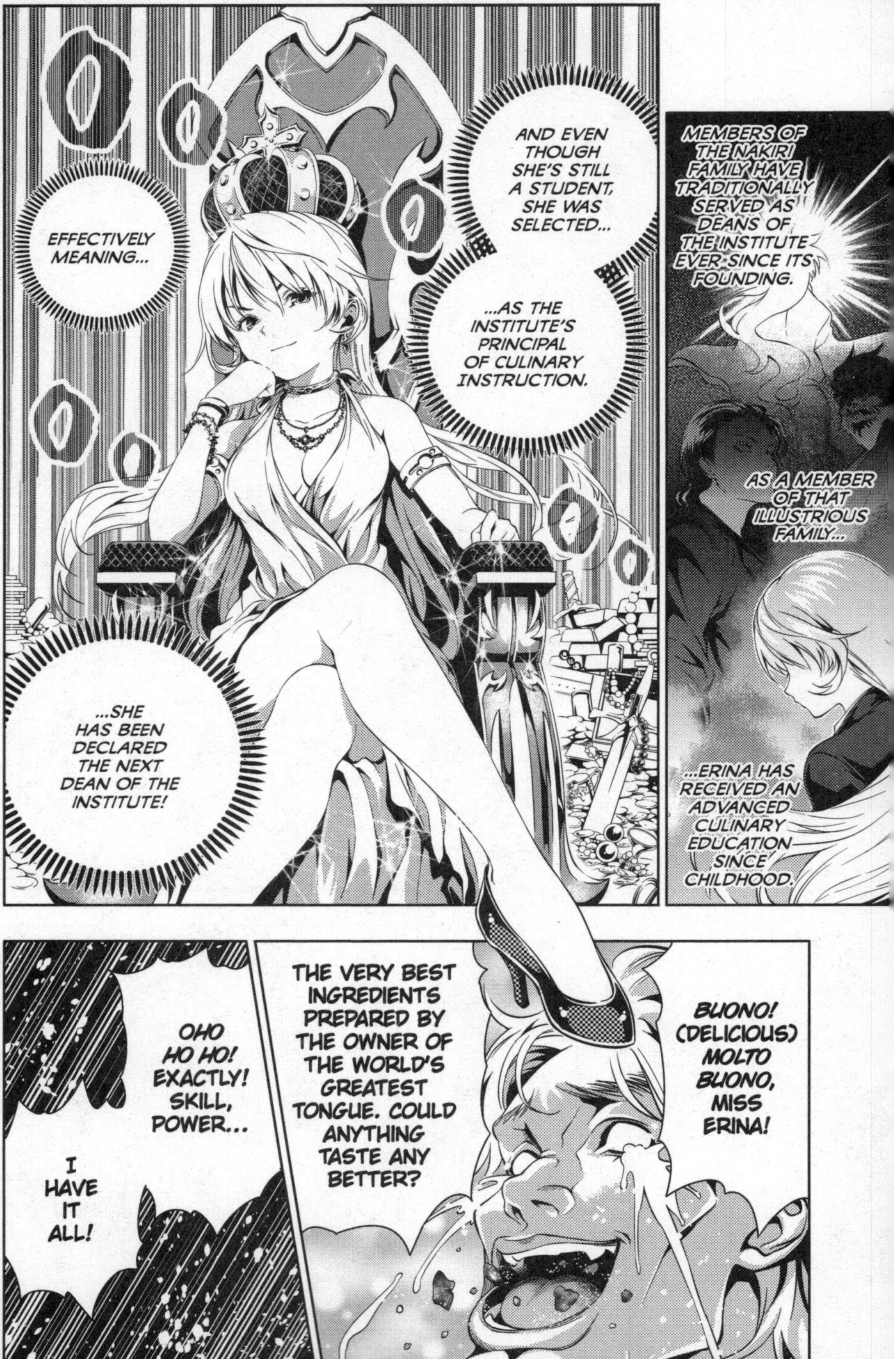
MEMBERS OF THE NAKIRI FAMILY HAVE TRADITIONALLY SERVED AS DEANS OF THE INSTITUTE EVER SINCE ITS FOUNDING.
AS A MEMBER OF THAT ILLUSTRIOUS FAMILY...
...ERINA HAS RECEIVED AN ADVANCED CULINARY EDUCATION SINCE CHILDHOOD.
AND EVEN THOUGH SHE'S STILL A STUDENT, SHE WAS SELECTED...
...AS THE INSTITUTE'S PRINCIPAL OF CULINARY INSTRUCTION.
EFFECTIVELY MEANING...
...SHE HAS BEEN DECLARED THE NEXT DEAN OF THE INSTITUTE!
BUONO! (DELICIOUS) MOLTO BUONO, MISS ERINA!
THE VERY BEST INGREDIENTS PREPARED BY THE OWNER OF THE WORLD'S GREATEST TONGUE. COULD ANYTHING TASTE ANY BETTER?
OHO HO HO! EXACTLY! SKILL, POWER...
I HAVE IT ALL!

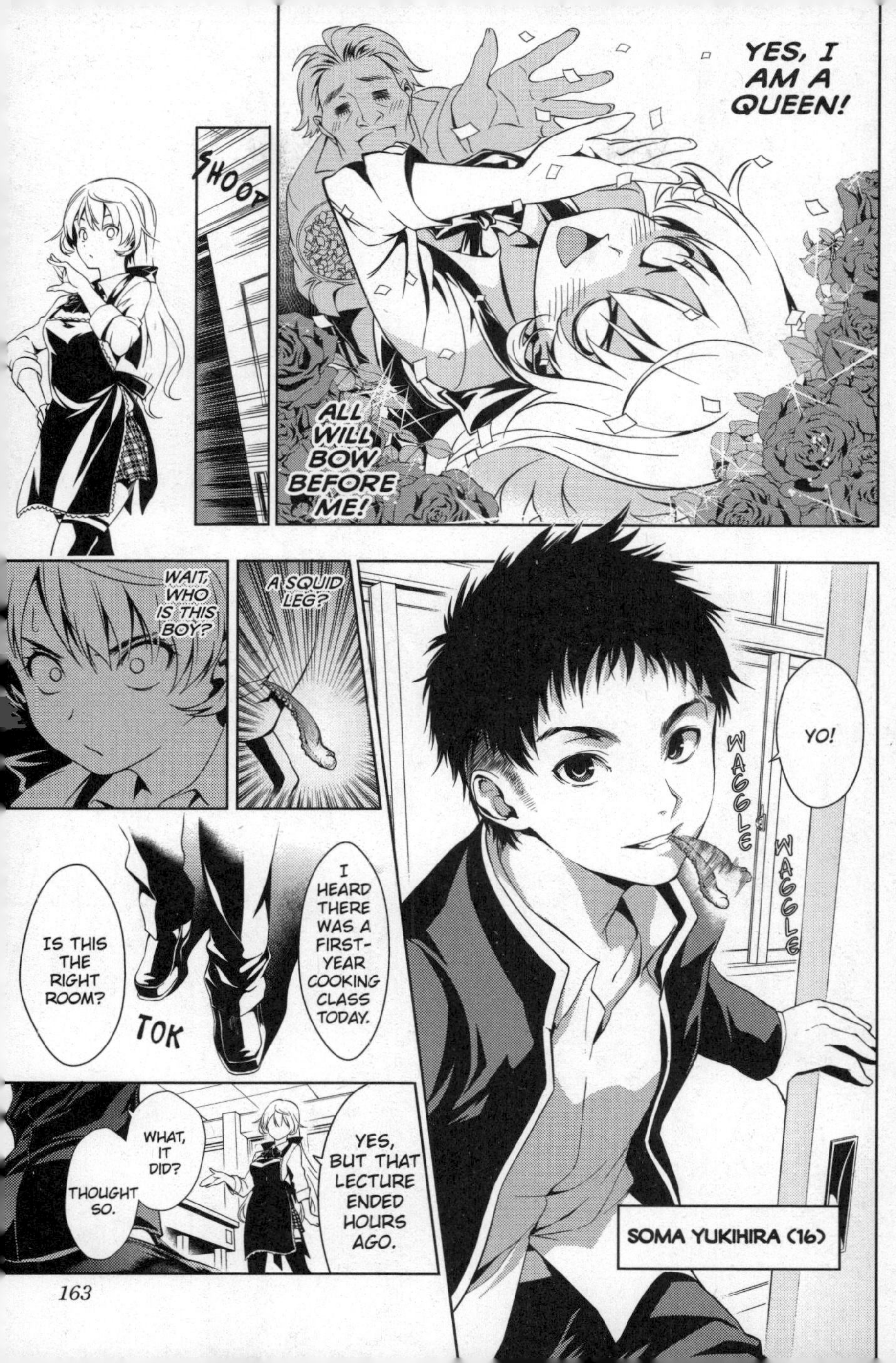
YES, I AM A QUEEN!
ALL WILL BOW BEFORE ME!
SHOOP
YO!
WAGGLE WAGGLE
SOMA YUKIHIRA (16)
A SQUID LEG?
WAIT, WHO IS THIS BOY?
I HEARD THERE WAS A FIRST-YEAR COOKING CLASS TODAY.
IS THIS THE RIGHT ROOM?
TOK
YES, BUT THAT LECTURE ENDED HOURS AGO.
WHAT, IT DID?
THOUGHT SO.

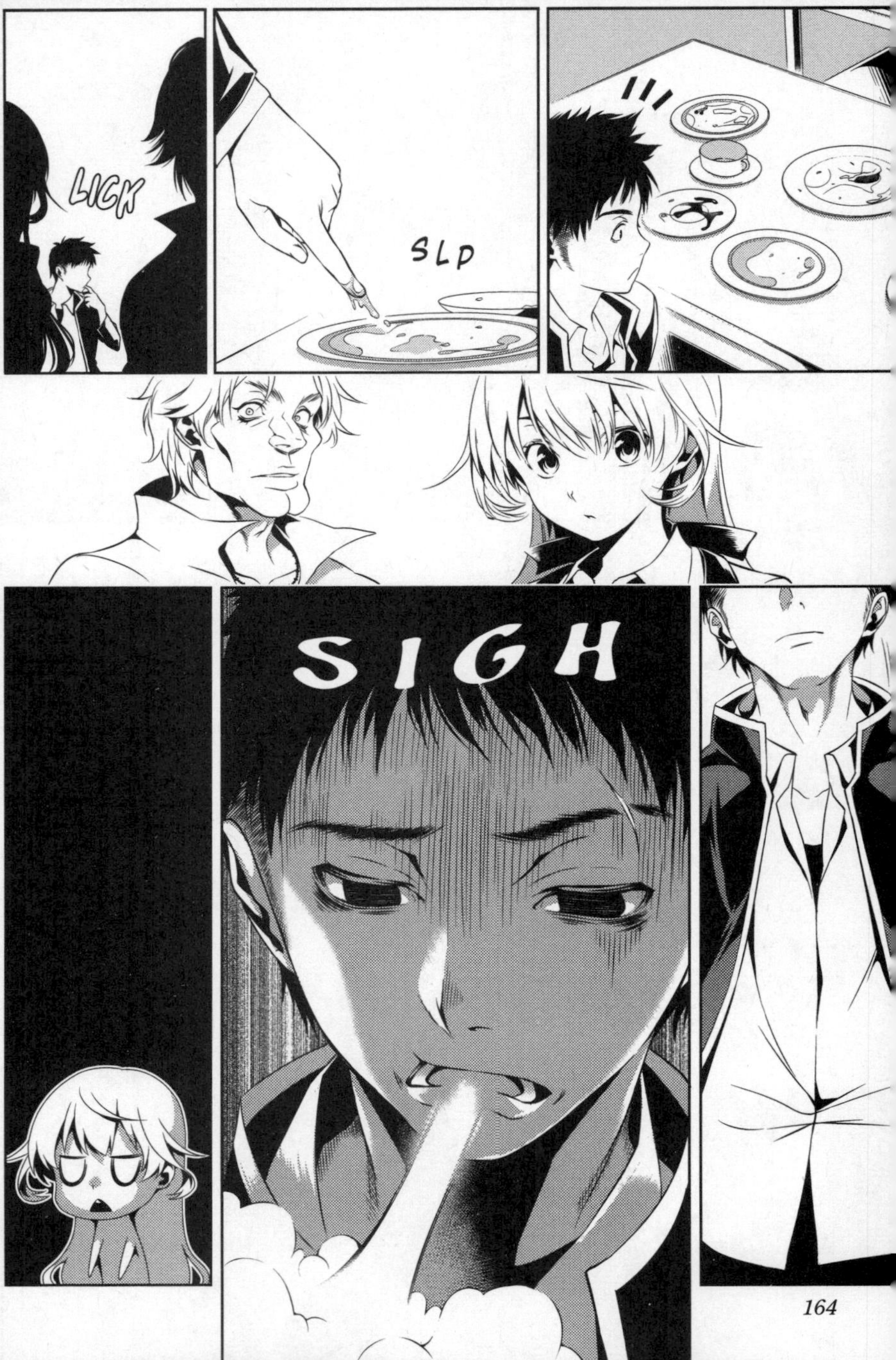
SLP
LICK
SIGH

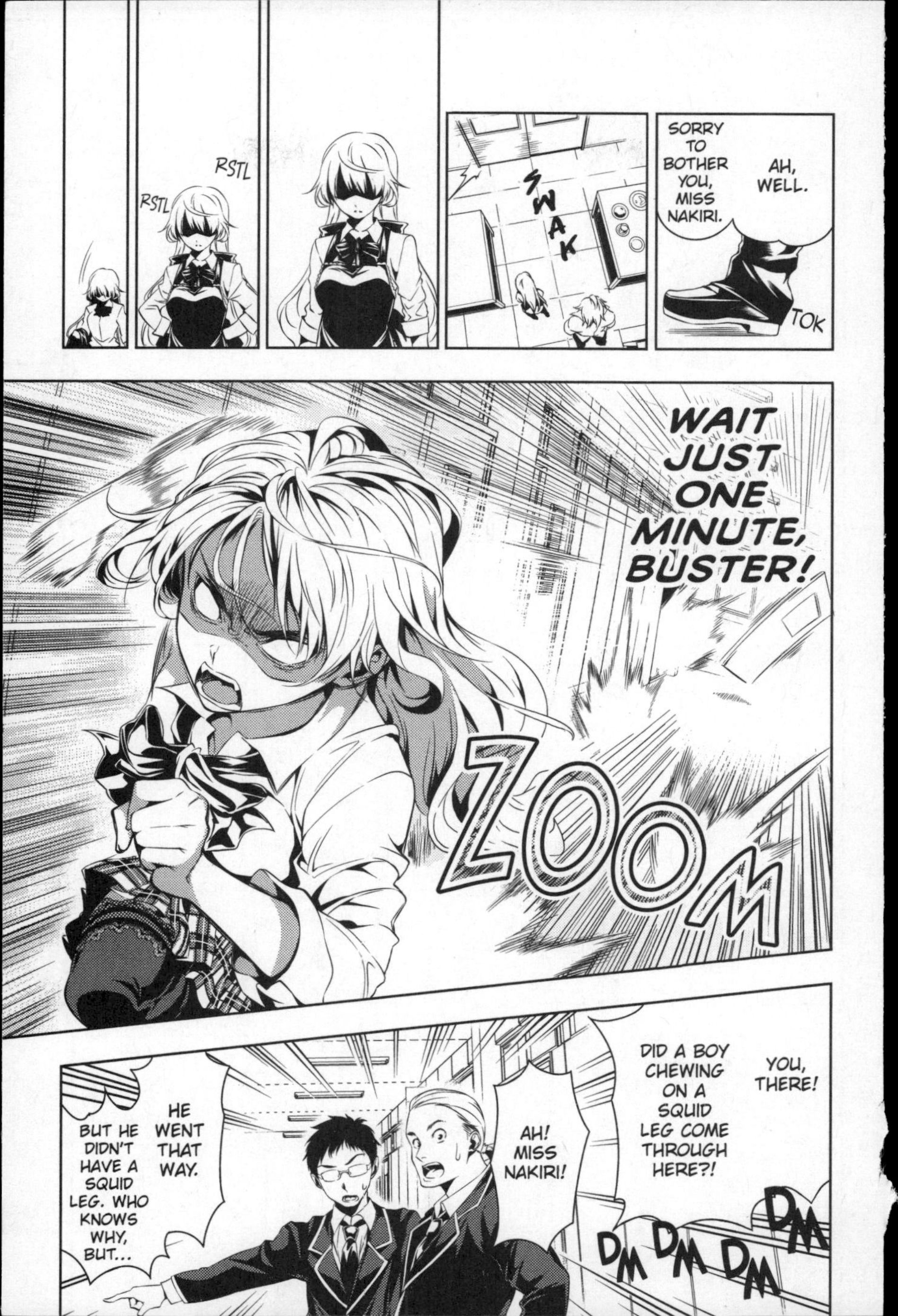
AH, WELL.
SORRY TO BOTHER YOU, MISS NAKIRI.
TOK
SWAK
RSTL
RSTL
WAIT JUST ONE MINUTE, BUSTER!
ZOOM
YOU, THERE!
DID A BOY CHEWING ON A SQUID LEG COME THROUGH HERE?!
AH! MISS NAKIRI!
HE WENT THAT WAY.
BUT HE DIDN'T HAVE A SQUID LEG. WHO KNOWS WHY, BUT...
DM DM DM DM DM DM

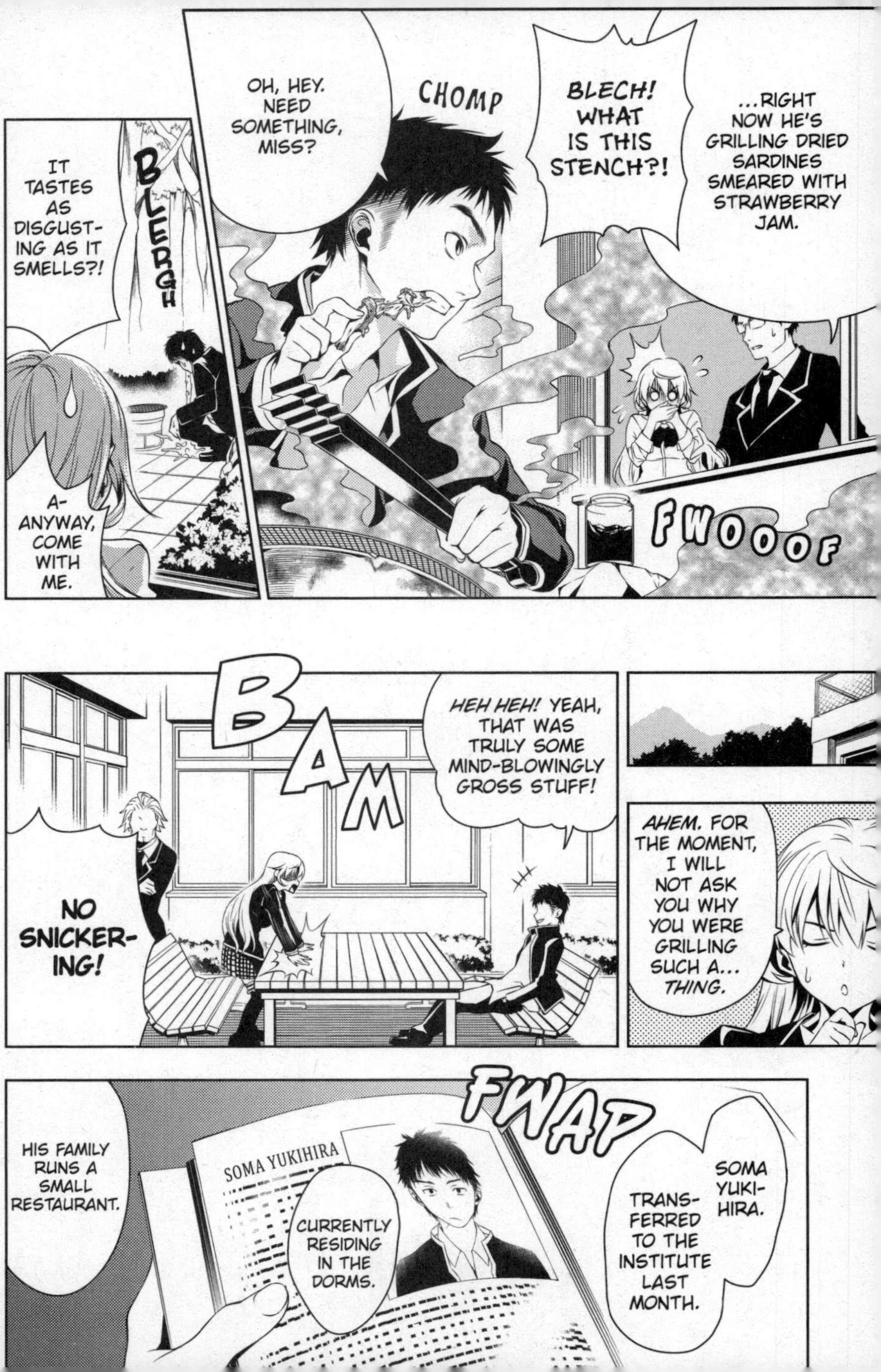
...RIGHT NOW HE'S GRILLING DRIED SARDINES SMEARED WITH STRAWBERRY JAM.
BLECH! WHAT IS THIS STENCH?!
CHOMP
OH, HEY. NEED SOMETHING, MISS?
FWOOOF
IT TASTES AS DISGUSTING AS IT SMELLS?!
BLERGH
A-ANYWAY, COME WITH ME.
AHEM. FOR THE MOMENT, I WILL NOT ASK YOU WHY YOU WERE GRILLING SUCH A... THING.
HEH HEH! YEAH, THAT WAS TRULY SOME MIND-BLOWINGLY GROSS STUFF!
BAM
NO SNICKERING!
FWAP
SOMA YUKIHIRA.
TRANSFERRED TO THE INSTITUTE LAST MONTH.
SOMA YUKIHIRA
CURRENTLY RESIDING IN THE DORMS.
HIS FAMILY RUNS A SMALL RESTAURANT.

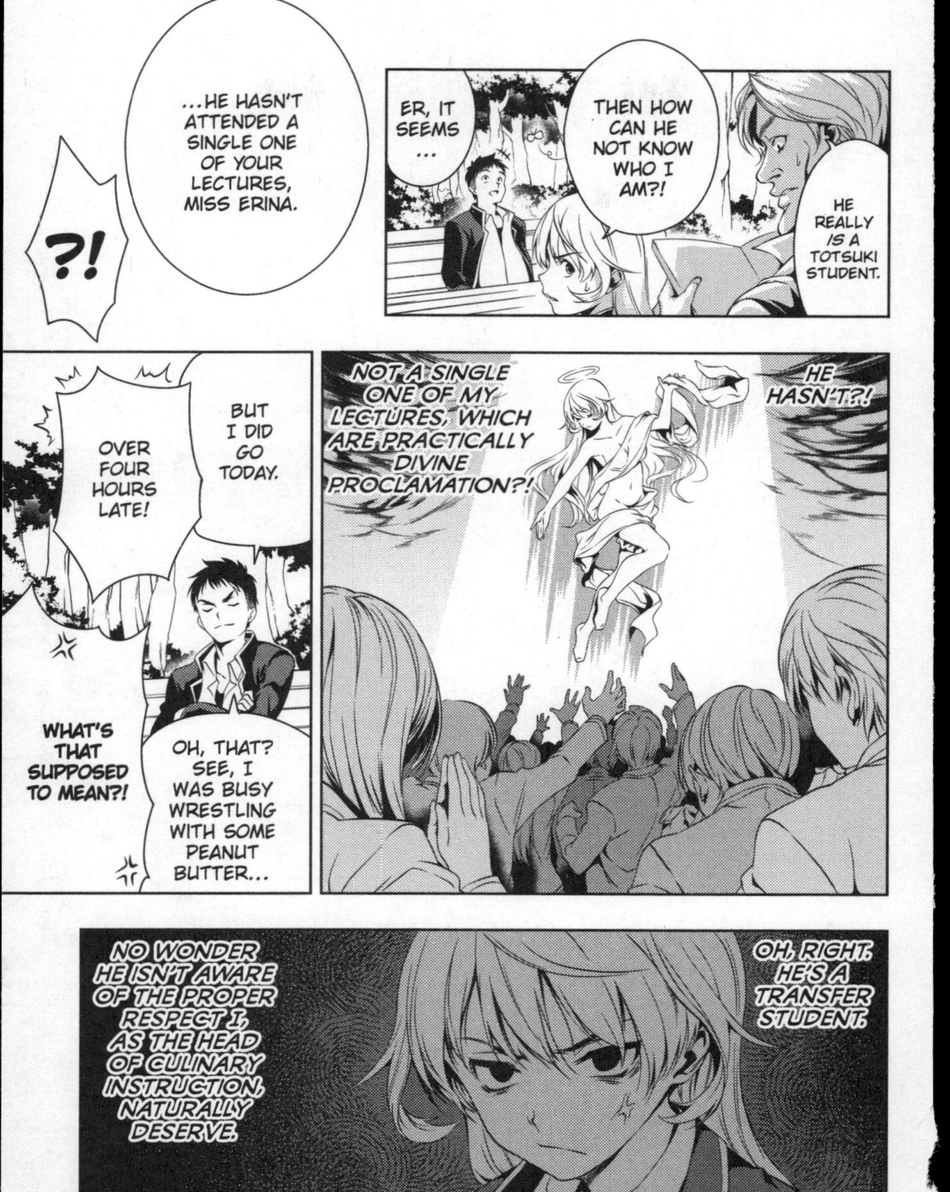
HE REALLY IS A TOTSUKI STUDENT.
THEN HOW CAN HE NOT KNOW WHO I AM?!
ER, IT SEEMS...
...HE HASN'T ATTENDED A SINGLE ONE OF YOUR LECTURES, MISS ERINA.
?!
HE HASN'T?!
NOT A SINGLE ONE OF MY LECTURES, WHICH ARE PRACTICALLY DIVINE PROCLAMATION?!
BUT I DID GO TODAY.
OVER FOUR HOURS LATE!
OH, THAT? SEE, I WAS BUSY WRESTLING WITH SOME PEANUT BUTTER...
WHAT'S THAT SUPPOSED TO MEAN?!
OH, RIGHT. HE'S A TRANSFER STUDENT.
NO WONDER HE ISN'T AWARE OF THE PROPER RESPECT I, AS THE HEAD OF CULINARY INSTRUCTION, NATURALLY DESERVE.

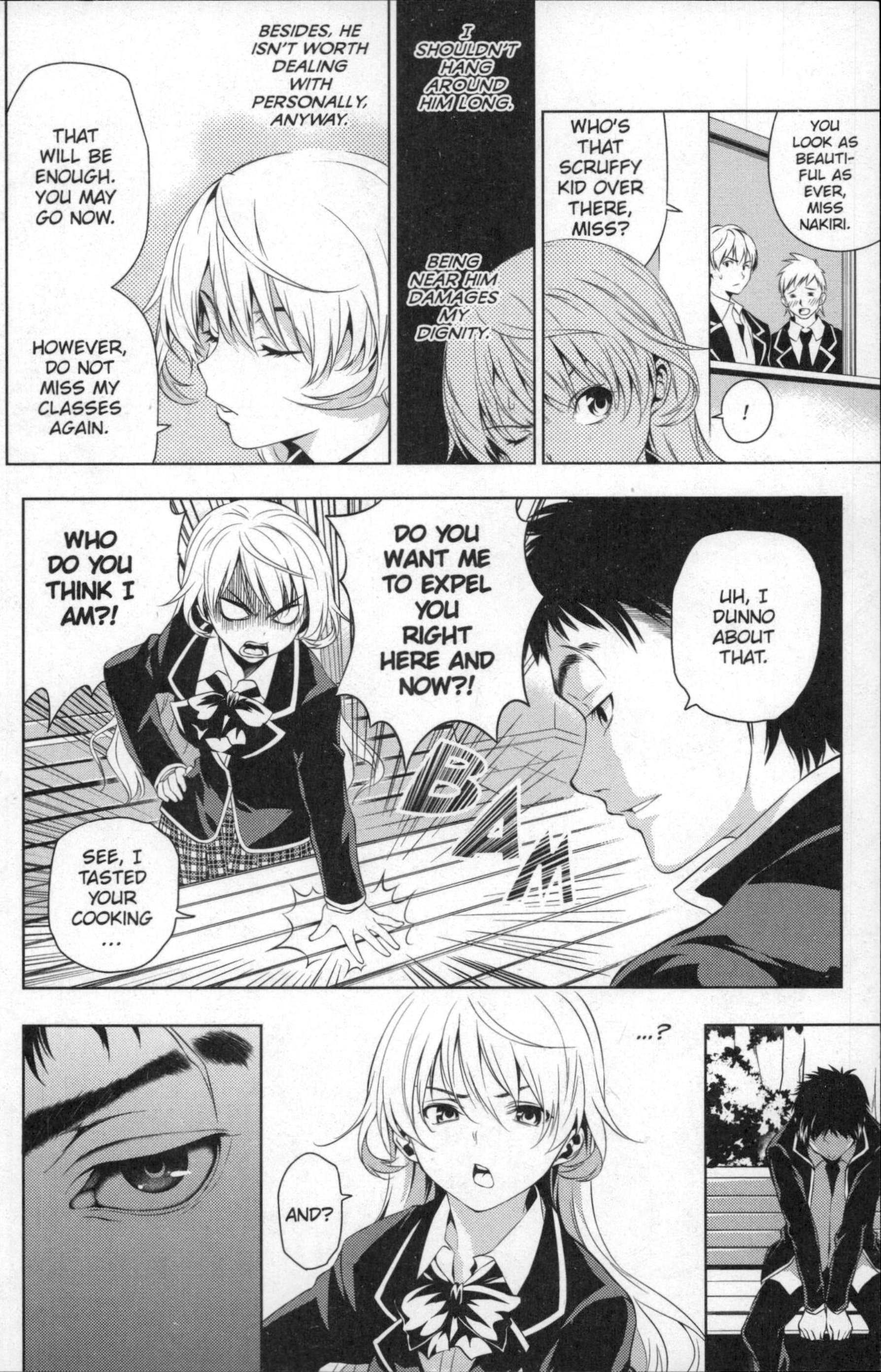
YOU LOOK AS BEAUTIFUL AS EVER, MISS NAKIRI.
!
WHO'S THAT SCRUFFY KID OVER THERE, MISS?
I SHOULDN'T HANG AROUND HIM LONG.
BEING NEAR HIM DAMAGES MY DIGNITY.
BESIDES, HE ISN'T WORTH DEALING WITH PERSONALLY, ANYWAY.
THAT WILL BE ENOUGH. YOU MAY GO NOW.
HOWEVER, DO NOT MISS MY CLASSES AGAIN.
UH, I DUNNO ABOUT THAT.
DO YOU WANT ME TO EXPEL YOU RIGHT HERE AND NOW?!
WHO DO YOU THINK I AM?!
BAM
SEE, I TASTED YOUR COOKING ...
...?
AND?

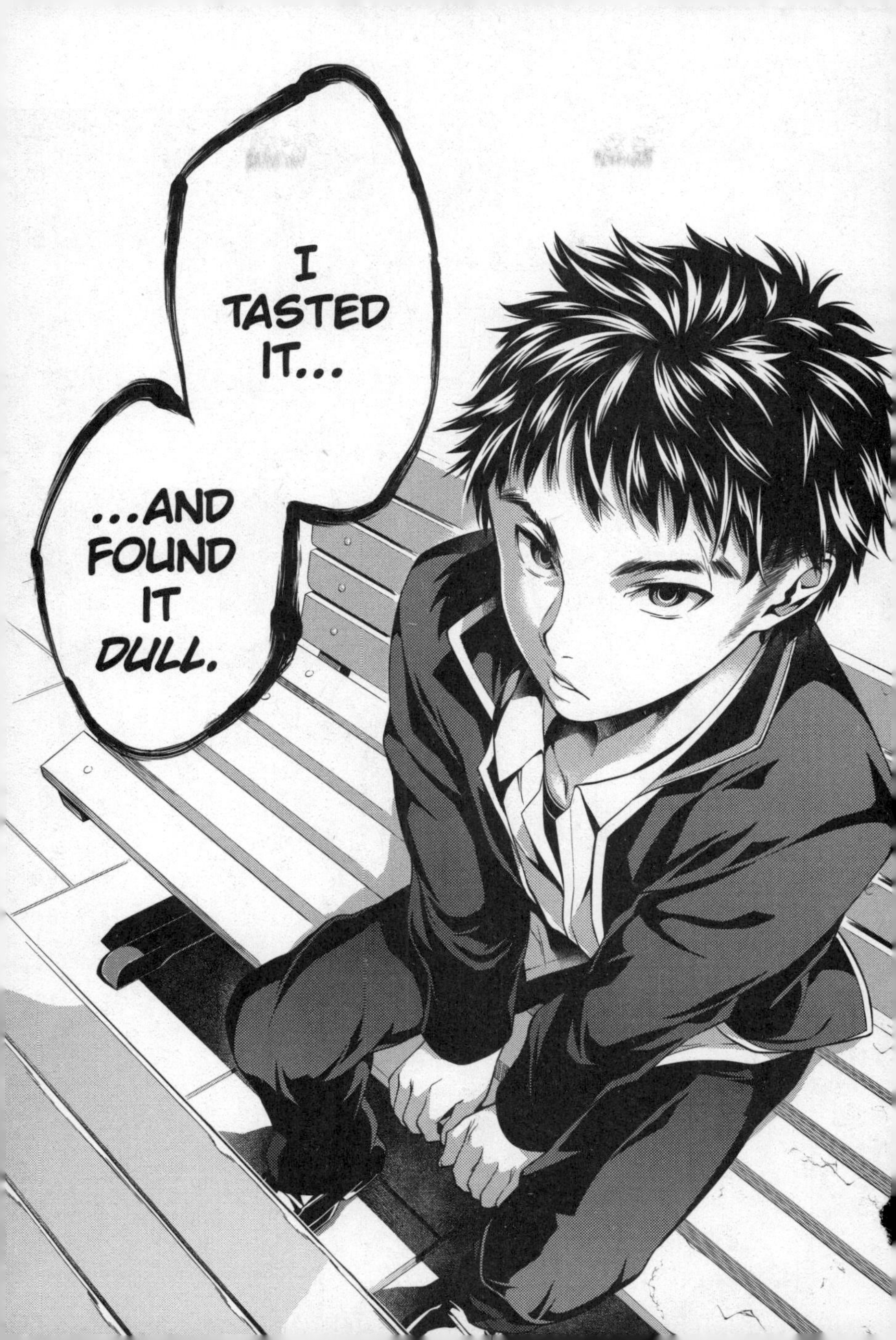
I TASTED IT...
...AND FOUND IT DULL.

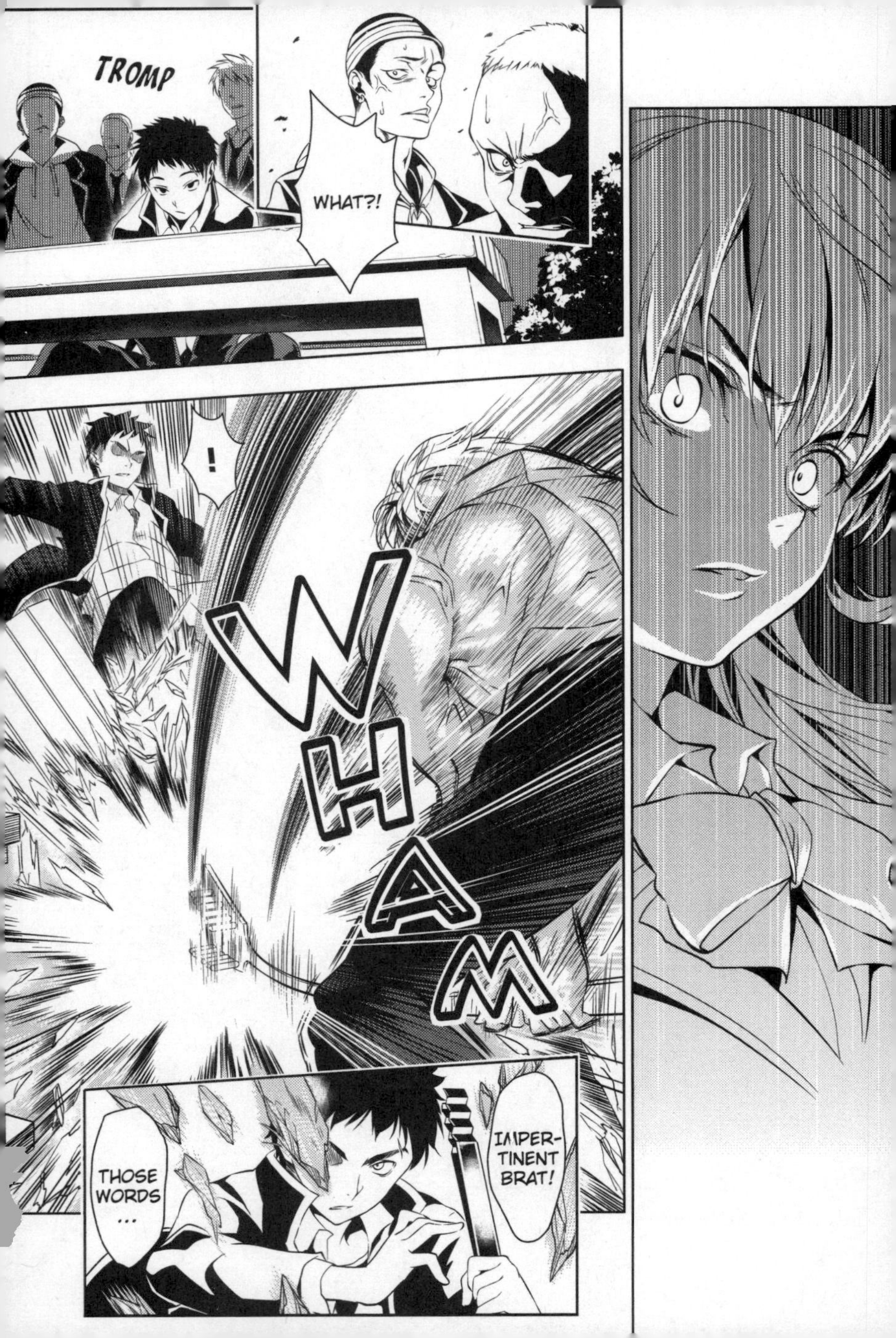
WHAT?!
TROMP
!
WHAM
IMPER-TINENT BRAT!
THOSE WORDS ...

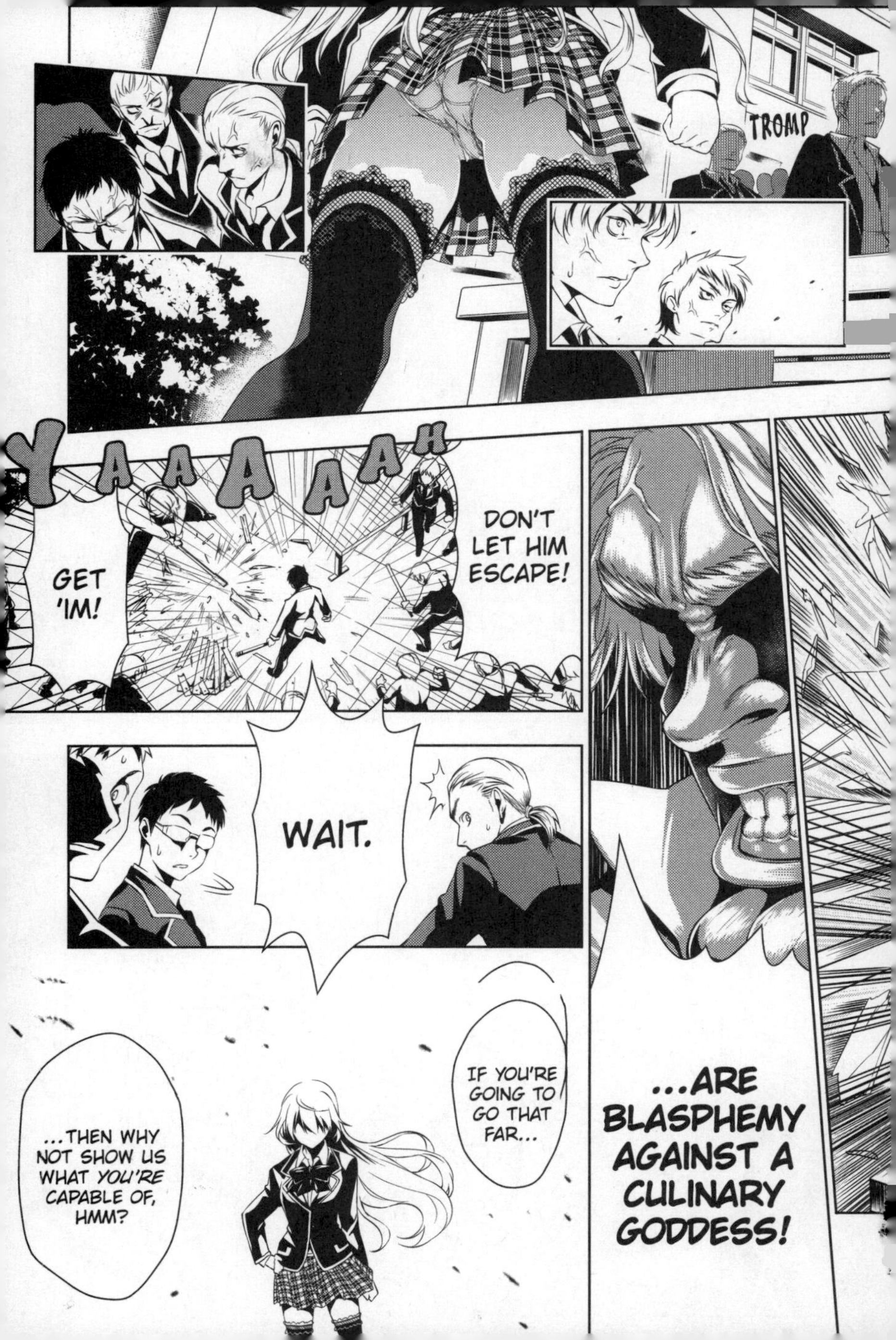

TROMP
...ARE BLASPHEMY AGAINST A CULINARY GODDESS!
YAAAAAH
DON'T LET HIM ESCAPE!
GET 'IM!
WAIT.
IF YOU'RE GOING TO GO THAT FAR...
...THEN WHY NOT SHOW US WHAT *YOU'RE* CAPABLE OF, HMM?

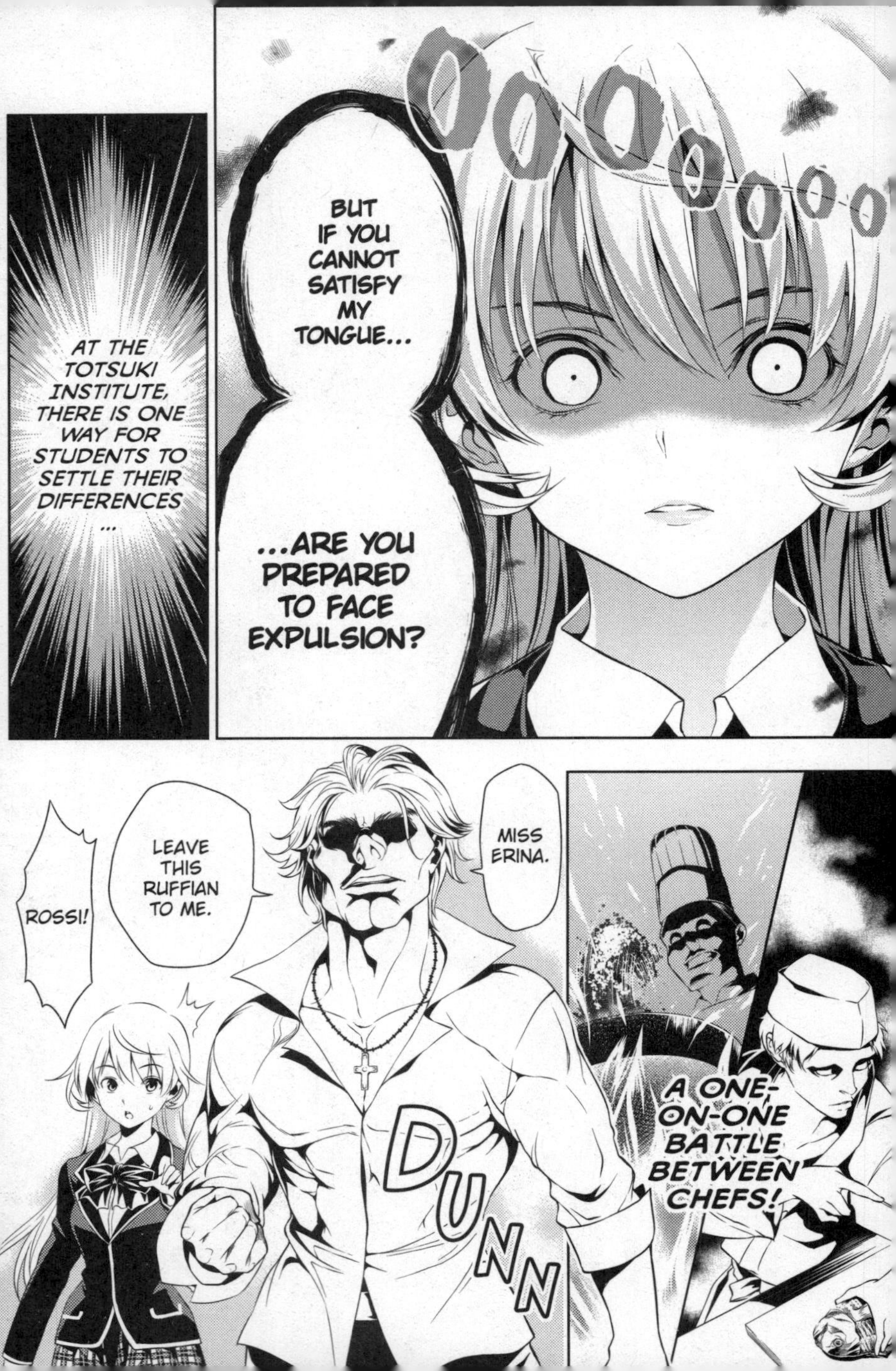
BUT IF YOU CANNOT SATISFY MY TONGUE...
...ARE YOU PREPARED TO FACE EXPULSION?
AT THE TOTSUKI INSTITUTE, THERE IS ONE WAY FOR STUDENTS TO SETTLE THEIR DIFFERENCES...
A ONE-ON-ONE BATTLE BETWEEN CHEFS!
MISS ERINA.
LEAVE THIS RUFFIAN TO ME.
ROSSI!
DUNN

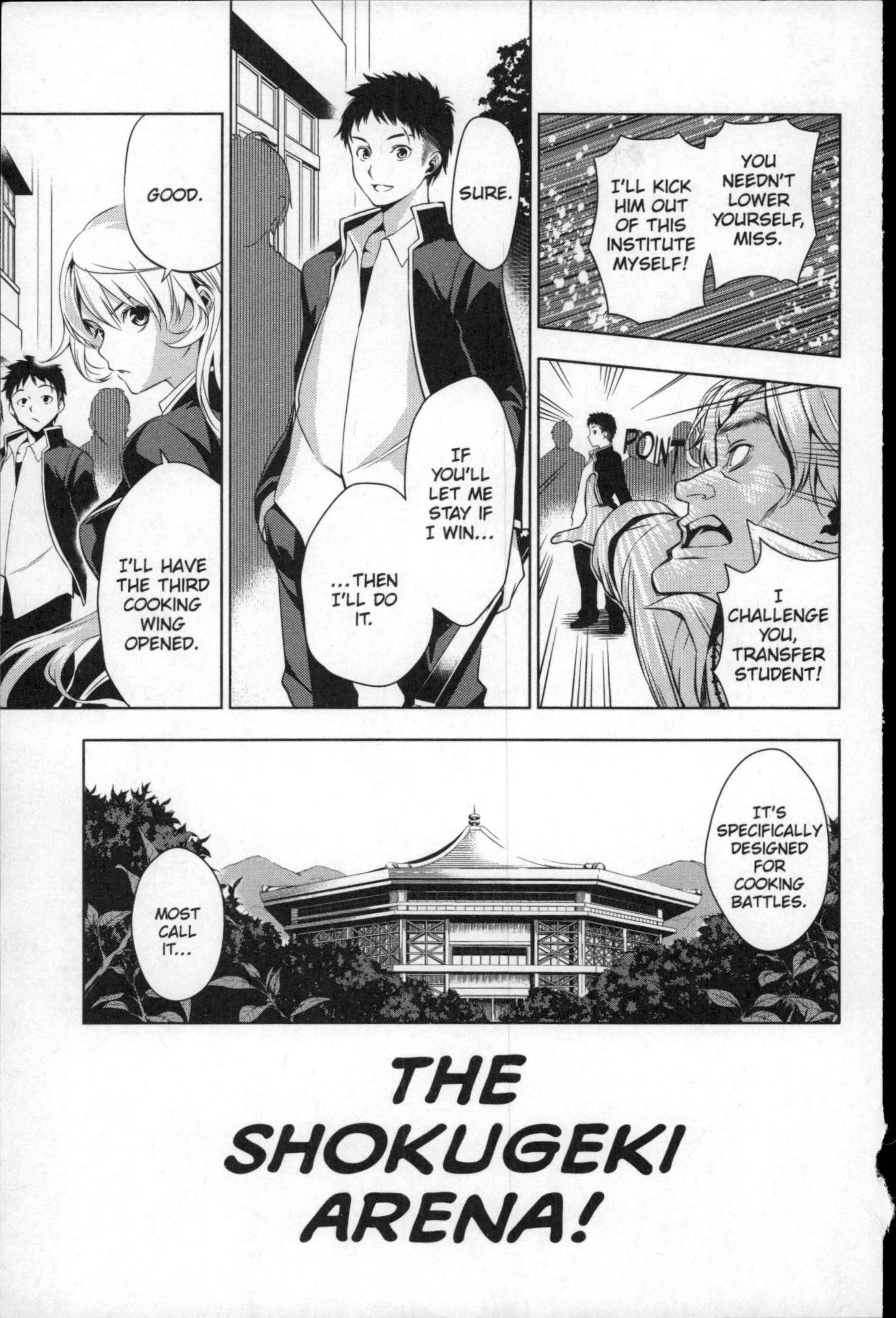
YOU NEEDN'T LOWER YOURSELF, MISS.
I'LL KICK HIM OUT OF THIS INSTITUTE MYSELF!
POINT
I CHALLENGE YOU, TRANSFER STUDENT!
SURE.
IF YOU'LL LET ME STAY IF I WIN...
...THEN I'LL DO IT.
GOOD.
I'LL HAVE THE THIRD COOKING WING OPENED.
IT'S SPECIFICALLY DESIGNED FOR COOKING BATTLES.
MOST CALL IT...
THE SHOKUGEKI ARENA!

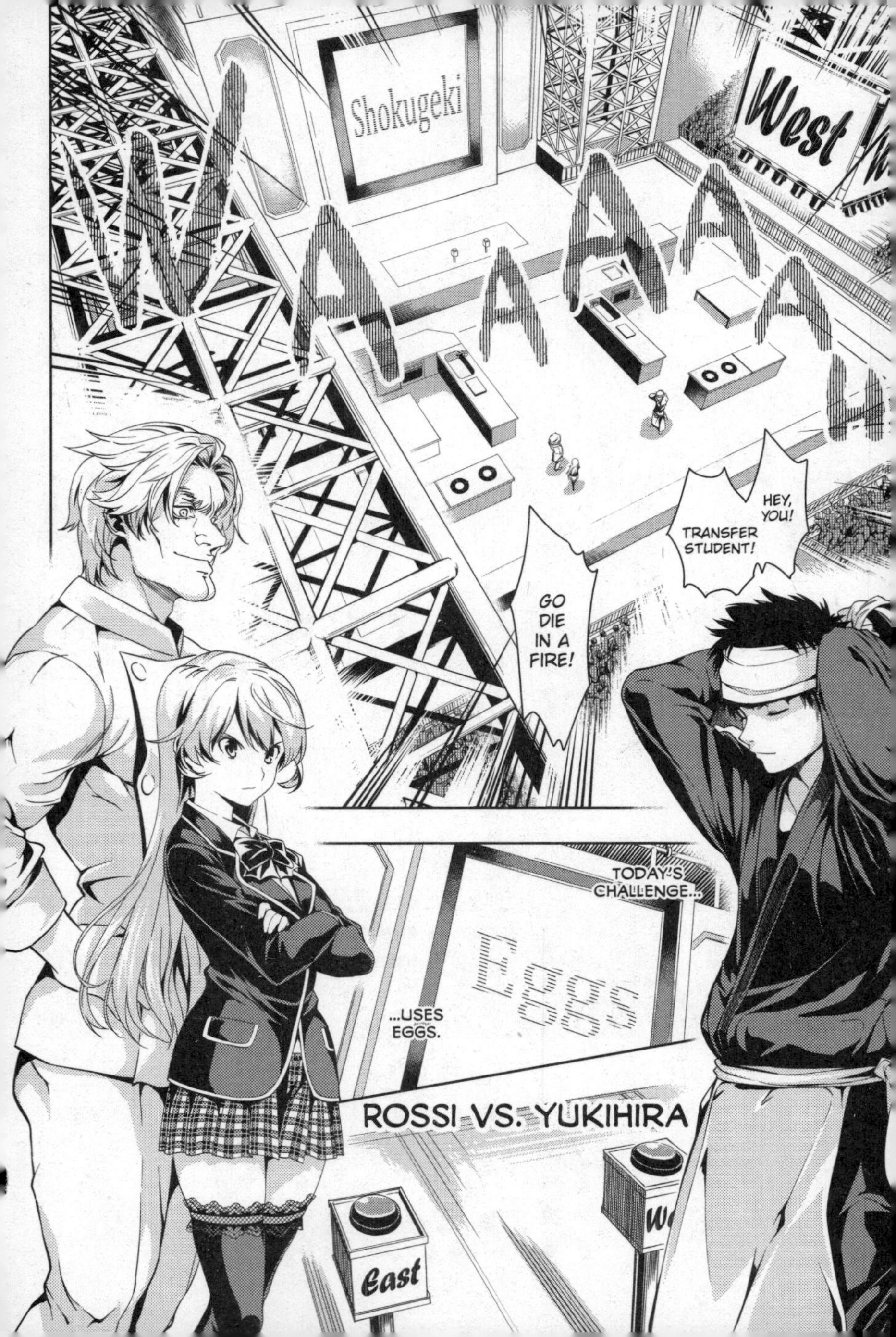

West
Shokugeki
WAAAAAH
HEY, YOU! TRANSFER STUDENT!
GO DIE IN A FIRE!
TODAY'S CHALLENGE...
Eggs
...USES EGGS.
ROSSI VS. YUKIHIRA
East

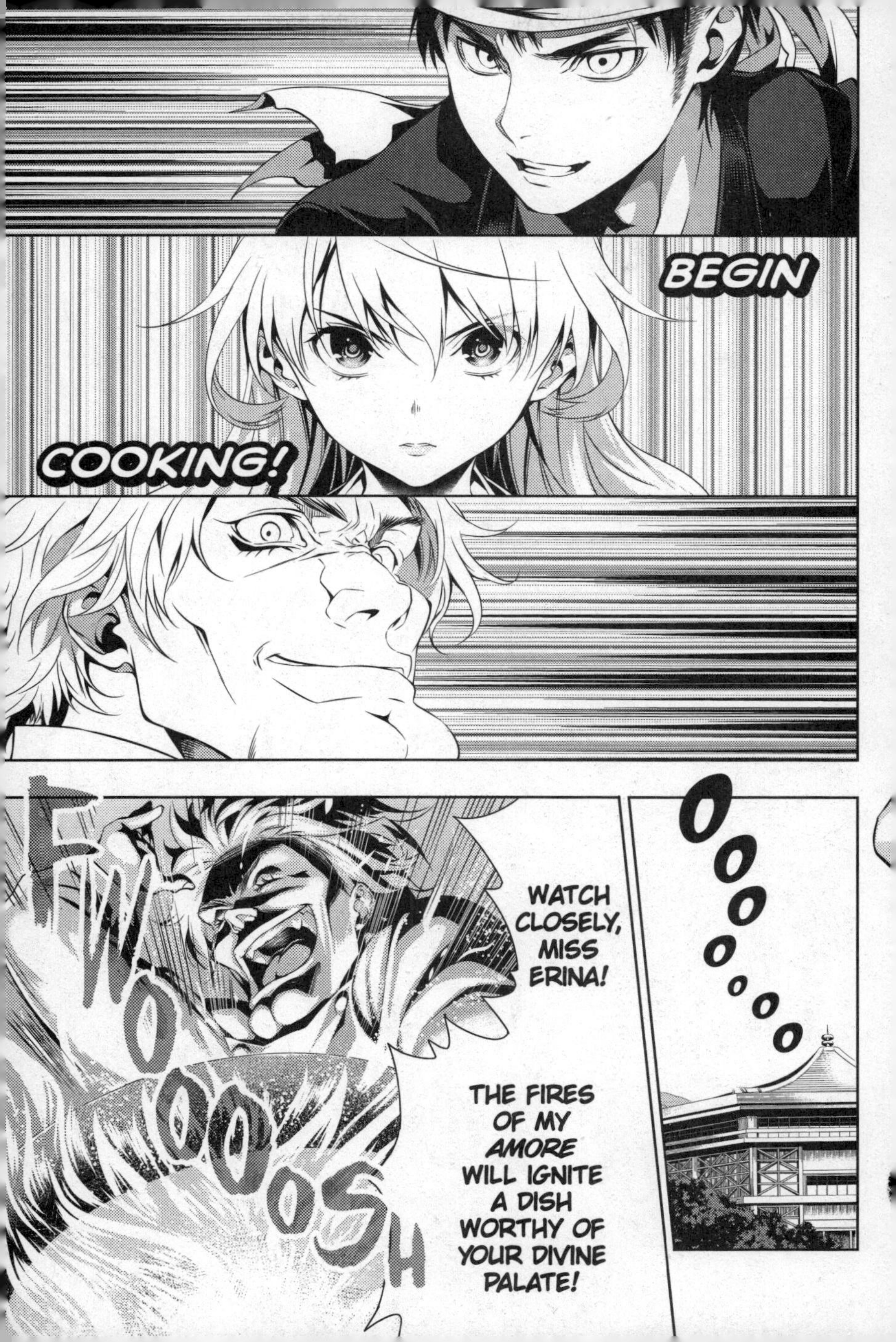
BEGIN
COOKING!
OOOOOOOOOO
WATCH CLOSELY, MISS ERINA!
THE FIRES OF MY *AMORE* WILL IGNITE A DISH WORTHY OF YOUR DIVINE PALATE!
FWOOOOOSH

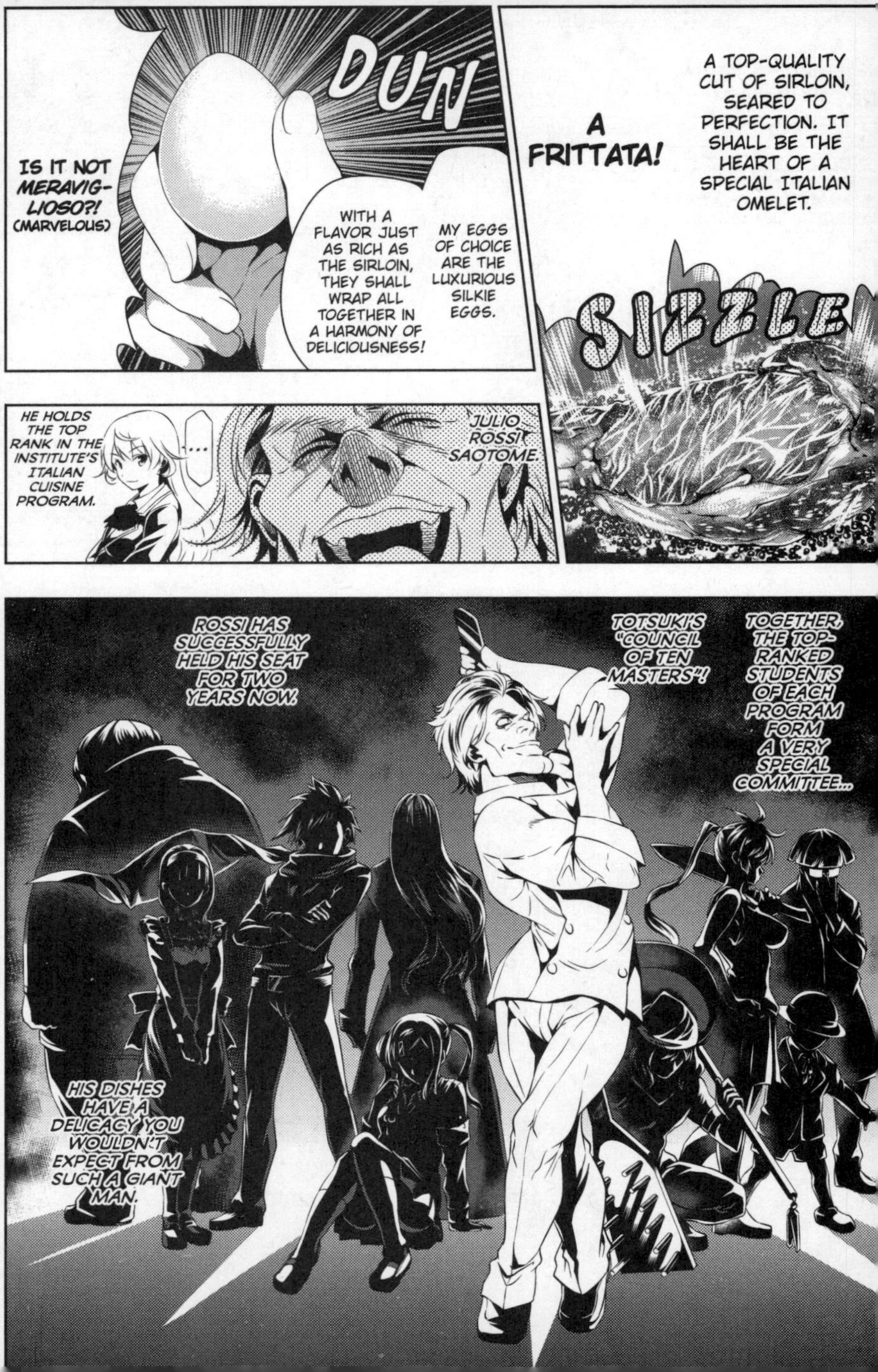
A TOP-QUALITY CUT OF SIRLOIN, SEARED TO PERFECTION. IT SHALL BE THE HEART OF A SPECIAL ITALIAN OMELET.
A FRITTATA!
SIZZLE
DUN
MY EGGS OF CHOICE ARE THE LUXURIOUS SILKIE EGGS.
WITH A FLAVOR JUST AS RICH AS THE SIRLOIN, THEY SHALL WRAP ALL TOGETHER IN A HARMONY OF DELICIOUSNESS!
IS IT NOT MERAVIGLIOSO?! (MARVELOUS)
JULIO ROSSI SAOTOME.
!
...
HE HOLDS THE TOP RANK IN THE INSTITUTE'S ITALIAN CUISINE PROGRAM.
TOGETHER, THE TOP-RANKED STUDENTS OF EACH PROGRAM FORM A VERY SPECIAL COMMITTEE...
TOTSUKI'S "COUNCIL OF TEN MASTERS"!
ROSSI HAS SUCCESSFULLY HELD HIS SEAT FOR TWO YEARS NOW.
HIS DISHES HAVE A DELICACY YOU WOULDN'T EXPECT FROM SUCH A GIANT MAN.

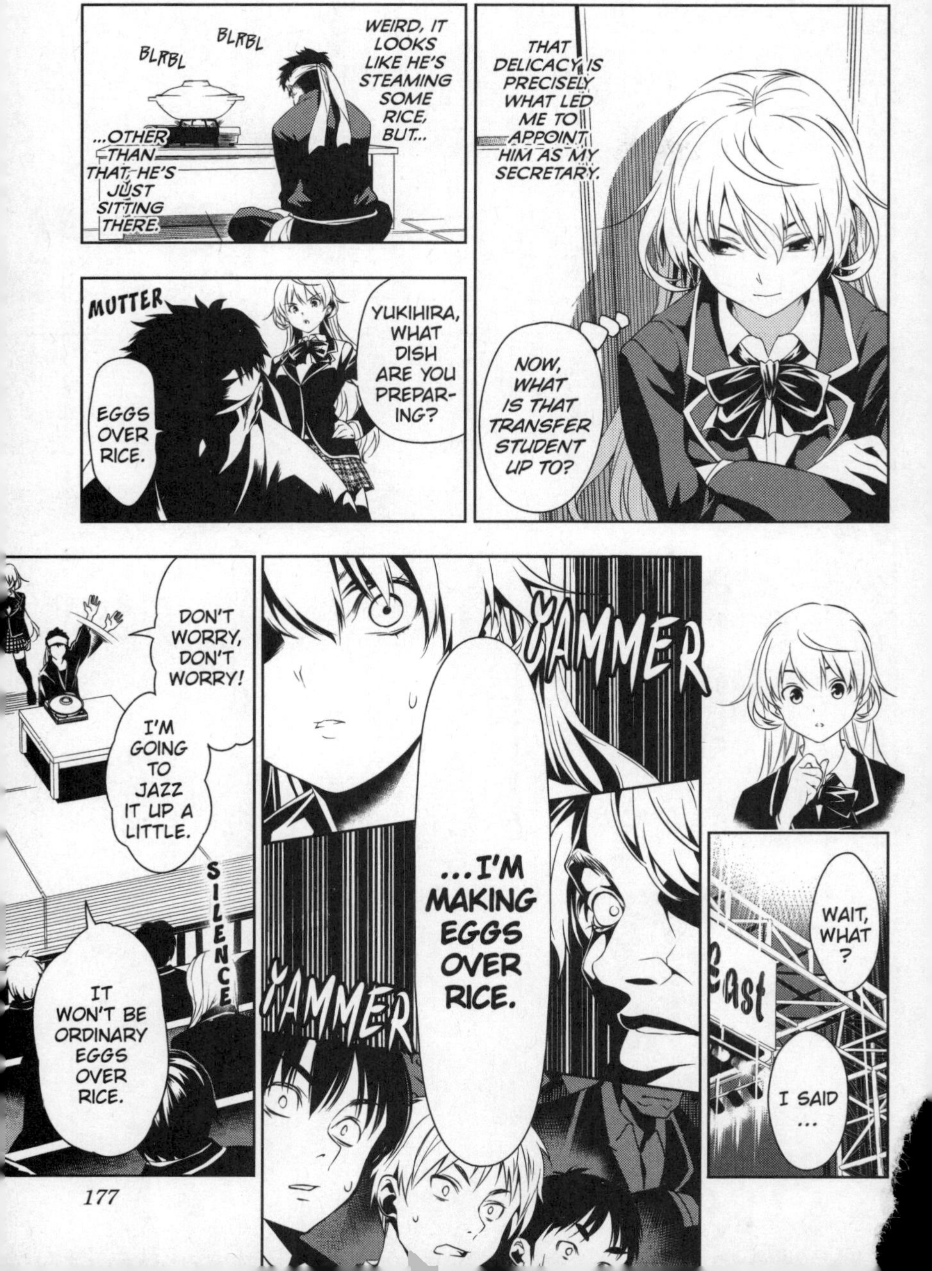

THAT DELICACY IS PRECISELY WHAT LED ME TO APPOINT HIM AS MY SECRETARY.
NOW, WHAT IS THAT TRANSFER STUDENT UP TO?
WEIRD, IT LOOKS LIKE HE'S STEAMING SOME RICE, BUT...
BLRBL
BLRBL
...OTHER THAN THAT, HE'S JUST SITTING THERE.
YUKIHIRA, WHAT DISH ARE YOU PREPARING?
MUTTER
EGGS OVER RICE.
WAIT, WHAT?
I SAID...
YAMMER
...I'M MAKING EGGS OVER RICE.
YAMMER
DON'T WORRY, DON'T WORRY!
I'M GOING TO JAZZ IT UP A LITTLE.
SILENCE
IT WON'T BE ORDINARY EGGS OVER RICE.

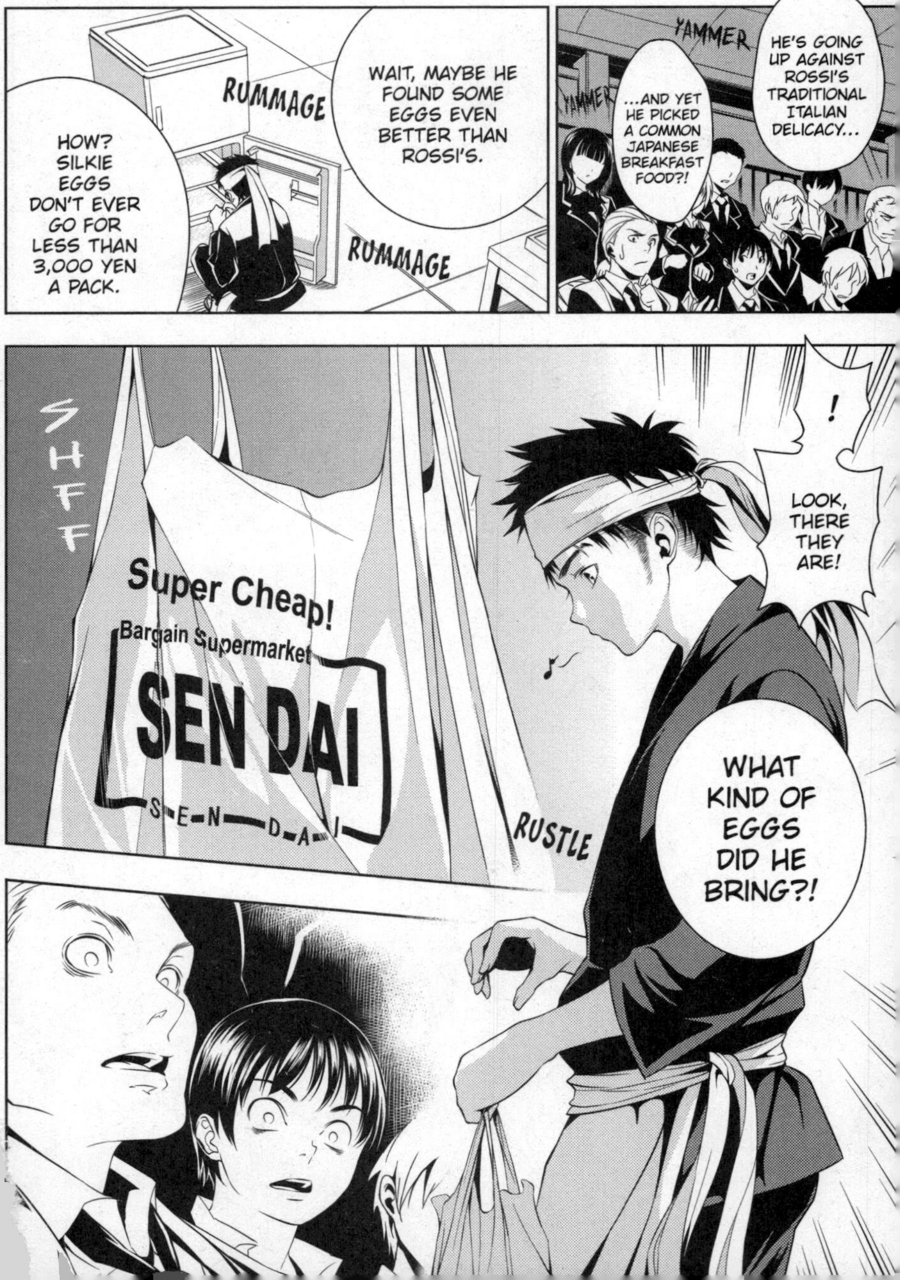
YAMMER
HE'S GOING UP AGAINST ROSSI'S TRADITIONAL ITALIAN DELICACY...
YAMMER
...AND YET HE PICKED A COMMON JAPANESE BREAKFAST FOOD?!
WAIT, MAYBE HE FOUND SOME EGGS EVEN BETTER THAN ROSSI'S.
RUMMAGE
HOW? SILKIE EGGS DON'T EVER GO FOR LESS THAN 3,000 YEN A PACK.
RUMMAGE
!
LOOK, THERE THEY ARE!
WHAT KIND OF EGGS DID HE BRING?!
RUSTLE
Super Cheap!
Bargain Supermarket
SEN DAI
S-E-N-D-A-I
SHFF

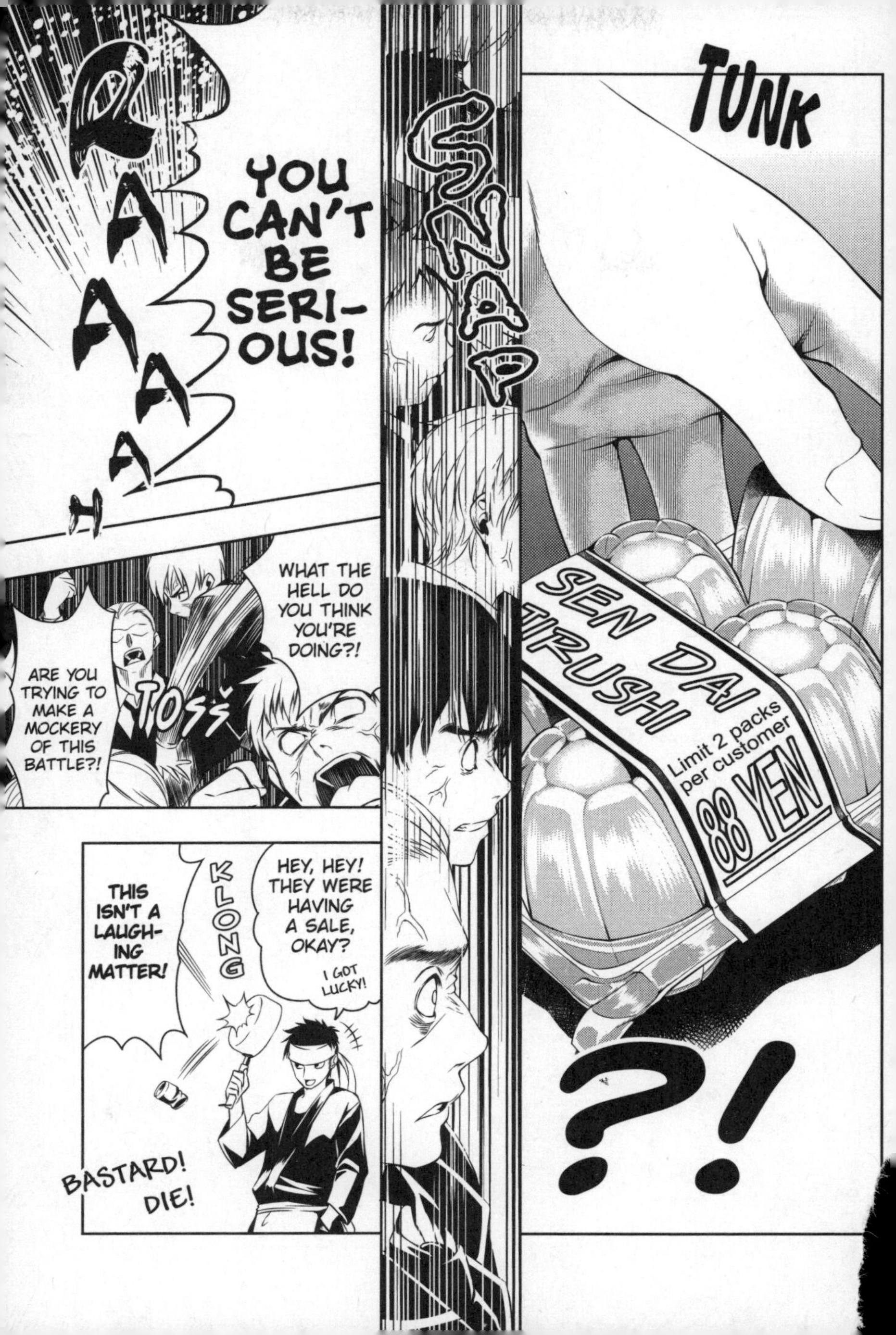
TUNK
SEN DAI TIRUSHI
Limit 2 packs per customer
88 YEN
?!
SNAP
YOU CAN'T BE SERI-OUS!
AAAAH
WHAT THE HELL DO YOU THINK YOU'RE DOING?!
ARE YOU TRYING TO MAKE A MOCKERY OF THIS BATTLE?!
TOSS
HEY, HEY! THEY WERE HAVING A SALE, OKAY?
I GOT LUCKY!
KLONG
THIS ISN'T A LAUGH-ING MATTER!
BASTARD! DIE!

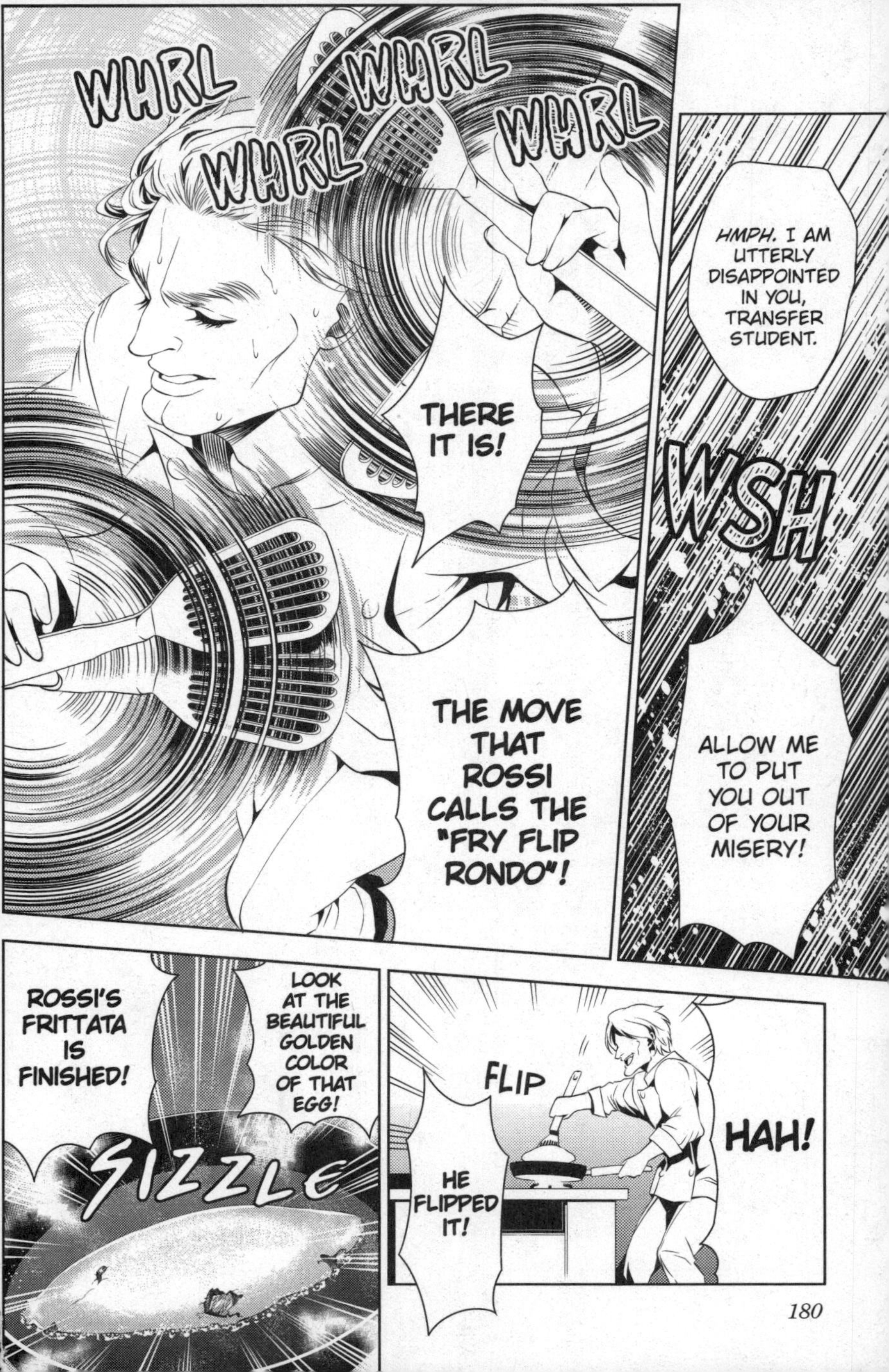
HMPH. I AM UTTERLY DISAPPOINTED IN YOU, TRANSFER STUDENT.
WSH
ALLOW ME TO PUT YOU OUT OF YOUR MISERY!
WHRL WHRL WHRL WHRL
THERE IT IS!
THE MOVE THAT ROSSI CALLS THE "FRY FLIP RONDO"!
HAH!
FLIP
HE FLIPPED IT!
LOOK AT THE BEAUTIFUL GOLDEN COLOR OF THAT EGG!
ROSSI'S FRITTATA IS FINISHED!
SIZZLE

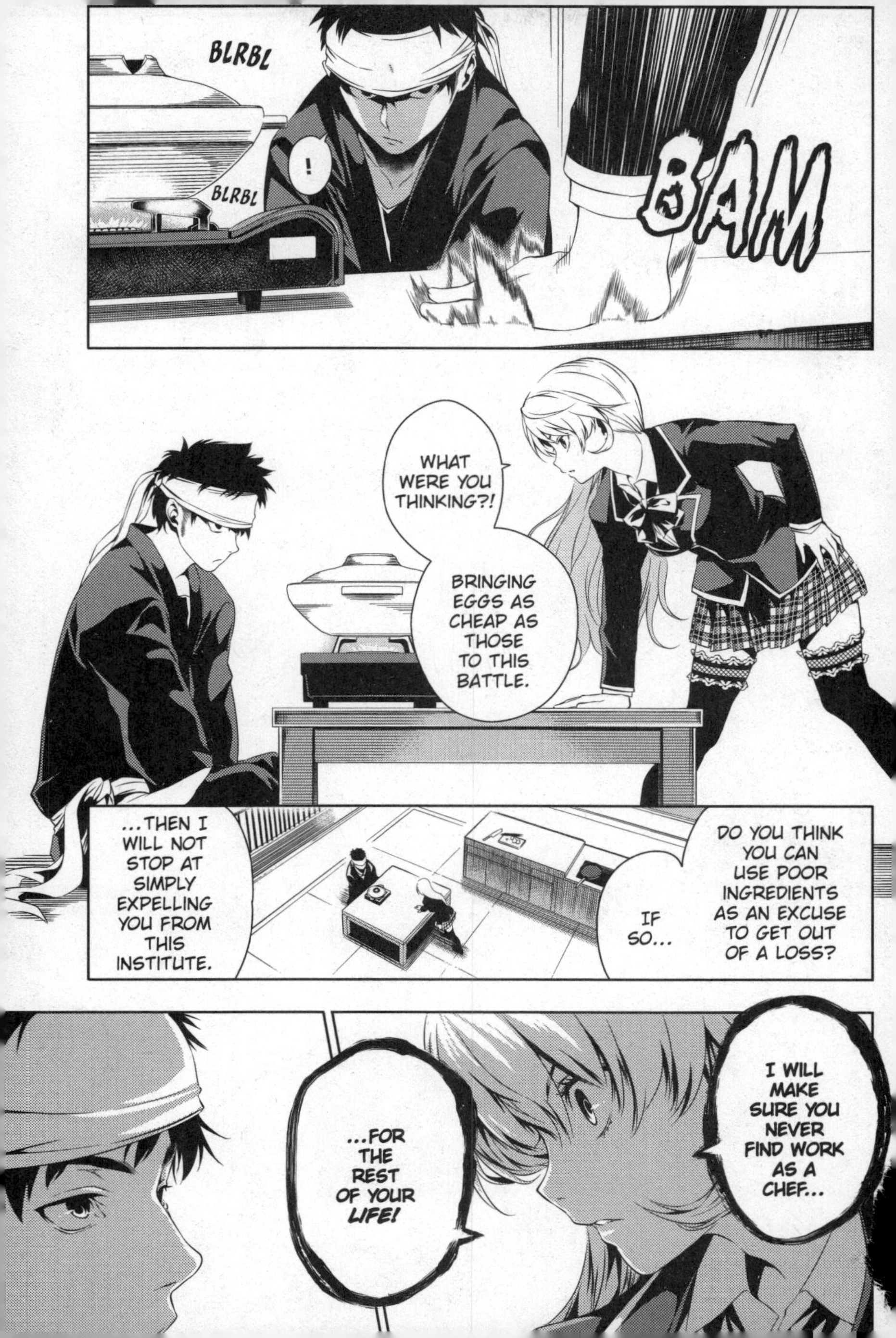
BAM
BLRBL
!
BLRBL
WHAT WERE YOU THINKING?!
BRINGING EGGS AS CHEAP AS THOSE TO THIS BATTLE.
DO YOU THINK YOU CAN USE POOR INGREDIENTS AS AN EXCUSE TO GET OUT OF A LOSS?
IF SO...
...THEN I WILL NOT STOP AT SIMPLY EXPELLING YOU FROM THIS INSTITUTE.
I WILL MAKE SURE YOU NEVER FIND WORK AS A CHEF...
...FOR THE REST OF YOUR *LIFE!*

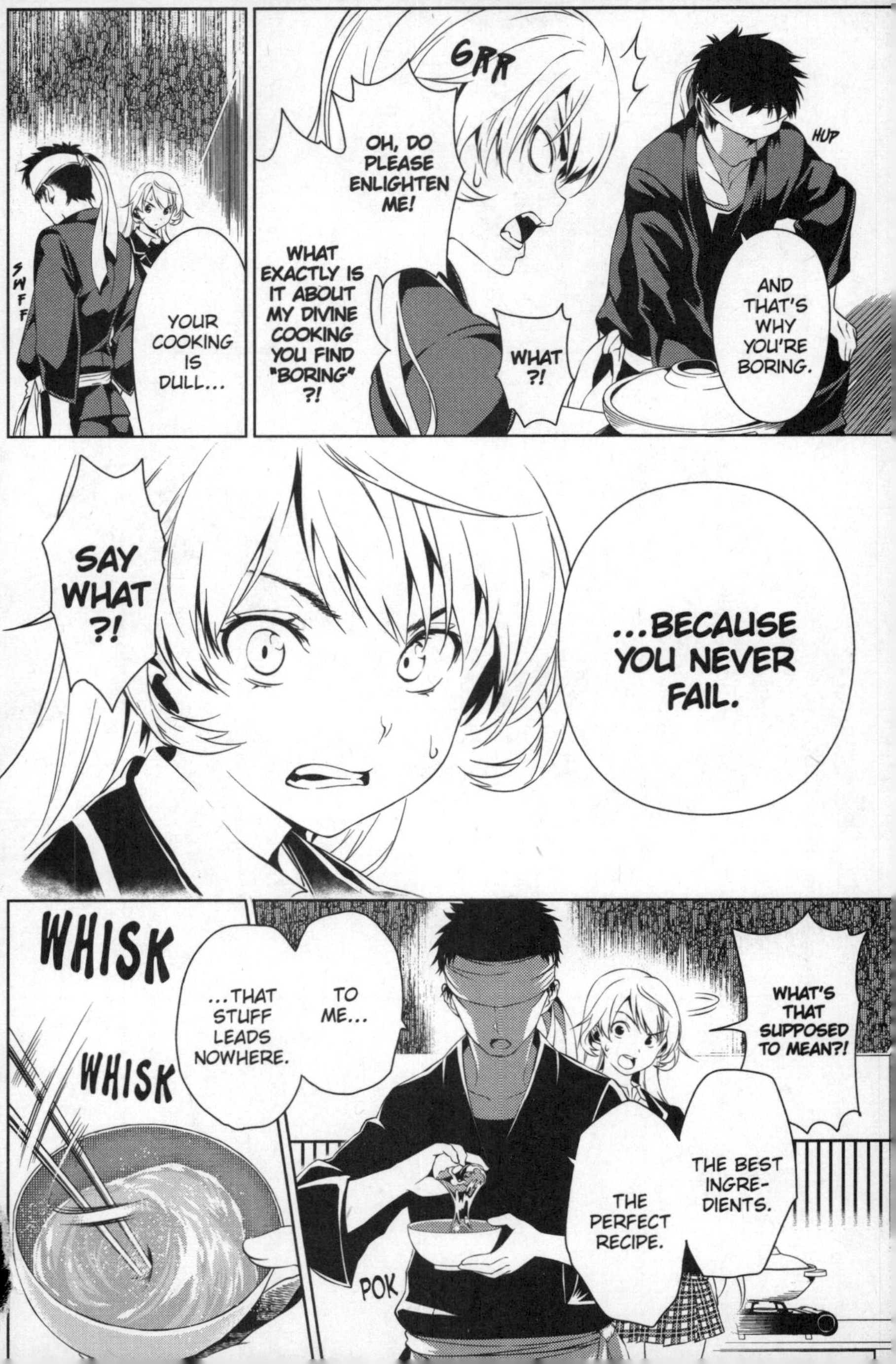
HUP
AND THAT'S WHY YOU'RE BORING.
GRR
WHAT?!
OH, DO PLEASE ENLIGHTEN ME!
WHAT EXACTLY IS IT ABOUT MY DIVINE COOKING YOU FIND "BORING"?!
SWFF
YOUR COOKING IS DULL...
...BECAUSE YOU NEVER FAIL.
SAY WHAT?!
WHAT'S THAT SUPPOSED TO MEAN?!
THE BEST INGRE-DIENTS.
THE PERFECT RECIPE.
TO ME...
...THAT STUFF LEADS NOWHERE.
WHISK
WHISK
POK

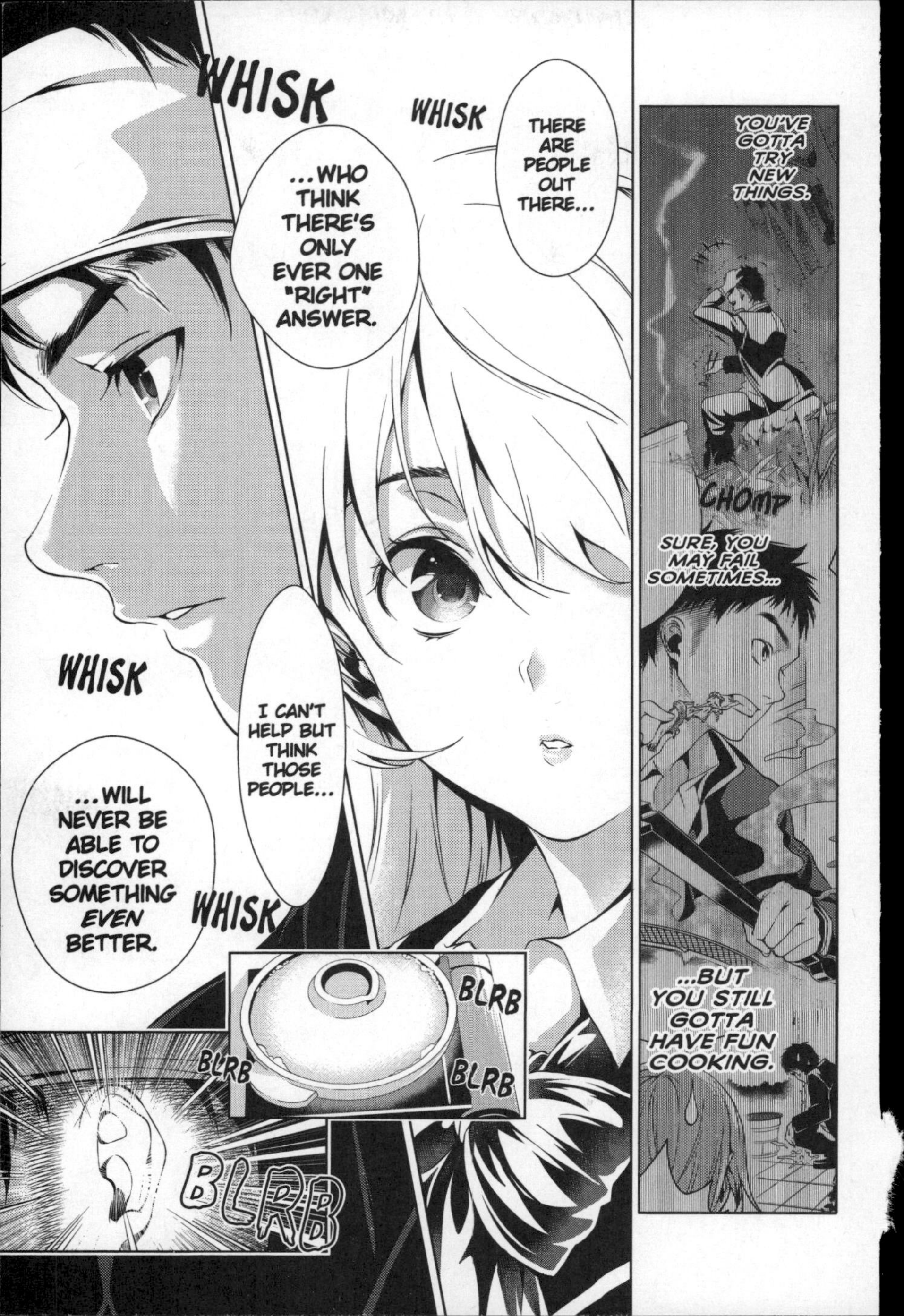
YOU'VE GOTTA TRY NEW THINGS.
CHOMP
SURE, YOU MAY FAIL SOMETIMES...
...BUT YOU STILL GOTTA HAVE FUN COOKING.
THERE ARE PEOPLE OUT THERE...
WHISK
WHISK
...WHO THINK THERE'S ONLY EVER ONE "RIGHT" ANSWER.
I CAN'T HELP BUT THINK THOSE PEOPLE...
WHISK
...WILL NEVER BE ABLE TO DISCOVER SOMETHING *EVEN* BETTER.
WHISK
BLRB
BLRB
BLRB
BLRB

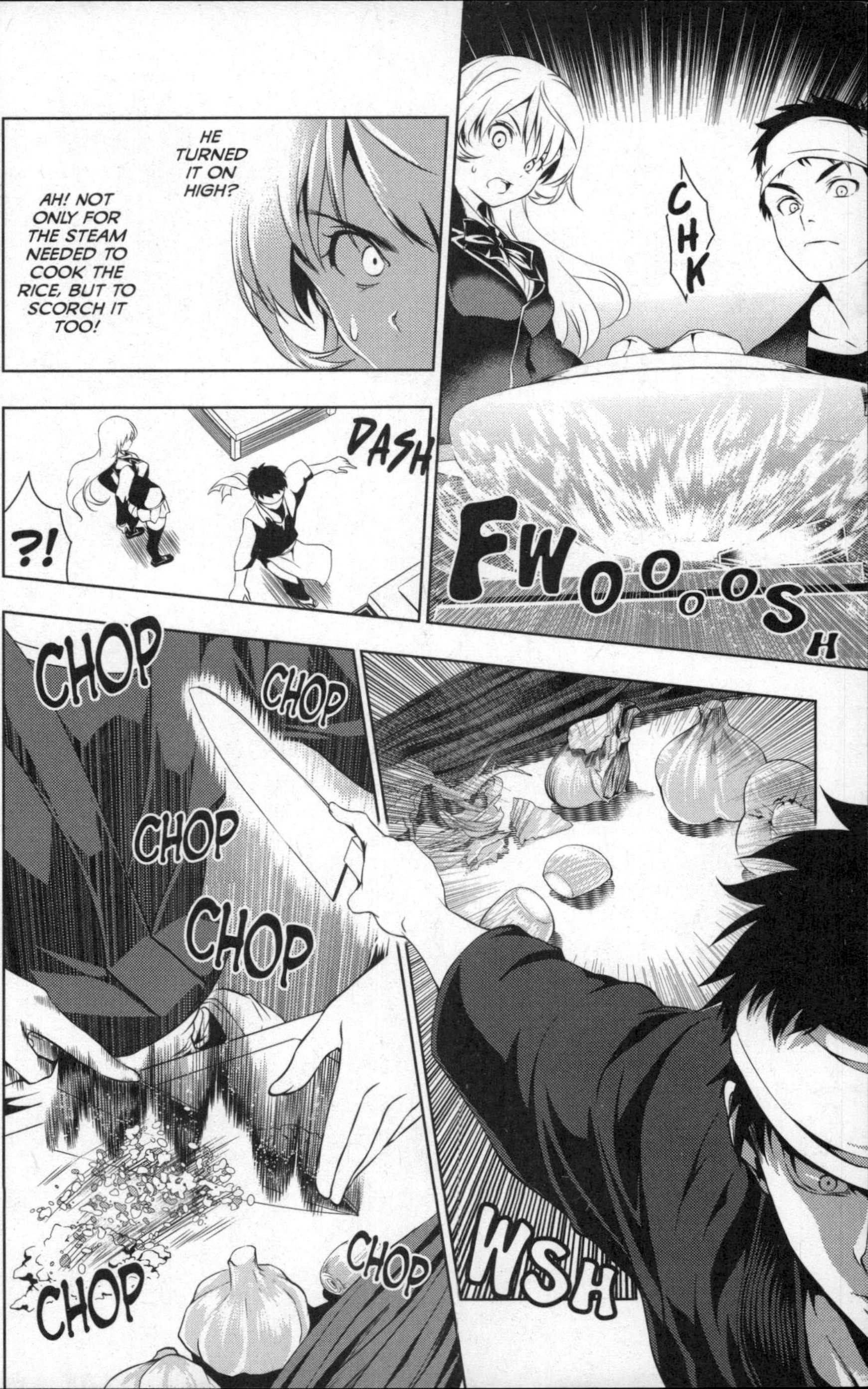

CHK
FWOOOOSH
HE TURNED IT ON HIGH?
AH! NOT ONLY FOR THE STEAM NEEDED TO COOK THE RICE, BUT TO SCORCH IT TOO!
DASH
?!
WSH
CHOP
CHOP
CHOP
CHOP
CHOP
CHOP

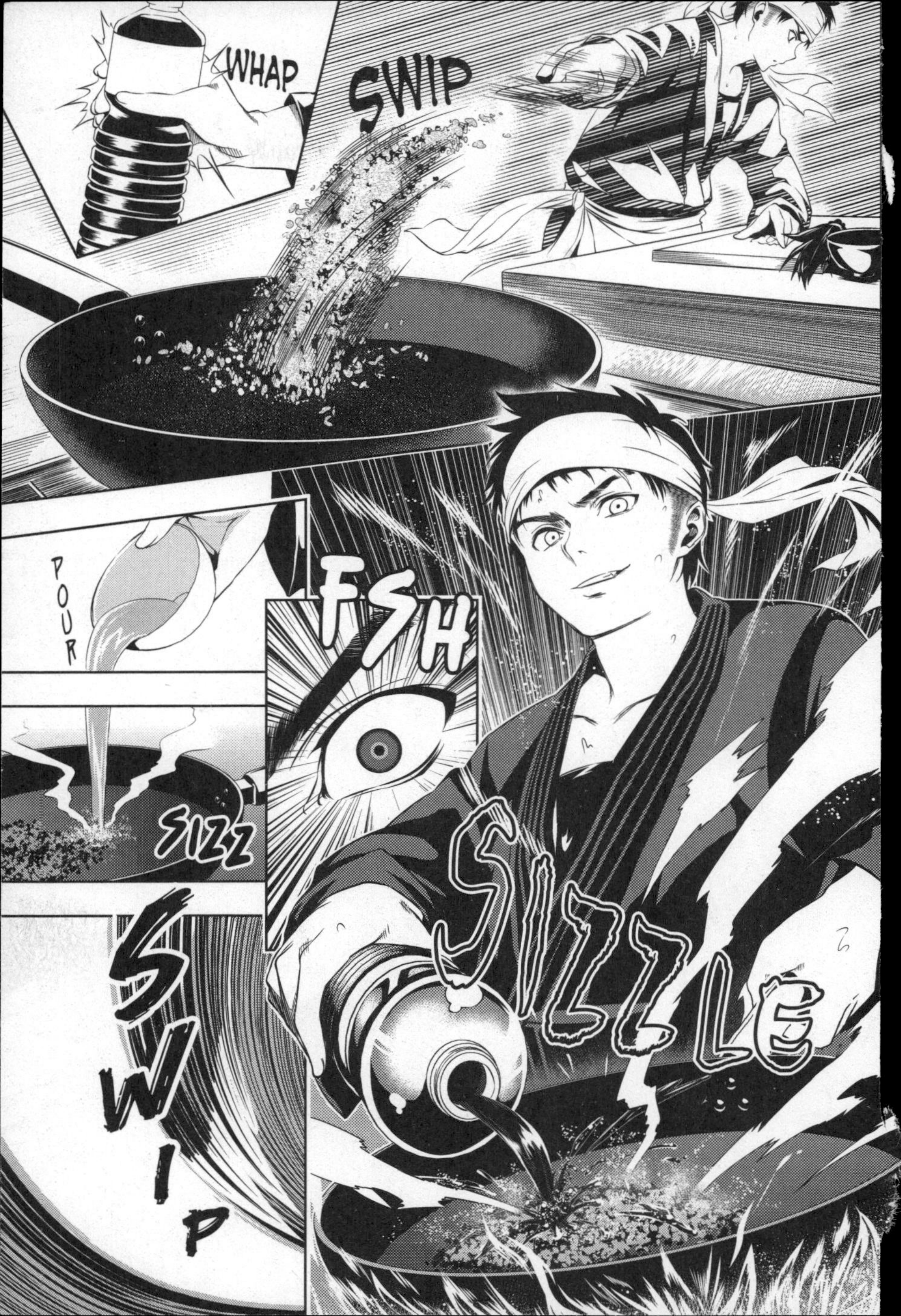
SWIP
WHAP
SIZZLE
FSH
POUR
SIZZ
SWIP

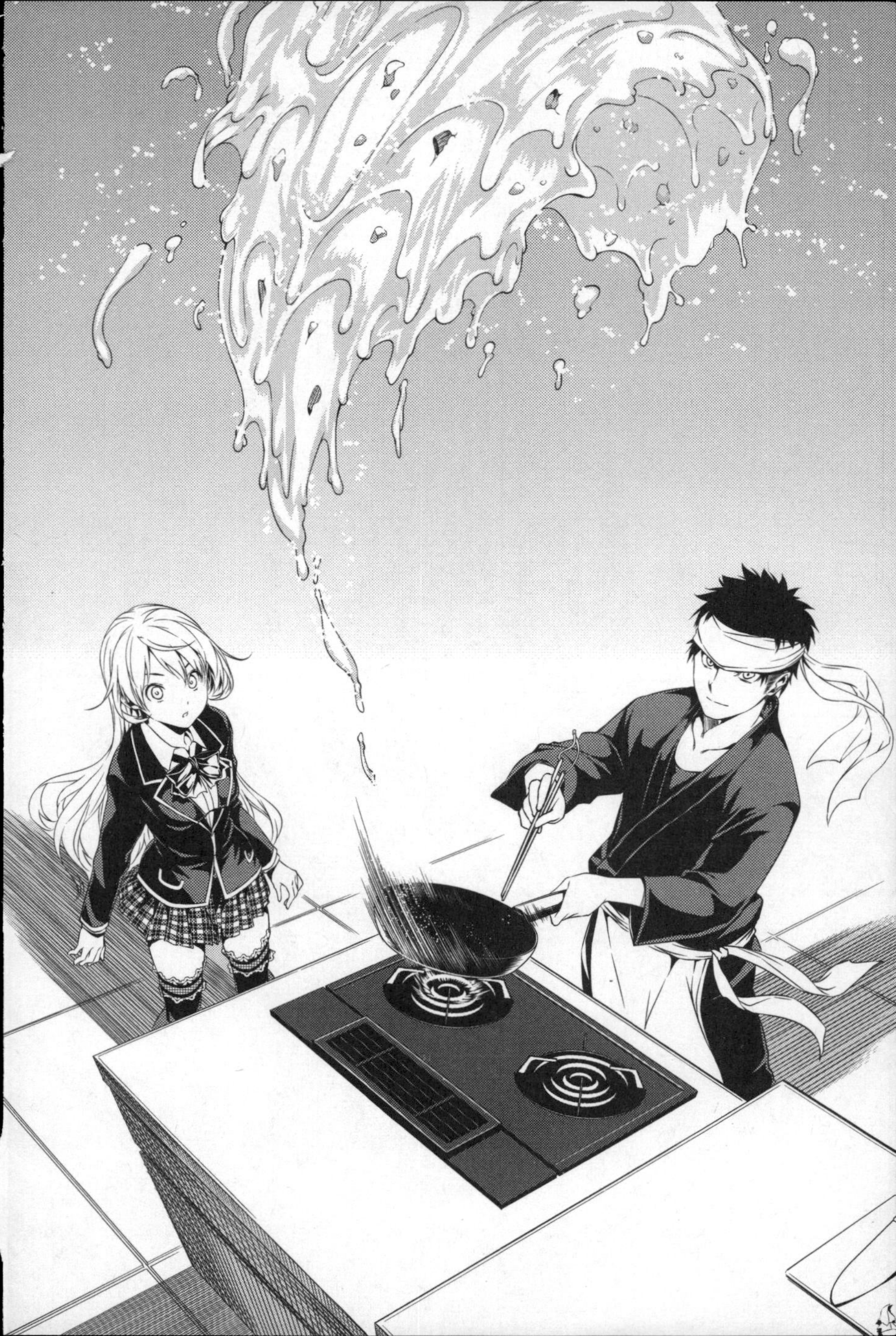

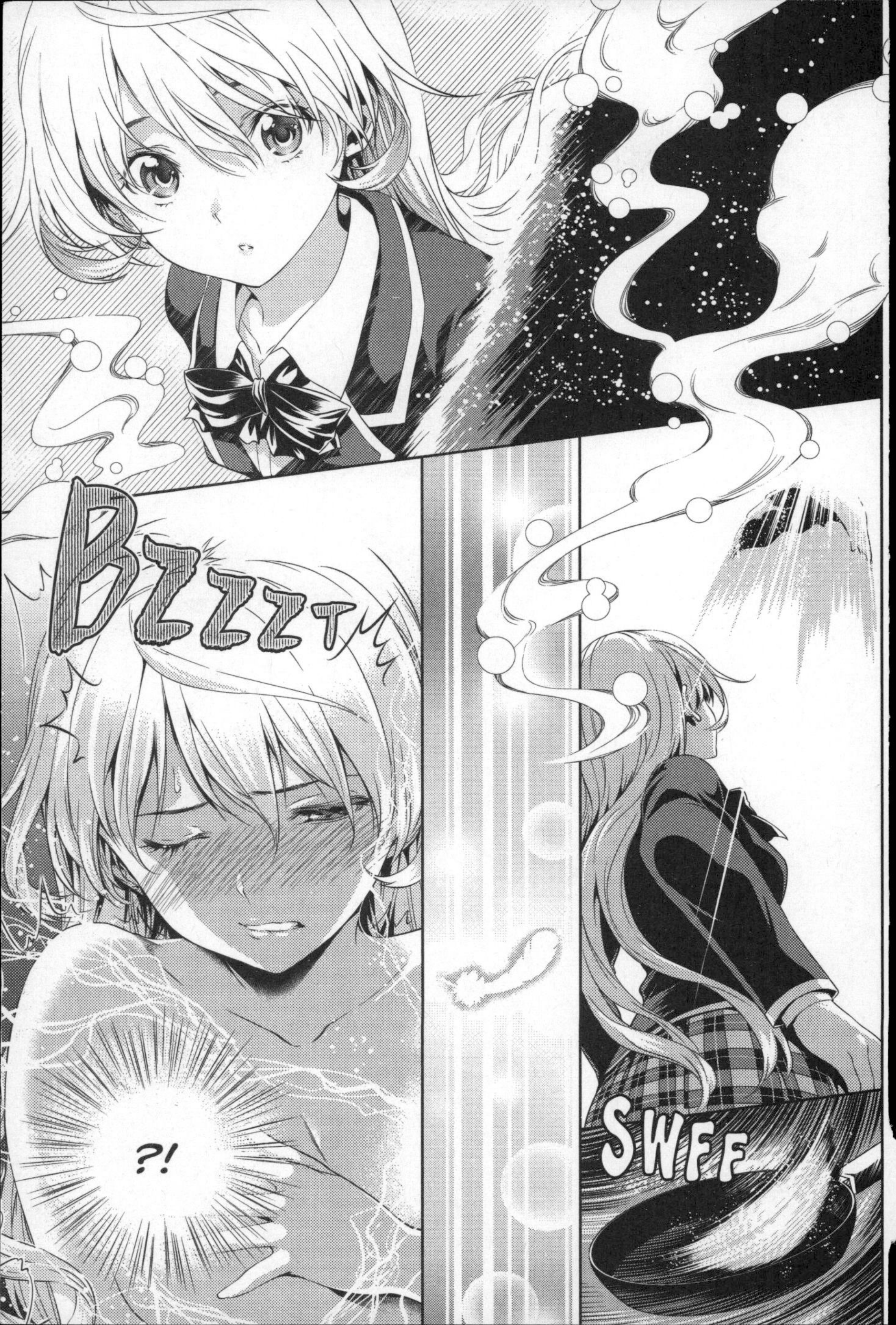

SWFF
BZZZT
?!

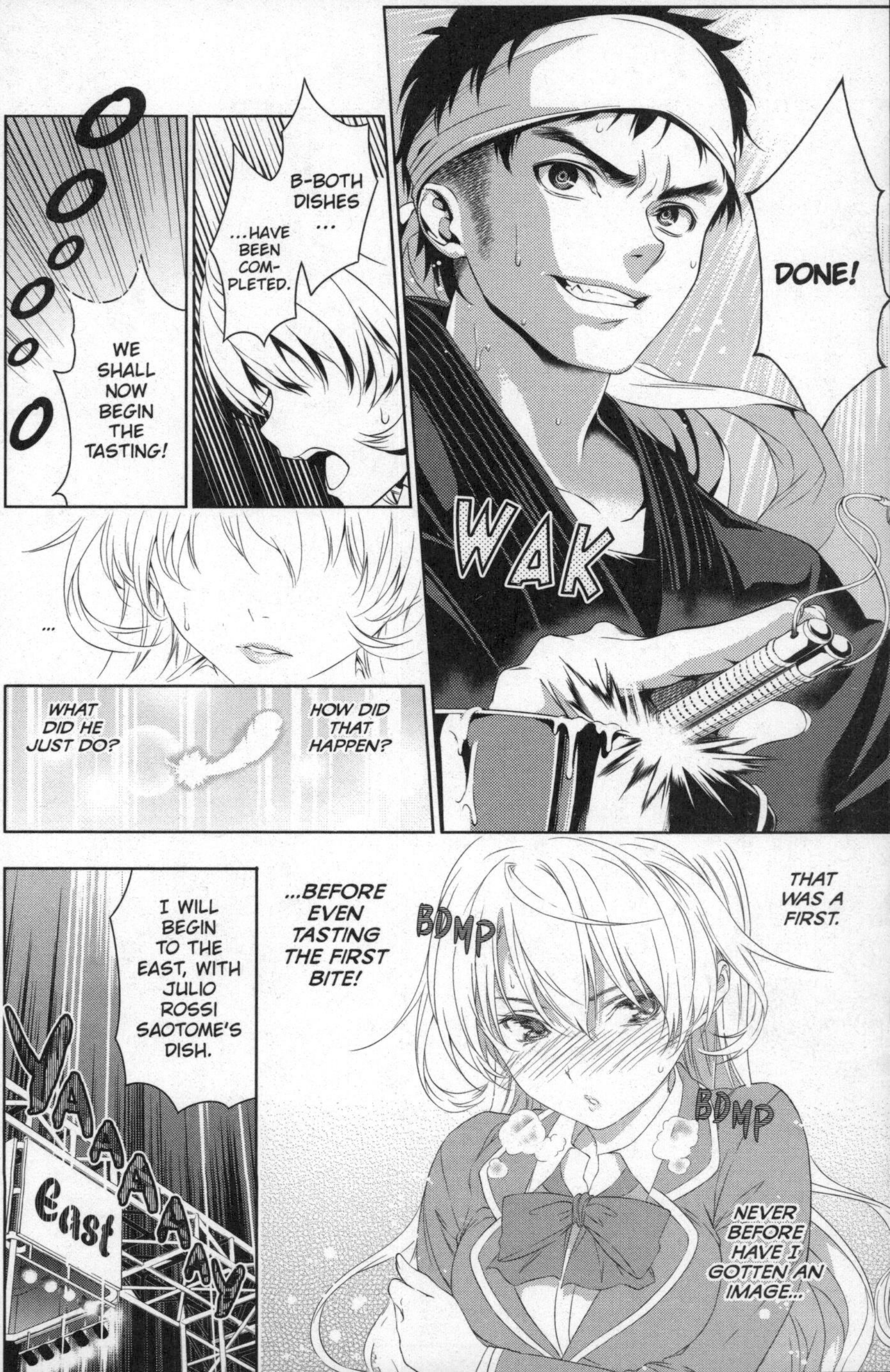
DONE!
WAK
B-BOTH DISHES ...
...HAVE BEEN COM-PLETED.
OOOOOOOO
WE SHALL NOW BEGIN THE TASTING!
...
HOW DID THAT HAPPEN?
WHAT DID HE JUST DO?
THAT WAS A FIRST.
BDMP
BDMP
NEVER BEFORE HAVE I GOTTEN AN IMAGE...
...BEFORE EVEN TASTING THE FIRST BITE!
I WILL BEGIN TO THE EAST, WITH JULIO ROSSI SAOTOME'S DISH.
YAAAAAAAY
East

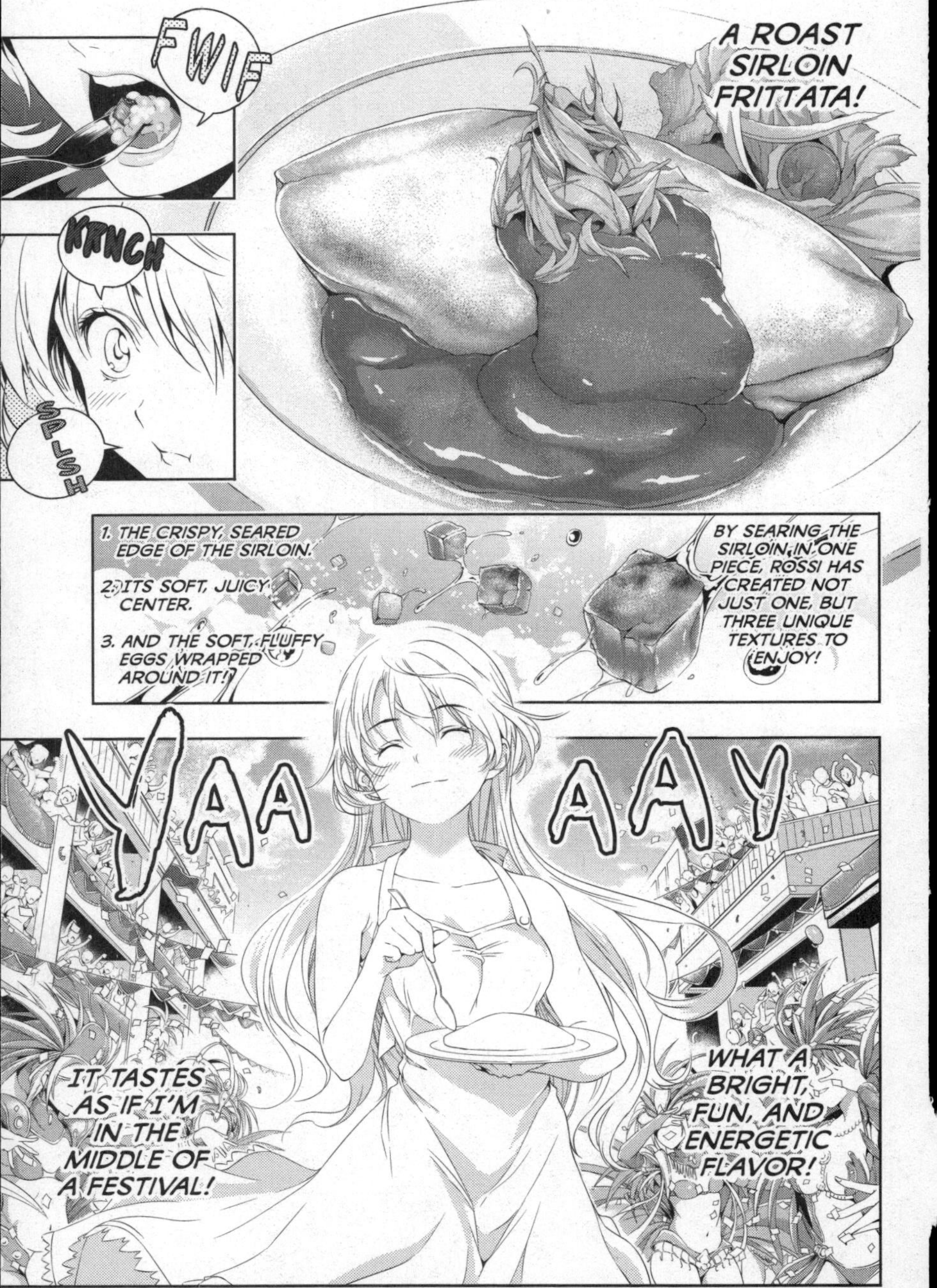

A ROAST SIRLOIN FRITTATA!
FWIF
KRNCH
SPLSH
BY SEARING THE SIRLOIN IN ONE PIECE, ROSSI HAS CREATED NOT JUST ONE, BUT THREE UNIQUE TEXTURES TO ENJOY!
1. THE CRISPY, SEARED EDGE OF THE SIRLOIN.
2. ITS SOFT, JUICY CENTER.
3. AND THE SOFT, FLUFFY EGGS WRAPPED AROUND IT!
YAAAAAY
WHAT A BRIGHT, FUN, AND ENERGETIC FLAVOR!
IT TASTES AS IF I'M IN THE MIDDLE OF A FESTIVAL!

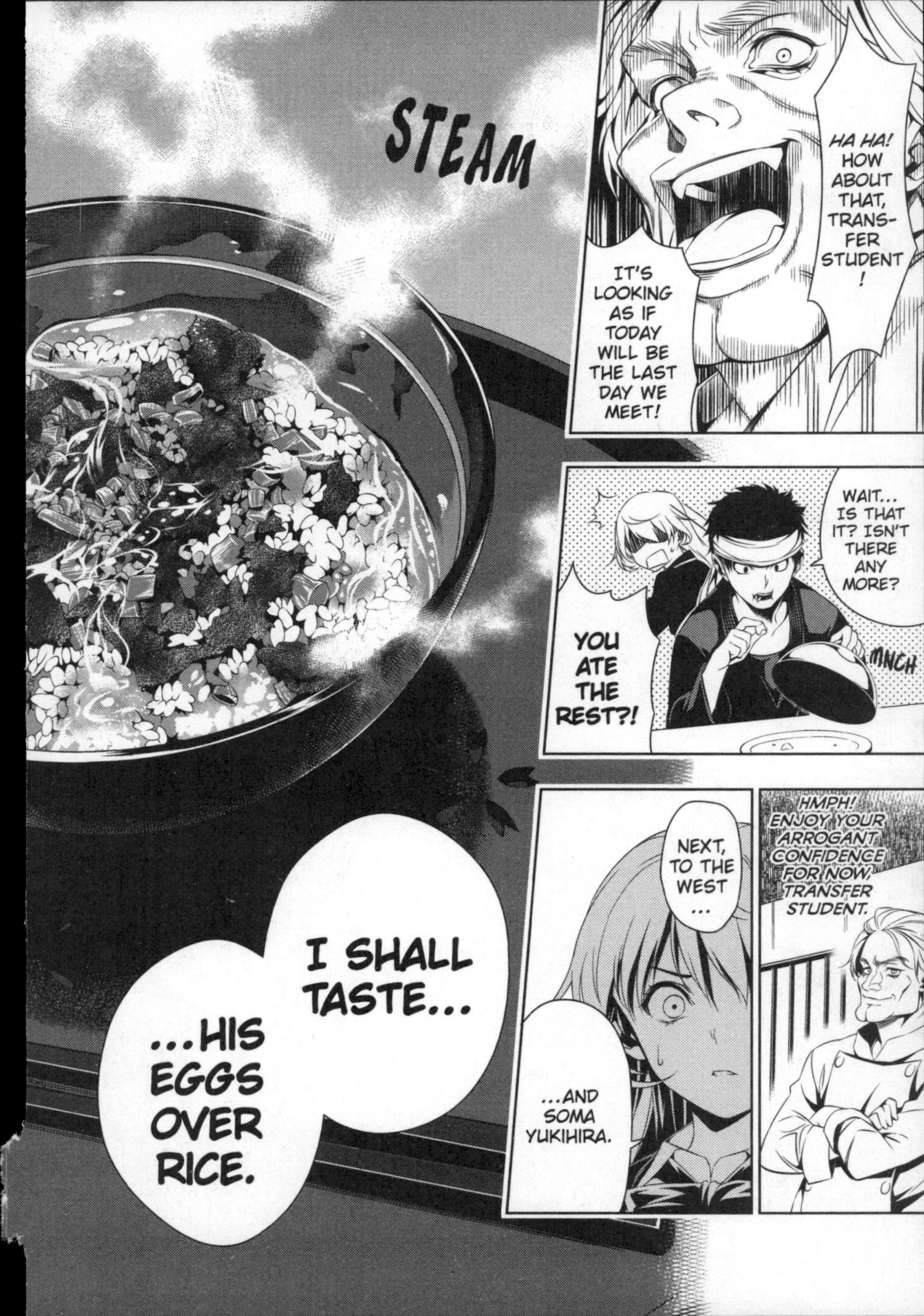
HA HA! HOW ABOUT THAT, TRANS-FER STUDENT!
IT'S LOOKING AS IF TODAY WILL BE THE LAST DAY WE MEET!
WAIT... IS THAT IT? ISN'T THERE ANY MORE?
MNCH
YOU ATE THE REST?!
HMPH! ENJOY YOUR ARROGANT CONFIDENCE FOR NOW, TRANSFER STUDENT.
NEXT, TO THE WEST...
...AND SOMA YUKIHIRA.
STEAM
I SHALL TASTE...
...HIS EGGS OVER RICE.

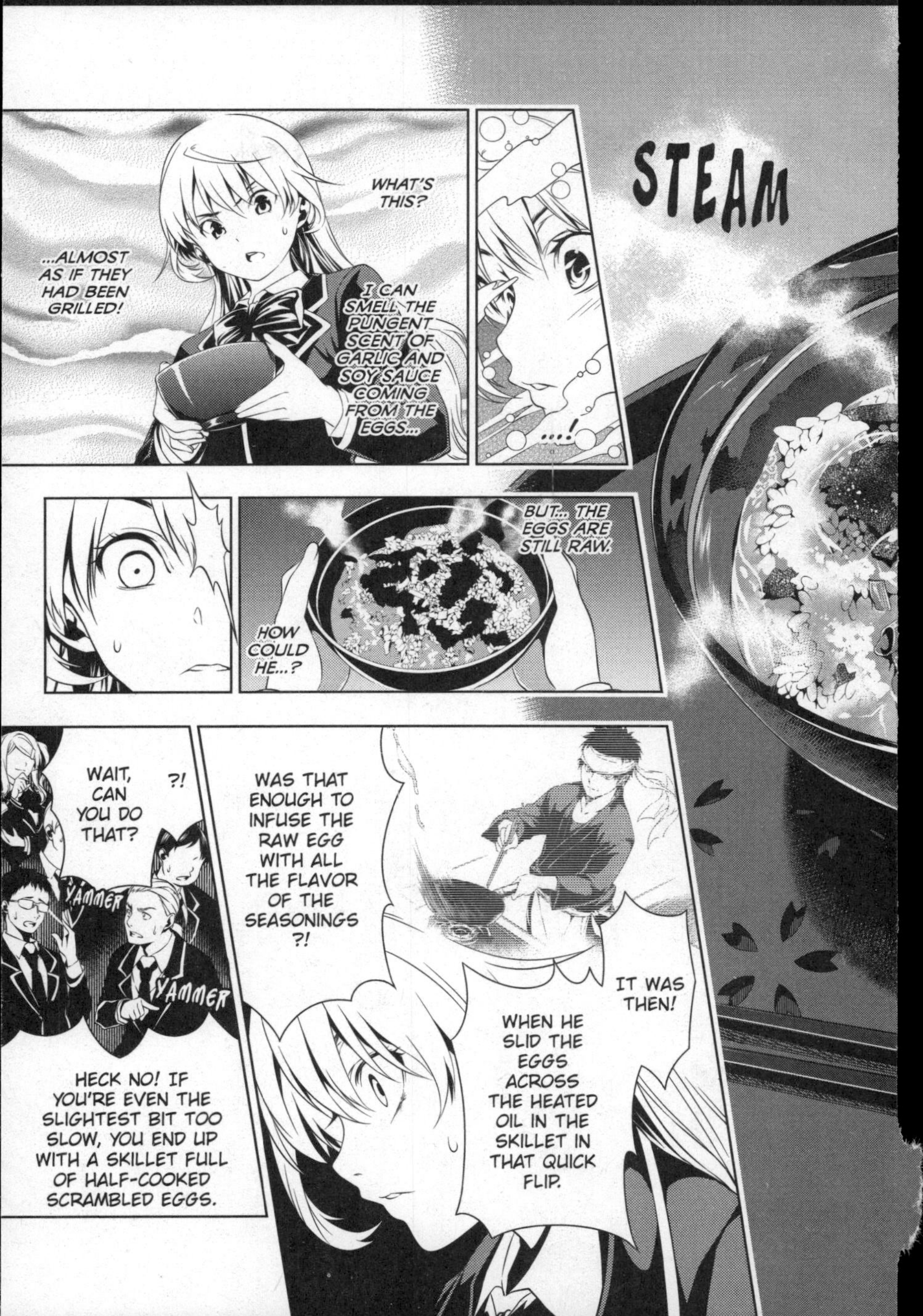

STEAM
....!
WHAT'S THIS?
I CAN SMELL THE PUNGENT SCENT OF GARLIC AND SOY SAUCE COMING FROM THE EGGS...
...ALMOST AS IF THEY HAD BEEN GRILLED!
BUT... THE EGGS ARE STILL RAW.
HOW COULD HE...?
WAS THAT ENOUGH TO INFUSE THE RAW EGG WITH ALL THE FLAVOR OF THE SEASONINGS ?!
IT WAS THEN!
WHEN HE SLID THE EGGS ACROSS THE HEATED OIL IN THE SKILLET IN THAT QUICK FLIP.
?!
WAIT, CAN YOU DO THAT?
YAMMER
YAMMER
HECK NO! IF YOU'RE EVEN THE SLIGHTEST BIT TOO SLOW, YOU END UP WITH A SKILLET FULL OF HALF-COOKED SCRAMBLED EGGS.

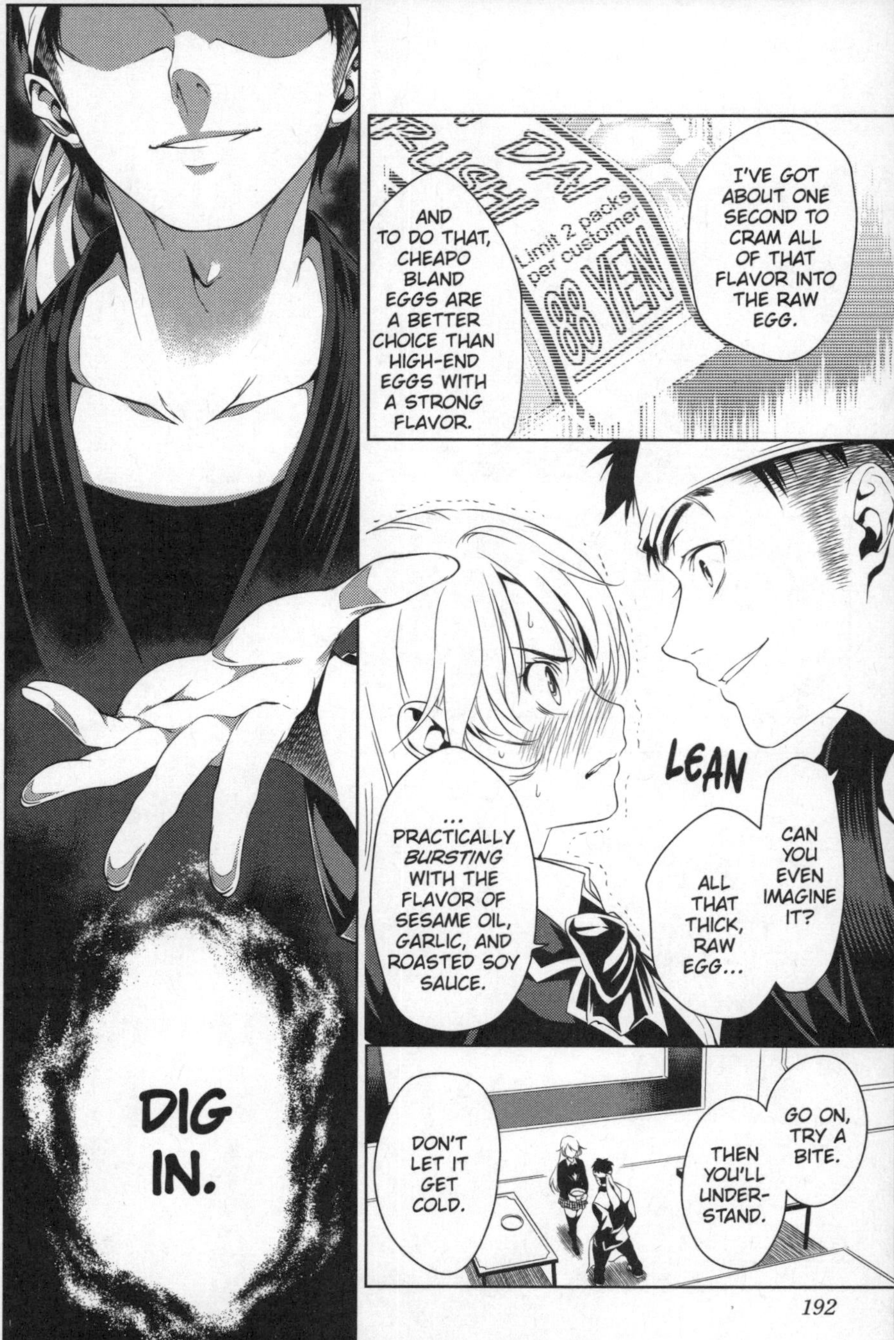
I'VE GOT ABOUT ONE SECOND TO CRAM ALL OF THAT FLAVOR INTO THE RAW EGG.
DAI
Limit 2 packs per customer
88 YEN
AND TO DO THAT, CHEAPO BLAND EGGS ARE A BETTER CHOICE THAN HIGH-END EGGS WITH A STRONG FLAVOR.
LEAN
CAN YOU EVEN IMAGINE IT?
ALL THAT THICK, RAW EGG...
... PRACTICALLY *BURSTING* WITH THE FLAVOR OF SESAME OIL, GARLIC, AND ROASTED SOY SAUCE.
GO ON, TRY A BITE.
THEN YOU'LL UNDER-STAND.
DON'T LET IT GET COLD.
DIG IN.

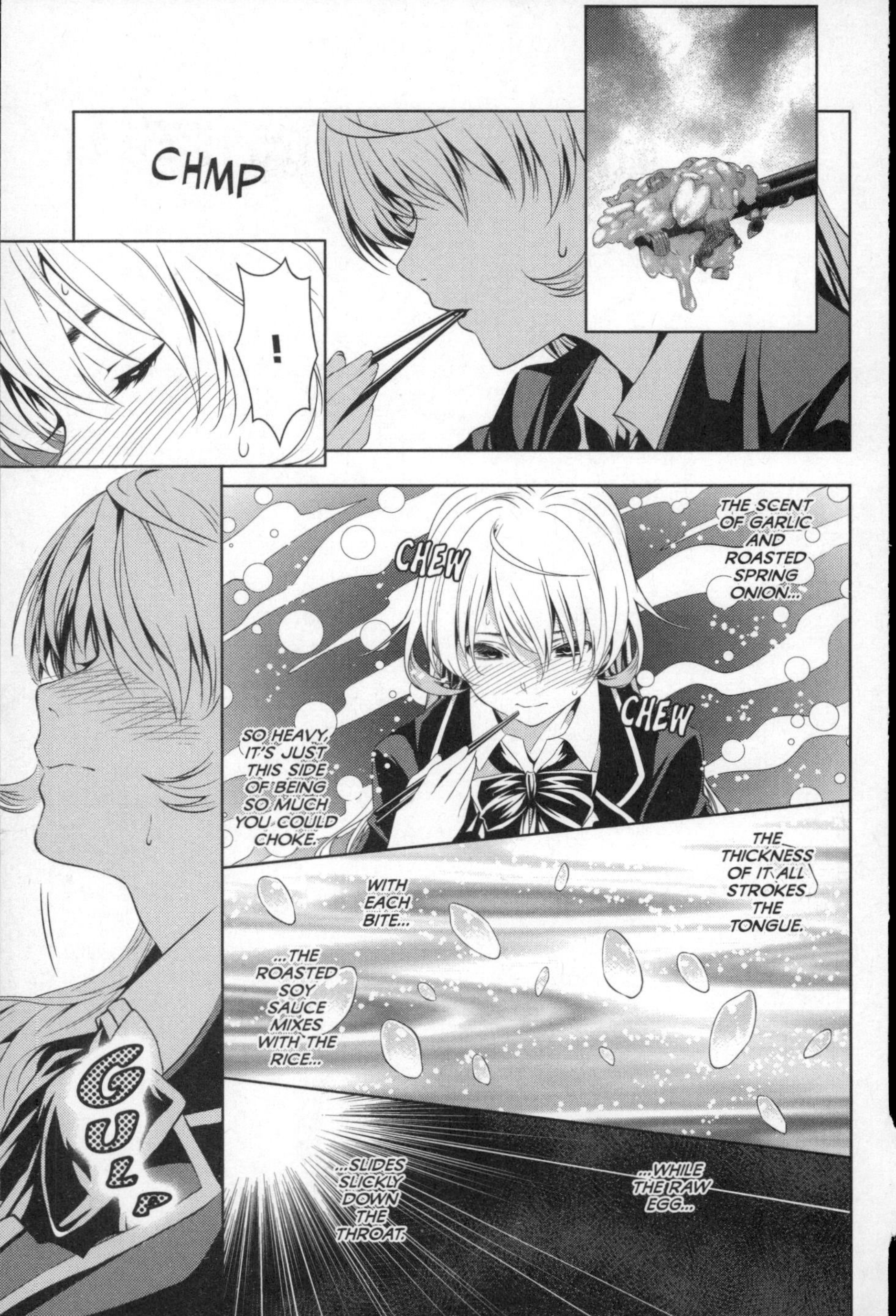
CHMP
!
THE SCENT OF GARLIC AND ROASTED SPRING ONION...
CHEW
CHEW
SO HEAVY, IT'S JUST THIS SIDE OF BEING SO MUCH YOU COULD CHOKE.
THE THICKNESS OF IT ALL STROKES THE TONGUE.
WITH EACH BITE...
...THE ROASTED SOY SAUCE MIXES WITH THE RICE...
...WHILE THE RAW EGG...
...SLIDES SLICKLY DOWN THE THROAT.
GULP

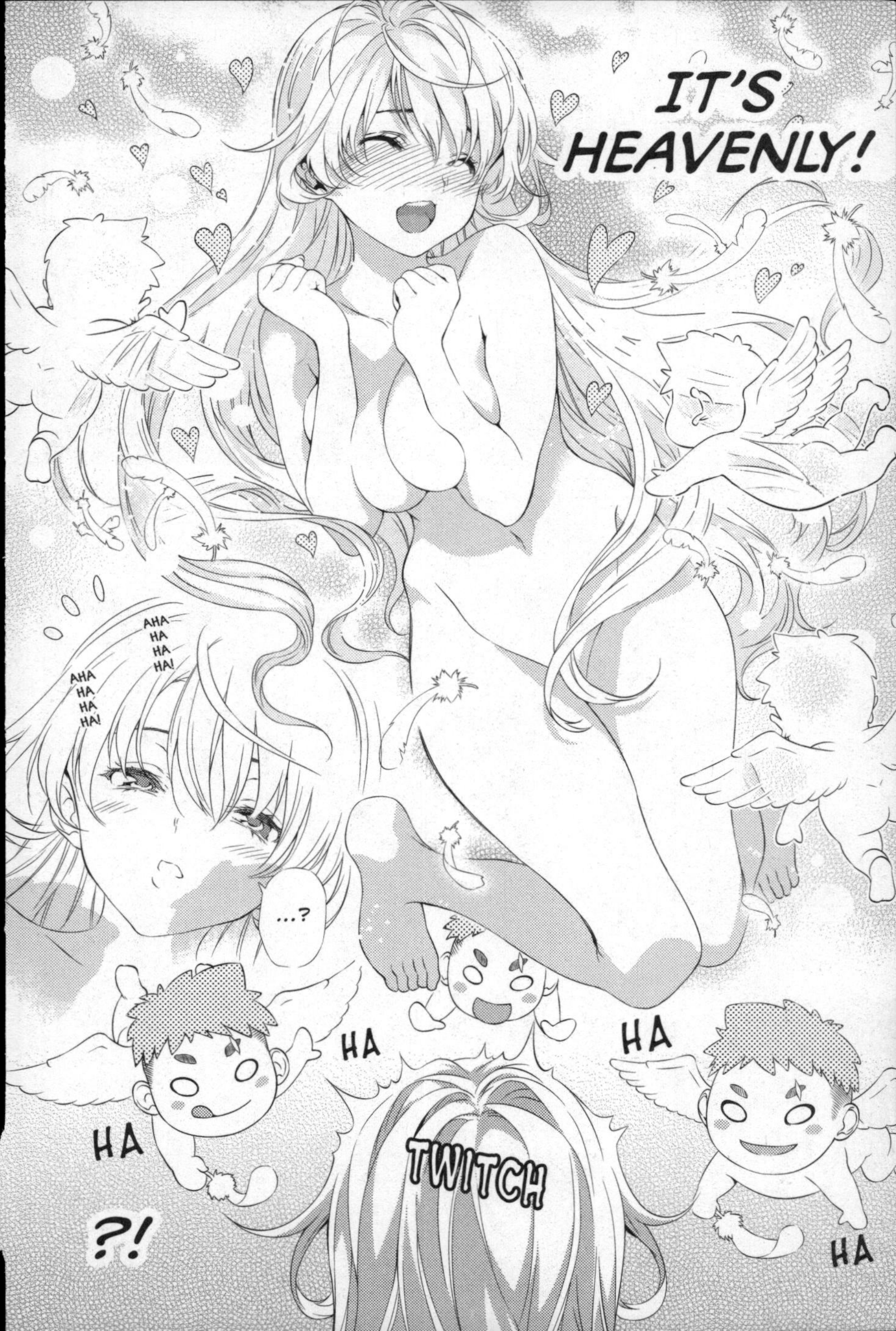
IT'S HEAVENLY!
AHA HA HA HA!
AHA HA HA HA!
...?
HA
HA
TWITCH
HA
HA
?!

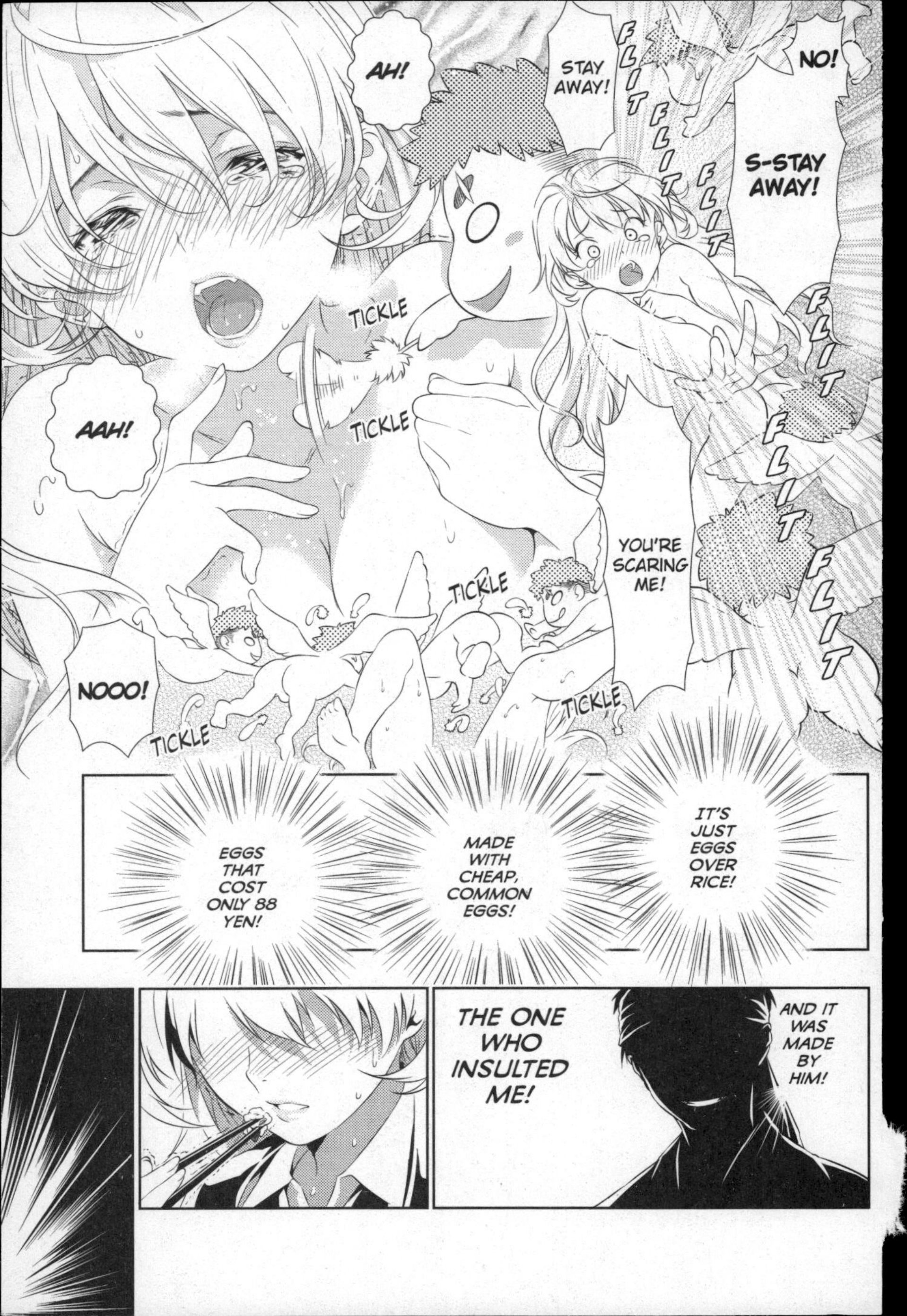
NO!
S-STAY AWAY!
FLIT FLIT FLIT
STAY AWAY!
FLIT FLIT FLIT
AH!
TICKLE
TICKLE
YOU'RE SCARING ME!
FLIT FLIT FLIT FLIT
TICKLE
TICKLE
AAH!
NOOO!
TICKLE
IT'S JUST EGGS OVER RICE!
MADE WITH CHEAP, COMMON EGGS!
EGGS THAT COST ONLY 88 YEN!
AND IT WAS MADE BY HIM!
THE ONE WHO INSULTED ME!

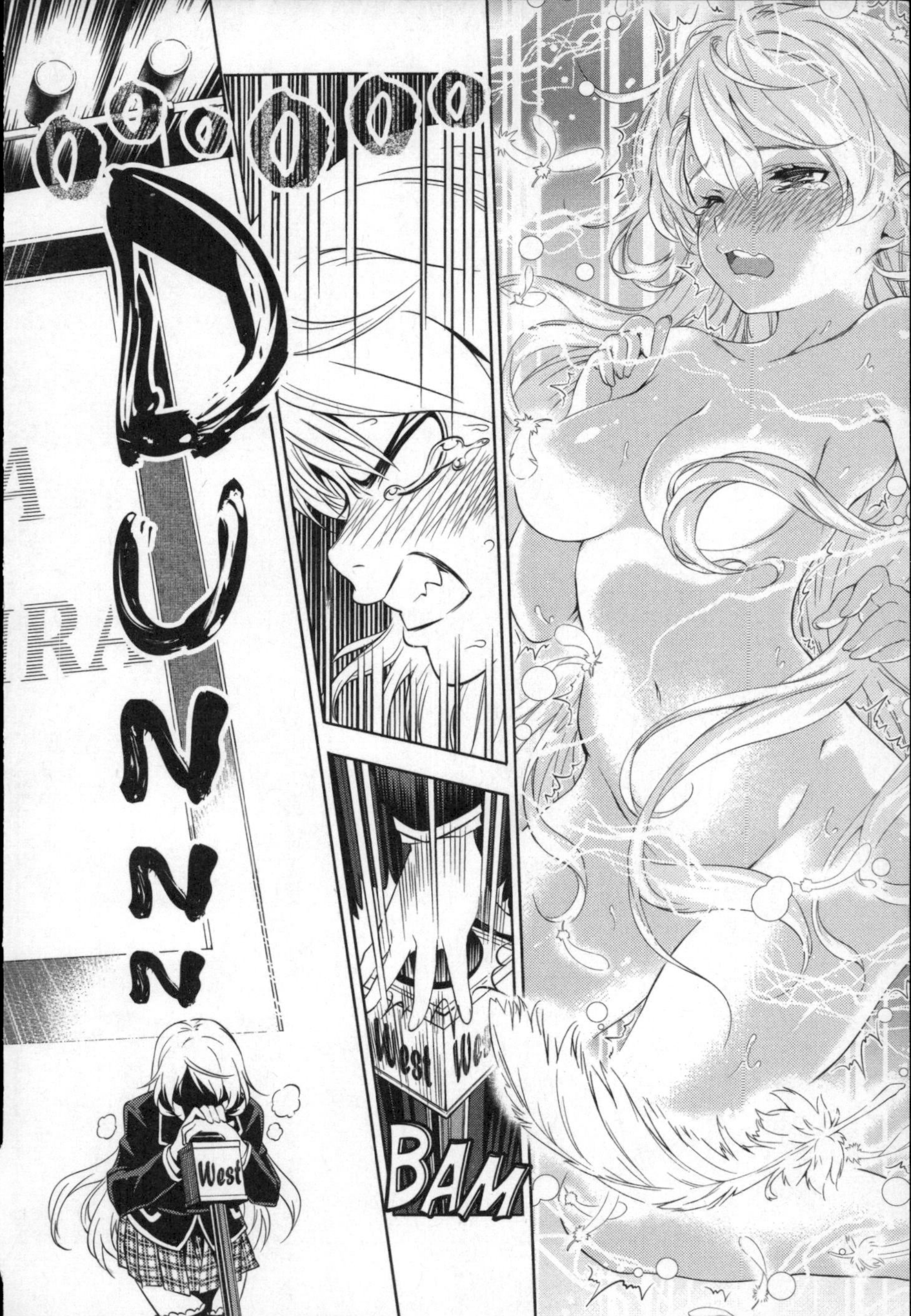
West
West
BAM
DUNNN
West

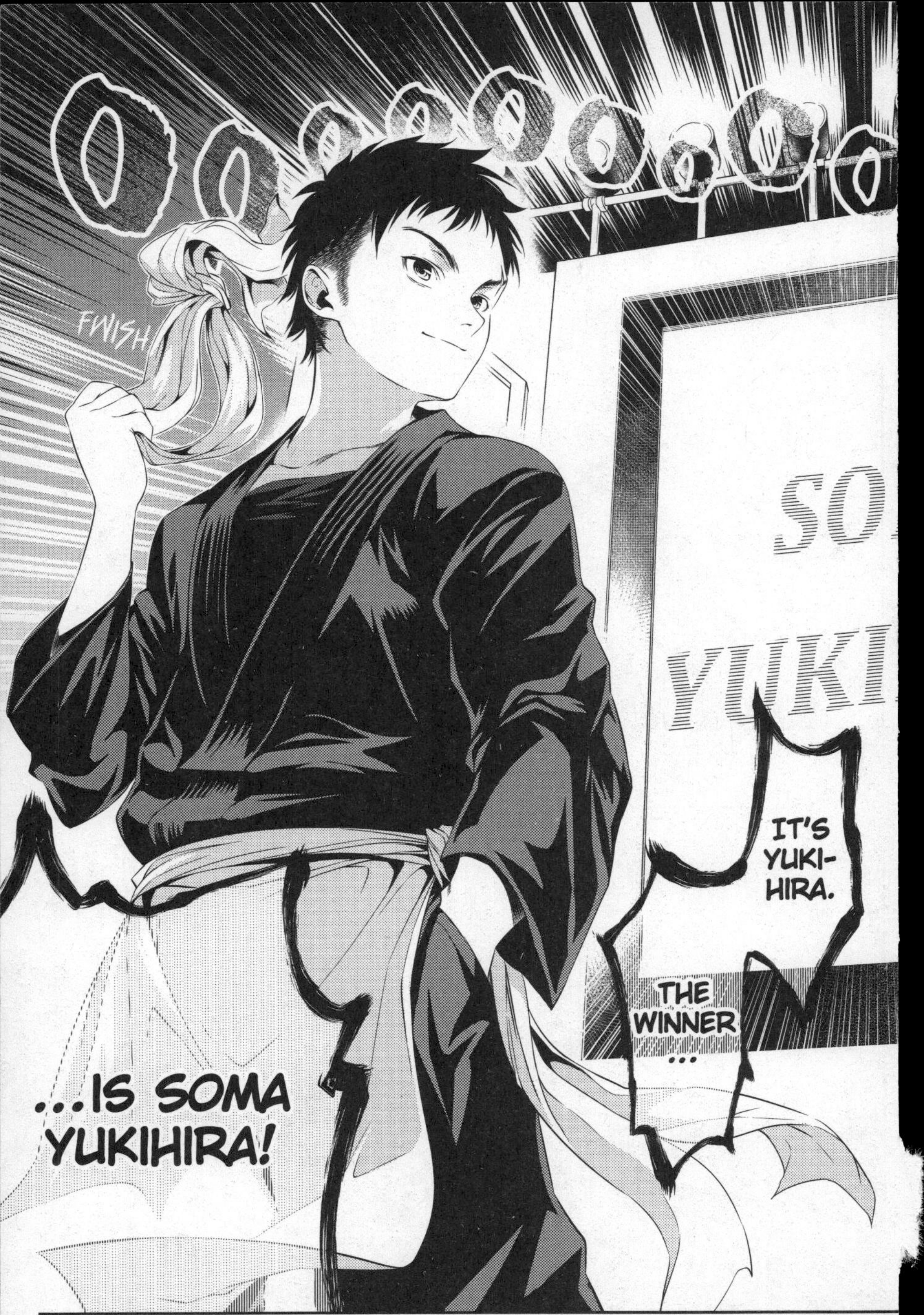
FWISH
IT'S YUKI-HIRA.
THE WINNER...
...IS SOMA YUKIHIRA!

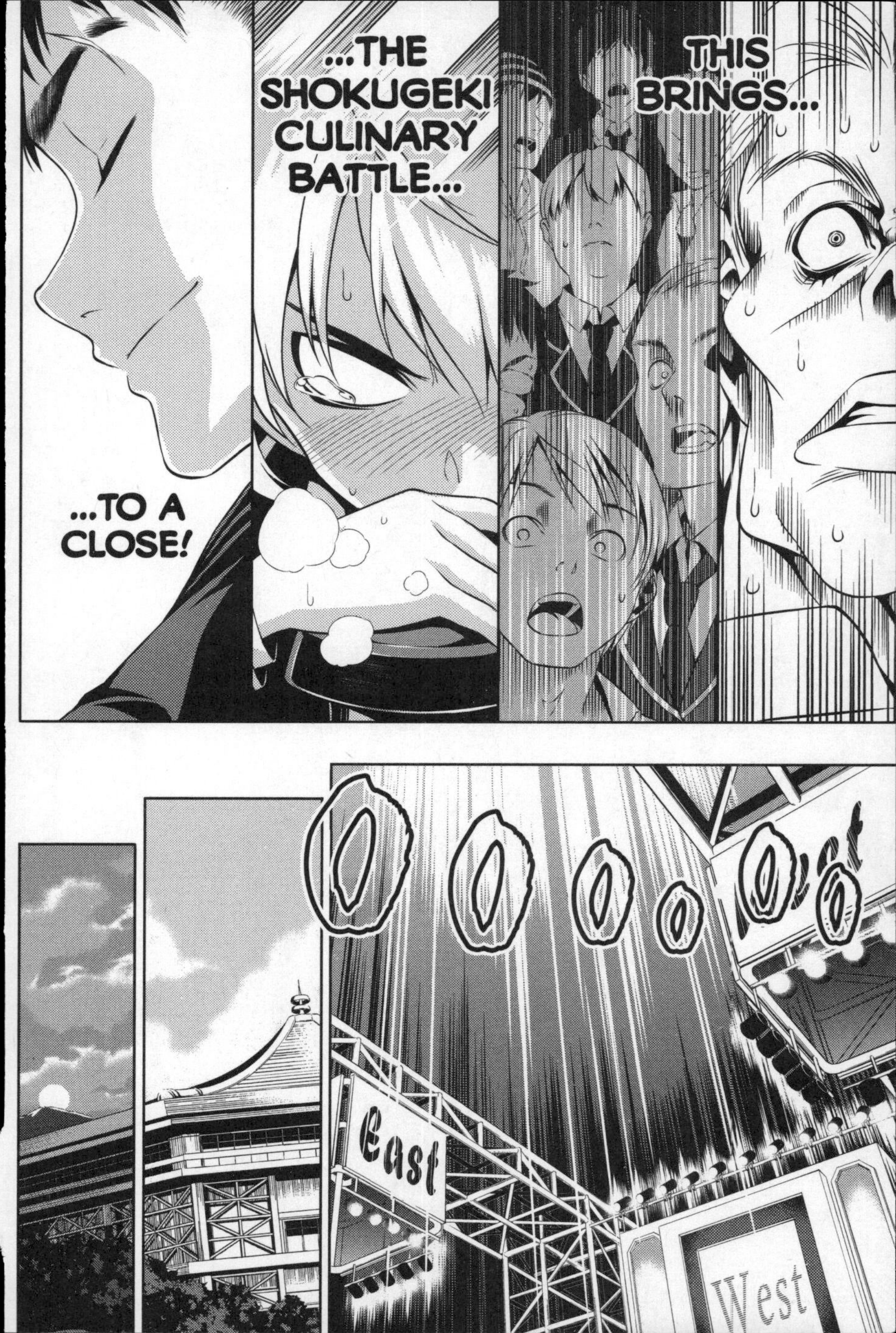
THIS BRINGS...
...THE SHOKUGEKI CULINARY BATTLE...
...TO A CLOSE!
OOOOO
East
West

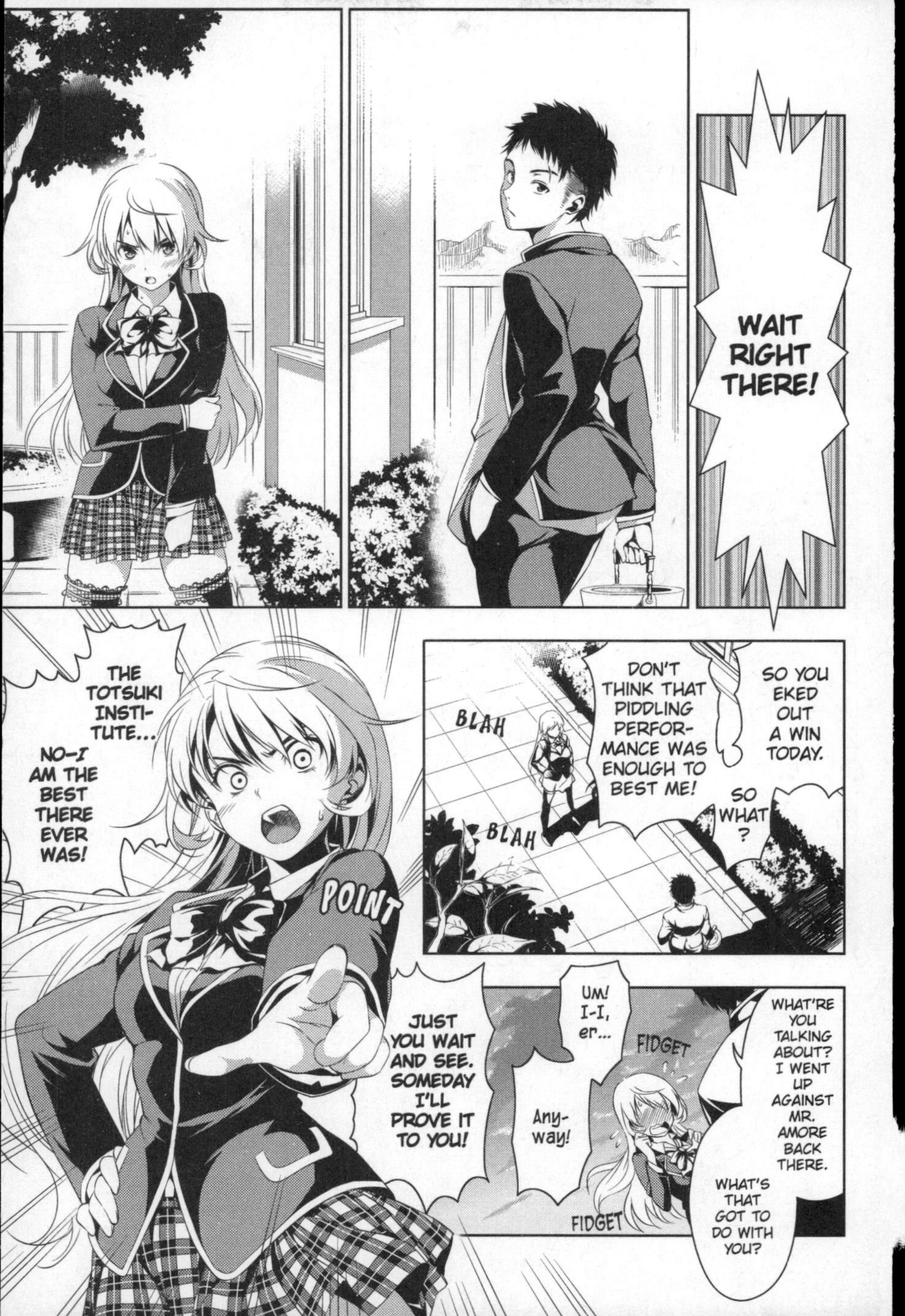
WAIT RIGHT THERE!
SO YOU EKED OUT A WIN TODAY.
DON'T THINK THAT PIDDLING PERFOR-MANCE WAS ENOUGH TO BEST ME!
BLAH
BLAH
SO WHAT?
WHAT'RE YOU TALKING ABOUT? I WENT UP AGAINST MR. AMORE BACK THERE.
WHAT'S THAT GOT TO DO WITH YOU?
Um! I-I, er...
FIDGET
Any-way!
FIDGET
JUST YOU WAIT AND SEE. SOMEDAY I'LL PROVE IT TO YOU!
THE TOTSUKI INSTI-TUTE...
NO—I AM THE BEST THERE EVER WAS!
POINT

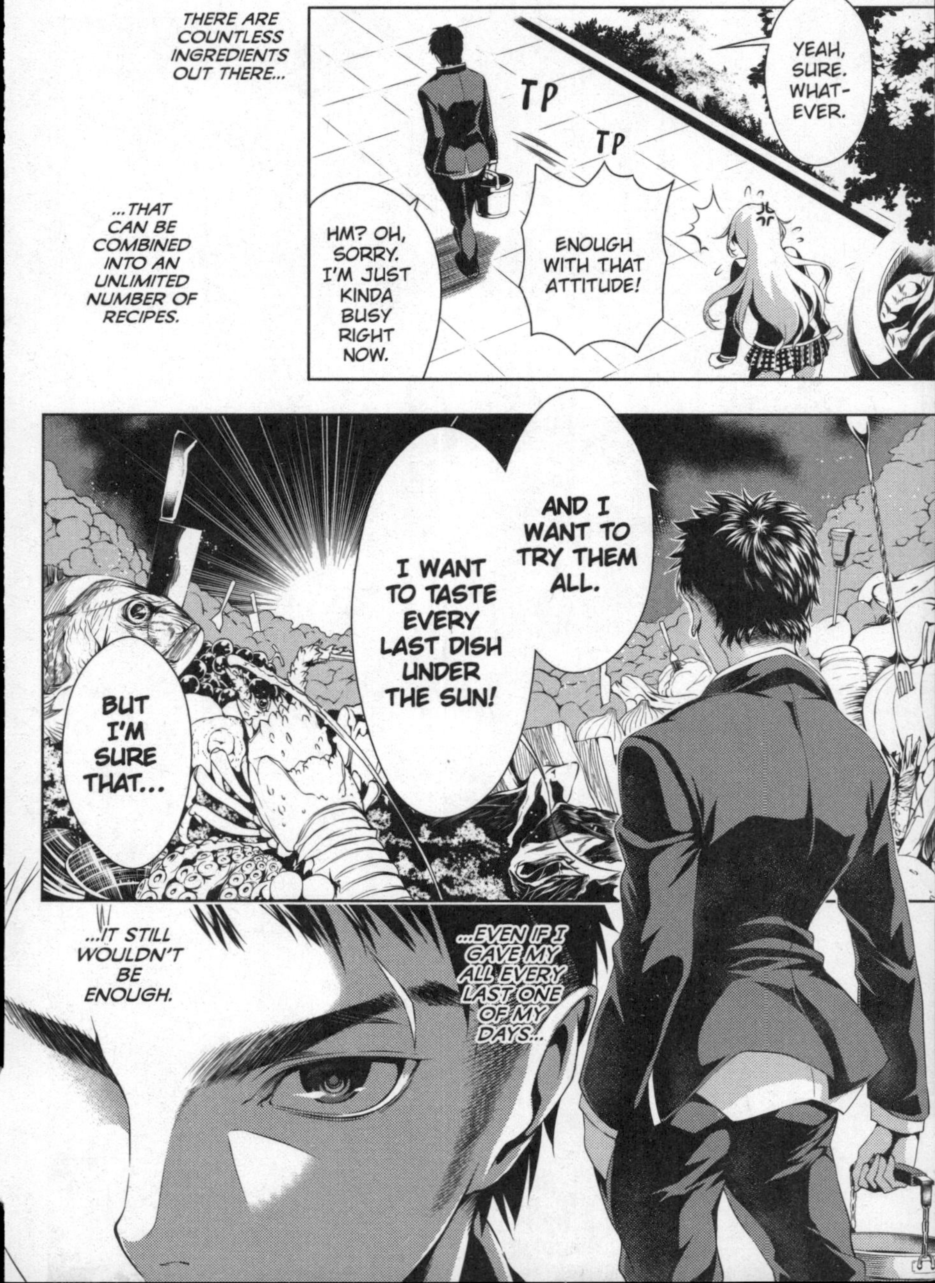
YEAH, SURE. WHATEVER.
TP
TP
ENOUGH WITH THAT ATTITUDE!
HM? OH, SORRY. I'M JUST KINDA BUSY RIGHT NOW.
THERE ARE COUNTLESS INGREDIENTS OUT THERE...
...THAT CAN BE COMBINED INTO AN UNLIMITED NUMBER OF RECIPES.
AND I WANT TO TRY THEM ALL.
I WANT TO TASTE EVERY LAST DISH UNDER THE SUN!
BUT I'M SURE THAT...
...EVEN IF I GAVE MY ALL EVERY LAST ONE OF MY DAYS...
...IT STILL WOULDN'T BE ENOUGH.

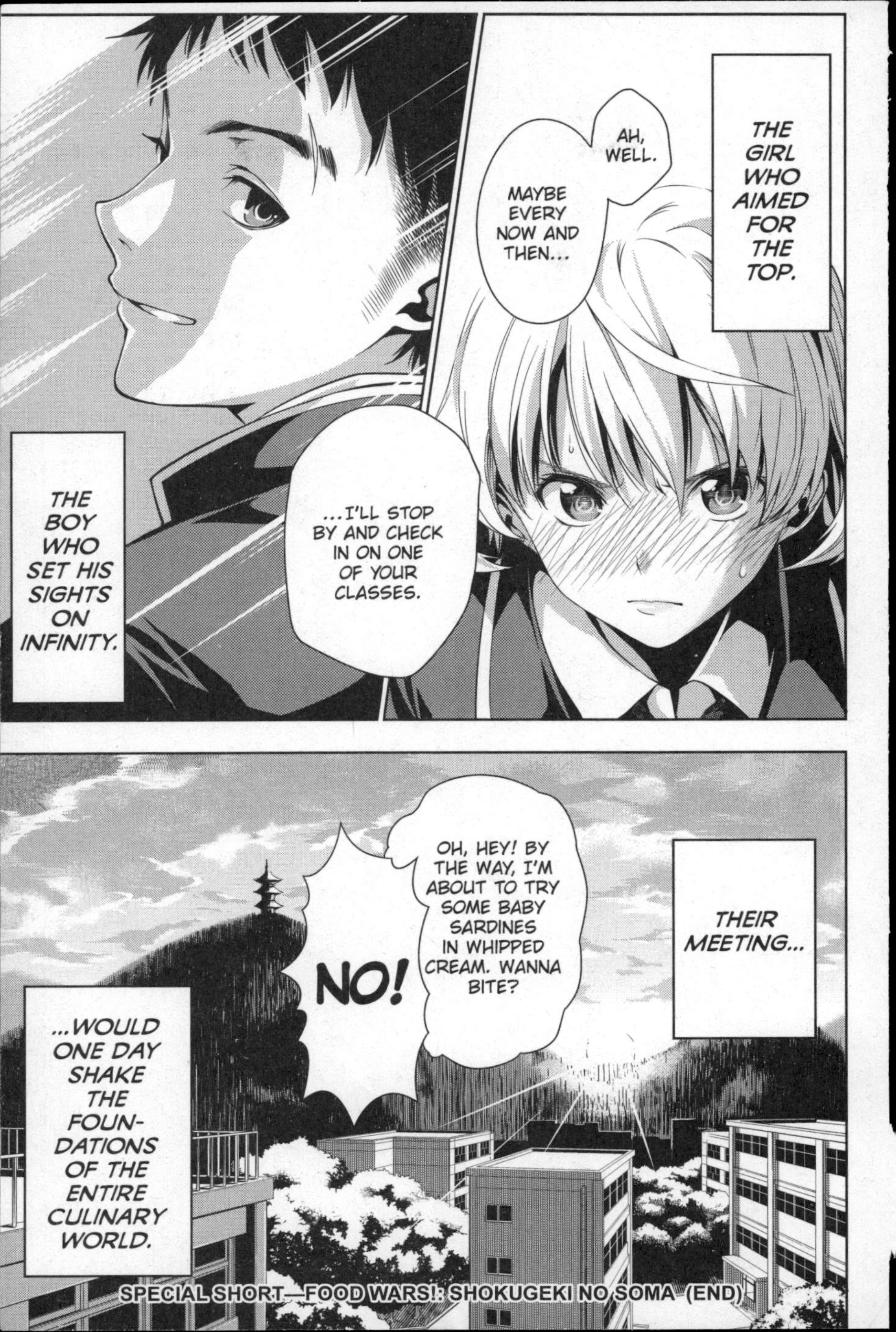
THE GIRL WHO AIMED FOR THE TOP.
AH, WELL.
MAYBE EVERY NOW AND THEN...
...I'LL STOP BY AND CHECK IN ON ONE OF YOUR CLASSES.
THE BOY WHO SET HIS SIGHTS ON INFINITY.
THEIR MEETING...
OH, HEY! BY THE WAY, I'M ABOUT TO TRY SOME BABY SARDINES IN WHIPPED CREAM. WANNA BITE?
NO!
...WOULD ONE DAY SHAKE THE FOUN-DATIONS OF THE ENTIRE CULINARY WORLD.
SPECIAL SHORT—FOOD WARS!: SHOKUGEKI NO SOMA (END)

THANK YOU VERY MUCH FOR READING VOLUME 1 OF *FOOD WARS!: SHOKUGEKI NO SOMA.* ON THE NEXT PAGE IS A SHORT BONUS STORY I DREW JUST FOR THIS VOLUME. I HOPE TO SEE YOU NEXT VOLUME!

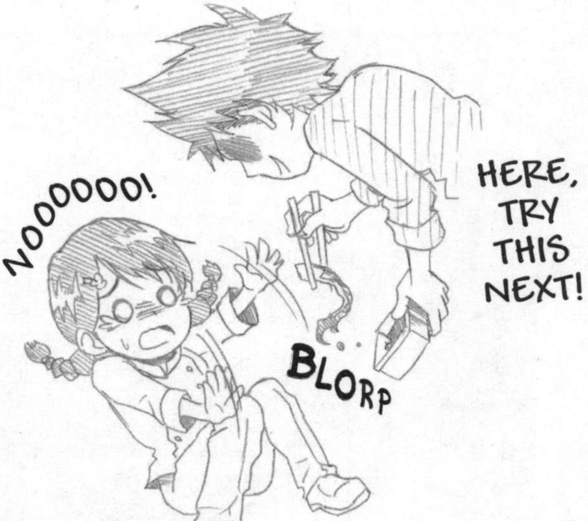
HERE, TRY THIS NEXT!
NOOOOOO!
BLORP

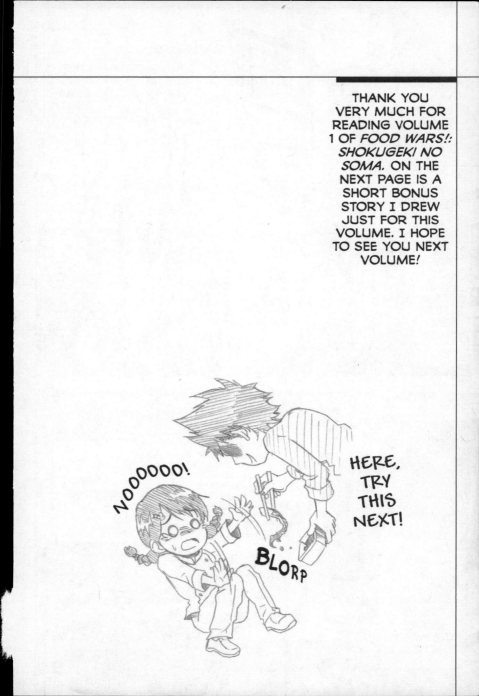

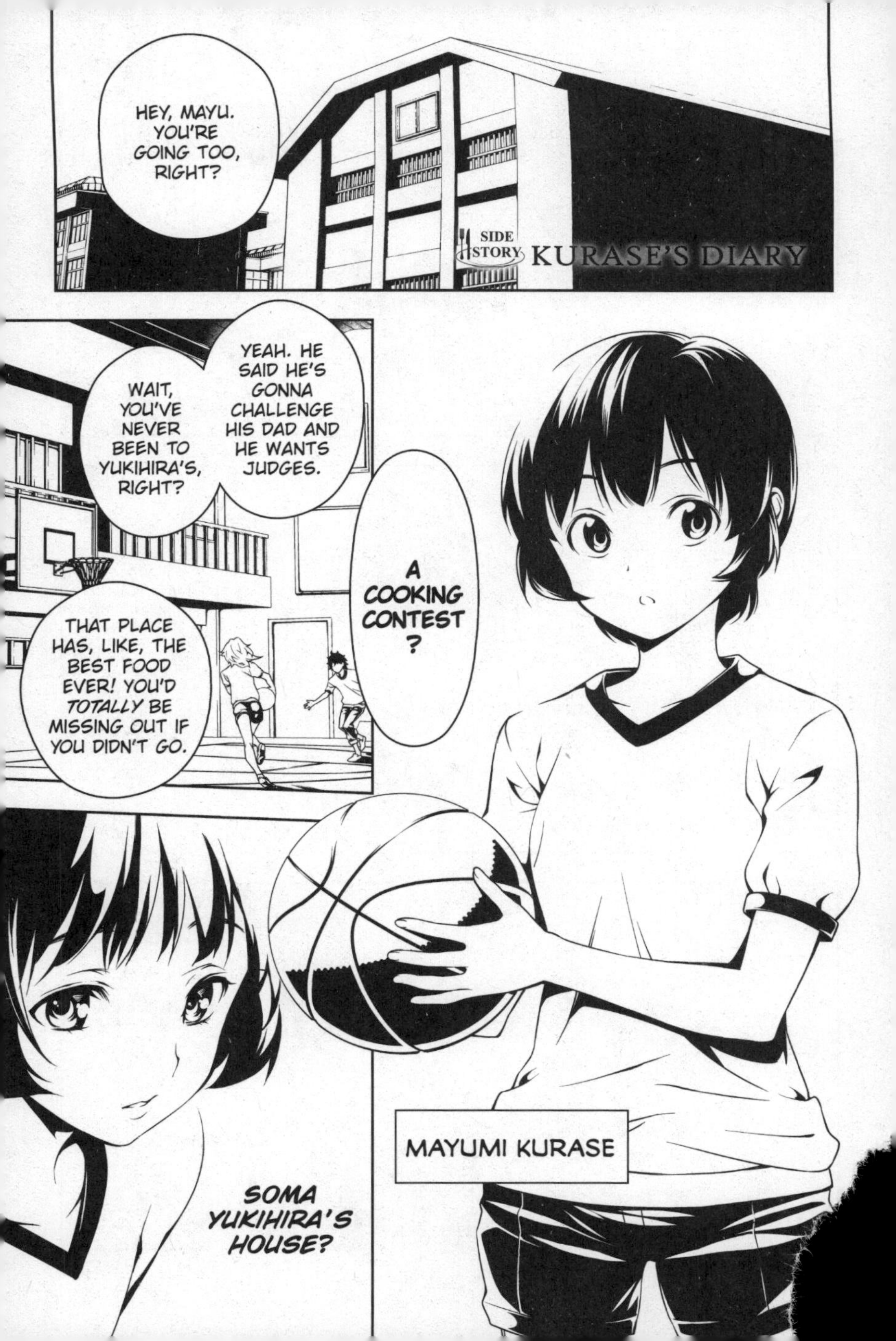
HEY, MAYU. YOU'RE GOING TOO, RIGHT?
SIDE STORY KURASE'S DIARY
A COOKING CONTEST?
MAYUMI KURASE
YEAH. HE SAID HE'S GONNA CHALLENGE HIS DAD AND HE WANTS JUDGES.
WAIT, YOU'VE NEVER BEEN TO YUKIHIRA'S, RIGHT?
THAT PLACE HAS, LIKE, THE BEST FOOD EVER! YOU'D *TOTALLY* BE MISSING OUT IF YOU DIDN'T GO.
SOMA YUKIHIRA'S HOUSE?

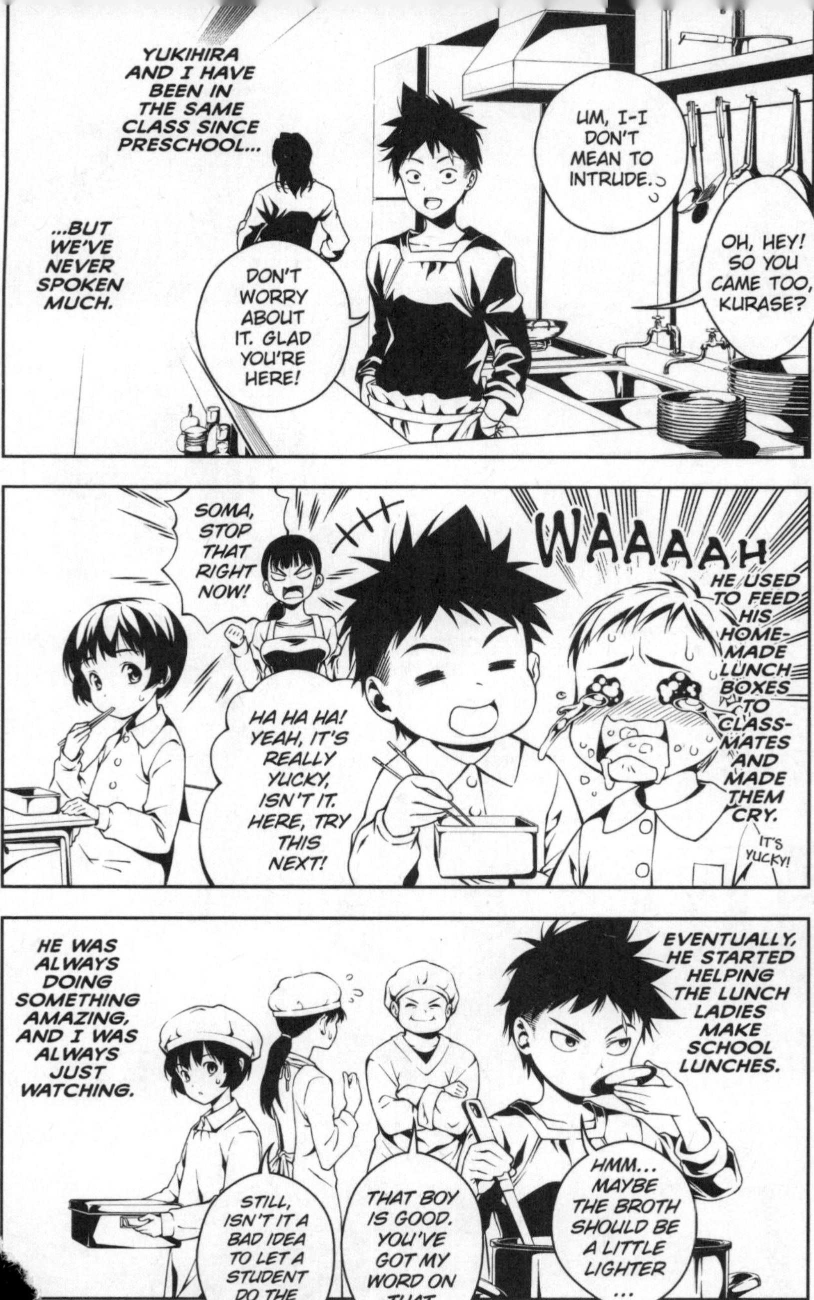
OH, HEY! SO YOU CAME TOO, KURASE?
UM, I-I DON'T MEAN TO INTRUDE.
DON'T WORRY ABOUT IT. GLAD YOU'RE HERE!
YUKIHIRA AND I HAVE BEEN IN THE SAME CLASS SINCE PRESCHOOL...
...BUT WE'VE NEVER SPOKEN MUCH.
WAAAAH
HE USED TO FEED HIS HOME-MADE LUNCH BOXES TO CLASS-MATES AND MADE THEM CRY.
IT'S YUCKY!
HA HA HA! YEAH, IT'S REALLY YUCKY, ISN'T IT. HERE, TRY THIS NEXT!
SOMA, STOP THAT RIGHT NOW!
EVENTUALLY, HE STARTED HELPING THE LUNCH LADIES MAKE SCHOOL LUNCHES.
HMM... MAYBE THE BROTH SHOULD BE A LITTLE LIGHTER...
THAT BOY IS GOOD. YOU'VE GOT MY WORD ON THAT.
STILL, ISN'T IT A BAD IDEA TO LET A STUDENT DO THE COOKING?
HE WAS ALWAYS DOING SOMETHING AMAZING, AND I WAS ALWAYS JUST WATCHING.

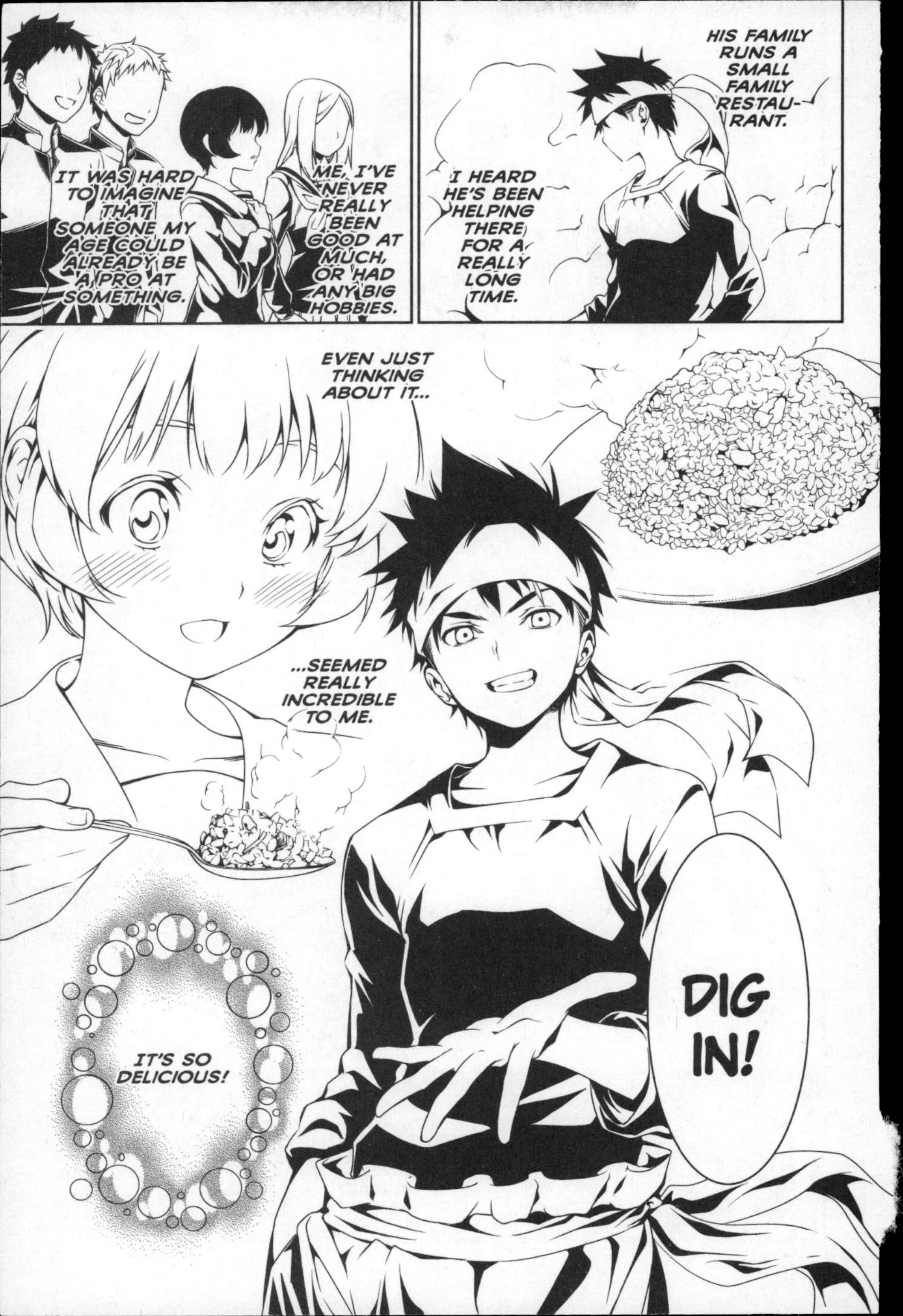
HIS FAMILY RUNS A SMALL FAMILY RESTAURANT.
I HEARD HE'S BEEN HELPING THERE FOR A REALLY LONG TIME.
ME, I'VE NEVER REALLY BEEN GOOD AT MUCH, OR HAD ANY BIG HOBBIES.
IT WAS HARD TO IMAGINE THAT SOMEONE MY AGE COULD ALREADY BE A PRO AT SOMETHING.
EVEN JUST THINKING ABOUT IT...
...SEEMED REALLY INCREDIBLE TO ME.
DIG IN!
IT'S SO DELICIOUS!

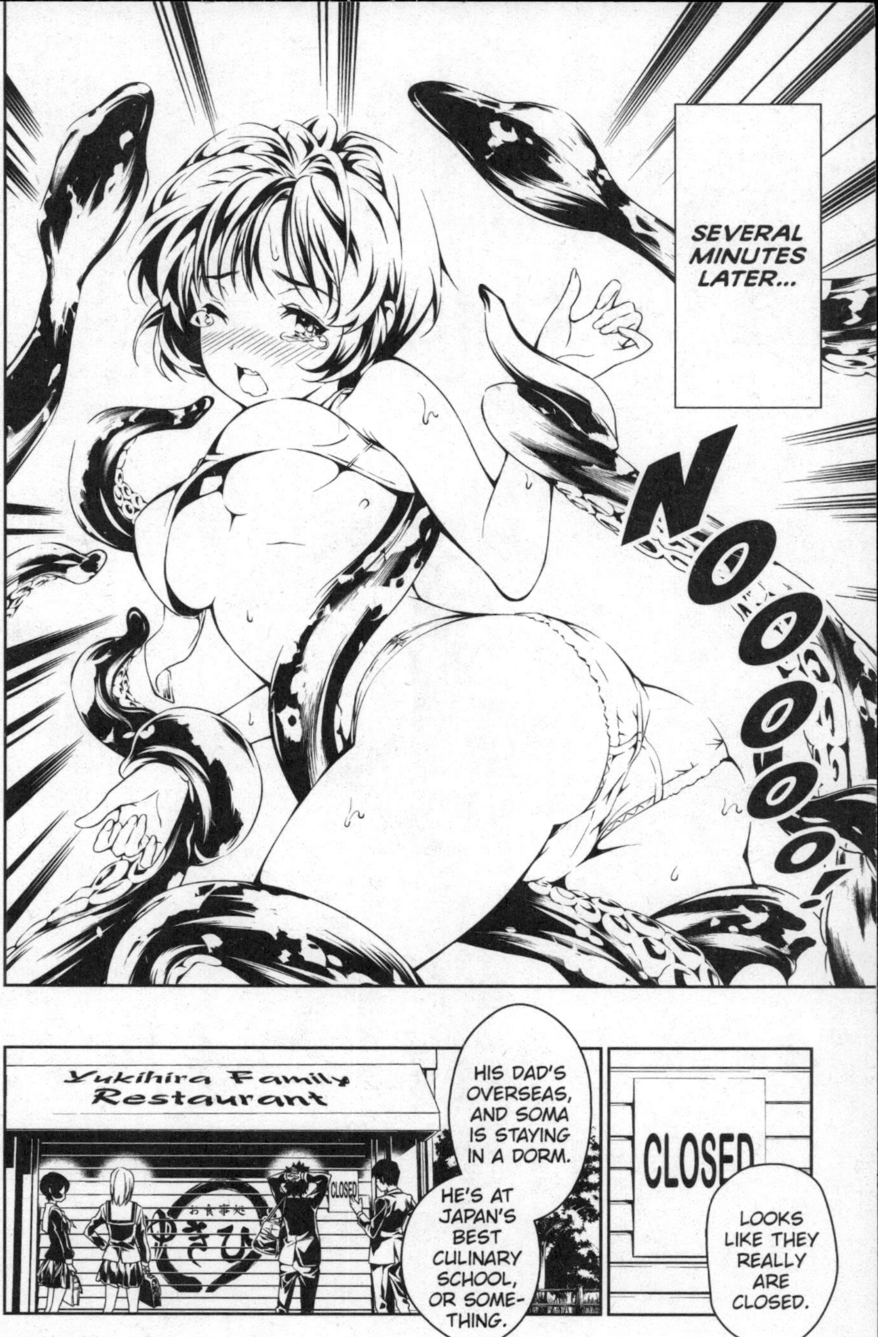
SEVERAL MINUTES LATER...
NOOOOOOO!
CLOSED
LOOKS LIKE THEY REALLY ARE CLOSED.
Yukihira Family Restaurant
お食事処
CLOSED
HIS DAD'S OVERSEAS, AND SOMA IS STAYING IN A DORM.
HE'S AT JAPAN'S BEST CULINARY SCHOOL, OR SOME-THING.

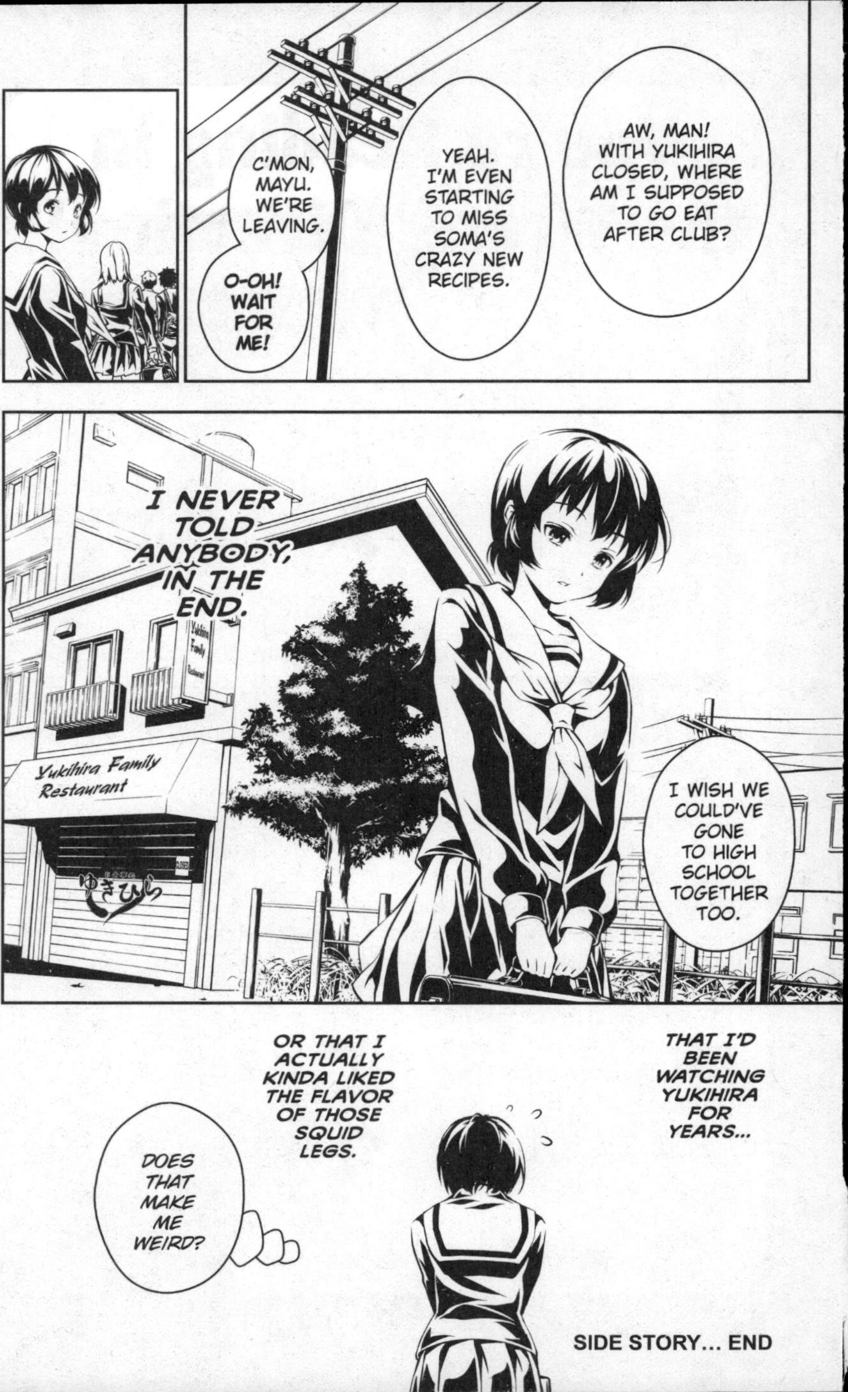
AW, MAN! WITH YUKIHIRA CLOSED, WHERE AM I SUPPOSED TO GO EAT AFTER CLUB?
YEAH. I'M EVEN STARTING TO MISS SOMA'S CRAZY NEW RECIPES.
C'MON, MAYU. WE'RE LEAVING.
O-OH! WAIT FOR ME!
I WISH WE COULD'VE GONE TO HIGH SCHOOL TOGETHER TOO.
I NEVER TOLD ANYBODY, IN THE END.
Yukihira Family Restaurant
Yukihira Family Restaurant
CLOSED
ゆきひら
THAT I'D BEEN WATCHING YUKIHIRA FOR YEARS...
OR THAT I ACTUALLY KINDA LIKED THE FLAVOR OF THOSE SQUID LEGS.
DOES THAT MAKE ME WEIRD?
SIDE STORY... END

You're Re[ading]
the Wrong Direction‼

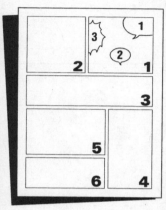

Whoops! Guess what? You're starting at the wrong end of the comic!

…It's true! In keeping with the original Japanese format, **Food Wars!** is meant to be read from right to left, starting in the upper-right corner.

Unlike English, which is read from left to right, Japanese is read from right to left, meaning that action, sound effects and word-balloon order are completely reversed… something which can make readers unfamiliar with Japanese feel pretty backwards themselves. For this reason, manga or Japanese comics published in the U.S. in English have sometimes been published "flopped"— that is, printed in exact reverse order, as though seen from the other side of a mirror.

By flopping pages, U.S. publishers can avoid confusing readers, but the compromise is not without its downside. For one thing, a character in a flopped manga series who once wore in the original Japanese version a T-shirt emblazoned with "M A Y" (as in "the merry month of") now wears one which reads "Y A M"! Additionally, many manga creators in Japan are themselves unhappy with the process, as some feel the mirror-imaging of their art skews their original intentions.

We are proud to bring you Yuto Tsukuda and Shun Saeki's **Food Wars!** in the original unflopped format.

For now, though, turn to the other side of the book and let the adventure begin…!

—Editor